Using
Networks

Frank J. Derfler, Jr.

A Division of Macmillan Computer Publishing, USA
201 W. 103rd Street
Indianapolis, Indiana 46290

Contents at a Glance

Using Networks

Copyright © 1998 by Que

International Standard Book Number: 0-7897-1596-1

Library of Congress Catalog Card Number: 98-84376

2000   99   98   3   2

Interpretation of the printing code: the rightmost double-digit number is the year of the book's printing; the rightmost single-digit, the number of the book's printing. For example, a printing code of 98-1 shows that the first printing of the book occurred in 1998.

Composed in Janson and MCPdigital by Macmillan Computer Publishing

Printed in the United States of America

Credits

Executive Editor
Laurie Petrycki

Development Editor
Jim Chalex

Technical Editor
Steve Rigney

Managing Editor
Sarah Kearns

Project Editor
Mike La Bonne

Copy Editors
Audra McFarland
Margo Catts

Indexer
Cheryl Jackson

Production
Marcia Deboy
Michael Dietsch
Jenny Earhart
Cynthia Fields
Maureen West

Cover Designers
Dan Armstrong
Ruth Harvey

Book Designer
Gary Adair

Contents

Dedication

To Steve Rigney and family. Isn't this fun?

About the Author

Frank J. Derfler, Jr. first appeared on the masthead of *PC Magazine* in its fifth issue—before *PC Magazine* was purchased by Ziff-Davis. Frank was listed as the "Communications Editor." At that time, in 1982, he was on active duty with the United States Air Force and stationed in the Pentagon. His writing career up until that time included several articles on nuclear arms proliferation and electronic warfare in professional military journals. He also had a regular column in *Kilobaud Microcomputing* magazine, a pioneering publication in the personal computer industry.

While he guided the readers of *PC Magazine* through modem communications, he also helped to guide the entry of microcomputers into the military. Frank led the development of what became known as the "Zenith contracts" that eventually delivered over 140,000 PCs into the Air Force and Navy. He also worked on a committee that created contracts with companies like IBM, Digital, Buroughs, and Univac for the development of TCP/IP software for specific computers. These were destined for use in something called ARPAnet—the precursor to the Internet.

In 1986, Frank opened the *PC Magazine* LAN Labs in Virginia. With his retirement from the Air Force in 1987, the LAN Labs moved to Destin, Florida. The LAN Labs developed the first widely distributed LAN benchmark tests and included both testing and editorial activities. *PC Magazine* continued to test networking equipment and software in this facility until the opening of ZD Labs in 1991.

Frank is the author or co-author of more than a dozen published books on networking and data communications. His most popular titles include *The PC Magazine Guide to Connectivity* and, with co-author Les Freed, *How Networks Work*.

Acknowledgments

To Steve Rigney for keeping me on track. To Jim Chalex for breaking new ground. To Laurie Petrycki for waving the green flag. Also to all the unsung heroes at MCP: Mike La Bonne, Audra McFarland, all the editors, the indexer, layout, and proofreading staff.

We'd Like to Hear from You!

Que Corporation has a long-standing reputation for high-quality books and products. To ensure your continued satisfaction, we also understand the importance of customer service and support.

Tech Support

If you need assistance with the information in this book or you have feedback for us about the book, please contact Macmillan Technical Support by phone at **317-581-3833** or by email at support@mcp.com.

Orders, Catalogs, and Customer Service

To order other Que or Macmillan Computer Publishing books, catalogs, or products, please contact our Customer Service Department:

Phone: 1-800-428-5331

Fax: 1-800-835-3202

International Fax: 1-317-228-4400

Or visit our online bookstore:

http://www.mcp.com/

Introduction

Intranets and the Internet! Internet access, multiple access, and remote access! What's it all about and how do you do it? My goal in writing this book is to show you both the big picture and the pieces and parts you need to make computer connections within your office or home and outside. In a sense, I want to make you a hero. I want to help you solve problems in your company or organization, improve productivity, leverage network technology, keep costs down, and make money. That's the stuff of modern heroes. With the information I've given you in this book, you can amplify, release, and focus the power that is available in modern PCs when you connect them to synthesize and distribute information across a local net or the Internet.

I've written this book with managers in mind, not just technicians or PC power users. I assume you're "PC-savvy" enough to click around in Windows, and that you know how to plug a printer into the parallel port of a PC, but otherwise you don't need any special information, background, or experience to use this book.

The book you have in your hands is different from most books, because it is more than just printed pages of text. The sidenotes, diagrams, and the decision tree chart bound into the book lead you to important information and recommendations that can help you make decisions without forcing you to wade through oceans of words.

What's in This Book

The first chapter, "Society + Commerce = Connectivity," introduces the concept of information as the raw material, inventory, and finished product of many organizations. Chapter 2, "Charting Your Network Courses," takes you through the networking decision tree, an innovative device that can help you find economical and effective ways to design, install, and operate a connectivity system. Chapter 3, "Connecting PCs for Printer Sharing and File Exchange," discusses a variety of ways in which you can link computers to share printers, exchange files, and use networked applications.

The networking field is broad. No other logical division of the computer industry encompasses as many different technologies as does networking. The world of local area networks—only one portion of the networking galaxy—includes many specialized elements such as cables, connectors, network adapters, network operating system software, and management tools. Chapters 4 through 9 give you an overview, specific details, and practical hints about all these different network elements.

Chapter 10, "LAN Portals," moves outside the local network and describes how to use long distance circuits to link LANs together and to the Internet. The discussions of Internet protocols, devices, and activities go through Chapter 12, "The Protocols of the Internet."

The next chapters go through a variety of topics covering specific aspects of networking technology. These include linking to mainframe computers in Chapter 13, modems in Chapter 14, remote access in Chapter 15, management and cost control in Chapter 16, and the whole subject of email and other forms of workgroup productivity in Chapter 17.

The book concludes with Appendix A, "Glossary," and Appendix B, "What's on the Web Page?"

The online portion of this book includes a Web page with the URLs of vendors marketing networking products and a few discussion groups that are good sources of information.

Throughout this book, I've clustered information together into related areas—sometimes allowing overlap between those subject areas—to make the concepts and hints as readily available to you as possible. You don't have to read this book from cover to cover or even from front to back. It's designed to act as a quick reference, a tutorial, and a friendly consultant. Please enjoy it.

Society + Commerce = Connectivity

Connected systems improve productivity

Connected systems change business and society

Open systems were a great idea

The layers of a structured market

The importance of the "–ilities"

"The Internet," "intranets," "telecommuting," "computing as a competitive advantage," "total cost of ownership"…these are the hot buzzwords going toward the year 2000, and they are all about networking. Puzzled, but willing? Intrigued, but anxious? I'm here to help! You don't have to be a corporate networking guru to be interested in linking computers or to benefit from the synergy that linked computers offer. As the senior networking editor of *PC Magazine*, I receive a lot of email from people who work in offices with five or six PCs and want to know the best way to connect their computers in order to share data, printers, and communications connections. If you're linking two computers or two hundred, many of the same rules apply.

Similarly, you don't have to be a power programmer to install a printer-sharing device or even a full network for a hundred or more PCs. Modern networking products make it easy and economical to install powerful and flexible networking systems. The purpose of this book is to show you the advantage of connected systems and to help you understand the practical basics. We'll even discuss the equipment from the biggest and, in some cases, the most enterprising companies in the business.

The Connection Advantage

Competing = intranets and the Internet

In these times, when companies like Cisco Corporation are selling tens of millions of dollars worth of merchandise per day through their web sites, you have to communicate to compete. Corporate networks (called *intranets*) and the Internet are new and necessary parts of doing business.

In many businesses, information is a necessary lubricant for trade. The speedy flow of information allows the movement of money, raw materials, and products with little waste; it greases commerce. In other businesses, information is both a raw material and a crafted product. Information technology has historically been the lubricant that allowed modern corporations to slide out from under management pyramids to become flatter, more streamlined, and more profitable organizations.

Computers hold and sort information, and communications networks transport information among computers. Computers and their networks form the manufacturing and transportation infrastructure of modern organizations and societies.

At certain stages in the development of a society, the majority of the people need practical skills in such areas as agriculture, herding, or fishing. As societies industrialize, a large percentage of the populace must learn how to drive a car, and many people master mechanical trades. In the United States, we are now at the stage when many of us must master the information trades. Most people have to know how to use information-delivery tools such as television sets, and an increasing number have to be able to put information into and take information from a computer. The need to use a computer connected to a communications network follows quickly after that.

Not every member of society needs the skills taught in this book to select, install, and manage networking systems, but someone in practically every commercial office and workgroup must have these skills for the enterprise to run efficiently and effectively. A hundred years ago, commercial organizations relied on horse-power and the skills of teamsters and farriers as they moved their products by horse-drawn wagons. Fifty years ago, commerce was centered around the train and the truck, as well as the skills of drivers and mechanics. Today, commerce is increasingly dependent on computers and their communications systems and on the skills of the professionals who create, install, and maintain them. Now is the right time for you to learn about computer connectivity systems. In fact, if you work with or around computers and aren't familiar with most of the material in this book, you're almost too late!

Visit our web page!

One of our goals is to help you find the information you need to succeed. To that end, we have established a web page containing contact information for major vendors and information on important discussion groups you can visit. See Appendix B, "What's on the Web Page," for more information.

Connectivity Is Dead

I used to begin my speeches to groups of PC users and managers by announcing, "Connectivity is dead!" Because I carried the title of connectivity editor of *PC Magazine* at the time, my audiences thought this was a strange thing to say. My point was this: Connectivity, with a capital "C," is an IBM term describing a method of interconnecting computers that inexorably laced people into IBM's proprietary web. If you connected using "Big Blue's" signaling, cabling, and software systems, it was difficult to integrate products from other manufacturers into your network.

That type of Connectivity is dead. The new world of connectivity, with a little "c," allows interconnection between computer systems made by many different manufacturers. Today, you can shop for components on the basis of features, price, service, support, and availability, and you generally know that the software and hardware products you buy will work together.

An Open World and Everybody's World

The escape from the "closed" meaning of Connectivity was an uphill trek. Many companies, institutions, and even governments took thousands of small steps to reach a system of "open" connectivity. In 1977, the International Standards Organization (ISO) established a subcommittee to define standards for products used to link heterogeneous computers.

Those standards make up the famous (or infamous) seven-layer networking model that you might have read about. Don't worry, though, this book provides more than just information about the seven-layer model, but it's polite to tip a hat in that direction. The open model did a lot to bring us into the world of practical networking—although not in the exact way that anyone envisioned.

The world of open connectivity specifications, or *protocols*, is a paradise with rules, in which all products work together in harmony because they conform to published standards for interoperability. The footsteps of mortals first echoed in this paradise in 1987, when companies like AT&T, Digital Equipment Corp., and others began announcing and releasing products conforming to certain sections of the ISO specification for Open Systems Interconnection (OSI).

An interesting thing happened on the way to paradise. Many companies learned to get along with each other even without conforming exactly to the ponderous ISO OSI seven-layer model. While companies learned how to create products for the structure of the open systems, they also learned that it was relatively easy to create products for each others' systems. So aggressive companies such as Microsoft, Performance Technology, and Artisoft created software that let their network operating systems interoperate with Novell's popular NetWare.

Soon after, Novell and Microsoft each fielded software that allowed interoperation between network servers and clients using either NetWare or various versions of Windows. In addition, each moved to link their operating systems more closely to UNIX. Then, in the 1990s, the work of the Internet Engineering Task Force (IETF) rose to prominence. Companies made products conforming to the IETF's standards and worked together to ensure interoperability. Chapter 12 discusses the IETF in more detail.

As a result of all this, modern network managers can mix network pieces and parts from different companies in a variety of ways. The open world—designed to be open according to certain guidelines—became everybody's world. And following the rules of openness became less important than working together directly.

SEE ALSO
➤ *The general theory of protocols can be found on page 195.*

LANs, WANs, and Intranets

It usually takes some time for an organization to evolve to the point at which it needs large open systems or, at least, cooperative computer systems made up of pieces supplied by many vendors. The need for connectivity often begins with a simple desire to share a single printer between two PCs or to move a file from one person to another without writing it to a disk and walking it down the hall. Today, the need to share expensive links to the Internet or to corporate intranets drives the shape of many local area networks. These modest networking challenges don't always require solutions that incorporate miles of wire and megabytes of programs. Although some connectivity problems cry out for local area networks, others yield to simpler solutions.

The terms "network" and "local area network" (LAN) are both overused and abused, so we should first be sure we have the same frame of reference.

A *network* is any type of interactive information-carrying system. Your body contains networks of sensors and nerve fibers, and your television set displays information from entertainment networks. The information-carrying aspect of networking is important. Information-carrying networks are the infrastructure—the roads and highways—of modern societies. Computer communications networks carry information between different computers and between computers and their peripherals.

A *LAN* is a computer communications network that spans a limited geographical area—usually no more than a few miles and often much less (see Figure 1.1). Other types of computer communications networks include the *metropolitan area network* (MAN) and the *wide area network* (WAN). Technical factors force these computer communications networks to trade speed for distance.

FIGURE 1.1

Local area networks link computers within about 1,000 feet of one another. Wide area networks link local area networks. The Internet and corporate networks are WANs that link many LANs (millions in the case of the Internet). If you dial into an Internet service provider, you are connecting to that ISP's LAN.

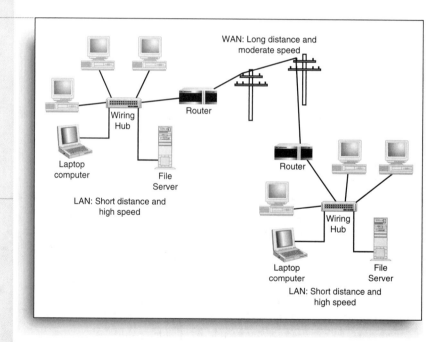

In a LAN, the data moves at tens or even hundreds of megabits per second within an office, throughout a factory, or across a campus. By contrast, data in a WAN typically moves at 1.5 megabits per second or less, but this kind of network can span continents and oceans. The Internet and corporate intranets are applications of wide area networks.

This book focuses primarily on local area network connectivity alternatives, but it also looks at the corporate intranet and the Internet WAN as important sources and destinations for LAN traffic. (An intranet is a system of web servers and similar services that operates only over your corporate network. It's useful for distributing many kinds of internal information to client computers using browsers.) We'll also tell you how to link your LAN to WANs like the Internet and private corporate networks (see Chapter 10) and how to protect your LAN from the threats on public networks.

SEE ALSO

➤ *For more information on network architectures like Ethernet, see the section "Ethernet the Elder," on page 133.*

Layers of a Structured Market

Overall, buyers of connectivity products seem to fall into four categories, based primarily on the complexity of the systems they need. The buyers of LAN systems can be divided into those with simple resource-sharing needs, those who need to link 2 to 20 PCs in a network, managers of larger networks with 20 to 400 nodes or even more, and the new priests of computing who practice the arts of the network infrastructure.

The first level, the most basic, buyers of connectivity are innovators who see a need to link computers and share information, usually in a small organization or workgroup, and who take action to fill that need. These buyers often include PC-savvy managers and people who are genuinely enthusiastic about personal computers. They often shop with a limited budget and look for practical solutions that don't involve a lot of training or support. Usually, they don't have to coordinate their decisions with a lot of technical specialists. These people often buy their products through catalogs or directly from magazine ads. They can buy printer-sharing and simple file-transfer systems and have them installed and operational in just a few hours.

How fast is fast?

Let's try to put these speeds into perspective. Without any diagrams, this chapter is about a 20KB file. In most transmission schemes, it takes about 200,000 bits to move a 20KB file. (In most schemes, it works out to 20KB×8 bits per byte×2 bits per byte of transmission overhead.) On a 10-megabit-per-second LAN, the actual transmission of the data takes about two one-hundredths of a second to move between nodes (writing the file to disk takes a lot longer). On a typical modem link, the transmission takes 8–10 seconds. On an ISDN link, the transfer takes about a second and a half. On a 1.5 megabit link, the transfer takes about one-tenth of a second. The bigger the file is, the larger the difference you see in transmission times.

Speed = higher cost

When it comes to wide area network connections, you can choose from fast, far, or inexpensive—pick any two. Fast long-distance connections (more than 128KB per second spanning more than a mile or so) can cost hundreds of dollars per month. The monthly cost rises as distance and speed increase.

Interoperability

It's perfectly fine to buy networking products like adapter cards and hubs through discount catalogs and big retailers. The standards in place just about guarantee interoperability. The predominance of Microsoft's Windows is also beneficial for interoperability.

The second level of buyers are those who know they need a high-speed network for a group of 2 to 20 users. These people are often engaged in what has been called "guerrilla networking." They bring in small networks in an underground "guerrilla" operation, sometimes under the noses of unresponsive corporate data-processing professionals.

The networking hardware and software for a group of 2 to 20 PCs runs about $100 per PC. Because this is within the discretionary limits of a middle manager, these buyers aren't strapped for cash, but they must carefully account for what they spend. With Microsoft's Windows operating systems, these people can install a network for 2 to 20 PCs in one afternoon, spend a couple of hours configuring the applications, and enjoy a functional network on the second day.

This class of network doesn't need a full-time person dedicated to the job of network management. But someone usually emerges or is appointed as the caretaker of the LAN.

The next category of connectivity buyers includes many graduates of the guerrilla school of networking and some of the corporate data-processing professionals who understand the importance of networked PCs. These folks need a multiserver network for 20 to 400 users or more. They operate from funds specially budgeted for the network, and they worry about speed, reliability, and support much more than they do about cost.

Buyers of networks with 20 to 400+ nodes might hire professional system integrators to supply and install their networks, but the buyers typically dictate the brands and components used in a system. Typically, organizations with networking requirements on this scale have a professional staff dedicated to maintaining and expanding the network.

Interestingly, contributions to the budget for the operation of larger networks often come from managers of the business side of an organization. In a growing number of companies, the business managers control items in their budgets for services such as copy machines, telephones, and the LAN, which gives them a lot of input into the activities of the technical staff.

How to get started

Need to link just 2–4 computers in a small office–maybe even at home? Look for starter kits of a few adapters and a small hub, which are available from 3Com, Bay Networks, Intel, Linksys, and other vendors. They're priced so that you, in effect, get one adapter free.

Information System money

If you're a middle manager, it's nice to have some money from the Information System department in your budget. It gives you flexibility and makes the IS department more responsive to your needs. Beware of an IS department that has its own budget and agenda.

Finally, at the top of the "connectivity buyers" stack are those managers who supply corporate infrastructures. These infrastructure builders come from several disciplines. First are the PC-savvy zealots who have hiked a long trail and learned many lessons. Second are people who specialize in communications systems and are often schooled more in telephone networks than in corporate computing networks. Last are the corporate data-processing managers and people whose whole line of work depends on computers (such as structural or mechanical engineers who use computers as tools every day). They have to learn the technology of their tools in order to use them well.

In many ways, these people are today's "priests" of computing, and they chant a litany that would be lost on managers and buyers of the lower-level systems. The step into the technology of corporate infrastructure is much bigger than the one from small- to medium-sized networks. The words are different, the concepts are sometimes arcane, and the arguments between factions supporting different protocols, architectures, and vendor-backed systems are fierce. Yet once you've mastered this technology of networking infrastructure, it becomes a powerful tool for commerce and education.

The priests of the infrastructure often control their own budgets. But because they must work with network systems that service and are financed by business managers, they worry about productivity and economy more than the corporate data-processing professionals of the 1970s and '80s ever did. They usually write the specifications for their own systems and often buy directly from manufacturers.

All of these consumers of connectivity products are trying to solve the problem of how to tap their organizations into the volume and type of information they need for successful operation. Working in and building up the infrastructure for modern commerce and society are the tasks of the modern connectivity worker.

Whatever category you fall into, when you are ready to make purchasing decisions, you look for products. These products will conform to certain protocols and follow certain technical strategies, but the decision finally comes down to a company name, a product name, and a price.

The Future Is in the "-ilities"

It's clear that the concerns we had about throughput and inter-operability in the early 1990s are past. For the most part, networking products are fast enough, and the local area network is seldom a bottleneck. Also, generally things work together well enough. Proprietary "extensions" to networking standards can still burn you, but if you stay with products that conform to standards, interoperability is a safe bet. The strategy for buying the products you need for the year 2000 and beyond should rely on a more sophisticated set of what I call the "-ilities." Specifically, this set includes scalability, upgradability, reliability, and affordability. Each of these factors is tough to measure, but important.

- *Scalability.* How well will a product grow? Few networking systems stand still; they tend to grow beyond all plans and forecasts. So it's important to examine how well the products you buy today will grow with your network installation. Avoid the problem of "one more port." (At some point, will the addition of one more network node force you to buy an expensive new chassis, server, or cable system addition?) Depending on the product, scalability is about power, capacity, and expansion.

- *Upgradability.* Scaling relates to capacity, but upgrading relates to the capability to meet new standards. Will the vendor be around to provide new revisions to software and firmware, and how drastic is the upgrade process? Erasable read-only memory is an important feature that adds to upgradability.

- *Reliability.* No one in the networking business has time to do the longitudinal studies required to prove the long term reliability of specific products. The best three indicators of reliability are your own experience, feedback from people you trust, and the manufacturing practices of the vendor. You can use two manufacturing data points: The first is published mean time between failure (MTBF) ratings for the equipment, and the second is whether the manufacturer's plant is certified by the International Standards Organization (ISO). The ISO has a set of standards, part of the ISO 9000 family, covering quality assurance, manufacturing, and product testing. ISO certification and MTBF testing add significantly to the cost of production, but they are useful indicators of product reliability.

- *Affordability.* The total cost of ownership (TCO) of a computer system is a lot more than the initial cost. Cost of ownership encompasses training, maintenance, and intangibles such as software upgrades. Networking products can require a lot of time and brainpower for installation, configuration, and maintenance. Unless you have a value-added retailer to lean on, you should consider formal training. The major vendors offer some type of on-site or classroom-based training classes. You can expect to pay approximately $500 a day for these classes, plus traveling expenses. Most of the vendors also offer training at your location. You should also investigate warranties, but most warranties are limited to two years and cover replacement parts only. Optional protection plans vary in features and price. Before purchasing any major networking products, you should closely evaluate the true cost of warranty and technical-support plans that don't provide much long-term help.

The good news is that you have many connection options. The following chapters are designed to help you sort those options and make the choices that are best for you.

SEE ALSO

➤ *For more on total cost of ownership, see the section "Keep a Low TCO" on page 422.*

Charting Your Network Courses

Connection = sharing

Distance makes the difference

Media-sharing LANs

Making outside connections

Linking LANs

LAN-management tools

I designed this chapter for folks who know they need a network—to link their PCs, access mainframe computer systems, get on the Internet, or simply share printers—but aren't sure how to do it. You've probably heard about local area networks (LANs), and you might even use one now. Yet, beyond what you'll learn to call *media-sharing LANs*, there are lots of different ways to link PCs to one another, to other kinds of computers, and to shared devices such as file servers, printers, communications gateways, and modems. Some of the alternatives actually cost less than traditional LANs and provide more flexibility. This chapter leads you through the alternatives and guides you toward other areas of the book that might offer greater insight.

The heart of this chapter is a chart called the Connectivity Decision Tree (see Figure 2.1). The chart consists of a series of yes-or-no questions leading to recommendations. At each branch of the Connectivity Decision Tree, I suggest an alternative connection scheme or service. In boxed comments, I outline the major advantages and drawbacks of each alternative. Overall, I give you a brief explanation of the major connectivity alternatives in this chapter; later chapters contain detailed explanations of nearly all the alternatives.

As we examine these alternatives, you can take advantage of our web site to find the URLs of companies offering products in each category. Flip to Appendix B, "What's on the Web Page," to find the address of our web page.

Connection = Sharing

The need to share inspires all of the connectivity systems, techniques, and alternatives discussed in this book. You link computers to gain shared access to resources such as printers, files, and communications gateways.

Sharing one or more printers is a major incentive to linking computers into a network. Even though the prices of very capable laser printers have declined in recent years, it still makes economic sense to share printers among PCs if you can do so without too much technical and managerial overhead.

Connecting to Print

Take a minute to study the Connectivity Decision Tree. Then let's start with the question in the upper-left corner of the Decision Tree: "Need to share more than printers?" If you answer "no" to this question, it means that sharing printers is all you need to do. Several kinds of products give you low-cost printer sharing.

You can share printers among a few people by using a manual switch that routes the printer connection from one PC to another. Typically, however, you would automate the process through a *printer-sharing buffer*. Such devices—usually small boxes roughly the size of this book (see Figure 2.2)—can give up to ten people shared access to the same printer at a cost of less than $50 per connection.

When a PC has something to print, the printer-sharing buffer routes the job to the printer. The person using that PC simply invokes an application's print function in the usual way, and the buffer does all the work. Buffers often have their own internal memory area where they can hold or spool print jobs until the printer can handle them. Some printer-sharing buffers include a small pop-up terminate-and-stay-resident (TSR) program or a Windows program that allows you to select the desired printer, but others use no software in the PC.

A printer-sharing buffer is attached to a serial or parallel port on each PC and to one or more printers. When you buy one of these products, you have to choose a model that has the appropriate types of ports for the PCs and printers you want to link. The dealers and manufacturers of these devices have a good handle on the technical specifications of devices you are likely to have, so ask for help in selecting the right buffer.

Refer to Appendix B for a list of companies offering these products, and see Chapter 3 for more detailed information on printer-sharing techniques.

FIGURE 2.1

The Connectivity Decision Tree.

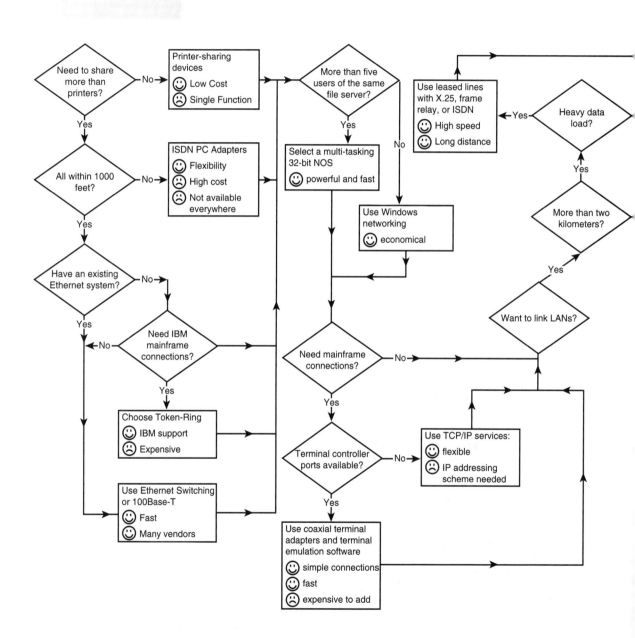

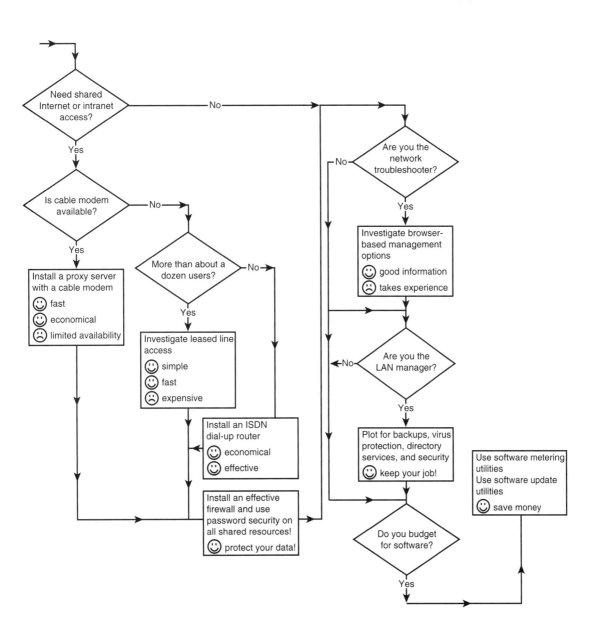

FIGURE 2.2

Printer-sharing products, like FastPrint from Rose Electronics, Inc., provide an inexpensive way to share several printers among as many as 32 PCs without adding LAN adapters or networking software to the computers.

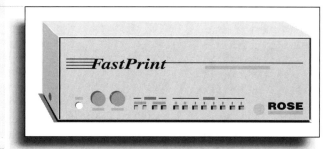

Distance Makes the Difference

By the time you get to the question "All within 1,000 feet?" in the Decision Tree, you've already established your need for a connectivity scheme fast enough to provide multiuser concurrent access to the same data files. Only the question of the distance between devices remains.

The laws of physics make it much more difficult—and therefore expensive—to send a fast signal over a long distance than to send a slow signal over a long distance or a fast signal over a short distance. If you want high-speed service over a mile or more, you'll have to pay for special signaling techniques and circuits. But it is relatively easy and economical to maintain a signaling rate of 10–100 megabits per second over 1,000 feet.

ISDN Moves Data over Distances

One technique you can use to link PCs over a distance is called the *Integrated Services Digital Network* (ISDN for short). The ISDN program, supported by funds from many governments and international companies, has the goal of digitizing the analog telephone systems of the world. ISDN is currently available in the major cities of North America, Europe, and Japan.

The devices that link ISDN and personal computers look exactly like regular modems. Generally they have the same task of linking the computer to the phone line, but technically they work much differently. Companies such as 3Com, Motorola, Eicon, and others offer terminal adapters that link your PC to ISDN telephone lines. When using an ISDN line, you dial and answer just as you would if you were using a regular telephone line, but data you send and receive is handled digitally all the way (whereas it must undergo at least one analog-to-digital conversion to be transmitted over a regular phone line).

ISDN provides 128KB per second computer-to-computer communications across thousands of miles at a cost of pennies per minute (plus a monthly base rate of about $30–$60). You can use ISDN to call an Internet service provider, a friend across the country, or your office from your home.

Media-Sharing LANs

Fasten your seat belt and tug on your helmet strap; we're about to enter the fast lane. Now you're in the world of *media-sharing LANs*. These networks use special adapter cards to let each computer on the network share access to high-speed cables or *media* connecting them.

The next stops on the Connectivity Decision Tree involve the selection of cabling schemes, adapter cards, and LAN software. Soon you'll have to be familiar with terms such as *Token-Ring*, *Ethernet*, network *operating systems*, and *gateways*. Don't worry though; you'll find the information you need in Chapter 5, which provides an introductory overview of media-sharing LANs. Later chapters cover topics such as adapter boards in even more detail.

Ethernet is a media-sharing LAN scheme that works great for most networks. Ethernet is very efficient in most installations. However, because it's a shared media, all the network nodes that have packets of data to send compete for time on the interconnecting cable. If you have a few very busy nodes, this contention can lead to collisions and slow access for all nodes.

Installing ISDN

ISDN used to be a nightmare to install, but many vendors of terminal adapters now provide excellent installation software and even a personal liaison service with your local telephone company. Although it's still not available everywhere, ISDN's flexibility and speed make it highly desirable.

If your existing Ethernet network system is running at more than 25 percent capacity, you should consider adding an Ethernet switch. An Ethernet switch provides each network station with a full 10 megabits per second of throughput without contention. You can add an Ethernet switch to the network without changing the adapters or other components.

If you don't have an existing Ethernet network and you need high-speed connections, you should investigate a 100Base-T or Fast Ethernet network system. This architecture carries data at 100 megabits per second, but it requires new adapters and hubs and the right kind of cabling.

Cables for Mainframe Connections

IS Managers and Mainframes

Corporate Information Systems managers aren't as omnipotent as they once were, but they still tightly and rightfully control access to mainframe computer systems. If mainframe access is one of your requirements, coordinating with corporate IS should be one of your first steps.

One important factor is to determine if the PCs on your network will need access to an IBM mainframe. Hence the question of whether you "Need IBM mainframe connections?" in the Connectivity Decision Tree. You should make this decision early because IBM designed one cabling and access scheme—Token-Ring—as the primary means of linking mainframes to a network. If you choose not to use Token-Ring (as well you might because it is ugly and expensive), there are other good ways to link PCs to mainframes. But Token-Ring is the route IBM wants you to use for this purpose. Therefore, if your organization will ever need connections between PCs and IBM mainframes, choosing a Token-Ring architecture now gives you the option to use special IBM connection equipment later.

If Token-Ring access to IBM mainframes is not critically important to you, you should use today's practical networking choice: Ethernet. You must consider many factors when you select LAN cabling. The construction of the building, existing wiring, the experience and knowledge of the people doing the installation, and several other factors influence this decision. Later chapters cover other less-critical aspects of various LAN wiring systems, but the questions in the Decision Tree cover the most important considerations.

SEE ALSO

➤ *To read about LAN wiring alternatives, see the section "Cables for Network Connections," on page 106.*

On to Software

The next question on the Decision Tree is "More than five users of the same files?" The number of people simultaneously sharing the same data files is a rough indicator of the workload placed on the computer that acts as a file server. Heavily loaded servers— those handling more than a dozen simultaneous users running word processing, spreadsheet, and accounting applications— need a network operating system that is capable of handling several tasks simultaneously. Lightly loaded servers can run efficiently using the resource sharing capabilities built into Microsoft Windows 95 and 98.

Multitasking Server Operating Systems

A server carrying the load of many busy client stations can receive hundreds of requests for file actions per second. The operating systems in these servers need special multitasking techniques to queue and satisfy these requests. The three most widely used server operating systems are the various versions of Novell's NetWare, Microsoft's Windows NT Server, and Sun's Solaris. These high-quality 32-bit multitasking operating systems have roughly comparable prices, capacities, and performance ratings, so choosing between them is largely a matter of selecting the product with the right features for your organization, bearing in mind the expertise of the local installers and support people.

Chapters 8 and 9 handle the basics and details of network operating systems.

Fighting the Power

Many people prematurely predicted the death of UNIX at the hands of Windows NT. Instead, Novell's largely self-inflicted wounds gave Sun breathing room to produce Solaris, a nice network operating system for the non-geek. Solaris is holding its own and has become a competitive operating system— particularly for the "anything but Microsoft" crowd.

Making Outside Connections

The next series of questions in the Connectivity Decision Tree deals with extending the network beyond the limits of its local high-speed cable. Extended links can go to mainframe computers, to other local networks, and to unlikely sounding devices such as distant facsimile machines. Because few companies do business in just one place anymore, developing extensions to other operating areas, to suppliers, to dealers, and even to

It all starts with LANs

It's useful to think of the local area network as a basic building block of connectivity. The LAN extends to employees working on the road or at home and links to other LANs through wide area networks—including the Internet. In this book, we'll start with the LAN, enhance its services and capabilities, and then build outward.

TCP/IP and LANs

The TCP/IP protocols were designed for wide area networks to stream data over long distances. Because of the popularity of the Internet, many network managers are using only TCP/IP for both WAN and LAN. These protocols are less efficient on LANs, but LANs typically have throughput to spare, so it makes little practical difference.

customers is an important part of networking in business. In large part, this is what the highly touted and little-explained "information highway" is all about—extending beyond physical limits to do business wherever the business might be.

Mainframe Links

At this point in the Decision Tree, you again encounter the question "Need mainframe connections?" If you selected IBM's Token-Ring wiring scheme when this question came up earlier, you already have a path to the mainframe.

If you don't have Token-Ring wiring, you have several other LAN-to-mainframe connection alternatives. If the computers follow the IBM 3270 communications architecture, you can establish a network gateway, or you can give each PC the capability to emulate a 3270 terminal and connect directly to the mainframe through coaxial cable or over modem-equipped telephone lines.

A negative reply to the question "Only IBM mainframes?" opens a path to the subject of linking computers with architectures designed by many companies through the *TCP/IP protocol services. Transmission Control Protocol/Internet Protocol*, or simply TCP/IP, is a standard set of communications protocols developed by the U.S. government and adopted by many companies and institutions around the world. Although it is the standard protocol of the Internet and intranets, its first role was as a universal method of transmission between different makes and models of large computers. If you properly select communications software designed to meet the TCP/IP standards, you can link computers with many different kinds of operating systems and internal architectures. TCP/IP utilities let you exchange files, send mail, and store data on different types of computers connected to local and extended networks.

SEE ALSO

➤ *Making connections to mainframe computers is tough stuff. For more information and definitions, see Chapter 13 on page 330.*

➤ *The TCP/IP family of protocols appears in many places throughout the book, but you'll find introductory information in the section "Networking Protocols," on page 195 and details in the section "The Heaven and Hell of IP," on page 317.*

Linking LANs

Organizations that have offices in many locations face the problem of linking widely separated local area networks. The Decision Tree question "Want to link LANs?" introduces more questions relating to how far apart the LANs are and how much data will flow between them. Solutions range from connections made over fiber-optic links (see Figure 2.3) to the use of ISDN.

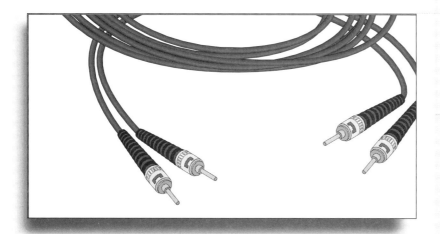

FIGURE 2.3

Fiber-optic cabling provides long-distance connections between PCs and between discrete networks of PCs using more typical copper wiring.

Those of you looking for ways to intermittently connect networks or to connect remote and portable PCs into a LAN should seriously consider using modems and *remote-access servers*. These servers effectively integrate distant computers into a local area network. If you need high-speed, full-period connections for heavy data loads, you have excellent options available from vendors called *value-added carriers*. Such carriers offer services like frame relay, which carries data around town or around the world with guaranteed quality of service.

The subject of shared Internet access is complex, but it shouldn't be terrifying. The number and type of users and the connection alternatives available in your neighborhood determine your connection choices. Cable modem service is always a good choice— if it's available to you. However, because cable modem connections aren't designed to be shared across a LAN, you must use a web-caching proxy server to share the cable modem's capabilities.

It pays to hunt for ISPs

It pays to hunt for the best ISP in your area. There are more than 3,000 ISPs in North America, and many small companies provide excellent service to customers within a limited geographical area.

If a cable modem isn't available, consider an ISDN dial-up router. This type of router can serve the connection needs of 20–30 average Internet users. (Bigger networks require leased lines and special contracts with Internet service providers.)

The most important step in installing an Internet access system is to make sure that you protect your networked resources from invasion. A firewall can keep persons with malicious interests out while letting friends through, which is harder than it sounds. Firewalls and good old-fashioned (but effective) password security are parts of the necessary precautions for protecting your network from Internet invaders.

SEE ALSO

➤ *Chapter 10 is stuffed with information on linking LANs; see page 247.*

➤ *Remote access is important enough to consume all of Chapter 15, which starts on page 383.*

➤ *Web-caching proxy servers are covered in the section "Caching the Web," on page 314.*

➤ *More information on firewalls can be found in the sections "Heavy Security" on page 324 and "Security" on page 416.*

LAN-Management Tools

LAN administrators in large and small organizations are coming under increasing pressure to back up their budgets, monitor LAN operations in real time, and safeguard against network abuse. Network management is a high-priority topic for anyone responsible for the tens of thousands of dollars invested in the typical network. Several categories of network-management software provide administrators with strong tools they can use to prevent abuse, collect statistics, and provide reports on network operations.

SEE ALSO

➤ *Network management is the sole topic of Chapter 16, which begins on page 399.*

Traffic Monitoring

If you answer "yes" to the question about being the network troubleshooter, you need some special tools. Network troubleshooters can use two types of traffic-monitoring systems. *Media-monitoring software* gathers statistical data from a centralized wiring hub and provides second-by-second control over the connections that servers and client stations make to the network. *LAN protocol analyzers* capture the packets of data flying across a network and decode them into more-or-less plain English.

Application-Metering Software

The question "Need to limit the number of application users?" refers to whether you must monitor and limit the number of people simultaneously using an application in order to stay within the confines of a software license. LAN *application-metering software* controls the number of people who can simultaneously access a networked application. This type of software enables you to buy only as many copies of an application as you really need yet eliminate the danger of abusing software licenses.

Similarly, *LAN-management software suites* are products that roll many functions together. They produce printed reports that administrators can use to plan LAN growth and justify expenditures, and they offer additional capabilities such as virus protection and backup.

Making the Right Choices

The Connectivity Decision Tree won't replace a good consultant, but it will help you organize your ideas and make some important early decisions about the best approach to take. An investment in a media-sharing LAN can pay big dividends in workgroup productivity, but such a complex system requires a great deal of investment, planning, and management. Less-complex alternatives and techniques might work fine for you. The Connectivity Decision Tree can help you manage the growth and operation of your network for years to come.

Connecting PCs for Printer Sharing and File Exchange

Simple switches

Printer-sharing buffers

Zero-slot LANs

Media-sharing LANs

Printer sharing alternatives

While networking is valuable because it makes telecommuting possible, reduces corporate overhead, and reduces inventory, we don't see much evidence that it reduces the amount of paper we use. Except in specific applications (such as document management, described in Chapter 17), the once longed-for "paperless office" remains a dream. Even the Internet doesn't help. We find that people often print out documents that they download through the Internet because they find it easier to read such documents on paper than on the screen. Because the primary output of computers seems to be paper, printing capabilities are both important and a major investment.

Sharing relatively expensive printers among several people has always been a primary objective of PC connectivity. In the mid-1980s, even dot-matrix printers with "near-letter quality" were expensive. As the cost of letter-quality printers declined, printers capable of producing the special fonts needed for desktop publishing appeared on the horizon as high-cost items. Now that we have reasonably priced printers suitable for basic desktop publishing, printers that can use large sheets of paper or print in high volume are the ones that demand sharing. But because one person probably won't keep a modern printer busy, it makes sense to share printers among as many people as possible.

SEE ALSO
➤ Document management is a workgroup productivity application described in Chapter 17, starting on page 427.

Simple Switches

To many people, printer sharing means having a box with a switch on the front and cables running to the PCs and printer. When you turn the knob, the switch establishes a connection to the printer from one of two or three PCs.

Manual printer switches (see Figure 3.1) are often called *A-B boxes* after the designation of the switch positions. Although they are simple to operate, they must be connected to each computer using a maximum of about 15 feet of parallel cable. Additionally, several printer manufacturers, including Hewlett-Packard, warn against using manual switches with shorting contacts that make one connection before they break the other because of the risk of an excessive voltage spike that might damage your printer when someone changes the switch setting.

A commercial A-B box offers a simple and effective way to share a printer among as many as three or four users. However, you trade the benefits of simplicity for the hassles of remembering to change the switch and coordinating with the other people using the system.

Printer-Sharing Buffers

Printer-sharing buffers automate the concept of the manual printer switch. Although printer-sharing buffers come in a variety of sizes and shapes, each device typically has a cabinet just big enough for all the connectors mounted on it and a separate power supply molded into the wall plug. As Figure 3.2 shows, the printer-sharing buffer uses the existing ports on the computers and printers and creates shared connections that don't involve adding hardware or software to the PC.

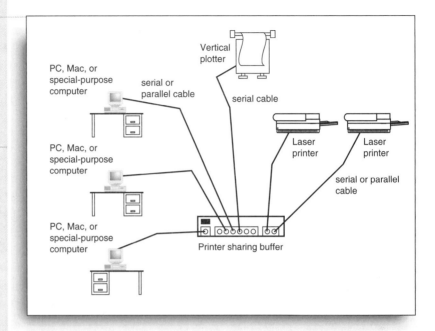

FIGURE 3.2

Printer-sharing buffers provide the simplest method of connecting computers and shared printers or plotters. These devices require little setup and no special hardware or software on the PCs.

You can often fit a printer-sharing buffer inconspicuously next to the printer. As Figure 3.3 shows, some companies even design them to fit inside popular printers like the Hewlett-Packard LaserJet. These devices connect to each PC and printer, switching print jobs and connections from the PCs to the printers.

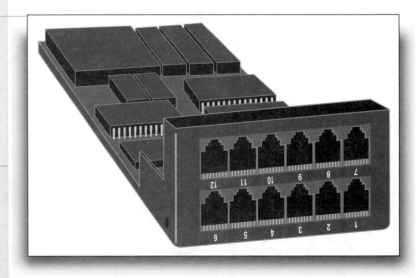

FIGURE 3.3

The ASP ServerJet is an interesting printer sharing product that slides into an I/O slot of an HP LaserJet and allows as many as 12 computers to share the printer without any other special software or adapters.

A printer-sharing buffer enables each person who shares the printer to send print jobs just as if the printer were attached directly to the PC. The device receives a job, checks the printer's availability, and either passes the job to the printer or stores it until the printer can accept it. The most sophisticated units can select from among several attached printers based on the print job's format and content. Once the buffer has the print job, the person who sent the job is free to turn to other tasks while the buffer works with the printer.

Because the buffer stores print jobs, it needs enough memory to hold the kinds of jobs that are being sent. Documents containing graphics print slowly and occupy a lot of memory, so if people on your network create a lot of graphical documents, consider adding four or more megabytes of memory to the print buffer. Adding memory raises the cost, but it also increases the speed even though the operation stays simple.

Printer-sharing buffers offer versatility and flexibility. They come in models that can handle a wide number and variety of computers running UNIX, Macintosh, DOS, and Windows operating systems, as well as different printing devices. They're useful for small installations in which you don't want to install a media-sharing LAN and for networked installations in which you don't want to load down the LAN with big print jobs. Note that printer buffers are particularly well suited to the problem of sharing a plotter. Plotters are typically serial devices, and the software you use to create plotted images often expects to directly address the PC's serial port hardware (particularly under DOS), so it's difficult to use these devices with LAN software and hardware. But because the printer buffer functions like a plotter connected to the serial port, all of the software works fine, and you're able to share the expensive plotting hardware.

You can find models of print buffers with up to 64 ports, but the price of these products typically stays at slightly under $50 per port. Most modern printer-sharing buffers can also handle problems such as mismatched speed between the PC and printer serial ports, or the need to convert between a PC's serial connections and a printer's parallel connections.

The cables used to attach PCs to printer-sharing buffers have distance limitations, particularly if you use a somewhat fast parallel-cable connection. You can count on a good connection if you use less than 50 feet of parallel printer cable, but the distance between the printer and the most distant PC can't be much more than that. Several products in this market, however, can carry serial-port connections to printers over several thousand feet of cable.

I've said that the print buffers don't need software loaded in each PC, but using a small piece of software in the client computers can improve flexibility. Typically, you can program a print buffer so it automatically sends print jobs to specific types of printers set up for envelopes, color, PostScript printing, or other special features. But if you want to manually select the printers, you can use terminate-and-stay resident (TSR) software under DOS, or you can use a Windows program to select the printer you want to use for your print jobs. The designers of these buffers know all sorts of necessary tricks about resetting printers between jobs and sending form feeds to kick out the last page of a job.

Printer-sharing buffers are practical devices. They don't do anything more than efficiently move print jobs to the printer or plotter. But if that is all you need, your worries are over.

Choosing a Printer-Sharing Buffer

If you decide a printer-sharing buffer is right for you, consider these things before you buy:

- How many PC and printer ports do you need?
- How much RAM is available for the print job queue?
- Do you want serial or parallel connections?
- Do the cables come with the unit?
- Does the unit allow PCs and printers operating at different speeds to be connected?
- What is the size of the unit and the type of cable connectors?
- Where will you get technical support?

Printer sharing is an important part of workgroup productivity. You should install a system that can provide all the capabilities you need, but don't pay for more than you require.

Zero-Slot LANs

I coined the phrase "zero-slot LANs" in a 1987 *PC Magazine* review of these low-cost but highly functional PC-connection products. To create a zero-slot LAN, you simply take two PCs, connect one cable between their serial or parallel ports, and load a small piece of software in each PC. The software lets the people using the two PCs share printers, exchange files, and even simultaneously access the same data file. In Microsoft Windows, there is even a capability to link PCs through their serial ports with properly configured cable connections.

But the days of zero-slot LANs are over because the prices of shared-media LANs have dipped so low. Any tiny cost advantage left to the zero-slot LAN doesn't outweigh its disadvantage in throughput, so I mention them here mainly as a historical note. LapLink from Travelling Software is the best surviving example of a zero-slot LAN.

The next section introduces media-sharing LANs, a very capable—perhaps overly capable—printer-sharing technique.

Media-Sharing LANs

The wide-ranging capabilities of media-sharing LANs are a major reason for their popularity. Before we learn about lower-cost alternatives to media-sharing LANs, let's briefly examine how these popular connection systems function.

Media-sharing LANs carry messages simultaneously from multiple stations over a shared high-speed medium. The most common medium today is unshielded twisted-pair copper wire, but many LANs still use coaxial copper cable. *Fiber-optic* cable is used primarily to link between major network segments on different floors or in different buildings. Media-sharing LANs use signaling and sharing schemes with names like ARCnet, Ethernet, and Token-Ring. An *adapter board* for these networks occupies a slot in each PC and performs the data handling and precise timing chores that become necessary when the media are shared among hundreds of stations.

Network operating systems like Windows and NetWare fool local programs into thinking that distant disk drives and printers—which actually reside on computers acting as servers—are really on the local computer. The redirection of service requests to the network allows standard applications to use shared resources like the network server (for file storage), networked printers (for printing), and communications links to the Internet and corporate intranets.

When you put together a card-carrying LAN, you need space in each PC and some technical skill to install the LAN adapter card, and you also need a good budget for the cabling and for special LAN software. The hardware and software for these networks will cost around $150 per station. Although that might seem like a lot, wide area network connections can have high initial costs and monthly recurring costs. Managing a media-sharing network with a dozen stations or more usually requires the talents of a full-time PC support person. You get what you pay for, though, because these LANs provide more functionality and speed than any other connectivity alternative.

SEE ALSO
➤ *To learn more about the cabling for media-sharing LANs, see the section "Cables for Network Connections," on page 106.*

Print Servers

Although the administrative details involved in making media-sharing LANs work correctly are often complex, the concept behind shared LAN printing is simple. A device called a *print server* accepts print jobs from client PCs on the network and queues those jobs until the printers controlled by the print server can accept them. Utility software included in a network operating system gives network users and administrators control over the priority of jobs in the queue.

Printers shared on the network might connect to a PC, or they might connect to a specialized standalone print server, or they might have their own network connections.

One or more PCs on a media-sharing LAN can take on the role of a print server. This PC makes its attached printers available to all other devices on the network. Software that resides in each PC using the network intercepts the print jobs that standard applications create and sends them to a network print server.

The PC acting as a print server might simultaneously act as a file server or as a personal workstation. There are no special hardware requirements for the print server except that it must have enough serial or parallel ports for the attached printers. An old cast-aside PC with a slow 80386 or 486 processor works just fine as a dedicated network print server. Modern LAN operating systems provide ways for any PC attached to the network to fill this function.

Standalone print servers offer better flexibility, economy, and reliability than do networked printers attached to PCs. Because each standalone print server is a small device about the size of a modem, you can put it anywhere that you can conveniently put the printers. If you share a printer that's connected to a networked PC, however, you must keep that PC running all the time. If the PC goes down, everyone on the network is unable to print. Standalone print servers are reliable and fit almost anywhere. For under $400, you can purchase a device that's capable of simultaneously connecting and controlling the activities of three printers.

Sophisticated tasks, such as downloading fonts to the printer for desktop publishing, often require several carefully executed steps. Because applications don't always reset the printer mode before and after executing a print job, some jobs might print with text in compressed form, with strange fonts, or sideways because one of these attributes was used in a previous print job.

Protocols for Printing

When you print across a LAN, you have to decide what set of *protocols* or communications rules you'll use for communication between the client computers and print servers. I'll explain this in much more detail in later chapters, but your choices include NetWare's NCP over IPX, the NetBEUI protocol from Windows, and TCP/IP. The first standalone print servers were designed to work with NetWare, and practically all the devices in this market still work with NetWare.

NetWare comes with two network print server applications, *Pserver*, which runs on a dedicated server, and *Nprinter*, which runs on a client PC. Typically, all products work with both the Pserver and Rprinter applications. However, in this mode, you must have a NetWare server on your network to handle the queues, and you must run the IPX/SPX protocol on the client PCs that need to print.

The TCP/IP set of protocols has two print utilities it inherited from UNIX called Lpr and Lpd. These utilities allow you to print directly to a device that understands TCP. While UNIX and Windows NT include an Lpr/Lpd utility, Windows 95 doesn't. In order to get around this problem, many products include a proprietary printer port driver that enables users to print from a Windows 95 PC using the TCP/IP protocol.

Browser management can't do it all

Browser-enabled management eliminates many arcane commands and techniques, but sometimes arcane knowledge wins out. For example, in some cases you still must use Novell's Pconsole to set up a NetWare print queue. The browser interface is sometimes more useful for monitoring and managing than it is for performing initial configuration and setup.

Another advantage of using these print servers is that you can manage them from a remote location. Most devices allow you to perform tasks such as verifying that the server is up and running, resetting a hung server, and changing basic information including the name of the device. A new trend in management is to use a web browser to manage and control a device. Typically, you must assign an IP address to the device and then point your browser at that address. Then you can perform almost every management task from across the web that you can with the product's proprietary management utility.

SEE ALSO

➤ *Chapter 9, which starts on page 191, tells more about the protocols for network communications.*

➤ *We talk a lot more about UNIX in the section "Digital and UNIX," on page 231.*

On the Bottom Line of LAN Printing

You get the best value in a media-sharing LAN when you use it to provide many people with simultaneous access to the same files. Media-sharing LANs shine when you use them to provide accounting services, inventory control, and other database applications. They also provide good value when you use them to share expensive communications links to intranets and the Internet or to different computer systems such as mainframes.

A Field Guide to LANs

How about a helicopter view? Let's look over the networking territory a little so you can find the areas you want to know more about and dip down into them. I've written this chapter to give you an overview of the pieces and parts in a media-sharing LAN system and to describe the important factors you need to consider when you're stringing together those pieces and parts. Later chapters deal with the features and foibles of specific cabling schemes and operating systems in more depth. This chapter gives you the strategic view, the buzzwords, and the background you'll need to get the most out of the material in later chapters.

As a first step in explaining these systems, I'll divide them into hardware and software. Even this seemingly simple division isn't clean, though, because some hardware elements have software on board in read-only memory (ROM). But it's a good way to start examining the pieces of the LAN puzzle. After we examine the real pieces and parts, we'll move from the material to the conceptual by introducing a number of networking acronyms and concepts.

Networking's Necessary Hardware

Servers, client PCs, adapter cards, and cables are the dry-bones hardware into which networking and application software breathe life. Because modern hardware products follow international standards, you can often mix and match hardware products from different vendors within the same network. Similarly, the hardware you buy does not determine your selection of application software for the network. But the selection of the right hardware isn't simple. You have to make up-front decisions with long-term consequences.

Servers and Clients

In a PC-based network, computers act in the functional roles of servers and client stations. The servers make their attached disk drives, printers, modems, and unique communications links (such as fax) available to the client stations. Software running on the client PCs gives network users access to the data and devices available on one or more servers. The type of networking software running on a server determines whether the server is dedicated to its service role or whether it also runs local application programs in what is termed a *peer-to-peer network*. In essence, a PC can be both a server for other clients and a client to other servers.

Practically any Pentium-class computer can act as a file server in a business office with as many as fifty clients. Even machines with 80386 and 80486 processors are suited for use as print servers and fax servers. But some network applications run partly in the server, so investing in a powerful processor today will pay future dividends. If you get into a line-of-business application such as inventory, reservations, or accounting, the act of designing the server quickly jumps from a casual back-of-the envelope exercise and becomes a fine art. It's best to consult the company selling the application to get guidelines for server sizing information.

Many companies sell computers with multiple expansion slots and disk drive bays as servers. But a computer with a lot of internal space, a fast processor, and a vertical mounting pedestal isn't necessarily a good server. Here is my advice on servers in a nutshell: Get fast drives and lots of RAM. First, price a good set of hard drives with triple the capacity you think you'll ever need and a compatible SCSI disk controller. A fast/wide SCSI-2 controller with its own on-board memory cache and processor can make a huge difference in server performance.

If reliability is a critical factor, you'll find it worth the extra cost of a RAID system. The acronym RAID stands for Redundant Array of Inexpensive Disks. The idea is to combine as many as five disks into a single system that writes data across as many as five drives. The *striping* of data across the drives has advantages in both performance and reliability. Because the data heads of each individual drive don't have to move as much during the read and write actions, these actions are faster. A technique called RAID 5 enables a feature called *parity checking*. Under RAID 5, if one drive in the array fails, the controller can use the parity information and the contents of the remaining drives to

What is a server?

The word "server" has several meanings in terms of both function and physical form. Some servers run inside PCs, and some are special-purpose standalone boxes such as print servers, fax servers, and communications servers. So "server" can refer to a function performed by software, or it can be a specific kind of beefed-up PC, or it can be a single-purpose box containing its own processor and programming.

Stay alive!

How's your UPS? A good uninterruptible power supply should be
something you buy with every computer (just like the monitor). It's
even more important to have a UPS
on every computer providing a network function, such as a server.
Even if some client PCs don't have
UPS protection, you want the server
to be alive when those PCs recover
from a power outage. And wiring
hubs need UPS protection, too,
because even if the PC and server
have power, they can't talk if the
hub is out.

determine and quickly reconstruct the contents of the bad drive. RAID 5 is one of the primary elements in what is called a *high availability server*.

You should choose a PC with a fast Pentium processor and then load it with a minimum of 64 megabytes of RAM (make sure you buy the RAM in a configuration that allows you to add more without throwing away what you already have). The speed of the processor is less important than is having a good disk controller and enough RAM. As a rule, file servers and web servers benefit from a PC having as much as 128MB of RAM. It's a good investment.

SEE ALSO

➤ *For more specifics on RAID and server hardware, perform a read action on the section "Software in the Client PC," on page 163.*

Interface Cards

The most frequent investment you will make in LAN hardware is to buy *network interface adapters* (generally called *interface cards* or *adapter cards*). In 1987, a typical network interface card cost $600. Today, the increased availability of these printed circuit boards has turned the interface card into a commodity product. Currently a no-frills Ethernet card is well under $100. ARCnet, which also used to be common, has now fallen into obscurity except in industrial applications. Its technology was kept propri-etary by Datapoint, Corp., and it didn't gather the industry-wide momentum collected by Ethernet.

Every computer on the network needs an interface card to trans-fer the serial signals on the network cables or media into the parallel data stream inside the PCs. Figure 4.1 illustrates the process. These adapters can also change the format of the data from parallel to serial and amplify the signals so they can travel over the necessary distances. In some cases, you will put two or more adapters in a server to split the load onto separate cables and reduce congestion.

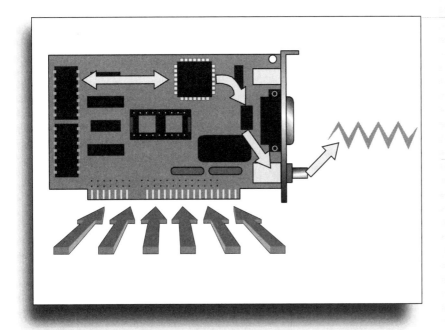

FIGURE 4.1

The network interface card changes the parallel signals inside the computer into serial signals that go over the network cable. The interface card determines what type of network cable system you will use.

These adapters also have the important job of controlling access to the media. This media-access control (MAC) function takes three general forms: listen-before-transmitting, sequential station number, and token-passing.

SEE ALSO

➤ *You'll find more about network interface cards and network architectures like Ethernet in the section "Ethernet the Elder," on page 133.*

Media-Access Control

The listen-before-transmitting scheme, called carrier sense multiple access (CSMA), operates like a CB, police, or other two-way radio system. A network node that has data to transmit listens to the LAN cable. If it doesn't hear the carrier or the transmitted signal of another network node, the station broadcasts its message. Various techniques handle the problems that arise when multiple stations hear the empty channel and start to transmit at the same time.

The MAC layer

You'll hear or read references to the "MAC-layer" address. Every LAN adapter card has a unique address. Ethernet and Token-Ring addresses are assigned at the factory. Some devices, like sophisticated wiring hubs and routers, use these addresses to control traffic.

ARCnet uses a different media-access scheme, sequential station number, which assigns a station number (0 to 255) to each node on the network. A station that has messages to send simply waits for its number to come up in turn.

The other popular media-access control scheme, token-passing, involves a special message called a token that is passed from node to node by active stations on the network. The station that has this token has permission to transmit.

LAN scientists and the people marketing LAN products can argue for days over the theoretical advantages of the CSMA and token-passing media-access protocols. My advice is not to worry about the question. Other factors, such as whether a company stands behind its products, are much more important than the type of media-access protocol that's used by the adapters you choose. But you do need to know what people mean when they talk about media-access schemes or MAC protocols.

SEE ALSO

➤ *For more information on the specifics of LAN adapters and how they work, check for transmissions in the section "Adapter Options," on page 86.*

Wire, Wire Everywhere...and Not an Inch to Link

The most important question associated with choosing an adapter board is what kind of cable or wire you want to use for the network. Modern Ethernet and Token-Ring adapters give you a wide variety of wiring choices. But remember, your network will never be any better than its cabling! This is the link that ties everything together, and poorly installed cabling is a sure prescription for frustration and failure.

What network interface card you choose determines the type of cabling you'll need to connect the servers and the client stations. Choices include coaxial cable, fiber-optic cable, unshielded twisted-pair wire, and shielded twisted-pair wire. If one of these types of wire is already installed in your building, you'll want to select an interface card that can work with the existing wiring. Figure 4.2 shows some wiring examples.

FIGURE 4.2
The major types of network wiring are (from left to right) thin coaxial cable with BNC connector, fiber-optic cable and connectors, shielded twisted-pair wire with an IBM Token-Ring connector attached, and unshielded twisted-pair wire with a modular connector attached.

Two electrical phenomena can disrupt your network: crosstalk and outside electrical noise. *Crosstalk* occurs when electrical fields in adjacent wires induce false signals in both wires. Outside electrical noise comes from lights, motors, radio systems, and many other sources. The negative effects of crosstalk and noise increase as the signaling speed of the network increases. Therefore, the goal of any wiring scheme is to keep crosstalk and noise to a minimum.

SEE ALSO
➤ *The section "Cables for Network Connections," on page 106, has LAN cabling all wired up.*

Coaxial Cable

Coaxial cable provides good protection from crosstalk and outside electrical noise. A woven metal or foil braid surrounding the outside of a single conductor presents a formidable barrier to electrical noise. Originally, thin Ethernet and ARCnet schemes used only coaxial cable.

One other version of Ethernet uses a thick coaxial cable—particularly, for example, as a backbone between workgroups on different floors of a building. *Thick Ethernet* cable (known in the trade as "frozen orange garden hose" because it's stiff and carrot-colored) is difficult to install, and its popularity is diminishing.

Overall, because coaxial cable is more expensive and takes up more space in wiring conduits, it is being superseded by unshielded twisted-pair wire for desktop connections and by fiber-optic cable for longer runs.

Fiber-Optic Cable

Fiber-optic cable allows for greater distance between stations: A fiber-optic link can run for several kilometers without the need for repeaters that regenerate the signal. In addition, fiber-optic cable provides total immunity to electrical noise: Radio transmitters, arc welders, fluorescent lights, and other sources of electrical noise have absolutely no effect on the light pulses traveling inside this kind of cable. Many vendors offer versions of their network interface cards adapted for fiber-optic transmission.

However, fiber-optic cabling is expensive. Depending on local labor rates and building codes, installing this type of cable can cost as much as $200 per network node. At one time, it was thought that fiber optic cabling would replace all copper cable, at least in heavy-duty commercial applications. But new developments in the engineering of cable schemes, particularly in the capability of unshielded twisted-pair wire to carry high-speed data, have reduced the technical advantages of fiber.

Unshielded Twisted-Pair Wire

Unshielded twisted-pair wire (UTP) used in networks can meet all of your networking needs. A number of organizations, including the Electronic Industries Association, the Telecommunications Industry Association (EIA/TIA), and Underwriter's Laboratories (UL), have standards for UTP wiring.

The EIA/TIA 568 standards describe a UTP structured wiring scheme that can handle the fastest network connections you'll run to the desktops. Some server connections might use a newer technology called Gigabit Ethernet, which requires fiber-optic cable, but Gigabit Ethernet will typically find its use as a campus backbone technology.

SEE ALSO

➤ *You'll learn more about Gigabit Ethernet on page 148.*

Shielded Twisted-Pair Wire

Shielded twisted-pair wire (STP) has a name similar to the more widely used unshielded twisted-pair wiring, but it has a very

---

UTP is the best investment

UTP is what you want for a new or expanded LAN. UTP installations are flexible and offer room for growth. However, you should still use only fiber-optic cable for network connections between buildings. Problems with the electrical grounds of individual buildings can translate into mysterious problems between networks. Always use fiber between buildings, and replace copper inter-building data connections if you have them.

different construction. Shielded twisted-pair wire is bound in an external aluminum-foil or woven-copper shield that's specifically designed to reduce electrical noise absorption. Different companies have their own specifications for such cables, although IEEE standards apply to systems like IBM's Token-Ring.

Shielded twisted-pair cables are expensive and difficult to work with, and because they are so thick, they often fill up wiring conduits. Still, IBM has successfully marketed a wiring plan that uses these cables for Token-Ring installations. The IBM plan adds reliability (and substantial cost) by using a separate run of cable between each server or workstation and a central wiring hub. This wiring plan significantly increases the amount of cable used, but it also ensures against the total failure of the network in the event that one cable breaks or shorts.

SEE ALSO

➤ *For more on Token-Ring, see page 149.*

Network Topology

Isn't *topology* a lovely word? Basically, in networking it means "the shape of things." A *physical topology* is a description of the route the network cables take as they link nodes; logical topology describes how the messages flow to the stations. The physical form and the logical path can be two different things.

ARCnet typically uses a wiring plan or topology in which every station links directly into a central wiring hub, which reduces the vulnerability of the overall network. Token-Ring uses a similar hub in its physical topology. Thin Ethernet, on the other hand, uses a station-to-station wiring scheme that is economical because it uses less cable than a hub-type scheme. However, it runs the risk of total network failure if any one link is severed or shorted. Because of this drawback, modern Ethernet networks use a hub topology, but many station-to-station installations still provide good service. The physical structure of the local network includes many elements: network interface cards, hubs, cabling, print server, file servers, and other devices working together. Figure 4.3 shows a typical configuration and provides hints about what to look for in networked devices and connections.

SEE ALSO

➤ *Chapter 7, which starts on page 131, takes on topology and describes the more practical aspects of network architecture.*

Why a hub?

All modern LAN installations should use a wiring hub. The hub isolates malfunctioning links and prevents problems on one individual link from taking down the entire network. The hub adds cost, and you run into electrical limitations when connecting hubs, but you should always plan for a wiring hub—even if your network consists of only two computers.

FIGURE 4.3

An integrated workgroup network has many elements, including network interface adapters, at least one wiring hub, and devices like access servers and routers to link to the outside world.

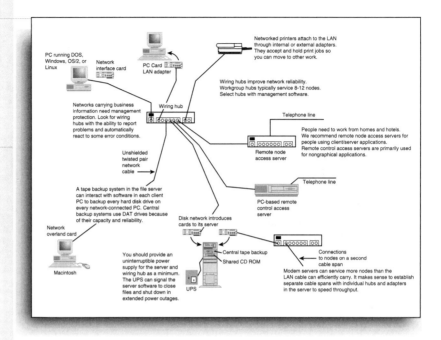

FIGURE 4.3

An integrated workgroup network has many elements, including network interface adapters, at least one wiring hub, and devices like access servers and routers to link to the outside world.

The Soft Side

Because of the current de facto standards and protocols, you can mix and match pieces—servers, network interface cards, cables, and software—in a myriad of ways to form an optimally productive and cost-effective network.

Many people worry more about network interface cards and cabling than they do about network operating systems. While they can usually specify that they want a server with fast disk drives and a fast processor, they don't know how to quantify, describe, or select networking software. But software can make or break a network.

Network operating systems make distant resources local. If you are interested in files residing on a computer down the hall, the networking software enables you to access those files as if they resided on a disk drive in your own machine. It enables you to use a printer located thousands of feet—or even miles—away as if that printer were snugly attached to your own LPT1 port. And it allows you to use network modems or links to other communications devices as if they were cabled to your own COM1 port.

Network operating systems have a multitasking and multiuser architecture. Your PC's desktop operating system takes requests from application programs and translates them, one at a time, into actions to be performed by the video display, disk drives, and other peripheral devices. Network operating systems, on the other hand, take requests for services from many application programs at the same time and satisfy them with the network's resources, in effect arbitrating requests for the same services from different users.

SEE ALSO

➤ *You can burrow more deeply into the structure of networking software in the section "Software in the Client PC," on page 163.*

Invisible and Modular

Ideally, networking software is invisible to users. When you use it, you know you have additional resources available, but you usually don't care where the resources are or how you attach to them.

Structurally, networking software has many modules. Most of them reside in the machine that acts as the server for data, printer, or communications resources. But, as Figure 4.4 shows, several important program modules must be installed in every workstation, or sometimes in devices posed between the workstation and the network.

Figure 4.4 illustrates how the operating software interacts with the hardware and software on the workstation (left) and on the server (right). For both workstation and server, the hardware is the bottom level of the diagram; everything above that is software. Arrows represent the flow of messages—requests for services and data and responses to those requests.

The workstation is only a "client," with no capabilities for contributing resources to other network stations. It has the same PC hardware (disk drives, monitor, keyboard, and so forth), BIOS (Basic Input/Output System, the software that links the hardware to DOS), and operating system that all PCs have, whether they are networked or not.

Making distant resources local

The importance of networking software is that it invisibly makes shared drives, printers, and communications ports seem like they're attached to the local computer. You use the same word processing, spreadsheet, web browsing, and other software that you would use on a PC with no local area network connection, and a disk drive shared across the LAN appears as just another drive letter, like D: or E:, to desktop applications.

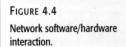

FIGURE 4.4

Network software/hardware
interaction.

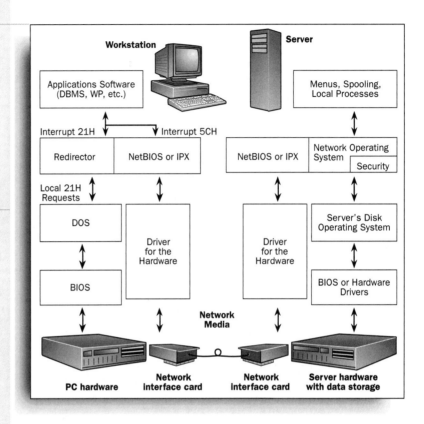

For LAN operation, several additional elements are necessary, both hardware (interface cards and cables) and software (redirectors, network layer software, and driver software). In addition, the application program running on the workstation might have certain added network attributes, such as the capability to issue record- and file-lock commands automatically. (This software enhancement is not strictly necessary because even application programs not designed for a LAN can run on a network.)

The *redirector* module is added to intervene between the application program and the desktop operating system such as DOS, Windows, or UNIX. It intercepts software calls from an application program asking the desktop operating system for a service such as file access. Each PC's redirector is programmed to switch certain calls out through the network for service (for instance, requests for data from drives that don't exist in the local PC's hardware). Thanks to the redirector, a PC application can easily use network resources just by addressing the correct disk drive.

Another added software module, the *interface card driver*, moves data between the redirector and the client PC's network interface card. This driver software is specifically designed for network interface card hardware. Many manufacturers have cooperated with Microsoft, and they have their drivers bundled into the Windows operating system. Other vendors provide the drivers on diskettes shipped with their products or on their Internet web sites.

The network interface card sits in the expansion bus of the workstation. In modern networks, the wiring and media-access protocol are almost always independent of the networking software. The interface card includes programs in read-only memory that manage the creation and transmission of packets over the network.

At the other end of the cable from the workstation interface card is the server, with additional specialized LAN software and its own interface card. Like any other computer, the server runs an operating system. Sometimes it's Windows 95 or 98, but often it's a more powerful multitasking operating system such as Windows NT Server, some version of Novell's NetWare, or Sun's Solaris. In some networks, you can run local application programs on the server and use it as a network terminal. Finally, network utility programs run on the server, offering print spooling, auditing, and other LAN features.

Working together, these program modules perform the basic actions of networking software. In a nutshell, networking software recognizes users, associates their preprogrammed privileges with their identities, and then reroutes their requests to the appropriate server for action.

Operating System Features

You'll want to consider the following features when selecting a particular system.

- *Dedicated servers versus a shared solution.* Windows 95/98-based network operating systems allow any networked computer to contribute drives, printers, and other resources to the network. Microsoft's Windows NT has the same capabilities. Other operating systems, such as Novell's NetWare and Banyan's VINES, require a computer dedicated to the server role.

The shared solution (also called *peer-to-peer resource sharing*) is appealing in small installations in which the cost of a dedicated machine is a factor. Sharing a workstation's resources always slows the operation of local programs, while dedicated servers give faster network performance. But many Pentium-equipped PCs have enough power to support both server and local processing tasks.

- *Fault tolerance.* If critical business, security, or safety operations run on a network, the operating system software can help improve survivability. So-called fault-tolerant operating systems mirror the operation of a disk drive or even an entire server on a duplicate resource. If the first drive or server fails, the mirror image takes over. NetWare and Windows NT provide a variety of options for system fault tolerance.

- *Server-based applications.* In the typical PC-based network, application programs run on the workstations, and the servers run special programs dealing only with security and resource sharing. This arrangement is usually efficient, but sometimes performing certain disk-intensive tasks on the network file server is more efficient (these tasks include indexing a database or compiling program source code). All modern network operating systems can run appropriate application tasks on the server, increasing the efficiency (and complexity) of operation for installations that are busy with disk-intensive applications.

- *Server software memory.* The amount of RAM the server software uses is important if you want to use a PC as both a workstation and a server in a peer-to-peer network.

- *Network administration.* Every successful network has someone who officially or unofficially acts as the system administrator. What kind of software tools are available to the system administrator for reporting on who is using the network and for monitoring the workload? These tools are important to both improving performance and controlling costs.

Redundancy and reliability

You can enhance the reliability of servers with hardware and with software. Disk arrays (RAID), redundant power supplies, and multiple processors add hardware survivability. Software that mirrors the operation of disk drives also adds reliability, as does software that *clusters* separate computers so they monitor each other.

- *Diagnostic utilities*. Some network operating systems give the network supervisor certain utilities he can use to find problems and configure the server for optimum operation. These utilities can supply reports of bad packets and network errors, and they include tools for the operation of disk-cache programs.

- *Security*. Security is usually maintained through the use of passwords. The best systems have different levels of access giving users various privileges (including read, write, modify, create, and erase). Other forms of security are password protection for facilities such as disk drives, subdirectories, or even selected files, and the ability to regulate access based on the time of day or day of the week.

- *Electronic mail*. A good electronic mail system alone might justify your investment in a LAN. But the simple email systems of yesterday that focused on storing and forwarding messages have evolved into more sophisticated messaging systems. A messaging system provides an underlying architecture that allows many kinds of application programs to identify users across the network and move information between programs. Messaging systems, led by Microsoft's Messaging Application Program Interface (MAPI), are an important part of modern network operating systems.

- *Print spooling*. When several LAN stations use a printer attached to a central server, the print jobs are saved in a special file called a *spool*. The print jobs are then queued for printer access. Each user should have a way to check the position of his job in the queue and to kill jobs sent there by mistake. The network administrator should be able to change the priorities of jobs in the print queue and assign specific priorities to certain users.

Security begins with a locked door

Although software can provide security tools, most security problems result from poor administrative business practices. Hackers are a very minor threat compared to the problems caused by improper handling of passwords, poor physical access controls, and poor structuring of access control.

CHAPTER 4

Networking Acronyms and Buzzwords

Before you can fully understand networking, you've got to speak the language. At the very least, the next time your boss asks whether you think the company should migrate to SAA, you should know that this doesn't mean moving corporate headquarters south of the border. The following guide should help demystify the acronyms and buzzwords that industry insiders toss around so glibly.

ISO's OSI Model

Because you need a structure to hang the acronyms and buzzwords on, you first have to know about the ISO and its OSI model. The International Standards Organization (ISO), based in Geneva, develops standards for international and national data communications. The U.S. representative to the ISO is the American National Standards Institute, or ANSI. In the early 1970s, the ISO developed a standard model of a data communications system and called it the *Open Systems Interconnection (OSI) model.*

The OSI model, consisting of seven layers, describes what happens when a terminal talks to a computer or when one computer talks to another. This model was designed to facilitate creating a system in which equipment from different vendors can communicate.

Other data communications models are IBM's Systems Network Architecture (SNA) and Digital Equipment Corp.'s DEC Network Architecture (DNA), both of which predate the OSI model.

The seven layers

The OSI model is a necessary evil. It gives us a way to discuss and diagram the major functions of networking. In the real world, the relationship between the model and real software blurs, but the functional descriptions remain valuable. You don't have to memorize the OSI model, but it is often helpful to understand the functions of the Network and Physical layers.

The OSI Layer Cake

Think of the OSI model as a layer cake like the one shown in Figure 4.5. At the bottom, holding everything else up, is the Physical layer, which is made up of the wiring or cables.

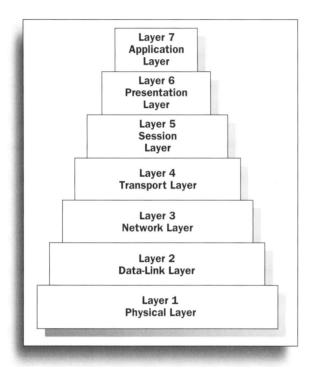

FIGURE 4.5

Layers of the OSI model.

These are the layers of the OSI model:

7) **Application layer:** At this level, software follows standards for look and feel.

6) **Presentation layer:** Here, data is formatted for viewing and for use on specific equipment.

5) **Session layer:** This layer provides a standard way to move data between application programs.

4) **Transport layer:** This layer of software is particularly important to local area networks. Transport layer software provides for reliable and transparent transfer of packets between stations.

3) **Network layer:** Software operating at this layer provides an interface between the Physical and Data-link layers and the higher-level software, which establishes and maintains connections.

2) **Data-link layer:** This layer provides for the reliable transfer of information across the Physical layer. It synchronizes the blocks of data, recognizes errors, and controls the flow of data.

1) **Physical layer:** The most fundamental layer is concerned with transmitting a stream of data over the physical cables and wires. Hardware and software operating at this level deal with the types of connectors, signaling, and media-sharing schemes used on the network.

The Physical Layer

The Physical layer furnishes electrical connections and signaling. Subsequent layers talk through this Physical layer. Twisted-pair wiring, fiber-optic strands, and coaxial cable are all part of the Physical layer.

Probably the most common standard in the Physical layer is RS-232, a wiring and signaling standard that defines which pin on the connectors does what, and when a voltage level on a wire represents a 1 or a 0. Europeans use an international standard called V.24, which is a lot like RS-232. All of these are Physical layer standards.

The Physical layer carries the signals for all the higher layers. Pull the plug, and you won't communicate at all. But without the higher layers, you won't have anything to say. The higher you go in the OSI model, the more meaningful the communication is to the end user.

Chapters 5, 6, and 7 focus on the Physical layer. This is the stuff of cables, adapters, and hubs.

The Data-Link Layer

Once you've made the physical and electrical connections, you must control the data stream between your system and the one at the other end. The Data-link layer of the OSI model works like the overseer of a railroad yard that's putting cars together to make up a train. This functional level strings characters together into messages and then checks them before putting them on the tracks. It might also receive an "arrived safely" message from the overseer in the other yard, or it might work with the other yard to reconstruct a message when a data disaster occurs. (Routing trains between yards is the job of the Network layer.)

The Data-link layer uses many protocols, including High-Level Data Link Control (HDLC), bisynchronous communications, and Advanced Data Communications Control Procedures (ADCCP). You don't need to know the details of any of these protocols; just picture them putting data trains on the right tracks and making sure they arrive safely. In PC-based communications systems, special integrated circuits on interface cards (instead of separate software programs) typically perform the functions of the Data-link layer.

Certain programs in PC communications act like Data-link layer protocols. If you use FTP, Xmodem, or Crosstalk's DART protocol for error detection and retransmission during a file exchange, you're using an application program that acts like a Data-link layer protocol while it is transferring a file.

The Network Layer

Larger wide area networks typically offer a number of ways to move a string of characters (put together by the Data-link layer) from one geographic point to another. The third layer of the OSI model—the Network layer—decides which physical pathway the data should take, based on network conditions, priority of service, and other factors.

The Network layer software usually resides in switches out in the network, and the interface card inside your PC must put the train together in a way the network software can recognize and use in routing.

Once there were many important products in the Network layer from companies like IBM and Digital, but this area is about conformity and performance, not variety and choices. Today, the Internet Protocol (IP) has won the Network layer competition. Most modern networks depend on the details of IP to address, route, and handle their packages of data. You'll typically find IP teamed with its Transport layer, TCP, and with other protocols in the large TCP/IP family.

SEE ALSO
➤ *IP and TCP are critical to networking today. You'll find them described in detail in Chapter 8, which starts on page 161.*

The Transport Layer

The Transport layer—layer 4 of the OSI model—does many of the same jobs as the Network layer, but it does them locally. Drivers in the networking software perform the Transport layer's tasks. This layer is the railroad yard dispatcher who takes over if there is a wreck out in the system. If the network goes down, the Transport layer software looks for alternative routes or perhaps saves the transmitted data until the network connection is reestablished. It handles quality control by making sure that the data received is in the right format and in the right order. This formatting and ordering capability becomes important when Transport layer programs implement connections among dissimilar computers. Whereas the Data-link layer counts boxcars to see if they are all there, the Transport layer opens them up to see if anything is missing or broken.

Networks of dissimilar computers can use several Transport layer protocols. One of the most common is the Transmission Control Protocol (TCP), developed by the Department of

Defense and now adopted and marketed by many companies as part of the TCP/IP protocol suite. Three commonly used software protocols that perform Transport layer functions in PC networks are NetBIOS, TCP, and NetWare's Internetwork Protocol Exchange (IPX). One or more pieces of software reside in every network station and pass calls between application programs on the network.

The Session Layer

Layer 5, the Session layer, is often very important in PC-based systems. It performs the functions that enable two applications (or two pieces of the same application) to communicate across the network, performing security, name recognition, logging, administration, and other similar functions.

Programs like NetBIOS and Named Pipes often jump the ISO model and perform both Transport layer and Session layer functions, so I can't name a piece of commonly used software that is unique to this layer.

The Presentation Layer

As soon as you see blinking characters, reverse video, special data-entry formats, graphics, and other features on the screen, you're in the Presentation layer. This layer might also handle encryption and some special file formatting. It formats screens and files so that the final product looks the way the programmer intended.

The Presentation layer is the home of control codes, special graphics, and character sets. The Hypertext Transfer Protocol, HTTP, used to format the information contained on web sites is an excellent example of a Presentation layer protocol. Presentation layer software also controls printers, plotters, and other peripherals. Microsoft Windows performs many Presentation layer functions.

The Application Layer

The top of the layer cake, the Application layer, serves the user. It's where the network operating system and application programs reside, performing everything from file sharing, print-job spooling, and electronic mail to database management and accounting. The standards for this top layer are new, like IBM's Systems Application Architecture (SAA) and the X.400 Message Handling specification for electronic mail. In a way, this layer is the most important one because the user controls it directly.

Some functions, such as file-transfer protocols, work from the Application layer but do jobs assigned to a lower layer. This is comparable to the president of a railroad sometimes sweeping out boxcars.

That's it: the top of ISO's OSI model. The concepts are pretty simple, but dozens of committees are working to define standards for little pieces of each layer, and great political fights are waged over whose ideas should prevail. But we're going to move on, hanging some buzzwords on the model and seeing where they fit.

Protocols

Many protocols are not standards!

There is a big difference between protocols and standards. Anybody can establish or suggest a protocol, and many people and companies do! Some companies are so powerful that their protocols become de-facto standards. But real standards are set by a few recognized organizations. Although the problem of proprietary protocols isn't as great as it used to be, you should always be wary of any product that claims to be better than the existing standards. You could wind up depending on an orphan product.

Most of the buzzwords I've listed here are protocols. Like the signals that a baseball catcher and pitcher exchange, *protocols* represent an agreement among different parts of the network on how data is to be transferred. Though you aren't supposed to see them, and only a few people understand them, their effect on system performance can be spectacular. A poorly implemented protocol can slow data transfer, but software following standard protocols can make communications between dissimilar systems possible. For instance, the TCP/IP protocol enables you to transfer data between computers that have different architectures and operating systems.

The key elements of a protocol are syntax, semantics, and timing. The *syntax* specifies the signal levels to be used and the format in which the data is to be sent. *Semantics* encompasses the information structure needed for coordination among machines and for data handling. *Timing* includes speed matching (so that a computer with a 33.6-kilobit-per-second port can talk to one with a 54-kilobit-per-second port) and the proper sequencing of data (in case it arrives out of order).

Protocols describe all these functions. Because protocols are implemented in real products, though, they often don't fit the full description of the OSI model—either because a product pre-dates the model or because its engineers couldn't resist adding that extra little tweak.

IEEE 802.X Standards

The Institute of Electrical and Electronics Engineers (IEEE) has developed a set of standards describing the cabling, physical topology, electrical topology, and access scheme of network products. The committee structure of the IEEE is numbered like the Dewey decimal system. The general committee working on these standards is 802. Various subcommittees, designated by decimal numbers, have worked on different versions of the standards.

These standards describe the protocols used in the lower two layers of the OSI model (the Physical and Data-link layers). They don't go above those layers; thus, using the common name of an IEEE standard (like Token-Ring) is an incomplete response to the question "What network do you use?" A complete reply would also specify the network interface, including the media and access protocol, as well as the networking software.

Let's look first at two IEEE 802 committee standards that relate to PC-based LANs: 802.3 and 802.5. Then I'll describe the work of the 802.6 committee.

SEE ALSO

➤ *The section "IEEE 10BaseT and 100BaseT," on page 140 explains the IEEE standards and provides more details about network operation.*

IEEE 802.3 and 802.5

IEEE standard 802.5 describes the Token-Ring architecture. The work of this committee received a lot of attention and leadership from IBM. This standard describes a token-passing protocol used on a network of stations connected in a special way, combining an electrical ring topology (where every station actively passes information on to the next one in the ring) with a physical hub topology.

IBM's Token-Ring system is important to corporate data-processing managers because IBM supports a number of mainframe-computer Token-Ring interfaces. Under IBM's Systems Application Architecture (SAA), mainframes and PCs share data as peers on networks.

Many vendors make Token-Ring interface cards for popular minicomputers. These allow easy interaction without the use of complex and expensive micro-to-mainframe links and gateways.

IEEE 802.3, on the other hand, describes a standard that owes a lot to the earlier Ethernet system. It uses carrier sense multiple access (CSMA) signaling on an electrical bus topology. The standard leaves room for several wiring options. One extension to the 802.3 standards introduced signaling at 100 megabits per second under what is commonly called Fast Ethernet or the 100Base-T standard.

You can buy 802.3 interface cards for the PC from dozens of manufacturers. Similar cards designed for popular minicomputers are also widely available. IBM even includes an optional Ethernet port on its mini/mainframe computer, the 9370.

IEEE 802.6

Metropolitan-area networks or MANs make up the 802.6 subcategory of the IEEE 802 standards project. Metropolitan networks can take many forms, but the term usually describes a backbone network of fiber-optic cables that could span hundreds of square miles. Local exchange carriers (the local telephone companies) provide a great deal of MAN connectivity, as do a growing number of cable television companies. While some organizations install their own microwave systems for MAN circuits, the majority lease circuits from local carriers. State utility commissions may regulate the tariffs for MAN services.

MAN carriers usually offer services in 1.544-megabit-per-second increments, and their backbone services provide throughput in the range of 80 megabits per second. The 802.6 MAN standard calls for a Distributed Queue Dual Bus topology that has drops at each service location. This topology uses multiple fiber-optic cables with special equipment at each service location to interleave messages into the cable.

Metro data services

In major cities, you can typically subscribe to MAN services offered by a variety of companies such as local telephone companies, cable television companies, and specialized carriers who have cables under the city. In smaller cities, the local telephone company is often the only carrier option.

Wide area networks (WANs) generally link cities. Specialized long-distance carriers lease circuits to organizations and communications companies to construct WANs. You can buy service at any speed, but speeds of 56 and 64 kilobits per second are the most economical, and 1.544-megabit-per-second service is common. The Federal Communications Commission has authority over the rates the long-distance carriers charge.

SEE ALSO

➤ *Numerous WAN connections are linked together in Chapter 11, which begins on page 271.*

IBM's Cable Plan

Another shorthand used by LAN writers and speakers is derived from IBM's cabling scheme. The major vendors—AT&T, DEC, Northern Telecom, and others—have their own wiring schemes. These vendors all want you to wire your buildings in certain ways that are advantageous for their equipment and will keep competing vendors away from your door.

The IBM cabling plan, like most things IBM, is comprehensive and capable, but expensive to install. IBM has developed standards for certain types of cables and certifies certain manufacturers that meet those standards. Here's a quick rundown of the IBM cable standards:

- *Type 1 cable.* Shielded cable with two twisted pairs made from solid wire (as opposed to the stranded wire used in Type 6. Used for data transmission, particularly in Token-Ring networks. Figure 4.6 shows Type 1 cable.

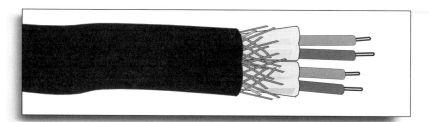

ISP, carrier, or what?

The market for WAN connections is confusing. Some Internet service providers (ISPs) have their own large cross-country networks and can offer a variety of private circuit and Internet access services. But other ISPs are only clients on the networks of bigger carriers. Ask several companies for bids on your WAN connection needs.

FIGURE 4.6

Many companies sell cable that follows IBM's Type 1 specification. This cable combines two separately shielded pairs of solid twisted wire. PVC and Teflon jackets provide different degrees of fire resistance.

- *Type 2 cable.* Four unshielded pairs of solid wire for voice telephone and two shielded data pairs in the same sheath (see Figure 4.7).

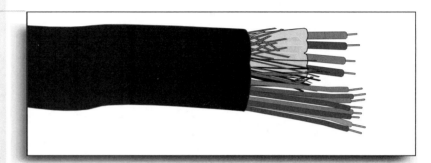

- *Type 3 cable.* Four unshielded, solid, twisted pairs of wire for voice or data. IBM's version of modern twisted-pair telephone wire.
- *Type 4 cable.* No specification published.
- *Type 5 cable.* Two fiber-optic strands.
- *Type 6 cable.* Shielded cable with two twisted pairs made from stranded wire. More flexible than Type 1 cable. Designed for data transmission; commonly used between a computer and a data jack in the wall.
- *Type 7 cable.* No specification published.
- *Type 8 cable.* A special "under-the-carpet" shielded twisted-pair cable designed to minimize the lump in the carpet that covers it.
- *Type 9 cable.* Plenum cable. Two shielded twisted pairs covered with a special flame-retardant coating for use between floors in a building.

Linking LAN Segments

Signals can travel only limited distances before losing power. On an Ethernet network, a signal can typically travel up to 1,000 feet; on a Token-Ring system, it can travel up to about 600 feet.

Networks use repeaters, bridges, routers, and gateways to relay and regenerate signals traveling long distances and to talk to other LANs or wide area networks.

Repeaters do what their name indicates: They repeat electrical signals between sections of networking cabling. You won't find many of these relatively simple devices in new networks. Repeaters relay signals in both directions with no discrimination. More modern devices, like bridges and routers, look at the messages the signals carry to determine whether they really need to pass each message to the next segment.

Bridges allow you to join two local area networks, and they allow stations on either network to access resources on the other network. Bridges use media-access control (MAC) protocols in the Physical layer of the network. They can link dissimilar types of media, such as fiber-optic cable and thin 802.3 coaxial cable, as long as both sides use the same MAC-layer protocol (such as Ethernet).

Routers operate at the Network layer of the OSI model. A router examines the address of each message and decides whether the addressee lies across the bridge. If the message doesn't need to go across the bridge and create traffic on the extended network, the router doesn't send it. Routers can translate between a wide variety of cable and signaling schemes. For example, a router could take your messages from Ethernet and put them out on a packet-switched network, operating through modems connected to high-speed leased telephone lines.

Gateways, which run on the OSI's Session layer, allow networks running totally incompatible protocols to communicate. In PC-based networks, gateways typically link PCs to host machines such as IBM mainframes. You'll find more information on bridges, routers, and gateways in Chapter 10.

Higher-Level Protocols

Moving up through the OSI model's layers, let's look at the techniques (and buzzwords) that different LAN software suppliers use for the Transport layer and Session layer protocols.

Routers rule

Repeaters and bridges were once commonly used as ways to link LANs. Although each still has its own uses, routers are now the primary components used between LANs. Advances in processing power and software made it practical to put full-power routers inside file servers, dial-up access devices, wiring hubs, and many other products. The router has become an important tool for reducing unnecessary traffic and providing added security.

If you don't specify the Transport layer protocols you want to use, you'll get whatever the vendor includes in its standard "protocol stack." Those protocols may or may not be available for the various mainframes or minicomputers in your network. For managers of large corporate networks, selection of the proper higher-level protocols is a complex, important task.

TCP/IP

The earliest large network systems were fielded by the Department of Defense (DoD). The DoD financed the development of interactive network communications software for many different mainframes and minicomputers. The standard core of the DoD-specified software consists of programs that implement two protocols: Transmission Control Protocol (TCP) and Internet Protocol (IP). The availability of TCP/IP software and the power of the biggest TCP/IP application, the Internet, make them attractive to managers who face the challenge of integrating dissimilar computer systems.

TCP and IP perform primarily what the OSI model terms layer-3 (Network) and layer-4 (Transport) functions. Particularly important is the capability to communicate and to order data among two or more different computer systems.

Companies like NetManage and Walker Richer and Quinn sell TCP/IP software customized for specific computers and controller cards. These software modules communicate through the network, recognize each other, and pass messages in a common format generated by the higher-level Session layer and application programs.

TCP/IP software is popular with managers of large networks because it works and is available for practically all computers.

NetBIOS

Another institutional solution whose grass-roots support is starting to slip is NetBIOS. NetBIOS started as an interface between the IBM PC Network Program (PCNP, superseded by PC LAN) and network interface cards provided by Sytek. When the IBM/Sytek team designed the interface, they also made it a programmable entryway into the network, which allowed systems to communicate over network hardware without going through the networking software.

A grass-roots movement of large-network users has been pushing a combination of NetBIOS (operating at the OSI Session layer) and TCP/IP. In this combination, application programs make calls to NetBIOS. Vendors like Novell don't actually use NetBIOS to drive network interface cards, but their operating systems can run NetBIOS emulators to furnish the same Session layer communications services NetBIOS offers.

NetBIOS modules establish virtual communications sessions with each other across the network. But NetBIOS uses a simple naming scheme that doesn't work well between networks or in a wide variety of operating systems. The Internet Protocol portion of TCP/IP envelops the NetBIOS modules so that they travel intact through multiple levels of network names and addresses. However, because of the growth of TCP/IP and because Microsoft now favors an implementation of Novell's IPX, NetBIOS is going to be less popular than it has been.

Layer 4 and Above

If you don't use TCP/IP or NetBIOS—or some rare layer-4 (Network) protocol complying with the OSI model—you enter a maze of vendor-specific protocols. If you use PCs only, and those PCs are working together in a network or perhaps using a gateway for mainframe file sharing, you won't care what protocols the networking software uses. But if you want computers from Digital, HP, IBM, and other vendors to treat each other as peers on the network, the network protocols you use become very important. (One caveat: These protocols don't make otherwise incompatible application files compatible; they just move them across the network and offer access to them.)

Each vendor engages other vendors to support its protocol in their products. What's important is that the set of vendors supporting a specific protocol matches the set of vendors whose equipment is used on your network.

IBM's SNA and APPC

IBM would like to wrap you in the Big Blue web called Systems Network Architecture. IBM's answer to the OSI model, SNA describes how IBM thinks a communications system should work.

Advanced Program-to-Program Communications (APPC) is a protocol within the SNA model that establishes the conditions enabling programs to communicate across the network. APPC is analogous to the Session layer of the OSI model. According to IBM, APPC is to be the communications basis for all the corporation's future applications and systems products.

Two other buzzwords from IBM (APPC /PC and LU 6.2) have the names of products that actually implement the APPC specifications. These programs, however, are large and cumbersome and have not caught on.

DECnet

The other company that can drown you in a sea of acronyms is Digital Equipment Corp. Digital developed its own protocol stack for interconnecting DEC systems, both locally and over wide area networks. The DECnet protocols are supposed to be heading toward compatibility with the ISO standards. It seems likely that DEC will adopt certain ISO protocols (as will many other vendors) to beat the drum for their compatibility.

Apple

Apple Computer has its own set of protocols in the AppleTalk family. The AppleTalk Filing Protocol (AFP) is the one that allows distributed file sharing across the network. AFP is attached to the Hierarchical File System (HFS) in the Macintosh operating system.

Distributed File Systems

SMB, RFS, NFS, and XNS are acronyms for some of the contending distributed-file-system network protocols. *Distributed file systems*, which are a part of every network, allow one computer on a network to use the files and peripherals of another networked computer as if they were local. The two operating systems link so that a subdirectory made available on the host is seen as a disk drive or as a separate subdirectory on the user's computer. Thus, application programs running on the user's computer can access the files and resources on the host without requiring special programming.

These protocols operate in approximately the same way, but they are not interchangeable. Typically, a major vendor develops a protocol for use within a product line, and other vendors license it to achieve compatibility.

SMB stands for Server Message Block, a protocol developed by IBM and Microsoft for use in the PC LAN program and in Windows networking. AT&T, Digital, HP, Intel, Ungermann-Bass, and others all support or accommodate this protocol to some degree.

RFS is the Remote File Service developed by AT&T. Because RFS was integral to many versions of AT&T's original implementations of UNIX, vendors in the UNIX market support it in their products. RFS introduced the *powerful streams* facility, which allows applications to open a stream to or from a device (in UNIX everything is a device: serial port, disk, and so forth) across any defined transport-level interface (TLI). The TLI can be the default UNIX transport services, or TCP, or some other protocol.

NFS stands for Network File System, an architecture developed by Sun Microsystems. Sun's PC-NFS is a complete but no-frills network operating system for the PC. This memory-resident module gives you access to files stored on UNIX-based minicomputers. Companies in the professional workstation market, including Harris Corp., HP, Texas Instruments, and many others, support the NFS architecture in their products.

SEE ALSO

➤ *The protocols are an important part of the discussion of networking software, starting on page 195.*

Now I Know My ABCs

Although this primer on buzzwords and acronyms just scratches the surface of networking terminology, it should help you gain a better understanding of the strange new language of connectivity.

LAN Adapters: The Hardware Heart of the LAN

Network adapters and what they do

Getting the adapter into the PC

PC Bus architectures

PC Card products

In this chapter, you begin your trip through the physical side of local area networking. One small piece of hardware is required to link a computer to the LAN: the network adapter card. It is critically important and carries many options.

In the next chapter, you will follow the path of the network cables that link the computers in a local area network and explore how to send signals using light. I've structured this information to help you buy the best adapters and make the right wiring choices for your installation. In later chapters, you'll learn about the Ethernet and Token-Ring cabling and signaling schemes, but here you'll learn the details of the pieces and parts all those schemes use.

Inside a computer, the low-powered electrical signals representing digital data travel on 8, 16, 32, or 64 thin parallel conductors, which are collectively called a *data bus*. The data bus carries signals between the central processor, random access memory (RAM), and input/output (I/O) devices. Modern computer designs put I/O devices, such as serial and parallel ports, both on the main board of the computer and in the expansion interface slots connected to the data bus.

A local area network *adapter card*, also called *a network interface card* or *NIC*, fits into an expansion interface slot or on the PC's system board. This adapter changes the low-powered parallel signals on the data bus into a robust stream of electrical 0s and 1s marching in single file through a cable connecting the stations on the network.

The concept of putting a special adapter inside the computer to communicate with devices outside the computer isn't new. In early personal computers, the serial and parallel port connections were always provided by separate extra-cost adapter cards. In the early 1980s, companies such as Zenith and Tandy began including serial and parallel ports in their computers to increase their value.

The industrywide acceptance of PC serial ports configured according to the IEEE RS-232C standard and of parallel ports following the de facto standard established by Centronics encouraged manufacturers to include these ports in their PCs. Designers knew these standard ports would be compatible with a wide variety of products, such as modems and printers.

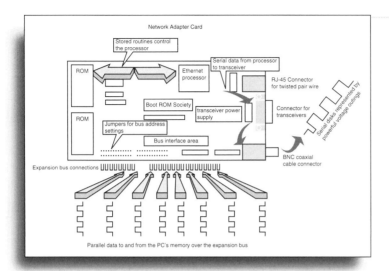

Network Adapter Card

Stored routines control
the processor

ROM

Ethernet
processor

Serial data from processor
to transceiver

RJ-45 Connector
for twisted pair wire

Boot ROM Society

transceiver power
supply

Connector for
transceivers

ROM

Jumpers for bus address
settings

Bus interface area

BNC coaxial
cable connector

Expansion bus connections

Parallel data to and from the PC's memory over the expansion bus

FIGURE 5.1

The LAN adapter translates between the low-powered parallel data stream inside the computer and the stronger serial data stream on a LAN cable. The adapter follows media-access control protocols to control the transmission of its data on the cable.

You've probably heard the terms Ethernet and Token-Ring mentioned frequently. Until the past few years, each of these terms encompassed a family of products that included specific types of wiring, connectors, network communications software, and adapter cards. But now, the products within these families have evolved beyond the original definitions. For all practical purposes, these terms currently define the techniques the adapters use to share the LAN wiring—the media-access control (MAC) protocols in LAN-talk—and the type of signals they send over the wiring. Which adapters you choose determine which media-access control and signaling parameters you'll be using.

SEE ALSO

➤ *We'll connect to the cables in the section "Cables for Network Connections," on page 106.*

➤ *Chapter 7, which starts on page 131, deals with the specific cabling and signaling schemes.*

Linking the Adapter to the PC

Although I spend a large part of this book describing how the cables and other external LAN connections work, the most important network connections are inside the PC. The best

Ethernet for new LANs

It's obvious that Ethernet has won the LAN battle. Token-Ring, ARCnet, and even ATM to the desktop will be footnotes when I sit down to write the history of networking. Any new installations should use Ethernet. However, in truth, a lot of you readers are still using the "legacy" Token-Ring and ARCnet schemes, and they work fine. I give those technologies full coverage in this book. If you're interested in only Ethernet, just consider the rest to be interesting antiques.

cabling and signaling schemes won't be of much use if data can't move quickly between the adapter and the PC. This is particularly true when the PC is acting as a file or communications server on the network. A *bottleneck* in a server slows the entire network's performance. Bottlenecks can occur in the software that integrates the adapter into the computer or in the way the adapter and computer electrically exchange information.

A LAN adapter has two sides: the expansion bus side and the LAN cable side. Both sides offer several types of technical alternatives. You have to find the right combination of alternatives in the system you buy.

Hot Drivers

Tests at *PC Magazine* clearly show the importance of the *network interface card driver*, a small piece of software loaded into every networked computer. The *driver* is the software that links the adapter to the PC's hardware and to a specific operating system. Drivers enable the movement of data between the computer and the LAN adapter. Specifically, they read and load hardware data buffers. Drivers also implement specific protocols that are part of the network communication process.

When you install a LAN adapter in a PC, you have to match the physical hardware characteristics, the operating system, and the network characteristics. This isn't a big problem under Windows 95/98 or Windows NT, but this three-way match can be a challenge if you are installing networking under Windows 3.x, UNIX, or some other operating system.

Hardware and software companies have taken several approaches to solving the problem of compatibility between the adapter and the operating system. Microsoft and 3Com developed the Network Driver Interface Specification (NDIS), which they hoped everyone would adopt. In theory, if the adapter company provides a disk with NDIS drivers, any NDIS-compliant LAN operating system could use the adapters. Microsoft's plan has been quite successful, and most LAN adapters come with NDIS-compliant driver software. In addition, Microsoft includes the NDIS drivers for several dozen popular LAN adapters in its Windows 95/98 and Windows NT products.

Novell developed a NIC driver interface it calls the Open Device Interface (ODI), which is a specification similar to NDIS in general concept. ODI is not as widely supported by the market as NDIS is, but Microsoft has adopted an ODI-compatible interface in its NDIS III description.

Some manufacturers of LAN adapters, such as Standard Microsystems and Intel, try to ensure compatibility by shipping a disk full of drivers for different network operating systems with their adapters. Artisoft and D-Link tried the reverse approach: They cloned the operation of an adapter with a wide range of support (the popular and venerable Novell NE2000) to take advantage of the large library of software already published for these boards.

When you shop for LAN adapters, make sure the adapters you buy will work with your operating system and computer bus architecture. You must be particularly careful if you're working with any brand of UNIX. A specification called the Packet Driver interface is valuable under UNIX. UNIX operating system designers recognize the Packet Driver interface, and many vendors offer interface software for their adapters that conforms to the Packet Driver specification. If you plan to use Novell's NetWare operating system, check for ODI drivers in addition to NDIS drivers.

Programmers use different techniques to create the driver software. Certain ways of moving data and using data storage buffers move the bits quickly between the adapter and the PC. Some programmers write small and efficient code using highly detailed assembly language, while others take the easier route and write less efficient drivers in the C programming language. Quite simply, some programmers write faster and more robust adapter-board drivers than others, and some companies spend more resources developing driver software than others.

While network adapter boards from different companies are alike in many ways, your safest bet is to buy adapters from name-brand companies. Typically, the drivers for these adapters are field-tested and incorporated in the installation packages of the major software vendors.

NDIS and ODI

When you install Novell's client software on a PC running Windows 95 or 98, it asks if you want to replace the Microsoft NDIS drivers with Novell ODI drivers. Generally, you should choose not to make the replacement. The two standards are now very close, and we advise against replacing Microsoft's drivers if possible.

Trouble? Get new drivers!

The troubleshooting action networking experts use most often to correct problems is to get the latest drivers for the LAN adapter. Companies update drivers with frightening frequency, and downloading the latest driver from a corporate web site can often solve troublesome and mysterious problems. On the other hand, sometimes loading a new version can introduce new problems, too!

SEE ALSO

➤ *I'll talk more about drivers under the specific operating systems in Chapter 9, which begins on page 191.*

I/O Options

The PC and adapter can communicate across the data bus using several techniques. You need to understand the different input/output options in order to balance performance, complexity, and cost when you select adapters.

To move data between the board and the PC's RAM, the designers of modern network adapters use one of four techniques: programmed I/O, direct memory access (DMA), shared memory, or bus-mastering DMA. Unfortunately, not every interface scheme works in every PC. For this reason, many adapters allow you to select from at least two schemes. In preparation for the challenge of interfacing adapters to PCs, I present the details of the four I/O techniques.

Programmed I/O

A technique called *programmed I/O* provides an efficient way to move data between the PC and the adapter. In this technique, the special-purpose processor on the adapter board controls a shared 8K, 16K, or 32K block of memory. The adapter's processor communicates with the PC's central processor through this common I/O location.

Both devices move data quickly by reading and writing to the same block of memory, which functions like the window between the kitchen and the counter in a fast-food diner. As in the diner, the processor on either side of the shared window rings a bell to signal the presence of something in the window. In the case of programmed I/O, the bell is a signal called *I/O Ready*.

The programmed I/O technique uses less memory than do some other data-transfer strategies. For this reason, many of the older and widely sold LAN adapters, such as Artisoft's AE-2, D-Link Systems' DE-250, and Novell's NE1000 and NE2000, use programmed I/O as their primary operating mode.

Direct Memory Access

Many adapters use a technique called *direct memory access* (DMA) to signal between the processor in the PC and the processor on the adapter. This alternative is particularly useful for older PCs that might still be working in an organization. When it receives a DMA request from an adapter or interface card, the PC's processor halts other operations to handle the data transfer.

Shared Memory

Shared memory is a method devised to overcome the shortcomings of the programmed I/O and DMA techniques. A shared-memory adapter contains memory that the host PC's processor can access directly at full speed with no wait states. You can buy such adapters with both 8- and 16-bit–wide interfaces to the PC's data bus, but the 16-bit adapters often run into memory conflicts with other devices in the PC.

Shared memory offers the fastest way to move data to and from an adapter, but installing a shared-memory adapter in a PC crowded with VGA video and other memory-hungry interfaces can be a frustrating job. You may run into memory conflicts that manifest themselves only when the LAN adapter and some other device try to use the same location at the same time.

Bus Mastering

Bus mastering enables an adapter board to send data to and receive data from the computer's memory without interrupting the processor. Bus-mastering DMA adapters take control of the data bus and move data directly between the network adapter and the PC's RAM while the processor continues its operations. Bus mastering LAN adapters are now widely available and are typically matched with the PCI bus described in the next section.

Inside the PC

Modern LAN adapters are pretty generic devices. Intel and 3Com, in particular, have evolved these products through heavy competition until they are both affordable and reliable. Despite that, you should understand certain differences and options.

The Bus Structure

The LAN adapter must match the bus structure inside the computer. Most PCs sold today use an expansion slot architecture called the Peripheral Component Interconnect (PCI), although many still come with slots configured for the Industry Standard Architecture (ISA). In addition, millions of computers still in use have other bus structures. Here's an overview of the bus configurations you might find:

- *ISA.* The original PC used an 8-bit bus (which transfers 8 bits simultaneously) known as the PC or XT bus. With the 286-based AT model, the bus was extended to 16 bits, and this became the Industry Standard Architecture, or ISA bus. ISA slots have connectors that are 5.5 inches long.

- *Micro Channel.* When IBM introduced the PS/2 line, it tried to capture customers through the introduction of the high-speed 32-bit Micro Channel (MCA) bus. If you have to network an old PS/2 with MCA slots, you'll have a hard time finding an adapter. ISA and MCA expansion boards are very different.

- *EISA.* To counter the Micro Channel and extend the ISA bus from 16 bits to 32 bits, the Extended Industry Standard Architecture (EISA) bus was introduced by a group of vendors led by Compaq. The EISA bus accepts both EISA and ISA boards, but it has been completely superseded by PCI.

- *Local Bus.* VESA's VL-bus was a very short-lived attempt at an improved data bus. However, the computers also had ISA bus slots, so if you must network one of these computers, use an ISA adapter.

ISA adapters

Even though those ISA adapters stacked on your shelves are obsolete, they're not useless. PCs used for the typical office tasks of word processing and email don't move a lot of network traffic. Those ISA adapters will work fine in the administrative office. Budget for PCI adapters in the computers running the ordering, inventory, and other line-of-business applications.

Peripheral Component Interconnect

PCI is a 32/64-bit local bus designed by Intel and used in PCs and Macintoshes. It uses 32- and 64-bit data paths and allows bus mastering. PCI can transfer data between the PC's processor and LAN adapters at up to 132MB per second, so it can service the fastest LAN adapters you're likely to use in a desktop PC. Most new PCs come with three or four PCI slots and a couple of ISA slots.

Some vendors ship a combination slot that can accept either PCI or ISA adapters. The ISA connector is 3.75 inches long. PCI provides Plug and Play capability, which enables the automatic configuration of the PCI cards at startup. If you mix PCI and ISA devices in the same PC, you have to tell the PCI setup utility about the configuration of the ISA cards.

The number of peripheral devices the PCI bus can handle is based on the electrical load on the bus. This load is a combination of inductance, capacitance, and other electrical characteristics. The basic PCI chip set uses about 33% of the available capacity. The PCI system can carry about four plug-in adapters, but a slightly greater number of adapters resides on the motherboard.

Sbus

Sun Microsystems uses an architecture called Sbus in most of the company's Sun workstations. The Sbus uses a 25MHz clock rate with 32- or 64-bit data handling. However, Sun has now introduced PCI-based computer systems into its product line, so the future of PCI seems bright.

USB: The Universal Serial Bus

Do your PCs have Universal Serial Bus ports? Vendors such as Gateway, Dell, Compaq, and HP have shipped PCs with USB ports since early 1997, but initially there were few USB peripherals to connect to those ports. Be careful because most of the very low-cost PCs are not USB-equipped; one that is USB-equipped might cost more than you think!

In a nutshell, USB is a 12Mbps bus for peripherals. One cable carries data between as many as 127 devices with no concerns about IRQ conflicts, DMA channels, or memory addresses. There are unique USB cables and connectors, and the port comes alive under version 4.00950B or later of Windows 95. You can get more vendor information and download a small utility to test your USB ports from `www.usb.org`.

Server segmentation is good stuff

The value of having multiple PCI LAN adapters in a server is that they enable you to segment the server to balance the networking load. I'll bring up LAN segmentation using multiple server adapters many times because it is the cheapest and quickest way to improve performance, reliability, and security.

Finding your USB

If you're not sure if a specific PC has USB, look on the back panel. If you see what looks like two coin slots for fat nickels and a logo that looks like the cherries on a slot machine, you've got USB. Note that you'll need USB cables to connect to any USB-equipped peripheral devices.

The hype about USB comes mainly from the multimedia game market. USB is touted as the connection for "force-feedback" digital joysticks and mice, CD-ROM drives, and new digital monitors. In the graphics market, USB provides a convenient and efficient way to connect scanners and digital cameras. Making a connection to a scanner without adding a mutliplexer for a shared printer improves economy and reduces complexity for the designers and users. Speeding and reducing the complexity of a download from a digital camera enhances its consumer appeal.

One important use of USB is as a connection for what some of the USB-bigots call *legacy devices*, the serial and parallel port products you're still buying today. Several companies offer USB modules with four high-speed buffered serial ports at the end of a USB cable. Changing USB to serial is an excellent way to connect a group of ISDN or high-speed modems to a PC.

USB is the obvious choice for ISDN, cable modem, and DSL connections. In addition, you can expect to see USB-to-Ethernet devices on the market, so USB can challenge the role of the internal LAN adapter card for some applications.

Interestingly, USB allows peripheral sharing. Devices like printers, scanners, and CD-ROM drives can serve more than one computer within the 5-meter cable length. And USB can be an alternative to Ethernet for small-office networking.

There is more to USB than a glorified game port, so watch your PC purchases to make sure you don't save a little and lose too much by buying PCs without USB.

SEE ALSO
➤ *I'll talk more about ISDN in the section "ISDN," on page 278.*
➤ *Chapter 14, starting on page 349, deals with modems.*
➤ *Chapter 15, starting on page 383, describes remote access—an important application for multiple modem systems.*

Intelligent I/O (I2O)

Another attribute of computers and interface cards to watch for is called the *Intelligent I/O* or *I2O port*. I2O is an internal architecture that uses specialized hardware to improve the way computers and operating systems interact with LAN, SCSI, and other I/O devices. It's important to note that you'll pay more for an I2O-capable computer, you'll have to use an I2O-capable operating system, and you'll want to make sure you buy adapters with the same capability.

Intel led the I2O initiative by establishing the I2O Special Interest Group. With members from the OS, server, and peripheral community, the I2O SIG has established standards that all members respect in their implementations. All pieces of the I/O puzzle (motherboard, NOS, and peripheral hardware and software) must work together to be effective. For more information on the SIG, check out www.i2osig.org.

The I2O architecture separates the operating system-specific modules that handle I/O from the hardware device-specific modules, and it puts a standard communications layer between the two. The operating system side of the software layer has several "classes" of devices—such as storage devices or LAN devices—with standard interface definitions. These standard interfaces eliminate the need for OS developers to write or obtain drivers for each make and model of hardware.

Similarly, the peripheral equipment manufacturers develop their internal code to communicate to a known interface, independent of the OS. This means that a company that provides LAN or RAID controllers can write to only one interface, the communications layer, yet all products will run on I2O-compliant versions of NetWare, SCO UNIX, or Windows NT with no additional work. Because developers no longer have to write separate drivers for each OS, the time to market for products is drastically reduced.

The extra investment in I2O buys you improved server efficiency. A server with an I2O-enabled NOS, motherboard, and peripheral cards can show system throughput increases of 3–5 times that of a server without I2O, even under heavily loaded conditions. In other words, I2O pushes up the top of the throughput and usability curves. I2O is also important because it makes developing and marketing new innovations in peripheral devices easier.

SEE ALSO

> *You can interface with more information on NetWare, UNIX, and Windows NT in Chapter 8, which begins on page 161.*

Is I2O worth it?

Is it worth paying more for I2O? The cost/value curve is difficult to plot, but it appears that I2O is a good investment for high-end servers. It isn't needed in most desktop computers, but it could cure bottlenecks in busy web servers and other devices that move a lot of small packets across the LAN.

Adapter Options

Along with the physical bus, appropriate drivers, and data handling options, there are other important features of LAN adapters. One option that's become almost a standard feature among LAN adapter manufacturers is an open socket for a remote-boot read-only memory (ROM) chip. This special ROM forces the host station to take its startup files from the server. PCs equipped with a remote-boot ROM don't need local floppy or hard disk drives. Diskless PCs eliminate the potential for theft of data files or programs stored on disks; this concept also cuts costs and reduces the minimum size of the computer. (The so-called "diskless workstations" that were available in the early 1990s are back again under the title of "thin clients." The popularity of the standard interfaces for browsers and the initial hype associated with the Java programming environment led to the reinvention of diskless workstations under a new name.)

Other useful features of LAN adapters include *light emitting diodes* (LEDs), which indicate operational status and different kinds of connectors.

What to do with AUI

You might run into certain devices, such as a router, that come with only an AUI port connection. In that case, you'll need a transceiver to link the AUI port to the wiring hub. Companies such as Allied Telesyn (www.alliedtelesyn.com) offer transceivers that can link AUI ports to different types of fiber-optic and copper cables.

Some buyers will want to know whether their Ethernet adapters include an *attachment unit interface* (AUI) port. The AUI port connects to a device called a *transceiver*, which has connections for thick and thin Ethernet coaxial cables and fiber-optic cables. Some companies call a transceiver a *medium attachment unit* (MAU), but that acronym has other meanings as well. A board with an AUI gives you more flexibility and greater potential for reuse with other wiring schemes. These boards might cost a few dollars more, but they offer a wider variety of connection options.

Finding Space in Crowded PCs

Technologies such as USB and I2O aim to eliminate the congestion and constriction at the point where the LAN adapter meets the PC. The PCI bus and the Windows Plug and Play standards took an earlier step in the same direction. But tens of millions of PCs and LAN adapters still in use don't have PCI or the more modern connection alternatives. Let's look at some tried-and-true techniques for merging LAN adapters and computers.

PCs have a limited number of expansion interface slots, memory addresses, IRQ lines, and DMA channels. High-density video adapters, mouse ports, and other communications boards all consume these resources in the host PCs. Table 5.1 shows some of the IRQ lines and I/O addresses standard PC devices use; these lines and addresses often interfere with the operation of LAN adapters.

TABLE 5.1   **Commonly used IRQ lines and memory addresses**

IRQ Line	Memory	Device
2	—	Shared with IRQ 9
3	2F8h	COM2
3	2E8h	COM4
4	3F8h	COM1
4	2E8h	COM3
5	280h	Tape controller
5	3Foh	Some PC XT hard disk controllers
5	278h	LPT2
6	3Foh	Floppy disk controller
7	378h	LPT1

My first advice about network adapter installation is to use the defaults recommended by the manufacturer of your adapter. The company chose those defaults to avoid typical problems.

If the adapter doesn't work at the default memory and I/O address, its installation manual will probably list at least two alternatives. Older adapters designed for the standard IBM PC AT expansion bus (the Industry Standard Architecture, or ISA bus) usually used slide-on jumpers to determine the shared RAM address and IRQ line. Newer adapters, particularly those designed for the PCI bus, change all parameters through special configuration programs provided on a disk that's shipped with each adapter or included in operating systems such as Windows 95/98 or Windows NT.

Document the installation!

Some professional installers consider the techniques they use to avoid interrupt and memory-address conflicts trade secrets, but the real secret is organization. Smart network administrators record the I/O and interrupt address of every device in every networked PC. You don't need a fancy database program—a three-ring binder works nicely—but having a quick reference to the I/O and interrupt addresses used in each machine can avoid frustration and save hours of installation time.

Remember, you must change the network driver in software to match the memory address and IRQ line set on the board; the software won't find the adapter if it doesn't know where to look. The first installation trick you should be aware of concerns IRQ3. The COM2 serial port on all PCs uses this IRQ line. But many LAN adapters come with the same IRQ line set as the default. Most PCs use electrical techniques to avoid a conflict, as long as both devices don't send signals on the same IRQ line at the same time. This means you can usually use a LAN adapter at IRQ3 even if a COM2 is in the machine, as long as you don't try to use the COM2 serial port and the network at the same time (as you might, for example, with a serially attached printer or modem).

Many manufacturers of PCs provide a method in either software or hardware to disable an on-board COM2 port, but there is no single standard technique. A smart LAN administrator asks how to disable COM2 and does so whenever a new PC comes into the office. Getting this information early can save problems later.

Because so many computers come equipped with an internal COM2, installers often use IRQ5 whenever they put LAN adapters in these computers. But because some hard disk controllers use IRQ5, you could introduce conflicts that seemingly appear at random. Similarly, the LPT2 port used in many PCs acting as network print servers also uses IRQ5.

Selecting IRQ2 for an 8-bit LAN adapter often works. However, this IRQ is actually served by IRQ9, so you might encounter conflicts if any devices in the PC use this higher-numbered interrupt. IRQ2 conflicts often sneak up on you when you try to add an internal device to a PC that has been happily operating with a LAN adapter at IRQ2.

You'll have to set an I/O address for the general operation of the board, and you might have to set one for a special auto-boot ROM. Many adapters use I/O addresses at 2A0h and 300h with success. Auto-boot ROMs use higher addresses, but they can still conflict with the ROMs in modern video adapters. Tests at the *PC Magazine* LAN Labs proved successful when using CC00h as the boot ROM address in many computers. But if you try that, note that you have to watch out for video system conflicts.

If you must install an adapter using a DMA channel, try DMA3 as the default. All PCs use DMA2 for the floppy disk drive controller, so someone simultaneously trying to use the floppy disk drive and a LAN adapter set to DMA2 will experience problems.

You usually won't have a problem setting up a LAN adapter in a typical client workstation if you use the defaults. The challenge comes when you want to put a LAN adapter in a PC equipped with a special adapter for a mainframe connection or with a tape drive controller. These devices (and to a lesser extent, devices such as add-on mouse adapters) often default to the same IRQ lines and memory locations used by LAN adapters. Some conflicts are insidious. You might not see a problem, for example, until you try to perform a tape backup and pull files across the network at the same time. In this case, one of the conflicting products must move—usually to IRQ5 with an I/O address of 320h.

Getting multiple boards to work together in tricky installations is often a matter of experience and luck. That's why many system integrators support only products that have a proven ability to work together. The craft of LAN installation involves some art, but it is primarily a skill, and you have specific rules and a road map of the PC's architecture that you can follow.

External Adapters

A LAN adapter normally resides in one of the PC's expansion slots. But notebook computers typically don't have standard expansion slots, and some PCs are already crowded with add-in options. If you don't have a spot for an internal adapter, or if you simply don't want to open up the PC, you can use an external adapter to link the PC to the LAN. Although external network adapters don't have the same fast throughput as internal adapters, they are adequate for 99% of all network client-station tasks.

Several companies, including D-Link Systems and Xircom, sell external network adapters that connect to your PC's parallel printer port. With special software, the parallel port—normally a one-way device—becomes a two-way path to the PC. Figure 5.2 shows Xircom's popular external adapter.

FIGURE 5.2

The Xircom external adapter attaches to the parallel port of a PC card and provides connections for Ethernet or Token-Ring networks. This kind of product is particular useful for laptop PCs and those with limited internal expansion slots.

The parallel adapter as a secret weapon

A parallel port adapter can be a network administrator's secret weapon. If you need to reconfigure a PC, update software, or troubleshoot a problem, you can almost always count on a parallel adapter to quickly give you a network connection without hassle. You can't say the same for internal adapters or PC card adapters. When you have to work on a PC, you can slap on a parallel port LAN adapter to get to the configuration server and then download a clean operating system or new software. It cuts the hassle.

Corp., the folks who developed the external LAN adapter in 1989, and Zenith Corp. have developed technology for a high-speed enhanced parallel port (EPP) that can achieve signaling rates as high as 2Mb (16 megabits) per second. Note that because they move data out the parallel port as single bytes, parallel port speeds are traditionally listed in bytes per second; however, the effective rate in megabits per second is really impressive.

When connected to older equipment, EPP hardware works at the typical 30–50Kbps of existing applications and ports, but when you connect one EPP device to another, they can move data at higher rates. Obviously, Xircom sees this higher parallel port speed as critical to eliminating the constriction that chokes the practical throughput of external LAN adapters to well under one megabit per second, depending greatly on the type and speed of CPU in the system.

EPP has rolled into a more comprehensive IEEE standard called EEE 1284. This standard defines the EPP and another type of parallel port supported by HP and Microsoft: the Extended Capabilities Port (ECP). The IEEE standard also defines the electrical connectors and cables that can extend parallel port signals at speeds of up to 5MBps across cables up to 30 feet long.

EPP provides fine control of the data for interactive communications such as LAN adapters, CD-ROM drives, or tape drives. ECP moves data in bigger blocks and is especially useful as a high-speed interface to printers and scanners. Both types of ports are more useful than the simple parallel port available on most PCs.

PC Card Adapters

A standard that emerged in 1991, *PCMCIA*, had a significant impact on LAN adapters—particularly for laptop computers. The acronym PCMCIA stands for the *Personal Computer Memory Card International Association*, and the PCMCIA standard describes several connection schemes for credit-card sized modules containing memory, modems, LAN cards, and other devices. However, for rather arcane reasons, the Association later changed its name and the name of the standard to the *PC Card* standard. New products say that they follow the PC Card standard, but people still talk about "pee-see-emm-see-eye-ay" devices.

But just when we all made the transition to PC Card, in 1995 the Association released a new version of the specification called *CardBus*, which is a 32-bit bus. (The previous specifications had been for 8- or 16-bit data paths.) CardBus is an extension of the PCI bus. CardBus products can theoretically carry data with a throughput of up to 132Mbps. Probably the best use of CardBus is for add-on storage devices.

At this time, most LAN and modem devices conform to the PC Card standard. The PC Card specifications describe the physical size of these devices, and most importantly, they set the standards for how these devices interface with the computer. If you have the right interface software, you can simply slide the device into a slot and start to use it.

The PC Card standard describes three sizes of cards. All cards are about 3.3 inches long and 2.1 inches wide and have a 68-pin connector on the end. Type II cards, the type used for modems and LAN adapters, are slightly less than one-quarter of an inch thick.

Two levels of interface software are at work between the device and the computer: socket services and card services. The socket services specification describes how the socket for the device interfaces with the computer. Software working at this level detects the insertion or removal of a PC Card while the system is on. Socket services are now a part of the Windows family of operating systems.

The card services specification describes how resources such as memory and interrupts interact with the device and provides a way for higher levels of software, like the network redirector, to talk to the PC Card hardware. In theory, the combination of the PC Card hardware, card services software, and socket services software allows you to add and remove PC Card devices without turning the computer off.

PC Card modems are easy to carry on the road, and combination modem and LAN adapter devices are common. For the most part, PC Card technology is through its growing pains, and these devices work well. If you have a problem, you can often obtain the cure by downloading whatever new driver is available on the vendor's web site.

Here are some things to look for in PC Card devices:

- *Inside:* Electrically, PCMCIA modems are similar to internal ISA bus modems and LAN adapters. Amazingly, the modems pack a serial port, a modem data processor, a line transceiver, and all other necessary parts inside a credit-card sized package. It's handy for resetting a hung modem: You can just pull it out and slide it back in.

- *Outside:* The telephone or LAN cable connection is the only part of a PC Card device you see, and vendors are even competing over that. Vendors differentiate their products by way of the PC Card to cable connection scheme they use. For example, some companies use the X-Jack, a telephone-cable connection device that retracts out of sight when it's not in use. Other vendors use special external connection cables, but if you misplace the cable you can't make a connection. However, these external cable systems are less fragile than the X-Jack, and they provide a link to the wall jack.

- *Power:* PC Card devices draw their power from the computer's battery. A modem draws about 7 watts when in use but drops to about 1 watt during sleep mode. A LAN adapter takes slightly less. In rough numbers, PCMCIA modem operation can be 10% to 30% of your laptop's total power requirement, so using this kind of modem can significantly reduce the runtime of your battery.

Also to its advantage, PC Card still provides a great way for the screwdriver-phobic to install LAN or modem hardware painlessly. In addition, tests show that the average desktop or laptop computer doesn't pay a penalty in throughput for using PC Card devices. Although these devices are more expensive than internal expansion cards because they cost more to fabricate, they do work well.

PC Card power

If you're trying to stretch your laptop's battery life to last on a coast-to-coast flight, you can pull out the modems and LAN adapters in the PC Card slots. Just pull them out a half an inch so they don't connect, and you'll save a lot of power. However, don't let them drop out on the cabin floor because they'll slide 42 rows forward during landing.

The Need for Speed

There are several possible choke points in any network. The speed of the file server's hard disk has the biggest influence on the server's response time. But once you've installed a fast hard disk drive and controller and sufficient RAM for caching, the server's LAN adapter card becomes the next most likely choke point. Busy client stations can ask the server to provide 3–7Mbps over a heavily loaded network, and this transfer rate taxes the whole data bus, driver software, and adapter system.

The easiest way to improve server performance on a busy network (after you're sure you have the best hard disk system you can afford), is to split the network load among two or more LAN adapters in the server, as shown in Figure 5.3. NetWare and Windows NT can host four or more adapters in the same server. Although it often takes some juggling to find an open combination of IRQ line, memory address, and DMA channel for more than one adapter, it's worth the effort.

FIGURE 5.3

You can split the network load among two or more adapters in the server, which significantly increases the throughput on heavily loaded networks—providing the hard disk subsystem can carry the load.

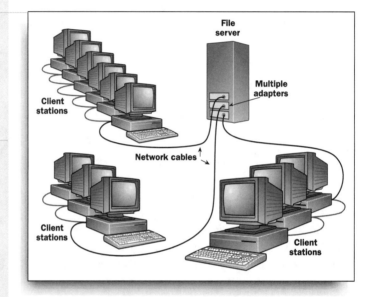

When you split the network load among adapters, you give each adapter interface a chance to make an orderly transfer of its data. This trick enables you to postpone the installation of another server in a growing network and can ensure fast response times in stable networks. As a side benefit, if one cable run or adapter fails, the stations on the other side of the network will still have use of the server.

In summary, LAN adapters take data from the PC and get it ready for transmission over the network cabling. The interface between the adapters and the PC is important, but the cabling system carries the serial data out into the hostile outside environment. The next chapter deals with that cabling.

Your Network Can't Be Better than Its Cable

The cables in your network carry everything. There is no such thing as a "bargain" in cable systems. You get only what you pay for. A LAN cable system installed by someone who's unskilled or uncaring can cause mysterious intermittent outages, slow down response times, and cause frustration during the frequent moves and changes every organization experiences. A good cabling system is an important investment because your network can never be any better than its cabling.

Cable systems are described by many cable and wiring plant standards. You'll find it useful to understand these standards and specifications when you write a request-for proposal or select a network cable system. It's important to carefully plan your network's cable system because it is probably the most expensive, and certainly the longest lasting, part of any network. Overall, a network can't be any better than its cable system.

A long list of companies, organizations, and even government bodies regulate and specify the cables you use. Some companies, such as AT&T, Digital Equipment Corp., Hewlett-Packard, IBM, and Northern Telecom, have volumes of detailed specifications that go beyond the cable to include the connectors, wiring and distribution centers, and installation techniques. These plans are called *premise distribution systems* (PDS).

National and international organizations, such as the Institute of Electrical and Electronic Engineers (IEEE), the Electronic Industry Association, and the newer Telecommunications Industries Association (EIA/TIA), Underwriters Laboratories (UL), and government agencies at various levels that develop fire and building codes, all issue specifications for cable material and installation. EIA/TIA has issued EIA/TIA 568 and 569 standards for technical performance, and the EIA/TIA has an active program to extend their requirements. The IEEE includes minimal cable requirements in their 802.3 and 802.5 specifications for Ethernet and Token-Ring systems, but some of the IEEE's work is being overshadowed by the popularity of the unshielded twisted-pair wire specified by the EIA/TIA and UL. The designations for coaxial cable had the benefit of being set in practice before most of the standards committees began their deliberations.

The National Electrical Code of the United States describes various types of cables and the materials used in them. The Underwriters Laboratory focuses on safety standards but has expanded its certification program to evaluate twisted-pair LAN cables for performance according to both IBM and EIA/TIA performance specifications as well as National Electrical Code safety specifications. UL has established a program to mark shielded and unshielded twisted-pair LAN cables that should simplify the complex task of making sure the materials used in an installation are up to specification.

National Electrical Code

In the event of a building fire, a cable running between walls, up an elevator shaft, or through an air-handling plenum could become a torch that carries the flame from one floor or one part of the building to another. Because the coverings of cables and wires are typically a form of plastic, they can also create noxious smoke when they burn. Several organizations, including Underwriters Laboratories, have established standards for flame and smoke that apply to LAN cables. The standard most widely supported by local licensing and inspection officials is the *National Electrical Code* (NEC).

The National Electrical Code was established by the National Fire Protection Association (NFPA). The language of the code is designed so that it can be adopted through legislative procedure. In general terms, the NEC describes how a cable burns. Among other things, the standards limit the maximum amount of time a cable may burn after a flame is applied. Other standards, developed by the NFPA and adopted by the American National Standards Institute (ANSI) also describe the type and amount of smoke a burning cable may generate.

While the industry recognizes and generally acknowledges conformance to the NEC standards, every individual municipality, city, county, or state can decide whether or not to adopt the latest version of the NEC for local use. In other words, the NEC standards might or might not be a part of your local fire or building codes. Regardless, I urge you to select cable that meets the NEC codes for your application.

You'll see NEC-type codes listed in catalogs of cables and supplies. These codes classify specific categories of products for specific uses. Generally, you'll find LAN cables listed under type CM for communications or type MP for multipurpose. Some companies choose to run their cables through testing as remote control or power-limited circuit cable CL2 or CL3 (class 2 and class 3) general tests, but the flame and smoke regulations for these categories are generally the same. The differences in these parts of the codes concern the amount of electrical power that could potentially run through the cable under the worst conditions. MP cable is subjected to tests that assume the most power-handling capability, with CM, CL3, and CL2 going through tests that assume decreasing levels of power handling. Type designations OFC and OFN cover fiber-optic cables. Type OFC fiber-optic cable contains metal conductors inserted for strength; type OFN cable contains no metal.

The cable types sometimes have an additional letter that designates the cable's use:

Pay for plenum only if you need it

Plenum cable costs considerably more per foot, so be sure your contractor uses it only where it's needed.

- The letter *P*—as in NEC Type CMP (Communications Plenum) cable—designates a cable that has passed tests showing a limited spread of flame and low smoke production. Plenum cable is typically coated with a special jacket material such as Teflon. The code defines a *plenum* as a channel or ductwork fabricated for handling air. (A false ceiling or floor is not a plenum.)

- The letter *R*, as in NEC Type CMR (Communications Riser) cable, shows that the cable has passed similar but slightly different tests for the spread of flame and production of smoke. For example, riser cable is tested for its burning properties in a vertical position. According to the code, you must use cable rated for riser service whenever the cable penetrates a floor and a ceiling. Riser cables typically have a polyvinyl chloride (PVC) outer jacket.

Company Plans

AT&T, Digital Equipment Corporation, IBM, and Northern Telecom, along with other companies, have developed and published complete architectures for premise distribution systems (PDS). AT&T calls their architecture the AT&T Systimax Premises Distribution System; Digital uses the name Open DECconnect; IBM calls their architecture simply the IBM Cabling System; and Northern Telecom has the Integrated Building Distribution Network (IBDN). IBM and AT&T fielded their systems in 1984 and 1985, and DECconnect came out in 1986. Northern Telecom's IBDN, which is quite similar to AT&T's Systimax, is a relative newcomer; it emerged in 1991.

Overall, the plans from IBM and AT&T have had the most profound effect on the industry. You'll often see cables in catalogs rated in terms of IBM or AT&T specifications. IBM's concept of cable *types* permeates the industry, while AT&T has influenced every cable and connector standard.

Other companies, particularly Amp, Anixter, and Mod-Tap, market and sell specific equipment for structured wiring systems. Anixter especially deserves praise for setting openly documented fair performance and electrical standards for twisted-pair wiring. Anixter's original concept of *levels* is used by EIA/TIA and UL in their standards.

AT&T Systimax

AT&T's Systimax PDS is deeply rooted in history. Before the breakup of the Bell System in the United States, the technical side of the telephone industry was controlled by a series of publications called the *Bell Standard Practices* (BSPs). Because it was largely a monopoly, the industry didn't need many standards beyond those in the BSPs. The BSPs described in detail how installers should cut, twist, and attach every wire and how to secure every cable span. The Systimax specifications are, at least, a spiritual and cultural offspring of the BSPs. They are detailed and, if followed, can give you a flexible, reliable, and expandable cable plant.

AT&T manufactures, sells, and installs the products in the Systimax family. The company also offers training, so you will find many installers in local companies who know how to work to Systimax specifications. The AT&T Systimax plan is based on unshielded twisted-pair wire for the *horizontal* cable (the cable that runs from the wiring closet to the desktop) and on fiber-optic cabling (for everything else). It takes about three inches of AT&T catalogs to describe all the products in the Systimax line, but the basic Systimax 100-ohm impedance cable for horizontal data wiring uses four pairs of unshielded twisted-pair 24 AWG copper wire, which provides two spare pairs in most installations. With an outside diameter of about .17 inch, these cables are easy to pull through conduits and inside walls. The Systimax specifications allow a cable run of 100 meters for data transmission at speeds of up to 16 megabits per second.

AT&T also specifies a cable combining copper and fiber-optic conductors. It provides a total of eight unshielded twisted pairs and two fibers inside one jacket. This combination offers plenty of bandwidth for data and voice telephone connections to any desktop and the capability to add fiber connections for higher-speed data, video, or other applications. If you have a big budget and plan to own the building forever, this is the right stuff to install—but it is expensive and bulky.

AT&T offers a variety of fiber-optic cables for use as backbone cable linking wiring closets or as horizontal wiring for special applications. Some products in this family group as many as 216 fibers together inside a protective jacket for the long trip up an elevator or air shaft. The AT&T fiber-optic standard calls for 62.5/125 micron multimode fiber operating at 850 nanometers (nm) and 1,300 nm and a bandwidth of 160MHz and 500MHz.

Cross connection and termination equipment give a PDS its flexibility; the cable system is no better than its connectors and terminators. The AT&T 110 Connector System has set the standard for the industry. This family of products includes several types of rack or wall-mounted connector hardware that typically goes into a wiring closet to terminate horizontal and backbone cable. Figure 6.1 shows the elements of a structured wiring system.

AT&T takes the wiring almost up to the desktop. The company offers a variety of wall outlets that terminate eight conductors for data and voice connections. The wiring sequence for these jacks (which wire goes to which terminal) is critical to the proper operation of the network. AT&T's Standard 258A is the most widely specified wiring sequence for four-pair plugs and jacks. It is also the same as the wiring sequence specified for ISDN and 10Base-T Ethernet over unshielded twisted-pair wiring. However, the AT&T 258A standard puts pairs 2 through 4 in a different sequence from the older Universal Service Order Code (USOC) sequence that's still used by many local telephone companies. This difference is a primary cause of problems when data networks are added to older wiring systems.

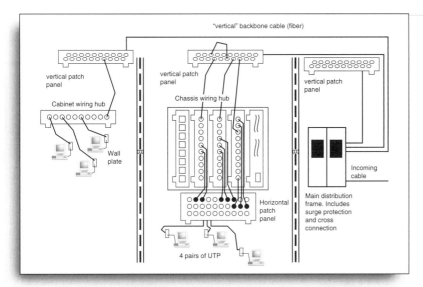

FIGURE 6.1

This diagram shows the elements of a structured building wiring system. The incoming cable is installed by the local telephone company or alternative carriers. Vertical wiring goes between floors and between wiring closets. Horizontal wiring goes out to individual stations.

Amp and Mod-Tap

Many companies manufacture or sell PDS components, but two companies, Amp and Mod-Tap stand head and shoulders above their competition in providing consistent quality, training, and support of their products. These companies don't attempt to set PDS standards. Instead, they market cable and connection products that conform to popular standards, while also innovating and providing improved convenience and quality. Both Amp and Mod-Tap have training programs for installers.

Among its many products, Amp markets the Ampix cross-connect system, a distribution system for voice and data that uses specially designed, high-quality wire terminations and printed

The value of wiring standards

This information about all of the standards is valuable because you're going to have to work with a cabling contractor at some point. Getting a guarantee that the materials and workmanship meet specific standards is your best strategy for getting a good installation.

circuit board connections between the wire termination and the RJ45 jack of the patch board system. Amp also offers a variety of fiber-optic cable splicing, terminating, and testing equipment.

Mod-Tap's product line stresses flexibility. The company markets products that meet the requirements of AT&T, IBM, Digital, and many other companies, as well as many standards committees. They also have an excellent line of fiber-optic products that range from the cable itself to connectors, splicing equipment, and supplies. The company is a single source of supply for products ranging from wall plates and connectors to all the components of a distribution frame.

Anixter's Cable Model

Anixter is a worldwide distributor of wiring system products. The company's place in history is assured as the developer of the multilevel model of performance for cables. Anixter's model includes five levels that describe the performance and electrical characteristics of cabling, ranging from the most common telephone cable used in residences to sophisticated twisted-pair cable capable of moving data at 100 megabits per second. The Underwriters Laboratories and EIA/TIA both developed new cable specification systems based on the Anixter cable model.

EIA/TIA

The Electronic Industry Association/Telecommunications Industry Association (EIA/TIA) is a U.S. standards body that has a long history of issuing standards for communications systems, including for example, EIA RS-232C and RS-232D for serial communications ports. The EIA/TIA tackled the problem of specifying LAN cables by starting with the Anixter five-level model, but the EIA/TIA calls the divisions "categories" instead of levels. Amp and other companies have worked in the EIA/TIA to expand the model to account for other categories of products including coaxial cable and fiber-optic cable. The result is the EIA/TIA 568 Standard for Commercial Building Telecommunications Wiring.

The primary advantage of EIA/TIA 568 is its publication as an open standard without the stamp of any single vendor. You can select and specify cable that meets a specific category of the EIA/TIA 568 standard and expect to get comparable bids from a variety of vendors. However, the EIA/TIA categories are not tied to the NEC specifications, and they don't deal with shielded twisted-pair wiring.

The EIA/TIA standard describes both the performance specifications of the cable and its installation; however, it leaves the network system designer room for options and expansion. The standard calls for two cables, one for voice and one for data, to be run to each outlet. One of the two cables must be four-pair UTP for voice. You can choose to run the data on another UTP cable or on a coaxial cable. If you elect to run fiber to the desktop, it can't displace the copper data cable.

Here is a capsule view of the EIA/TIA 568 standards:

- *Category 1.* Overall, EIA/TIA 568 says very little about the technical specifications in Category 1 or Category 2. The descriptions that follow are for general information. Level 1 cable is typically untwisted 22 AWG or 24 AWG wire, with a wide range of impedance and attenuation values. It is not recommended for data in general and certainly not for signaling speeds of more than 1 megabit per second.

- *Category 2.* This category of cable is the same as the Anixter Level 2 cable specification and is derived from the IBM Type 3 specification. This cable uses 22 or 24 AWG solid wire in twisted pairs. It is tested to a maximum bandwidth of 1MHz and is not tested for near-end crosstalk. You can use this cable for IBM 3270 and AS/400 computer connections and for Apple LocalTalk.

- *Category 3.* This category of cable is the same as the Anixter Level 3. Generally, it is the minimum level of cable quality you should allow in new installations. This cable uses 24 AWG solid wire in twisted pairs. It displays a typical impedance of 100 ohms and is tested for attenuation and near-end crosstalk through 16MHz. This wire is useful for data transmission at speeds up to 16 megabits per second. It is the lowest level wire standard you should use for 10BaseT installations and is sufficient for 4 megabit-per-second Token-Ring.

- *Category 4.* This cable is the same as the Anixter Level 4 cable. It can have 22 AWG or 24 AWG solid wire in twisted pairs. This cable has a typical impedance of 100 ohms and is tested for performance at a bandwidth of 20MHz. It is formally rated for a maximum signaling speed of 20MHz. Although it was popular for a while, Category 4 cable has been superseded by Category 5 in most new installations.

- *Category 5.* This is 22 or 24 AWG unshielded twisted-pair cable with a 100 ohm impedance. This cable is tested at a bandwidth of 100MHz and can handle data signaling under specified conditions at 100 megabits per second. Category 5 cable is a high-quality media with growing applications for transmitting video, images, and very high-speed data. I recommend Category 5 cable for all new installations.

Category 5 is what you want!

It bears repeating: Any new cable installation should meet the EIA/TIA and UL Category 5 standards. Using Cat 5 qualified cable, parts, and techniques is the only way to ensure the long and useful life of your network. This cable will work for Ethernet, Fast Ethernet, and Token-Ring.

Trying to describe the EIA/TIA 568 standard and the category system is like trying to paint a moving train. The standard evolves through an interactive committee process, and change—particularly expansion—is constant. For example, because IBM's 150 ohm shielded Type 1 and Type 9 cable are so important in the market, we expect to see them accommodated in the standard. There are also proposals that integrate Thinnet Ethernet coaxial cable, 62.5/125 micron multimode fiber, and single-mode fiber cable used for long-distance connections into the specification.

Underwriters Laboratories

Local fire and building code regulators try to use standards like those of the National Electrical Code, but insurance groups and other regulators often specify the standards of the *Underwriters Laboratories.* UL has safety standards for cables similar to those of the NEC. For example, UL 444 is the Standard for Safety for Communications Cable, and UL 13 is the Standard for Safety for Power-Limited Circuit Cable. Network cable might fall into either category. UL tests and evaluates samples of cable and then, after granting a UL listing, conducts follow-up tests and inspections. This organization's independent status makes the UL markings valuable tools for buyers.

In an interesting and unique action, the people at UL have tied safety and performance together in a program designed to make it easier to select or specify cable. UL's LAN Certification Program addresses both concerns. IBM authorizes UL to verify 150 ohm STP to IBM performance specifications, and UL has established a Data-Transmission Performance-Level Marking Program that covers 100 ohm twisted-pair cable. UL adopted the EIA/TIA 568 performance standard and, by evolution, the Anixter cable performance model. There is a small inconsistency: The UL program deals with both shielded and unshielded twisted-pair wire, while the EIA/TIA 568 standard focuses on unshielded wire.

The UL markings range from Level I to Level V. You can tell a UL level from an Anixter level because the UL uses Roman numerals. As you learned earlier in the chapter, IBM's cable specifications range from Type 1 to Type 9, while the EIA/TIA has Categories 1 through 8. Of course it's easy to become confused by the similarly numbered levels and types. The UL level markings deal with performance and safety, so products that merit a UL level also meet the appropriate NEC MP, CM, CL, or FP specifications along with the EIA/TIA standard for a specific category. Cables that earn these UL markings can have them printed on the outer jacket as Level I, LVL I, or LEV I, for example.

Here is a quick summary of the UL markings:

- *UL Level I.* Meets appropriate NEC and UL 444 safety requirements. No specific performance specifications.

- *UL Level II.* Meets performance requirements of EIA/TIA 568 Category 2 and IBM Cable Plan Type 3 cable. Meets appropriate NEC and UL 444 safety requirements. Acccptable for 4 megabit Token-Ring, but not for higher-speed data applications such as 10BaseT.

- *UL Level III.* Meets performance requirements of EIA/TIA 568 Category 3 and NEC and UL 444 safety requirements. Lowest acceptable marking for LAN applications.

- *UL Level IV.* Meets performance requirements of EIA/TIA 568 Category 4 and NEC and UL 444 safety requirements.
- *UL Level V.* Meets performance requirements of EIA/TIA 568 Category 5 and NEC and UL 444 safety requirements. This is the right choice for most modern LAN installations.

A Star to Steer By

As you navigate through the landscape of your network's cabling system, it's often difficult to see the forest for the trees. Structured architectures like a premise distribution system, the EIA/TIA guidelines, or the UL marking system provide some assurance that you can pick the right path to network success.

But simply using the right materials doesn't ensure that a cable installation meets the performance specification. Many factors, including how much the wire is untwisted before it reaches a termination, the type of termination equipment, the electrical noise in various frequency bands, and the near-end crosstalk (NEXT) caused by wires in proximity to each other, determine the quality of the total installation. You can get a good start on a high-quality installation by using the correct cable, but good cable does not guarantee a good installation. The actions of the installer are critical to the overall quality of your cable plant.

Cables for Network Connections

The type of adapter you buy dictates the types of cable that will work in the network, the physical and electrical form of the network, the type of electrical signaling used on the network, and how the networked PCs share access to the connecting cable. People in the network business generally refer to the path of the cables as the *physical topology* and to the route of the messages on those cables as the *logical topology* of the network. There is no fancy turn of phrase to describe *electrical signaling*, but sharing the cable is known as *media-access control*.

In the remainder of this chapter, I discuss the general characteristics of cables, their physical topologies, and the signals they carry. In the next chapter, you'll look at the logical topologies and media-access control schemes specifically associated with the Ethernet, Token-Ring, and ARCnet networking systems.

The larger the area your LAN covers, the more critical cabling design becomes. You must look at the issue of cabling first to determine whether it will drive your network budget and planning cycles, or whether it is only a minor consideration. The type of cabling you have installed or want to use might be a deciding factor in the design and layout of your network, or it might be a minor factor that you can handle quickly.

There are five possible cabling choices: unshielded twisted-pair, shielded twisted-pair, coaxial, fiber-optic, and no wiring at all. Wireless LANs, or at least wireless segments of LANs, provide a way out of difficult wiring problems in many installations as you'll see later. First, let's focus on physical cabling.

You can have the wiring for your LAN installed by contractors as big as AT&T or GTE, by your local telephone company, by a local electrical contractor, or by your own employees. In any case, be sure to consider the need for a final electrical inspection when you plan your installation.

Major vendors including AT&T, Digital Equipment Corp., IBM, Northern Telecom, and many smaller vendors have developed their own premise distribution system (PDS) plans. These cabling architectures provide for an integrated telephone and data cabling plant using hardware components from a single supplier. The advantage of having one source of supply is that there is only one place to point the finger of responsibility; the disadvantage is that you become wedded to that vendor. If you are planning a new building or major renovation, shop for a PDS, but plan for a long-term relationship with the supplier you select.

If you start from scratch, the cost of LAN wiring is divided between the costs of material and labor. Prices vary with the amount of cable you buy, but here are some general estimates for cable purchased in reels of 1,000 feet or more; these prices skyrocket for shorter hunks of cable.

- Typical fiber-optic cable should cost just under $2 per foot.

- Shielded twisted-pair wiring used for Token-Ring networks runs about 40 cents per foot.

Finding a contractor

If you don't have a good LAN cable contractor, you're starting at a great disadvantage. Big companies like AT&T can supply lists of their certified contractors, but there are also two professional organizations that can help. The Association of Cabling Professionals (ACP) and the Building Industry Consulting Services International (BICSI) maintain lists of design and installation professionals.

- Thin coaxial cable used for Ethernet costs about 15 cents per foot.
- Four-pair twisted wire costs 10 cents per foot.

A lot of contractors know how to install twisted-pair wiring, and the cable television industry has taken the mystery out of installing coaxial cable. There are very few good fiber-optic contractors or people who know how to wire Token-Ring networks, however. Labor costs for cable installations vary widely, driven by locale and the availability of knowledgeable contractors. Horror stories about expenses of $1,000 per networked PC continue to come out of New York City and other major metropolitan areas, but the average cost per drop in more normal areas is about $150 per drop.

Companies often elect to have their own computer resource people plan and even install LAN cabling with the help of a licensed electrical contractor. Involving your own people in LAN wiring can save money, avoid mistakes, and facilitate expansion. Several companies, including AT&T, Mod-Tap, and Northern Telecom, offer courses in wiring techniques.

SEE ALSO
➤ *Chapter 5, page 75 describes LAN adapters and their electrical signaling.*
➤ *Chapter 7, page 132 lays out the physical and logical topologies.*

The Harmonics of Square Waves

The signals on LAN cables are electrical square waves. A signal that rises quickly to a level of 15 volts represents a binary 0, and one that falls rapidly to a negative 15 volts represents a binary 1. The voltage transition from 0 to the positive or negative level signals the transmission of the bit to the receivers on the network. This signaling scheme works well, but it encounters two problems: radiation and interference. The various network cables take different approaches to these problems.

The problem with radiation comes from the harmonics generated by the rising and falling voltages. A simple rule of physics states that the harmonics of square waves are infinite. This means that the square waves generate radio signals all the way up the radio-wave spectrum. The radio-frequency emissions generated by the data signals on a LAN cable can cause interference with a wide range of radio and television devices located miles away. So LAN cables and equipment must somehow prevent radiation of the unwanted harmonics. Government organizations set limits on the allowed amount of radiation for all computer products. The U.S. Federal Communications Commission sets two standards: Class A and Class B, for office and home use respectively. Class B requirements are more stringent than those for Class A.

Organizations engaged in commercial or international espionage can use the radiated electrical signals to intercept the data moving across LAN cables. Some cable systems meet a stringent set of specifications called the Transient Electromagnetic Emanations Standard (TEMPEST) designed to make it very difficult for any unauthorized party to receive signals from the cable.

The second problem cable designers must deal with is outside interference. The effect of electrically radiated signals works in the other direction, too. Electrical signals from motors, power lines, fluorescent lights, radio transmitters, and many other sources can distort and override the desired signals on the LAN cable. LAN cables must somehow protect the signals they carry from disruption by such outside electrical interference. Fortunately, the same techniques that work to cut down unwanted radiation also reduce incoming interference.

Coaxial Cable

Coaxial cable consists of a core of copper wire—either solid or stranded—surrounded by an external shield of woven copper braid or metallic foil. The braid and central conductor have the same axis (thus the term *coaxial cable*). Flexible plastic insulation separates the inner and outer conductors, and another layer of insulation covers the outer braid. Figure 6.2 shows the shielding on thin and thick Ethernet cabling.

The outer conductor shields the inner conductor from outside electrical signals and reduces the radiation of interior signals. The distance between the two conductors, the type of insulation, and other factors give each type of cable a specific electrical characteristic called *impedance*.

Crosstalk will get you fired!

The real sticker about problems like crosstalk is that they are intermittent. It's potentially career-limiting to have LAN traffic pile up for no apparent reason. There are tools that you and your cable contractor can use to detect crosstalk, crossed pairs, and other problems. But the best defense is a good initial cable installation.

FIGURE 6.2

These pieces of thick and thin coaxial cable have multiple layers of braid and foil shielding.

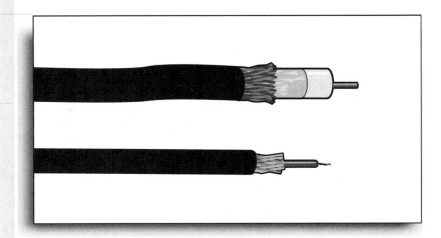

Different LAN signaling schemes, such as Ethernet, ARCnet, and IBM's 3270 cabling scheme, use cables with specific impedances, and they aren't interchangeable. You can't judge a coaxial cable's impedance by looking at it unless you read its type on the outside of the cable. The cables follow a letter and numeric designation scheme. If you just remember that Thin Ethernet uses a cable called RG-58 and ARCnet uses a cable called RG-62, you'll have as much knowledge as you're ever likely to need.

It takes a little experience and practice to install the connectors on coaxial cable, but the skill is important because one bad connection can halt the operation of an entire network. It pays to invest in good connectors that are plated with silver, not tin. It also pays to invest in a good crimping tool to install the connectors. Figure 6.3 shows a BNC connector attached to a piece of coaxial cable.

Watch particularly for cheap Ethernet T-connectors. Use only connectors that meet military specification UG-274. If a T-connector meets this specification, it will say so on the body of the barrel or on the lip of the male connector; be sure to look for that mark before you accept or install Ethernet T-connectors. I also recommend replacing unmarked generic connectors. With good connectors retailing for $6 to $10 each, and crimping tools selling for $150, you'll feel an urge to scrimp. But believe me, it's a bad gamble. Figure 6.4 shows two T-connectors.

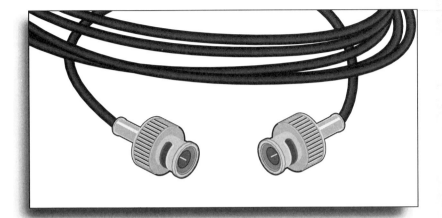

FIGURE 6.3

The connectors on the ends of this coaxial cable are typical of those used for thin Ethernet.

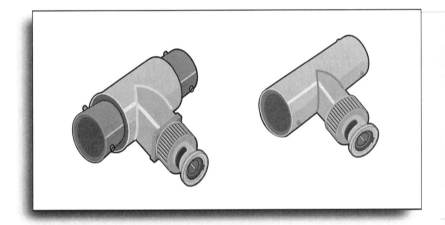

FIGURE 6.4

The quality of the T-connectors you use can have a major impact on the reliability and efficiency of your Ethernet network. The connector on the left shows its MIL SPEC numbers and has a reinforced junction at the center. Time has shown that connectors, like the one on the right, fail at the junction due to mechanical stress from the cable, and such failures are often difficult to detect.

Similarly, don't scrimp on the cable itself. Markings on thin Ethernet cable should identify it as RG-58/A-AU or as conforming to IEEE 802.3 specifications. (Don't confuse 53-ohm-impedance RG-58/A-AU cable with the 73-ohm RG-62/A-AU cable used in ARCnet, IBM's 3270, and other systems.) The radio industry is plagued by low-quality coaxial cable that allows unacceptable power losses at high frequencies. LAN cables aren't asked to carry high frequencies, so this problem might not show up for a few years until the insulation breaks down and the cable changes electrical characteristics. Always insist on brand-name cable that is clearly labeled with the standards it meets. An investment in good connectors, tools, and cable pays dividends for years.

That old coax ain't so bad!

Okay, I admit it, I still like coax. If you put it in right, it works forever. The modern standards call for a mix of UTP and fiber, but if you already have coax in your walls, perhaps from an earlier IBM mainframe installation, you can avoid spending tens of thousands of dollars on new wiring by adapting the existing cable to Ethernet. Check in places like the Black Box Catalog for the special adapters you'll need.

The thick backbone cable used in classical Ethernet networks requires some special handling. Known as "frozen orange garden hose," Thick Ethernet cable has the distance markers on the outside of the jacket to show the quarter wavelength points. It's important to get the terminators installed exactly on a black mark at each end; then, when you tap into the cable at the points marked between, the transceiver sees the correct impedance. If you miss the point by more than a few inches, theoretically the impedance mismatch could set up reflections within the cable that might cause problems.

However, in practice people report that Thick Ethernet works despite all types of mishandling. Instead of worrying about problems with the backbone cable, I'd watch out for smaller glitches, like a bad adapter or a transceiver with the Signal Quality Error (SQE) switch turned on. SQE is an old feature that causes more problems than it solves. (Installers say that SQE has three letters just like "OFF," and that tells you what to do with the switch.)

Thick Ethernet is difficult to install because of the size of the cable and the complex hardware involved in every connection. However, once it is in the walls, it should work until the building falls down.

Unshielded Twisted-Pair

As the name implies, *twisted-pair wiring* is made up of pairs of wires insulated from each other and twisted together within another insulating sheath. The twisting of the wire pairs produces a mutual shielding effect. Although this effect cuts down on the absorption and radiation of electrical energy, it is not as effective as an external wire braid or foil.

People often associate the term twisted-pair wiring with telephone wiring, but not all telephone wiring is twisted-pair. The wires in each pair of a twisted-pair cable are twisted together to reduce the electrical coupling between them and the amount of outside electrical noise they pick up. Figure 6.5 shows UTP wire pairs, and Figure 6.6 shows the most typical type of UTP termination: the RJ-45 plug. But there are many types of telephone wire that are not twisted. *Quad*, the wiring found in residences, has four parallel wires in one cable. The telephone wiring plants in many older buildings were designed for a key system, which uses phones with multiple line buttons and thick *multiconductor* cables. A few modern buildings are wired with something the industry calls *silver satin*. Silver satin cable is flat and typically has a silver vinyl jacket. None of these wiring systems—quad, multiconductor, or silver satin—is adequate for modern LAN data services.

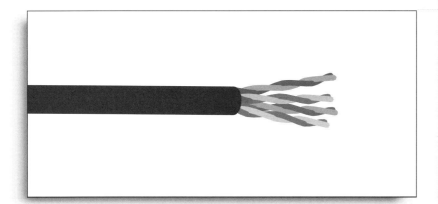

FIGURE 6.5

Unshielded twisted-pair wire offers an economical alternative for both Ethernet and Token-Ring networks. The twist of the wire provides a degree of shielding from external electromagnetic currents.

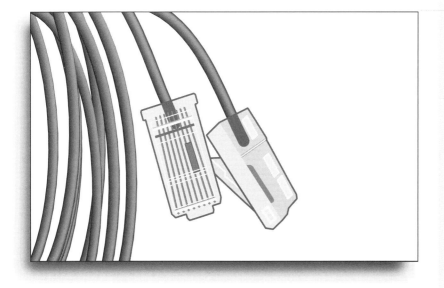

FIGURE 6.6

Unshielded twisted-pair wiring typically terminates in RJ-45 modular connectors like those shown here.

Unshielded twisted-pair wiring is very popular with network buyers, but much of its popularity is based on misconceptions or outdated information. Before you decide to string along with UTP, see if your decision is based on any of these ideas:

- *UTP is cheap.* Maybe, but while the wire itself is low in cost, the cost of the labor used to pull the wiring is the major portion of the bill. Fiber can cost ten times as much as UTP, but even at slightly more than $1 per foot, the cost of installation by a licensed electrical contractor can dwarf the cost of materials.

- *I can use the UTP that's already in the walls.* Again, maybe, but you need to analyze every wire run to be sure it meets the length, noise, and other electrical specifications for the networking architecture you want to use.

- *UTP gives me the reliability of the star wiring scheme.* Sure it does, but this arrangement is not unique to UTP. Modern wiring concentrators allow you to arrange any type of wire in a star physical topology.

The EIA/TIA and UL standards for UTP have made UTP practical for all network installations. My personal favorite wiring plan is still a system that uses thin coaxial cable in a star-wired configuration, but most organizations find UTP to be a more comfortable solution.

On close inspection, low cost and the chance to use existing wiring aren't the major advantages of using a twisted-pair setup. Let's examine its real benefits.

Even if you must pull additional twisted-pair wiring to install a LAN, at least the same wiring can be used for the telephone system (although I don't recommend running voice telephone and data signals on wire pairs in the same outside sheath because of crosstalk problems). The technology of twisted-pair wiring, unlike coaxial Ethernet alternatives and Token-Ring's shielded twisted-pair, is familiar to technicians you already have on staff or under contract. If an installer abides by a few rules (for example, keeping to a maximum wire length of 330 feet between computer and hub and avoiding sources of electrical noise), the installation is simple. Also, choosing unshielded twisted-pair wiring doesn't introduce complex and ugly cabling or the need for wall jacks and desktop attachments in your office.

Avoiding Twisted-Pair Problems

Telephone system suppliers such as AT&T, Northern Telecom, the regional Bell operating companies, and other PBX companies have standards for telephone wiring systems. Their standards and the resultant wiring systems are not identical, but they are close enough that you can usually assume their wiring systems can carry your data—assuming there are enough vacant wire pairs in the cables.

The heart of all the systems is the same: a wiring closet with rows of *punch-down blocks*. Some companies call them *Telco splice blocks*, and veterans know them from the old AT&T monopoly days as *Type 66 blocks*. Whatever their name, these central wiring points often become central failure points in wiring plants.

A punch-down block gets its name from the act of using a special hand tool to punch a wire down between the jaws of a retaining clip. The clip slices through the wire's PVC insulation and makes electrical contact. Punch-down blocks make installations and modifications simple, while avoiding the major problem of telephone system short circuits. However, the quality of the electrical connection made by the punch-down process varies considerably. The contact area between the clip and the wire is small, and moisture, crystallization, electrolysis, and corrosion can all degrade the electrical connection. On a voice system, a bad connection manifests itself in lower volume and perhaps frying or popping sounds. The human ear and brain deal with those problems admirably; unfortunately, computer data systems have less-than-human flexibility.

AT&T and other companies have new wire-splice blocks. AT&T calls its design the *Type 100*; it uses wire-wrap techniques and gold contacts for better connections. If you have transmission problems using unshielded twisted-pair wire, and if re-punching or wiggling the wires on the existing splice block changes the condition, you should consider retiring the old punch-down blocks in favor of more modern (and higher-priced) wire connection alternatives.

UTP Connectors

The connectors used on UTP are low cost and, with a little practice and care, easy to install. 10BaseT uses only two pairs of wires. Although that's all you really need, equipping your wall jacks with the full capacity of four pairs is a smart move as long as you don't use those spare pairs for anything else (like voice telephone systems).

The 10BaseT standard uses pins 1 and 2 for the first pair and pins 3 and 6 for the second pair. There is never any need for transposed pairs or cross-wiring in 10BaseT standard data systems. In fact, you should take care to make sure that the connections are straight-through all the way; otherwise, you'll lose the effectiveness of the electrical shielding generated by the twisting of the wires in each pair.

Eight wire sequences are commonly used for wiring an RJ-45 jack in the U.S. Among those sequences, the Preferred Commercial Building Cabling Specification of the Electronic Industries Association (thankfully referred to in the trade as the EIA standard), AT&T 258A, AT&T 356A, and the 10BaseT standard are now the most popular. These standards are all very similar, and you won't run into problems if you follow any one of them. However, an older Universal Service Order Code (USOC) was once the most popular wiring sequence, and it is not compatible with 10BaseT. You can quickly identify a USOC sequence because the pairs work their way into the center (as in 1–8, 2–7, and so on) instead of using the 1–2 sequence of 10BaseT.

Your best bet is to hire a cabling contractor to do your installation even if it's just a dozen nodes. But, even with a contractor on call, there will be days when you'll want to build your own short station cables. It's very difficult to do a good wiring job with a poor tool, so I urge you to invest in a good RJ-45 plug presser. The press looks like a giant pair of pliers. It aligns the plug and applies the correct pressure to seal the contacts. Make sure that you buy and use the proper RJ-45 plugs for the specific wiring segments. You'll need plugs for solid wire on the main runs, and you'll need plugs for stranded wire on the jumper cables and the cables that run between the walls and the PCs.

The solid wire and stranded wire plugs have different types of tiny internal contacts. Using the incorrect type of plug on a given type of wire practically guarantees intermittent operation as the system ages.

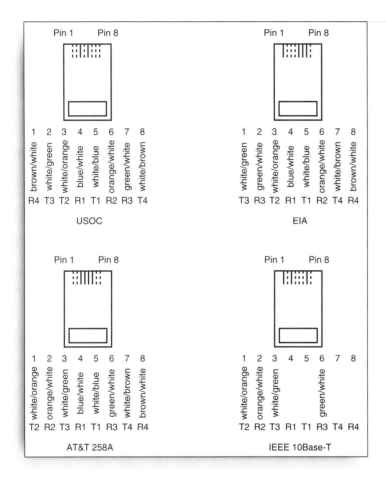

FIGURE 6.7

There are several different standards for wiring the RJ-45 plug used on UTP. Your network should use the 10BaseT standard unless it was wired for a proprietary telephone system.

Finally, keep the twists in the wires. It's tempting to untwist them, but don't do it. Keep the twists in each pair all the way to the plug or jack in order to retain as much shielding effect as possible.

I've devoted a lot of space to unshielded twisted-pair wire as a LAN connection scheme because this method of connecting network nodes is the clear choice in most installations. However,

Don't split those pairs!

Professional and amateur cable installers both commonly make a mistake called "installing with split pairs." It is possible to improperly install connectors so that the circuit still works but doesn't work well. Typically, the installer connects the correct signal wire (the T wires shown in Figure 6.7), but he pairs it with the incorrect R wires. The connection will work, but the electromagnetic shielding gained from twisting isn't effective, and the wires will absorb any electromagnetic interference. Take care!

you will still run across a technology called shielded twisted-pair wiring, particularly because it was once IBM's choice for its Token-Ring network system.

Shielded Twisted-Pair

Shielded twisted-pair wire carries an external aluminum-foil or woven-copper shield specifically designed to reduce electrical noise absorption. Thus, it combines the shielding properties of both coaxial cable and unshielded twisted-pair wire. Figure 6.8 shows the foil and braid shielding on shielded twisted-pair wire.

Shielded twisted-pair cables are relatively expensive and difficult to work with, and they require custom installation. Nonetheless, IBM has successfully marketed a wiring plan using these cables for Token-Ring installations. The IBM plan adds reliability (and substantial cost) by using a separate run of cable between every server or client station and a central wiring hub. This wiring plan significantly increases the amount of cable used, but it also ensures against the total failure of the network in the event that one cable breaks or shorts out. IBM uses special connectors, shown in Figure 6.9, for connection to the central wiring hub.

FIGURE 6.8

Shielded twisted-pair wiring combines the shielding of coaxial cable with the twisting of unshielded twisted-pair wire. However, this kind of wiring is bulky, expensive, and tricky to install properly.

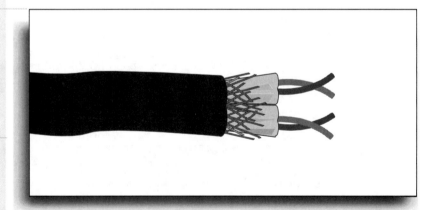

Coaxial cable, particularly the thin RG-59 or RG-62 type, is easier to install than shielded, data-grade, twisted-pair cable, and it has many of the same noise-resistance advantages. But if you want real data security and immunity from noise, you can't beat signals sent with light.

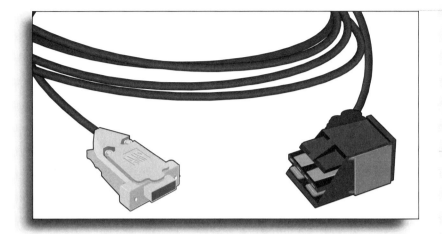

FIGURE 6.9
The D-shell connector shown here connects the cable to the Token-Ring adapter card. The larger, darker connector is an IBM Data Connector, which attaches the two twisted pairs of wire and shielding to an IBM medium attachment unit.

Fiber-Optic Cables

Fiber-optic cables, shown in Figure 6.10, are made of glass fibers instead of wire. These lightweight cables run many channels of stereo sound to airline passengers' seats, eliminating hundreds of pounds of wiring. Certain automobiles (such as Chevrolet's Corvette) rely on fiber-optic strands to route light from exterior lights to the dashboard so drivers can monitor safety conditions. Many PC-based local area networks, particularly those in critical line-of-business applications, use fiber-optic cables.

Fiber-optic cabling is made of a hair-thin strand of glass surrounded by strengthening material such as Kevlar. Small lasers or light-emitting diodes send pulses of light representing the 0s and 1s of the digital message through the fiber.

Fiber-optic cable has many advantages over copper wire, including complete freedom from electrical interference, a small diameter so you can reclaim your building's conduits, and the potential for carrying large amounts of data at high speeds over longer distances.

Practically all fiber LAN technologies use two strands of fiber going to each node, so some of the size advantage of fiber cable over small copper coaxial cable is lost in real installations. Each strand carries data in one direction for full-time two-way communications.

Dreaming in fiber optics

"Fiber to the desktop" was once a dream of network administrators. Fiber's high bandwidth and resistance to interference made it attractive. However, the spiraling cost of processing power resulted in increasingly low-cost transceivers for unshielded twisted-pair copper, while the cost of fiber-optic transceivers stayed high. Moore's Law won again, and now few planners believe that the clearly higher cost of running fiber to the desktop is worth the mainly theoretical gains. However, fiber is the clear winner for links between wiring closets because it provides for much greater distance than copper does.

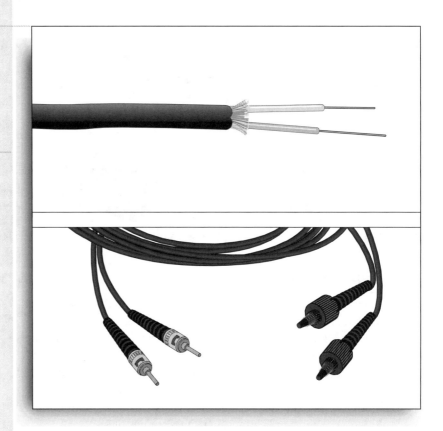

A couple of years ago, the big promise of fiber-optic systems came from their bandwidth. Hundreds of simultaneous telephone conversations or high-speed data transmissions can travel down a single fiber of glass that's a couple of times the diameter of a human hair. The telephone companies are making good use of fiber technology in this way as they expand and replace their systems.

Most people imagine data moving through fiber-optic cables at never-before-possible speeds. But speed is not one of the major advantages of PC-based fiber-optic local area networks. (EIA/TIA Level 5 UTP installations can carry data at 155 megabits per second.) The biggest advantage of fiber comes from increased distance. Fiber allows longer connections without requiring the installation of devices to repeat the signals, and it provides total immunity from interference in noisy electrical environments. But it doesn't move data any faster.

Distance and reliability are the primary assets most people value in fiber-optic cable; in addition, security is equally important to many users.

Distance

Although signals on a copper cable and light in a glass fiber travel at approximately the same speed, the light meets less resistance as it moves along. Therefore, light signals go farther with less attenuation. Fiber-optic links from simple PC-based LAN systems can run without a repeater to distances of more than 3.5 kilometers. This is more than 11 times the maximum distance for coaxial cable, and 15 times the distance for twisted-pair systems such as 10Base-T. (Architectural criteria other than the media limit Ethernet networks to 2.5 kilometers overall.)

Reliability

The primary reason for the reliability of fiber systems is that they don't pick up electrical signals and impulses. Despite shielding, bypassing, and grounding, copper cables become antennas. The longer they are, the more energy they absorb from sparking motors, radio transmitters, power wires, and other electrical devices. Additionally, metal cables can develop different voltage potentials to the electrical ground, leading to electrical ground loops that can induce interference and even sparking from metal cables. The energy from all these sources modifies and smothers the data signals in the metal cable, causing bad packets and sometimes transient unreliability. Fiber cables are immune to all electrical fields, so they carry clean signals and never spark or arc.

All fiber is not alike. AT&T favors a fiber with a core diameter of 62.5 microns (a micron is 1/25,000 of an inch), while IBM specifies a 100-micron core. You must match the equipment and the fiber, but if you install fiber before you buy the equipment, you'll be safe specifying the 62.5 micron size. Expect to pay about $1,100 for a 1,000-foot roll of cable with two fiber strands.

Security

Fiber LANs offer improved security because they carry light, and that light is precisely controlled. If I can get my hands on a

Copper can kill you

If you have an existing installation that links networks in two or more buildings using copper cable, it could be dangerous. Each building's electrical system has its own electrical ground. Unfortunately, disasters can happen. If a person were to inadvertently disconnect, dig into, run over, or otherwise damage a building ground, the electrical system could seek ground through your inter-building cabling, and equipment or people could be damaged. For that reason, you should link buildings, and even sections of large buildings, with fiber for safety as well as clean data.

coaxial cable LAN, I can tap into it and read all the data passing over it—including unencrypted passwords. Some coupling techniques let me intercept the signals without even piercing the cable; this is because copper cables radiate signals as well as picking them up. Fiber-optic cables often play a major role in voice and data communications systems approved under TEMPEST criteria because they radiate their light only at the ends of connectors.

If the amount of light going through the cable is precisely adjusted, the insertion of an unauthorized device to tap off some of the light causes the entire link to fail. System failure indicates that something unusual has happened to the cable. Because they don't leak, and it's difficult or impossible to insert a physical tap, fiber-based systems are practically immune to interception.

Who's Buying Fiber Optics?

The people buying fiber-optic LANs, or fiber-optic links for their LANs, aren't necessarily computer scientists and engineers with huge amounts of data to send. Instead, they are likely to be stockbrokers, bankers, medical technicians, and people in the fields of security or intelligence who need extended-distance coverage, absolute reliability, and perhaps confidentiality for their networks.

Fiber optics has moved quickly from a young technology with great promise to a set of mature, practical products that have significant advantages over other methods of connecting computers. At the same time, fiber systems bring some unique installation problems, and they cost more than alternative systems that use copper cables.

The price of connectors and the skill needed to install connectors on fiber-optic cable is much less of a problem than it once was. In the late 1980s, installers needed special equipment and expensive training to properly attach a connector to a piece of fiber, but now connections cost approximately $5 per connector, installation takes about two minutes per connector, and installers can quickly learn to use the simple installation tools.

FDDI

You have probably heard the acronym FDDI, which stands for *Fiber Distributed Data Interface*. FDDI is a standard specified by ANSI (the American National Standards Institute) as ANSI X3T9.5 for transmission at 100 million bits per second. Don't assume that all LANs using fiber conform to the FDDI standard, because actually very few of them do.

FDDI is something completely different. The FDDI standard defines two physical rings that simultaneously send data in different directions. The configuration is designed for reliability and flexibility as well as high throughput. The primary role of FDDI today is as a corporate or campus backbone linking LANs. Gigabit Ethernet is actually a spin-off of FDDI that uses FDDI signaling with the traditional Ethernet media-access control scheme.

Wireless LANs

This name is misleading. Wireless LANs typically aren't totally wireless, but instead use either radio or infrared technology to connect a node or group of nodes into the main body of the network. It's difficult to categorize wireless LAN systems because they have many different architectures. Some products work only with Ethernet or only with Token-Ring cabling, while others replace the cabling on certain segments. *Wireless* may be the hottest word in networking, but nobody owns the term and it means very different things to different people. There are at least five major types of wireless network connectivity:

- Conference room
- Building/campus
- City/region
- Continental
- Worldwide

Each type of wireless networking involves a different group of companies, and to make things even more confusing, there are overlaps between the categories. But before you get too far into this topic, I want to make one point clear: *Wireless networks in every category are always extensions of cabled networks, not replacements of them.* If any totally wireless networks actually do exist, they are rare exceptions.

The rules of physics apply to wireless connections just as they do to cable, but they are more confining in the wireless environment. Radio waves traveling through space face a much more hostile environment than do electrons traveling through copper. You can have long-distance connections, fast connections, or inexpensive connections over wireless, but not all three. Distance and signaling speed always work against one another, and raising either of those parameters while keeping the other one steady always raises the cost. This relationship makes it very difficult to field a wireless system that is less expensive or faster than one based on copper cables.

So, for wireless systems to succeed, they must be deployed in niche situations where copper is at some disadvantage. The two most fruitful applications for wireless are in areas where it is difficult to install copper cables and where people need or are willing to pay for, mobility.

SEE ALSO
➤ *We talk more about long distance wireless networking on page 272.*

Building and Campus Connections

Any number of situations can arise that make it difficult to install cable in a building or in a campus environment. For example, you might want to extend the network out to a lone PC in a warehouse or to a LAN in some other building, only to find that the distance limitations exceed a single span of LAN cable. A pair of routers would solve the problem, but they would also substantially increase the cost of connecting that single node. In such a case, a wireless link could be less expensive than copper and a lot easier to install.

As another example, you might also run into situations where the type of building construction or the inability to get a construction right-of-way blocks the cable installation. Wireless connections work in these cases too.

There are two classic ways to extend network coverage to other buildings: installing cables and leasing circuits. Installing cables (which, today, almost always means fiber-optic cables) requires an up-front investment for labor and materials, a small continuing cost for maintenance, and potentially large problems in getting right-of-way for installing the cable either above or below ground. You can take any number of strategies, including renting space on poles from power companies ($4 per pole per month is a common charge) or digging trenches through leased land (usually more than $100 per foot). However, the labor charges for these installations almost always exceed the cost of materials. Once the cables are in, your costs are sunk—in real and accounting terms.

If you don't want the up-front challenges of installing your own cables, you can try to lease circuits between your buildings from local telephone and cable companies. If this kind of service is available, your costs include an installation charge plus monthly charges (anywhere from $100 to $800 or more for T1). You should plan for delays while the carrier conducts engineering studies and perhaps installs or upgrades its own cables and equipment. The best you can say for this arrangement is that you don't have to maintain anything. You'll pay added fees, however, when you need to improve or move service or if you require greater reliability. You can deduct these costs and charges from your taxes as you pay them instead of using depreciation as you would for cables you own, but after a few years, the privately owned cables provide lower life-cycle costs.

SEE ALSO

➤ *We talk more about leasing circuits on page 271.*

➤ *The important role of Internet service providers in delivering circuits and service is discussed on page 312.*

The Third Way

There is one way to link buildings without cables, right-of-way hassles, or monthly costs: the wireless way. Wireless alternatives include both radio and optical systems. Optical systems, from companies such as SilCom and TTI Wireless, are very fast and are priced in the $10,000–$20,000-per-link range. They have signaling speeds of up to 155Mbps out to a maximum range of

2,000 feet. Although poor visibility, caused by weather or pollution, is a major limiting factor, if you have only a short inter-building link, optical systems are an attractive alternative.

Radio systems offer much greater range than optical systems do, and radio speeds are going up. As with optical systems, radio is fast and easy to set up. In one afternoon, you can establish a radio link between buildings separated by up to 20 miles and move data faster than it will go over a 1.5Mbps T1 circuit. One-time costs for these radio systems run anywhere from about $5,000 to more than $12,000 per link, but the equipment is reusable and requires practically no maintenance after installation.

Low-powered wireless systems don't require licensing for each site. You do need a line-of-sight path between the antennas, but there are tricks you can play by moving antennas and using repeaters that can bend the line-of-sight rule.

The list of major contenders in the building/campus wireless environment include Lucent and Aironet. Both companies offer flexible product lines with the ability to flexibly connect individual PCs and to separate large LANs. Unfortunately, these companies have been depending on proprietary signaling schemes for their products. PC Card and central point radios from one company won't work with those from another company.

An important development in this category of products is the IEEE 802.11 standard, which is designed to promote interoperability among wireless LAN products. As the vendors refine their 802.11-compliant products, they should have the ability to interact as reliably and efficiently as modern Ethernet products.

Bridges

The building/campus wireless systems typically act as linking devices called *bridges*. Unlike routers, bridges don't care about the network protocol you use (such as IPX or IP), and they don't require much time to set up and configure. Unfortunately, because a bridge passes all network protocols, it is usually not a great solution for linking LANs—owing to all the unnecessary traffic it sends. Better news is that most new bridges learn the

MAC addresses of all the PCs on both sides of the link, and they send the remote PC or LAN only the traffic that's really destined for the other side. These "learning" bridges eliminate any unnecessary traffic that could slow down performance.

If you set up a bridge to reject a group of specific MAC addresses, it can also serve as an internal security device. If you don't want certain PCs to connect to your bridged segment, for example, you can just connect a terminal to the bridge and enter the address of those PCs onto the filtered list. You may also want to filter some PCs or servers manually to cut down on the amount of traffic traveling across the bridge.

Wireless bridges use a radio technique called *spread spectrum* to send data through the air. Spread spectrum is a method of modulating or changing a data signal so that it occupies more of the radio band than is actually necessary to transmit the information. This spreading of the data secures the signal from eavesdropping and protects it from outside interference. Another benefit of spread spectrum is that it uses a portion of the electromagnetic spectrum known as the ISM (industrial/scientific/medical) bands. The ISM bands cover the frequencies of 902MHz–928MHz and 2.4GHz–2.484GHz and don't require an FCC license.

There are two types of spread-spectrum radios: frequency hopping and direct sequence. Most wireless bridges use the frequency hopping type. With frequency-hopping-spread-spectrum (FHSS) radios, the radio transmitter hops or jumps from one frequency to another at a specific hopping rate and in a specific hopping sequence. For example, a frequency-hopping transmitter may use a hopping pattern that goes from channel 20 to channel 3 to channel 15. The channel is the frequency width determined by the FCC.

FHSS transmitters are limited to 500KHz-channel bandwidths in the 900MHz band and to 1MHz-channel bandwidths in the 2.4GHz band. The receiving radio must know the transmitter's hopping sequence in order to recover the data safely. And because only the receiving station knows the hopping sequence of the transmitter, the data is safe from eavesdroppers.

Wireless bridges use surprisingly small antennas that are easy to mount and conceal. There are two types of antennas:

omnidirectional and unidirectional. An omnidirectional antenna sends and receives data in all directions. A unidirectional antenna sends and receives data in a single direction. Omnidirectional antennas are good for networking several PCs surrounding the bridge; unidirectional antennas are used to connect two locations across a great distance. The antennas are connected to the bridge (a small modem-sized box) using a special coaxial cable. The longer the cable, the less distance you can get between antennas, so you want to put the bridge as close to the antenna as possible.

Although wireless bridges are a great solution when you can't run cable, there are some things you must consider. These products are not cheap. You can plan to spend approximately $3,000 to $10,000 for each location to which you connect using a wireless bridge, depending on the type of antenna you use. If you can't run cable or if you have to run a lot of cable, however, a wireless bridge is your best solution.

SEE ALSO

➤ *You can route yourself over to much more information about bridges and routers on page 254.*

Longer Reach

You can expect more wireless connection options in the future. In some areas, it will be less expensive to deliver the "last mile" of telephone and data service across wireless systems than it is to bury cables. Constellations of low Earth-orbiting satellites will deliver worldwide roaming connections for data and voice. Cellular telephones are already considered "thin clients" for certain computer systems. The right interface software makes their limited screens and keyboards very useful computing tools. Wireless connectivity is one of the most important options in your networking tool kit.

Cabling Recommendations

What's the bottom line of these connection options? After you sort things out according to cost and benefit, it's pretty clear. First, if you have a large installation, always use fiber between wiring closets in the building and around the campus, regardless of what cabling you run between the wiring closets and the desk-tops. Pull plenty of spare fibers between buildings and between the floors of buildings, and let them sit dark until you need them.

Second, plan for plenty of wiring closets. You'll find plenty of small spaces associated with concentrations of workgroups where you can cluster the wiring hubs, routers, and Internet access devices that are a part of modern networks. The term *closet* sur-vives, even though these may be large rooms with their own air conditioning and power systems. Whether your wires come together in a special room, in a real closet, or under someone's desk, I urge you to provide backup power for the wiring center: It won't do much good to have backup power for the server and client PCs if the wiring center fails.

Third, take advantage of management features. As your network grows, the management capabilities of your cabling system become increasingly important. Hubs and routers often have microprocessors in the 80186 class dedicated to management duties. These processors can count the packets of data as they fly by, recognize errors in the data stream, and generate reports. Even network interface cards have management capabilities. These devices can hold data in a *management information base* (MIB) until it is polled by a computer running management soft-ware. These processors can protect the network by automatically disconnecting nodes generating bad data, and in some cases, they can even enhance security by restricting the day of the week and time of day specific nodes may enter the network. They can also send special messages, called *alerts*, to computers running network management software.

A signaling and reporting scheme called the *Simple Network Management Protocol* (SNMP) provides an architecture for net-work reporting and management that includes agent devices, which gather data in wiring centers and other network devices, and computers that act as management stations. The manage-ment computers can be PCs (typically running Windows), or they can be other platforms like Sun workstations running UNIX.

The Yin and Yang of server hubs

In late 1991, some companies, including Novell and Artisoft, delivered wiring hubs designed for installation in PCs acting as file servers. The products didn't successfully sell. We saw the idea come out again around 1996, but the products failed again. Merging the server and the hub always sounds like a good idea, but network man-agers are conservative, and hubs are small and cheap. I predict that this will again be a hot idea in 2000, but it won't fly then either.

Finally, run plenty of Category 5 unshielded twisted-pair cable between the wiring closets and desktops. Use patch panels for the UTP in the wiring closets in order to simplify the moves and changes that inevitably are a part of life in any organization.

SEE ALSO

➤ *There is a lot more information on SNMP and management tools on page 399.*

Putting It All Together

The next chapter describes the combinations of physical topologies, cables, and adapters used in three standard network architectures. As you'll see, these architectures continue to evolve and expand to include a variety of alternatives. Now, with a solid grasp of the features underlying each of these systems, you'll be able to master the array of options each alternative provides.

The Story of Ethernet, Token-Ring, and ARCnet

The physical elements of LAN cabling—the adapters, cables, and connectors—are defined by sets of standards that have been evolving since the early 1970s. These standards, which have undergone many revisions, ensure the interoperability and compatibility of network devices. Committees established by such organizations as the Institute of Electrical and Electronics Engineers (IEEE), the Electronic Industries Association (EIA), and the International Telecommunications Union typically labor for years to develop agreements and adopt standards on how electronic devices should signal, exchange data, and handle problems. However, it's companies that develop products conforming to those standards. Some companies, particularly IBM, used to establish their own proprietary standards and products (at least partly because they wanted to lock customers into their technology), but today, "open systems" are built around standards established by national and international committees prevail.

In theory, if any company develops a product that operates according to a standard, it will work with products from all other vendors meeting the same standard. In practice, however, companies often implement the standards in such different ways that the products don't work together without a lot of adjustment on both sides. Nonetheless, the concept is sound, and constant efforts to improve compatibility among LAN products are succeeding.

Three standard protocols for LAN cabling and media-access control should interest you: Ethernet, Token-Ring, and ARCnet. Each LAN standard combines physical and logical topologies, signaling, and media-access control techniques in different ways. I'll describe the important features of each one in this chapter.

How the Standards Got That Way

The IEEE assigns numbers to its active committees. Committee 802 is a very large organization that includes members from industry and academia interested in a broad range of wide-area and local-area network systems. Subcommittees of Committee 802 develop and maintain standards for several LAN topologies.

The subcommittees use decimal numbers to identify their work. The glossary (Appendix A) describes many 802 committee standards in addition to 802.5 and 802.3, which I will discuss here.

IEEE standard 802.5 covers the Token-Ring architecture. This standard describes a token-passing protocol used on a network of stations connected in a special way, combining a logical ring topology (in which every station actively passes information to the next one in the ring) with a physical star topology.

IEEE 802.3 describes a standard that owes a lot to the earlier Ethernet system. Networks conforming to IEEE standard 802.3 use a carrier sense multiple access (CSMA) media-access control scheme on an electrical bus topology. This standard leaves room for several wiring options, including thin coaxial cable and unshielded twisted-pair wiring.

ARCnet is not an IEEE standard. Because of this and the self-defeating overly protective actions of Datapoint Corp., ARCnet isn't chosen for new installations. ARCnet is still in use, but as changes, moves, mergers, and acquisitions take place, ARCnet networks will disappear.

Ethernet the Elder

Ethernet was one of the first LAN architectures. This network cabling and signaling scheme entered the market in the late 1970s and is still a respected standard. The reason for Ethernet's longevity is simple: The standard provides high-speed transmission at an economical price, offering a broad base of support for a variety of LAN and micro-to-mainframe applications. Companies marketing Ethernet adapters have kept their products up to date, and today Ethernet is the best network choice. There is a clear and reasonably economical migration path from 10-megabit-per-second Ethernet to systems with faster throughput, such as Ethernet switching, Fast Ethernet (100-megabit-per-second networks), and Gigabit Ethernet.

These days, you can buy an adapter card that will let you plug your PC into an Ethernet network for as little as $50, although retail prices can go slightly over $100. Figure 7.1 shows an Intel adapter designed for use in a server. Of the more than 20 companies that market Ethernet adapters, 3Com and Intel are probably the best known and most competitive. Until the mid 1990s, most adapters were made from the same set of function-specific chips—usually from National Semiconductor Corp. Today, many Ethernet adapters have custom processors. Some adapters are better for use in a server than in a PC client, and there are other important differences in features, performance, and cost.

FIGURE 7.1

This Intel EtherExpress% PRO/100 Server Adapter has an Intel i960 processor that takes the data-handling workload off the computer's central processor. It's an example of a modern and very capable LAN adapter.

People often associate Ethernet with network elements beyond the scope encompassed by the cabling and signaling scheme co-invented by Robert Metcalfe and David Boggs at Xerox's Palo Alto Research Center (PARC). According to Metcalfe, the name "Ethernet" derives from "the luminiferous ether thought to pervade all of space for the propagation of light" (a.k.a. electromagnetic waves).

Actually, Ethernet is a specification describing a method for computers and data systems to connect and share cabling. Ethernet encompasses what the International Standards Organization calls the Physical and Data-link layers of data communications.

The IEEE 802.3 family of standards includes the specifications of the older Ethernet protocols, but the committee's work also includes changes to the basic structure of the data packets. So technically, the term "Ethernet" doesn't include all of the options outlined under 802.3. "Eight-oh-two-dot-three" is a more complete description of the standard, but more people understand the term "Ethernet."

The primary characteristics of the early physical Ethernet link include a data rate of 10 megabits per second, a maximum station separation of 2.8 kilometers, a shielded coaxial cable connecting the stations, and a specific kind of electrical signaling on the cable called *Manchester-encoded digital baseband*. The latter specification describes the electrical signals that make up the digital 0s and 1s that are constantly passing over the network. Although the data rate in modern systems has skyrocketed to a gigabit, and the shielded coax has given way to less-expensive UTP and fiber, the distance limitations, encoding scheme, and media-access control scheme stay the same.

The major part of the Data-link layer specification for Ethernet describes the way stations share access to coaxial cable through a process called *carrier sense multiple access with collision detection* (CSMA/CD). CSMA/CD is the kind of operational scheme that modern standards committees call a *media-access control* (MAC) protocol. The medium is the cable connecting the network nodes, and the MAC protocol determines how nodes on the network share access to the cable.

SEE ALSO

➤ See *"Networking Acronyms and Buzzwords" on page 58 for a more detailed explanation of the ISO's OSI architecture.*

➤ *Chapter 6, which starts on page 95, guides you through the loops and twists of network cabling.*

Ethernet the Perennial

For many years Ethernet has been the fastest-growing network system and the first choice of many data managers and system integrators. For a while, IBM dangled new ways of using Token-Ring to connect PCs and mainframes in order to promote Token-Ring networking, and this slowed the growth of Ethernet. But, in terms of new installations, Ethernet now far outshines any other LAN networking scheme.

Token-Ring installations are very expensive compared to Ethernet, and Ethernet offers efficient ways to connect to DEC, Hewlett-Packard, IBM, Xerox, and many other computer systems.

As befitting a network scheme with its tenure, Ethernet has many offspring. Ethernet adapters using fiber-optic cable are available from companies like 3Com and Optical Data Systems. The biggest growth area is in Ethernet adapters operating over unshielded twisted-pair wire at data rates of 100 megabits per second.

The coaxial cable cabling scheme found in PC-based networks installed during the late 1980s and early 1990s uses a thin, 52-ohm coaxial cable between each two network stations. This cable, commonly called Thin Ethernet (and sometimes "cheapernet"), is typically limited to 305 meters (1,000 feet) between repeaters, but an IEEE specification limits it to 600 feet. The network interface card in each station usually attaches to this cable through a T-connector, which facilitates connecting and disconnecting stations on the network without breaking the continuity of the cable (see Figure 7.2).

FIGURE 7.2

The thin Ethernet coaxial cable runs from PC to PC in a physical daisy-chain topology. The cable connects to each node through a coaxial T-connector. The terminating resistors at each end of the cable are critical to proper operation. You should use only Ethernet T-connectors that meet military specification UG-274.

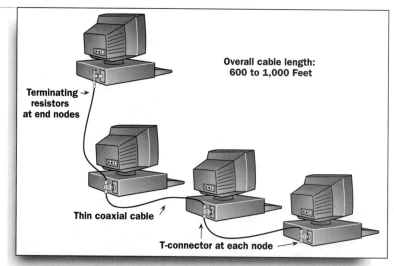

The oldest Ethernet cabling scheme is more frequently found in installations with larger computers. This scheme uses heavily shielded coaxial cable (informally named "frozen orange garden hose," which aptly describes its size, color, and ease of installation) to serve as a backbone among the clusters of nodes scattered around a building. Here the maximum length of cable between repeaters is 500 meters (1,640 feet), and the cable attaches to devices called *transceivers*, which transform the cable's connections into something more suitable for a PC or terminal. A flexible transceiver cable made up of a shielded twisted-pair wire runs between the transceiver and the AUI port on the network adapter. Transceiver cables can be up to 15 meters (45 feet) long; they connect to the network card through a 15-pin D-connector (see Figure 7.3).

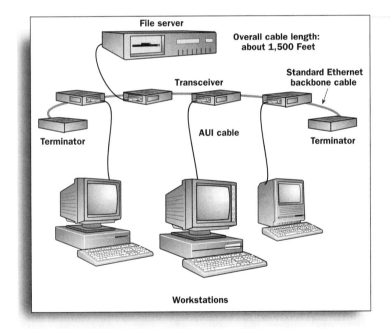

FIGURE 7.3

Standard Ethernet cable is thick coaxial cable that usually remains hidden behind walls. Transceivers connect directly at the cable and then extend the connection to each node through AUI cable.

SEE ALSO

➤ *I link Token-Ring to mainframe systems beginning on page 339.*

Packaging and Moving Data: The Ethernet Way

Ethernet uses a communications concept called *datagrams* to get messages across the network. The CSMA/CD media-access technique makes sure that two datagrams aren't sent out at the same time, and it serves as a method of arbitration if they are.

Ethernet's datagram concept is based on the simple premise that a communicating node will make its best effort to get a message across. The datagram concept does not include a guarantee that a message will arrive at any specific time or that it will be free of errors or duplications. The datagram system does not even guarantee that delivery will occur. If you want any of these assurances, you have to implement them in higher-level software.

The Ethernet datagrams take the form of self-contained packets of information. These packets have fields that contain information about their destination and origin, the sort of data they contain, and the data payload itself. Because the data field in each packet can be no larger than 1,500 bytes, large messages must traverse the network in multiple packets. (Articles statistically describing the efficiency of "best effort" packet-transmission systems have been the favorite filler of professional journals since Bob Metcalfe published his Harvard Ph.D. thesis, "Packet Communications," back in 1973.)

One element of the Ethernet packet structure, shown in Figure 7.4, differs from that codified by the IEEE 802.3 committee. The committee saw a need for a user ID in the packet; thus, its specification trades the byte count field for a user ID field. Fortunately, the network interface cards don't care as long as they take their data from higher-level software that sets up the packets. Ethernet and 802.3 packets can traverse the same network, but nodes operating under one format can't exchange data with nodes designed for the other without software translation at some level.

SEE ALSO

➤ *For more information about the layers of software above datagrams that add reliability, see Chapter 8, "The Structure of Networking Operating Systems," page 161.*

Datagrams aren't for certain!

Ethernet genuinely tries to get every packet from source to destination, but the attempt often fails, and the Ethernet cards and hubs don't recognize or respond to a failed delivery that isn't caused by a collision on the wire. It's up to software in the sending computer, which typically conforms to a standard like TCP, to recognize the need to resend lost packets. Different pieces of networking hardware and software have different interdependent functions.

Framing up packets

Despite the legitimate lineage of the term "packet," there is a current move toward calling modern Ethernet packets "frames." Someone always has a better idea. Whether you use the word packet or the word frame, you mean basically the same thing: the package of data created by the Ethernet adapter.

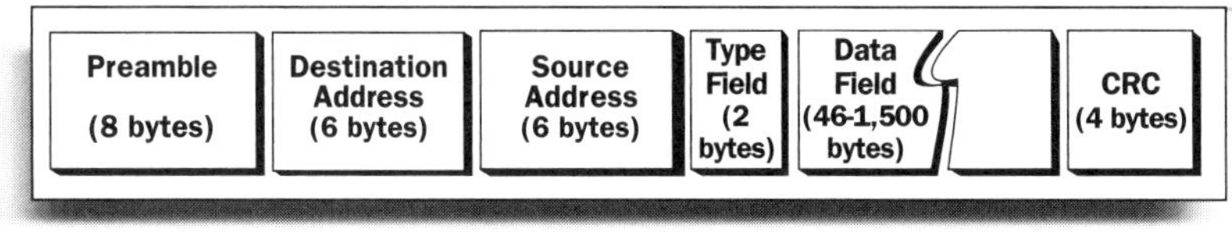

Preamble (8 bytes)	Destination Address (6 bytes)	Source Address (6 bytes)	Type Field (2 bytes)	Data Field (46-1,500 bytes)	CRC (4 bytes)

FIGURE 7.4

In the Ethernet protocol, messages are sent between workstation nodes in the form of "packets," or frames. Each packet measures 72 to 1,526 bytes long and contains six fields, five of which are of fixed length. The preamble field allows the receiving station to synchronize with the transmitted message. The destination and source address fields contain the network ID of the nodes receiving and initiating the message. The type field indicates the type of data in the data field that contains the actual data. The CRC field helps the receiving node perform a *cyclical redundancy check*—an error-checking analysis of the total packet.

Listen Before Transmitting

Before packets can traverse the coaxial cable of the Ethernet network as datagrams, they must deal with CSMA/CD, the media-access control protocol that determines how nodes on the network share access to the cable. CSMA/CD works in a listen-before-transmitting mode: If the network adapter receives data to send from higher-level software, it checks to see whether any other station is broadcasting on the cable. Only when the cable is quiet does the network adapter broadcast its message.

CSMA is a great system, but it has the following limitations:

- The listen-before-transmit mode assumes that each station can hear the same packet on the network at the same time. If some part of the packet must appear at all nodes at the same instant, the packet's overall length is critical.

- Short packets can cover less distance at one time than long packets can. Therefore, the length of the shortest packet determines the maximum distance between any two nodes on an Ethernet network.

- If the packet incurs any delay in route, as it does when it passes through a wiring hub, that delay shortens the maximum distance even more.

Later in this chapter you'll get deeper into wiring hubs, their delays, and ways around the problem.

Ten-four, over and out!

The familiar model of CSMA/CD is a radio system like a police, fire, or citizen's band device. Anyone with a message to send listens to the channel, waits until it's clear, and then transmits. Failure to wait can disrupt everyone's traffic.

CSMA/CD also functions as a mediator when the inevitable happens: when two or more nodes simultaneously start to transmit on an idle cable and the transmissions collide. The adapters can detect such collisions because of the higher electrical-signal level that simultaneous transmissions produce. When they detect a collision, the network adapter cards begin transmitting what is called a *jam signal* to ensure that all conflicting nodes notice the collision. Then each adapter stops transmitting and turns to its internal programming to determine a randomly selected time for retransmission. This "back-off" period ensures that the stations don't continue to send out colliding signals every time the cable grows quiet.

IEEE 10BaseT and 100BaseT

In late 1990, after three years of meetings, proposals, and compromises, an IEEE committee finalized a specification for running Ethernet-type signaling over unshielded twisted-pair wiring. The IEEE calls the 10-megabit UTP 802.3 standard 10BaseT.

The IEEE 802.3 family of standards generally describes carrier sense multiple access signaling, like Ethernet, used over various wiring systems. The name 10BaseT indicates a signaling speed of 10 megabits per second, a baseband signaling scheme, and twisted-pair wiring in a physical star topology (see Figure 7.5). In the mid 1990s, the perceived need for speed drove the development of a new standard called 100BaseT. In truth, developments in the chips that send and receive the signals over copper wire made signaling at 100Mbs over UTP possible, and marketing took over from there. 100BaseT is also called Fast Ethernet.

Where does Fast Ethernet go— really?

It's very clear that the best use for Fast Ethernet is as a big pipe for file and web servers. Many hubs combine 8–12 10Mbs ports with one or two 100Mbs ports. Of course, the hub has a lot of internal processing power to mediate the speed differences. A fast connection to a server eliminates a potentially serious bottleneck.

LAN cards able to handle either speed are marketed as 10/100 cards. While most 100BaseT connections go to servers today, the affordable price of 10/100 cards makes them a good investment for all new PC nodes.

Importantly, the "home run" wiring scheme of 10BaseT or 100BaseT—running a single wire from the central wiring hub to the desktop—improves the reliability of the system over the older daisy-chain Ethernet wiring scheme. The strong practical appeal of 10BaseT and 100BaseT products is in their commonality. You can safely mix and match adapter cards and wiring hubs from different companies and use them together on the same network. This commonality assures you of multiple sources of supply, competitive pricing, and confidence in long-term support.

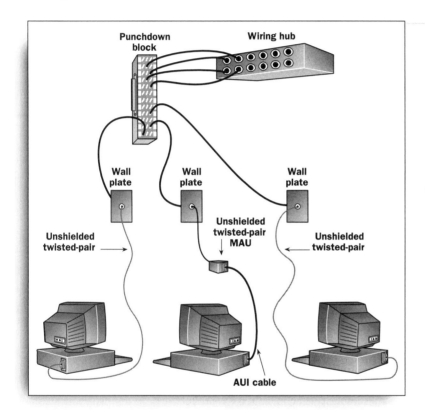

FIGURE 7.5

10BaseT is the IEEE designation for Ethernet running on unshielded twisted-pair (UTP) wire in a physical star topology. The UTP can run directly to the adapters in each node or to an unshielded twisted-pair media attachment unit (MAU) connected to the node through the AUI cable.

For a network manager, the biggest practical advantage of the 10BaseT or 100BaseT wiring installation comes from the star wiring scheme, which provides both reliability and centralized management. Like the spokes of a wheel, the wires radiate from a central wiring hub out to each node (see Figure 7.6). If one wire run is broken or shorts out, that node is out of commission, but the network remains operational. In Token-Ring or thin Ethernet wiring schemes, one bad connection at any point takes down the entire network.

Cables for hubs

In the previous chapter, we introduced the categories of cabling. As you examine the value of hubs, you should keep in mind that it takes specific types of cables, installed according to specific criteria, to make these hubs work correctly. Typically, modern installations will conform to the Category 5 UTP standards.

FIGURE 7.6

The 10BaseT and 100BaseT twisted-pair wiring systems gain flexibility and reliability through the use of a wiring hub. Note that these hubs require a power source and that it's smart to supply them with a UPS battery backup.

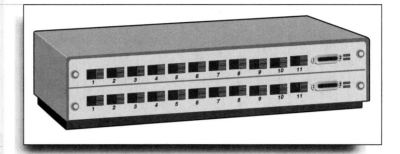

The central wiring hub is also an ideal place to install a monitoring microprocessor and network management software.

SEE ALSO

➤ *We manage to pull together everything about management starting on page 400.*

Wiring Hubs

The cabling system for 10BaseT and 100BaseT gives each network node its own discrete wire connection to a central wiring hub (see Figure 7.7). This topology provides excellent reliability, and the central wiring point is a natural location for network management and security activities. Firmware in the wiring center can monitor activity levels, recognize and report on problems, and even stop intrusion by limiting access on a port to a single authorized MAC layer address. You can also program a sophisticated wiring center to prevent access during certain periods (such as evenings and weekends).

You can typically access and control the firmware program in the wiring center from across the network. Many products also contain an RS-232 serial port so you can remotely control the wiring center through a modem.

Another important advantage of this topology is *operational survivability*. The concentrator, or hub, isolates the individual cables from each other so that, in the event of a broken line or connection, only that particular node loses service; all the other nodes on the network remain up and running. The concentrator can also recognize error conditions and disconnect—or in 10BaseT terminology "partition"—the offending node. The 802.3i 10BaseT standard requires that the wiring center must actively partition the individual node lines.

FIGURE 7.7

This Bay Networks BayStack 150 10BaseT hub provides 24 ports and a huge array of lights and management options. It can ensure that you have a good link to each node, monitor traffic levels, and detect several types of problems.

The IEEE 802.3i specifications also require that a 10BaseT wiring center act as a signal repeater by regenerating and retiming the packets, thus reshaping the digital square waves and cleaning off the line noise before broadcasting the signal to the other connected nodes. However, this regeneration process takes a finite time, which results in a small delay or *packet latency*. Latency limits the number of hubs you can string in a series.

Physically, each 10BaseT wiring center follows one of two models. A common configuration is a single closed cabinet with built-in RJ-45 jacks for 8–12 node connections. This type of closed box without an internal expansion capability and with fixed connections is usually referred to as a wiring *hub*.

The second type of wiring center consists of a modular cabinet with a common back plane and slots capable of accepting various electronic hardware modules for different wiring connections, management modules, and devices such as routers. This type of flexible and expandable wiring center, typically much more expensive than a hub, is commonly referred to as an *intelligent concentrator*.

The distinction between the two types of 10BaseT wiring centers is not set in stone. For that reason, you will see both terms used interchangeably in advertisements and technical literature.

The main advantage of a concentrator over a hub is the ability to link different media types such as UTP, thin Ethernet, thick Ethernet, and fiber-optic cable. But this flexibility is not cheap. Concentrators can cost $10,000 or more, compared to several hundred dollars or less for a simple hub.

One problem inherent in this design is the cost of adding one more node when you're all out of ports. These devices all have trip points where adding just one more node requires the purchase of an additional wiring center. For example, for a 30-node network, you might logically expect to purchase three 10BaseT hubs with 10 ports each. But because you have to interconnect the wiring concentrators, four ports are used for the inter-concentrator connections (A–B and B–C). This means that you must buy four 10-node hubs to connect 30 nodes. Note that if one of the hubs goes down due to power loss or some other malfunction, all the nodes on that hub go down, and the hubs on either side of it become isolated.

Another important thing to remember about 10BaseT installations is that the wiring hubs need backup power. If you provide UPS support for your servers and client PCs, you must also install backup power for the wiring centers to ensure continuity of operation.

Stackable Hubs

If you need any more than 8–12 node connections, you'll soon come across a category of products called *stackable hubs*. As the name implies, these hubs stack, typically in some kind of frame or cabinet. But stacking is driven by more than physical convenience—it's an electrical necessity. Both 10BaseT and 100BaseT devices use collision detection to determine when it is safe for a node to transmit on the network. A hub, technically called a *repeater*, transmits all network traffic between the network segments. It takes time for electronic signals to travel across all of the repeaters, but all nodes must simultaneously sense the same packet to avoid collisions. Greater device delay and smaller packet size drive down the permissible size of the network. The concept behind stacking hubs is to use a special high-speed connection between the hubs in the stack to reduce device delays.

The delay caused by repeaters forces rules limiting their use. The 10BaseT standard allows four repeaters on a single LAN segment, but 100BaseT is limited to one or two depending on something called the *Class type* of the repeaters (see Figure 7.8). There are two types, or classes, of 100BaseT repeaters: Class I and Class II. Class I devices have a higher latency, and the rules of CSMA allow you to place only one repeater on a single

100BaseT segment. Class II repeaters have a lower latency, and the rules allow you to cascade two together on a single segment, but you can't place them further than 5 meters apart. Most 100BaseT hubs are Class I devices.

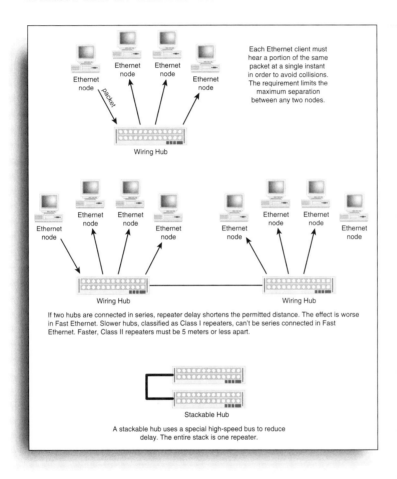

Each Ethernet client must hear a portion of the same packet at a single instant in order to avoid collisions. The requirement limits the maximum separation between any two nodes.

Wiring Hub

If two hubs are connected in series, repeater delay shortens the permitted distance. The effect is worse in Fast Ethernet. Slower hubs, classified as Class I repeaters, can't be series connected in Fast Ethernet. Faster, Class II repeaters must be 5 meters or less apart.

Stackable Hub

A stackable hub uses a special high-speed bus to reduce delay. The entire stack is one repeater.

FIGURE 7.8

Stackable hubs have a high-speed backbone that makes the stack appear as one Ethernet repeater.

The value of a hub stack hub is that the fast backbone between the hubs means the stack is only one repeater, regardless of how many hubs it holds. Stacking gives you flexibility. The vendors also often provide options for the stack, such as a management module or redundant power supplies.

Ethernet Switching

Ethernet's CSMA/CD media-access control scheme is both its weakness and its strength. In most networks, particularly those that transmit bursts of data, CSMA works well. When the work done across the network consists of opening and saving files and making queries against databases, CSMA works fine. But some modern applications, like video conferencing and transferring of very large multimedia files, generate a constant stream of data. If you get more than one of these on a segment, the result is an extremely high average traffic load and many CSMA collisions. When you have a lot of collisions, the overall throughput of the network degenerates.

A technique called *Ethernet switching* can improve the network throughput of individual nodes without forcing you to upgrade the LAN adapters installed in the PC or the cabling system. Switching hubs don't provide faster signaling, but they essentially remove the contention for the cable at each node. As a result, your network enjoys faster throughput, and the results are the same as if you were providing faster signaling. When you move to switching, you can keep your present Ethernet LAN adapters and hubs, but each adapter performs as though it were the only one on the network. Unlike the other networking alternatives described in this chapter, switching hubs don't divide the network bandwidth among all active nodes. Instead, a fast processor in the hub moves the packets across a backplane operating at hundreds of megabits per second. This is called a *collapsed-backbone architecture* because it acts as a series of individual wiring hubs connected by a fast backbone link.

In practice, older computers can't take advantage of the full 10-megabit Ethernet channel, so most companies offer Ethernet switching products in versions that allow you to share 10 megabits of bandwidth among one to eight nodes.

Generally, you can install switching hubs in one of four configurations: server front end, back end to a group of hubs, high-speed wiring concentrator, and FDDI concentrator.

Video: Do you care?

The problems of moving the streams of data created by video conferencing, film clips, and other video and audio systems seem to occupy the fantasies of some engineers. Frankly, I haven't seen streaming video pervading office networks. Video conferencing, for example, continues to be a solution looking for a problem. The same is true of asynchronous transfer mode (ATM) technology. Techniques like segmentation, switching, and Gigabit Ethernet will handle our real data requirements for a decade.

- As a server front end, a switching hub is the only connection point for one or more servers. Each server gets the maximum bandwidth it can use while the client computers compete for more limited bandwidths.

- As a back end to a group of nonswitching wiring hubs, a switching hub acts as a very fast yet economical backbone. As many as a dozen hubs can have 10-megabit bandwidth with no competition for the channel.

- As a high-speed wiring concentrator, a switching hub allows the administrator to give each node the necessary amount of bandwidth. This is the classic collapsed-backbone architecture.

- As a concentrator for a high-speed system, a switching hub can feed an FDDI, ATM, or Gigabit Ethernet link or some other type of backbone technology.

Switching hubs are now widely available and affordable. You don't need to worry about changes in emerging standards or losing an investment you've already made. Even though they don't meet every requirement for fast networking, they can offer the equivalent of hundreds of megabits per second of connectivity over an area as wide as any Ethernet network using existing adapters and cabling.

Segmentation Is the Key

When increased traffic starts to slow down the network, you don't necessarily have to give every user a dedicated port on an Ethernet switch or install 100 adapters in every desktop PC. Chances are, if you just add more segments to your LAN, you'll be able to increase performance and avoid a lot of extra costs. For example, if you have one network adapter in your file server and 40 users are connected to it, all 40 clients are sharing a single 10Mbps or 100Mbps pipe to the server. By adding another network adapter to the server and dividing the 40 clients among

If it ain't broke, switch it!

If you're running into a lot of collisions, try segmenting your network. If that's too complex, introduce switching. Importantly, switching prevents you from having to go into PCs that are running fine in order to put in a new 100BaseT adapter. Opening the cover on a PC that isn't broken is the surest way to make sure it will break. Switching adds speed, reduces wait times, and keeps the covers screwed on to perfectly good PCs.

segments, you effectively double your available bandwidth. Unfortunately, segmenting your LAN can require a lot of thought and effort, especially if you have dozens or hundreds of users and multiple servers.

However, one technology will automatically segment your network to increase performance. Products called *port switching hubs*, available from companies such as 3Com, HP, and LANart segment your network without using multiple hubs. And the best part is that they include software that will figure out the best way to partition your ports. In a nutshell, they do the math for you.

Almost no one understands port switching hubs. Many people confuse a port switching hub with a standard 10BaseT hub and an Ethernet switch. In the most basic definition, port switching hubs are 10BaseT hubs that include several internal 10Mbps LAN segments. The hub can automatically move traffic between the segments to balance the load. Although a port switching hub can do nothing about a total overload, it can take care of the typical problem of one or two nodes becoming very busy at certain times of day.

Load balancing allows the port switching hubs to monitor the traffic in the hub and then use that information to decide which ports belong on which segments. A few products can balance loads in real-time. The software monitors the network all the time or at specified intervals and then moves a port to a different segment if the traffic changes and shows a need for such. But the software takes action only if a specified threshold is exceeded. For example, if the number of errors or collisions on a specific port exceeds a number you have defined, that port is moved to another segment in an attempt to solve the problem.

The price is just right

Isn't is amazing? The vendors of these port switching hubs managed to bring them in at a price just slightly less per-port than 10 Mbs switching. So you have a nice continuum of improvement. You can go from a plain 10Mbs hub for under $50 per port to a port switching hub for about $65 per port. The ten megabit switches are about $85 per port, and 100-megabit-per-second systems top out at higher prices—particularly if you have to buy a new adapter for each node. The actual prices will drop every 6–12 months, but the relationships between the prices will probably remain the same.

Gigabit Ethernet

Gigabit Ethernet is a member of the 10 and 100Mbps 802.3 Ethernet standards family. It runs in both half- and full-duplex modes, and the half-duplex mode uses the same CSMA/CD access method as the rest of the Ethernet family. The first products into the market rely on the Fiber Channel physical signaling topology, using fiber-optic cable. In the future, developments in the copper wire transceivers should allow Gigabit Ethernet to use copper UTP Category 5 wiring over reasonable distances (in the range of 25–100 meters).

Multimode fiber-optic cable connections up to 500 meters away using full-duplex and single-mode fiber work for up to 2km. These distances limit the usefulness of Gigabit Ethernet to campus-wide or intrabuilding backbones.

You might be thinking, "What would I do with 1,000Mbps bandwidth on our LAN?" The fact is that it's always nice to plan for zero backbone contention for your streaming data. Most networks still use 10Mbps Ethernet on the desktop and use 100Mbps Ethernet for backbones, server connections, and true power users. However, as 100Mbps connections proliferate, their data becomes a bigger percentage of a gigabit. Gigabit Ethernet will be a good alternative for linking multiprocessor super-servers.

There are other alternatives for campus and building backbones, including Asynchronous Transfer Mode (ATM) switching. But it seems clear that the appeal of Ethernet will rub off on the Gigabit clan.

Token-Ring: The IBM Way

The IEEE 802.5 subcommittee, with a firm lead from IBM's representatives, developed a set of standards describing a token-passing network in a logical ring topology. IBM also put identical standards into place within the structure of the European Computer Manufacturers' Association. The original implementation of the standard used 4-megabit-per-second signaling, but faster 16-megabit signaling is also part of the standard.

The Token-Ring network is to networks what the Boeing 747 is to airplanes. It makes strange noises and requires special handling, but it can carry heavy loads; it offers power and flexibility, but it demands skilled management and control; it is one of the fastest things flying, but it's not one of the prettiest. In 1989, IBM introduced the equivalent of a supersonic 747 when they adopted the 16-megabit-per-second signaling scheme for Token-Ring. The higher signaling speed moves data more quickly, but it also requires more careful installation. The basic techniques of 4- and 16-megabit-per-second Token-Ring operation are the same.

The Token-Ring structure is the keystone of IBM's wide area and local area network architecture. IBM provides optional Token-Ring connections on its mainframe computer hardware and software to make PCs and mainframes act as peers on the same network. Don't assume that you must use only IBM hardware and software on networks with Token-Ring adapters, though. Madge Networks and other companies also sell Token-Ring adapters. You can use networking software from Microsoft, Novell, and other companies on adapters from IBM or from the other Token-Ring hardware manufacturers.

IBM didn't invent the concept of tokens or the idea of the ring configuration. Indeed, IBM paid a fee—allegedly in the area of $5 million—to clear a patent on Token-Ring networking filed by Olof Soderblom of the Netherlands. Other companies in the Token-Ring business have to decide whether to fight or accommodate Soderblom's claim of proprietary rights.

The multiple standards and IBM backing have apparently nurtured the faith of the semiconductor companies. Texas Instruments leads a pack of companies who sell relatively inexpensive chip sets like the TMS 380 that can perform all the functions of the 802.5 standard.

Token Technique

In a token-passing ring network, a stream of data called a *token* circulates like a freight train through the network stations when they are idle. This technique defines both the sequential logical topology and the media-access control protocol.

A station with a message to transmit waits until it receives a free token. It then changes the free token to a busy token and transmits a block of data called a *frame* immediately after the busy token. The frame contains all or part of the message the station has to send. The system does not operate by having one station accept a token, read it, and then pass it on. Instead, the stream of bits that make up a token or a message might pass through as many as three stations simultaneously.

When a station transmits a message, there is no free token on the network, so other stations wishing to transmit must wait. The receiving station copies the data in the frame, and the frame continues around the ring, making a complete round trip back to the transmitting station. The transmitting station then purges the busy token and inserts a new free token on the ring.

The use of the token-passing media-access control system prevents messages from interfering with one another by guaranteeing that only one station at a time transmits. Unlike Ethernet, token-passing ensures delivery of the frame.

This streaming of data makes Token-Ring networks better suited to fiber-optic media than are broadcast-type systems such as Ethernet and ARCnet. Optical media typically carry one-way transmission, and the token travels in only one direction around the ring, so there is no need for optical mixers that divide power or for expensive active repeaters.

Ring Around a Star

The physical topology of a Token-Ring network isn't what you might expect. Although the tokens and messages travel from node to node (client station, gateway, or server) in a sequential logical topology, the cables actually use a physical star topology, as shown in Figure 7.9.

FIGURE 7.9

Token-Ring uses shielded wire to connect each node to a central Multistation Access Unit (MAU). This diagram also shows two-port hubs, which are used to reduce wiring costs. Wiring hubs can connect through optional fiber-optic cable links.

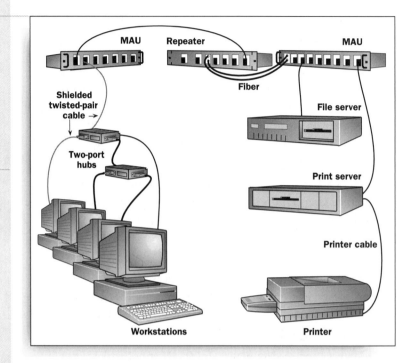

Token-Ring systems use a wire center (hub) that houses electro-mechanical relays to make the physical star into a logical ring. (Note that IBM's name for the Token-Ring wiring hub is Multistation Access Unit, or MAU. Don't confuse this MAU with the medium attachment unit, a transceiver connecting to the AUI port on an Ethernet adapter.)

When a station tries to join the ring, a voltage passes from the adapter board through the cable to the hub, where it activates the relay for that wire run in the hub. The action of the relay reconfigures the ring in milliseconds and adds the new station. Token-Ring networks are the only networks you can hear oper-ating because there is an audible click from the relay in the wire center whenever a station joins the ring.

If the cable from the station breaks, or if the wires in the cables short together, or if the station loses power, the relay opens and the station drops out of the ring. This arrangement prevents one bad cable from taking the entire system down (a major selling point for Token-Ring, ARCnet, and 10BaseT systems using a physical hub topology).

The typical Token-Ring wiring hub (Figure 7.10) accommodates eight nodes. The hubs stack on top of one another in a rack and are connected by patch cords running from one hub's "out" port to the next hub's "in" port. Because these cables extend the logical ring from one hub to another, nodes are on the same ring even if they are attached to different wiring hubs. Provisions are also available for linking the hubs through fiber-optic cable. Figure 7.11 shows a hub for small workgroups that can extend connections to other hubs.

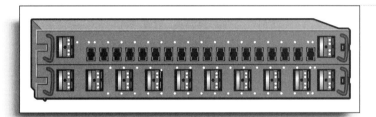

FIGURE 7.10

This illustration shows an unshielded twisted-pair wire Token-Ring wiring hub on top of a wiring hub for shielded twisted-pair wire. The RING-IN and RING-OUT connectors used to link hubs are clearly visible.

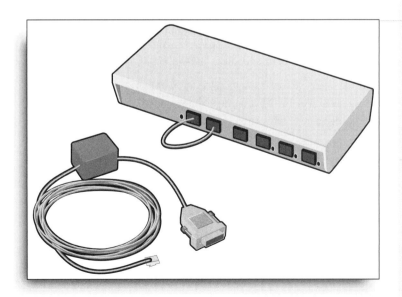

FIGURE 7.11

This Token-Ring wiring hub economically connects four nodes using unshielded twisted-pair wiring. Its RI and RO jacks can be used to make connections to other hubs located several hundred feet away.

When the Ring Stops

While the hub topology improves the network's chances of surviving a disrupted cable, the token-passing media-access protocol has its own unique survivability problem. If one adapter fails in an Ethernet or ARCnet system, only that node loses network access. But the malfunction of one adapter in a Token-Ring network can bring down the whole network because every node in the ring must actively pass every token and message. If the receiver or transmitter in one Token-Ring adapter fails, the token stops there. Modern Token-Ring hubs and adapters include active management capability and controlling software. These products immediately alert a manager to problems such as malfunctioning adapters and provide a means of forcibly disconnecting nodes from the ring.

Cables for the Ring

The original cable recommended for Token-Ring installations contains two pairs of twisted wire covered by a foil shield. The maximum length of cable between the Token-Ring hub and the attachment point for the network node can't exceed 150 feet (45 meters). However, you can have another 8 feet of cable between the attachment point (for example, a jack in a wall plate) and the node itself. The cables are connected to the hub using a special data connector that requires a certain level of experience for attaching it to the cable.

Today, any new Token-Ring networks typically go in using Category 5 UTP cabling. A device called a *media adapter* provides a way to connect older adapters and hubs to UTP.

Ring Speed

The original IBM Token-Ring product uses a 4-megabit-per-second signaling speed on the network cable. In 1989, IBM released a Token-Ring version using 16-megabit-per-second signaling. The 16-megabit adapters also work at 4 megabits on networks with the slower adapters. Other companies tried to follow IBM's high-speed lead, but they took over a year getting their products to market.

Although the signals representing 0s and 1s move faster across the wire, don't assume that 16-megabit-per-second Token-Ring will provide faster responses on your network than does the 4-megabit-per-second variety. On the other hand, don't assume that 4-megabit-per-second Token-Ring will give slower responses than does 10-megabit-per-second Ethernet. Many factors other than the network signaling rate limit throughput—particularly the speed of the servers. Note that installing 16-megabit Token-Ring over unshielded twisted-pair wire introduces new problems. The allowed cable lengths and number of nodes on each ring are determined by a complex chart. The faster signals are much more difficult to decode and are more easily masked by cumulative noise on the cable system.

Caught in the Ring

Many companies, spurred by IBM's sponsorship, choose Token-Ring as their wiring and media-access control architecture. While the operational benefits of Token-Ring over Ethernet are still the subject of esoteric debate, you need to look for the real benefits—particularly the potential for direct mainframe attachments—and weigh them against the cost of installing Token-Ring adapters, cables, and wiring hubs. As I explain in Chapter 12, "The Protocols of the Internet," there are effective ways to interface with mainframe computers that don't require a Token-Ring installation.

ARCnet: A Good Thing Caught Wanting

Using tokens or messages to regulate when a station can transmit over a shared wire isn't unique to IEEE 802.5. The ARCnet system, originated by Datapoint and fostered in the microcomputer world by Standard Microsystems, uses *transmission permission* messages addressed to specific stations to regulate traffic. The acronym ARC stands for Datapoint's Attached Resource Computing architecture.

Unfortunately, ARCnet networks are mostly relics. The system works well but at a relatively slow speed, and Datapoint was too slow to update the technology. In the end, except for some use in industrial systems, ARCnet was overtaken by the surge of support for the 802.3 Ethernet standard. However, because ARCnet systems still deliver the data in many networks, I'll outline the specifics of the technology.

ARCnet Topologies

ARCnet uses a broadcast-type logical topology, which means that all stations receive all messages broadcast into the cable at approximately the same time.

The ARCnet scheme traditionally uses RG-62 coaxial cable in a physical star topology that allows for a hierarchy of hubs. Small two- or four-port wiring hubs can feed other large and small hubs in an economical wiring scheme that retains the resistance to total outage that's inherent in a star topology. Modern versions of ARCnet can also use coaxial cable or unshielded twisted-pair wire in a station-to-station physical topology.

A complex set of rules regulates how big an ARCnet network can be. Generally, the maximum length of cable from one end of the network to the other is 20,000 feet. The maximum cable length between powered, or active, hubs that can regenerate signals is 2,000 feet. The maximum length between a powered hub and a network node is also 2,000 feet. Unpowered (passive) hubs can connect to nodes over 100 feet of cable. As you can see, ARCnet systems can cover a large geographical area.

The RG-62 cable specified for ARCnet is the same cable IBM uses in its 3270 wiring plan, which links terminals to mainframe terminal controllers. Because this plan also uses a physical star topology, many companies find it easy to install ARCnet when they downsize their computer systems from IBM mainframes to networks of PCs.

High-impedance ARCnet adapters allow a physical daisy-chain topology identical to that of thin Ethernet networks. The daisy-chained nodes can also connect to active powered hubs, for an overall network of 20,000 feet of cable.

ARCnet Access Control

The technical literature describes ARCnet as a token-passing system, but ARCnet operates very differently from IEEE 802.5 Token-Ring. Instead of passing a token from station to station, it has one station broadcast the transmission permission message to the others on the network.

Each Ethernet and Token-Ring adapter has a unique adapter identifier assigned by the manufacturer and drawn from a common pool established by industry associations. ARCnet adapters don't come with assigned identification numbers, however; instead, you set an identification number, from 1 to 255, using switches located on each adapter. The identification numbers have no relationship to the position of the nodes on the cable or to other physical relationships.

When activated, the adapters broadcast their numbers, and the lowest-numbered active station becomes the controller for the network. This controller sends a token to each active station granting permission to transmit. When each station receives the permission token, it either sends its waiting message or remains silent. Then the controlling station sends a permission token to the next station in numeric sequence.

When a new station enters the network, the stations all rebroadcast their station numbers in what is called a *reconfiguration* or *recon*. Like potential collisions in Ethernet, the concept of a recon bothers people who worry about esoteric matters of network efficiency. In reality, a recon takes no longer than 65 milliseconds at worst, and it scarcely disturbs the flow of traffic on a network.

Here are a couple of practical hints for all ARCnet installers:

- There are two things you can't afford to lose: the instruction manual telling you how to set the adapter numbers and the list of adapter numbers active on the network. If you know what station numbers have been assigned, it's easy to add more stations. If you don't know what station numbers are active, you face a frustrating session of research or trial-and-error installation.

- Keep your assigned station numbers close together, and put PCs with the most powerful CPUs in the low-numbered slots. The polling task takes a tiny bit of CPU power, so position your husky servers and other fast PCs to take on that role.

Speed

Traditional ARCnet operates at a signaling speed of 2.5 megabits per second. While many installations will never find this speed a limitation, it doesn't keep up with the capability of modern servers to deliver data. However, an economical solution to this problem also improves overall network reliability: You can divide the ARCnet network into sections by installing several adapters in the server and splitting the output into multiple channels.

ARCnet Standards

In October 1992, the American National Standards Institute (ANSI) specified the ARCnet protocol as the "ATA/ANSI 878.1 Local Area Network Standard." No IEEE committee worked on ARCnet because the formal role of the IEEE is to design a standard; ANSI standardizes an existing specification, and the ARCnet specification is now about two decades old.

Moving Data Faster

"Faster is better!" is an American credo. In networking, the increased use of audio and full-motion video in applications is driving some of the push toward faster networking. Even if you don't currently need faster network signaling, you'd better understand the emerging options for fast local area networking because it's virtually certain you'll be ordering a testbed or a trial system within a year or so and doing an operational installation within three years. But right now, the options are confusing and surprises are likely, so it's a little early for most organizations to make major strategic investments.

Still, there are already some valid uses for network signaling in the range of 100 megabits per second. Fast and accurate transmission of digitized x-ray images from a treatment facility to a consulting room requires high throughput, as does mirroring two servers using NetWare or Windows NT. One channel of broadcast-quality video requires about 8 megabits of bandwidth using the best available compression techniques, and audio takes just under 1 megabit per second. So companies planning multimedia and network teleconferencing projects will need LAN connections in the 100-megabit range.

If you do need higher speed throughput than 10-megabit Ethernet or 16-megabit Token-Ring provide today, I advise that you place a bet on switching hubs. With these devices, you can give a dozen nodes access to a full 10-megabit bandwidth without contention and still keep your existing network interface cards, cable, and hubs.

Networking Alternatives

To a large degree, the type of network adapter you choose dictates the logical and physical topologies, the type of media, and the access protocol scheme your network uses. These choices do not, however, dictate the type of networking software you use. The LAN hardware and the network operating-system software are important but separate decisions. The next two chapters describe the operation and selection of LAN operating-system software.

CHAPTER

8

The Structure of Network Operating Systems

This chapter reviews and elaborates on the concepts behind network operating system software described in Chapter 4. Here, you'll explore the functions of the various kinds of server software, client workstation software, and the underlying communications protocols. This chapter sets up an important framework for understanding networks. The next chapter provides more specific product details.

One important feature of LAN hardware like the Ethernet, ARCnet, and Token-Ring systems described in the previous chapters is its complete independence from the networking software. If you stick with IEEE- and industry-standard hardware and avoid proprietary cable and signaling schemes, you can choose practically any network operating system for your client workstations, servers, and other functional elements. Your decision on cabling and your decision on LAN software are separate.

SEE ALSO

➤ *Chapter 7, starting on page 131, describes the basics of Ethernet, ARCnet, and Token-Ring.*

➤ *Chapter 6, page 95 tells you all about cabling.*

➤ *Chapter 5, page 75 describes the interface between LAN adapters and PCs.*

➤ *Looking forward, page 202 will take you specifically though NetWare and Microsoft Windows NT.*

LAN Software Functions

Four concepts you've encountered in earlier chapters are worth repeating here.

- The primary purpose of networking software is to let you share resources such as printers, hard disks, and communications links among client stations.

- The primary function of networking software is to make distant resources appear local.

- Networking software performs the same functions, regardless of the operating system. The names of the products and protocols might change, but the concepts are the same for Windows, UNIX, Macintosh, and other operating systems.

"Protocols" one more time!

I explain the term *network protocols* several times in this book, but the explanation bears repeating in different contexts. *Network protocols* are agreements on how data will be packaged, accounted for, and transmitted across the network. Vendors and industry committees develop the agreements, and then individual companies try to write software that conforms to them. Some initial attempts at developing conforming software are more successful than others, but after a few months of trial-and-error (often with end-users performing the trials and suffering the errors), companies usually manage to get the software right. There's nothing mysterious about protocols. They're just agreements about how things should work.

- The network operating system uses layers of software that conform to specific rules of behavior or protocols to format data, address it, and reliably carry it across a local or wide area network.

A network operating system is not one program, but rather a series of programs. Some of these programs run in PCs acting as servers of various types, and others run in PCs acting as client workstations. Today, software modules designed to perform networking functions seem to be an integral part of operating systems like Microsoft's Windows or Sun's Solaris, but their functions are still separate and unique. Networking software comes on the CD with such programs, but it often isn't loaded if the computer isn't going to be on a network. The bundled networking software modules perform specific functions and can be unloaded or even replaced by software from another vendor.

The networking software in servers provides and controls multiple simultaneous access to disk drives, printers, and other devices such as modems and facsimile boards. The networking software in client stations intercepts and redirects the requests for service that application programs generate and then sends each of them to the appropriate server for action.

Software in the Client PC

We call computers that use a network's resources *clients*. A client PC uses hard disks, communications lines, and printers on a server as if these things were part of the user's own workstation. That redirection capability is the prime power of networks. Under some network operating systems, client stations can also act as servers, but today many computers on the LAN act as some form of a server. A desktop PC can make a CD-ROM drive, a printer, or a communications port available to other client PCs across the LAN.

Here are some important points to understand about how networking software does its job:

- Client PCs use shared resources provided by servers.
- You don't always need special applications on client PCs.

When is a server not a server?

Terms like "server" and "client" describe the *function* of a computer on the network; they don't tell you anything about the power or capacity of the PC acting in that role. Also, they aren't mutually exclusive terms: A PC will often act as a server of some kind–particularly as a print server–and as a client workstation at the same time. Hardware manufacturers sell products designed to be servers, but they aren't really servers until their drives and ports are made available for sharing. The function is more important than the hardware.

- Redirection software routes requests to servers.
- Transport layer software carries data across the cable.
- There are many kinds of servers.

The following sections explain these points in greater detail. A special diagram titled "Networking Protocols and Standards" provides a graphical view of the layers of networking software in Microsoft, Novell, and generic TCP/IP networks. Hook your thumb into the diagram because you'll want to refer to it through most of this chapter.

The Redirector

The redirection software in each client computer makes the resources available on the network look like local devices and connections to the programs and people using them. Commands sent from the keyboard and from programs to drives with names like D:, E:, and F: are redirected over the network to the appropriate file servers. Similarly, programs sending output to a network printer see that printer as a port selection that's listed with the local PC's ports.

Operating-system modules in the client stations include the redirector and the software elements that carry the redirector's output through the network. The redirector works within the client's operating system so that certain specifically programmed types of requests made by applications or from the keyboard go out through the network adapter for action instead of going to local disk drives or I/O ports. The network administrator programs the redirector through a menu or a command-line prompt to route all requests addressed to a specific drive letter or I/O port to a selected network resource.

For example, in a network using Novell's NetWare you would enter the following command to route requests sent to the F: drive out to a subdirectory called ACCOUNTS in a disk volume called VOLUME1 residing on a server named SERVER1:

```
MAP F: = SERVER1/VOLUME1: ACCOUNTS
```

Commands like this are usually part of the login script for an individual user, which gives each person a customized view of the network resources. Network administrators have the important task of creating and maintaining customized login scripts and batch files for each user. If you work through the graphical user interfaces found in operating systems like Windows and Macintosh, you select the resource you want to share by clicking on icons or menu entries, but those processes use the same concept of *mapping* local drive letters or port names to distant resources.

Transport Layer Software

Additional layers of networking software in the client move an application's request for service from the redirector to the network adapter and onto the network cable. This software has three parts:

- An application program interface (API)
- A network communications section that follows a specific protocol
- Drivers customized for the LAN adapter

Figure 8.1 shows the relationship of the redirector and Transport layer software.

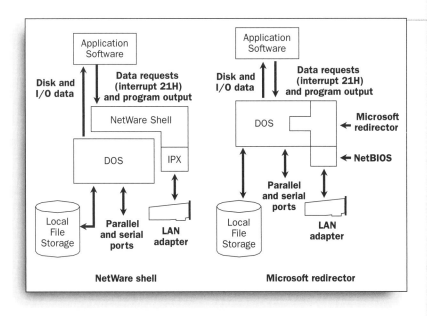

NetWare shell   **Microsoft redirector**

FIGURE **8.1**

Novell calls its client redirection software a "shell" to indicate that it wraps around the operating system and intercepts all data requests and commands coming from application programs and the keyboard. Under Windows, the Microsoft redirector is an integral part of the desktop operating system. The NetWare shell and the Microsoft redirector move the messages they receive to the network adapter card through transport-layer software such as NetBIOS, IP, or Novell's SPX/IPX. Each driver is configured specifically for the brand and model of LAN adapter.

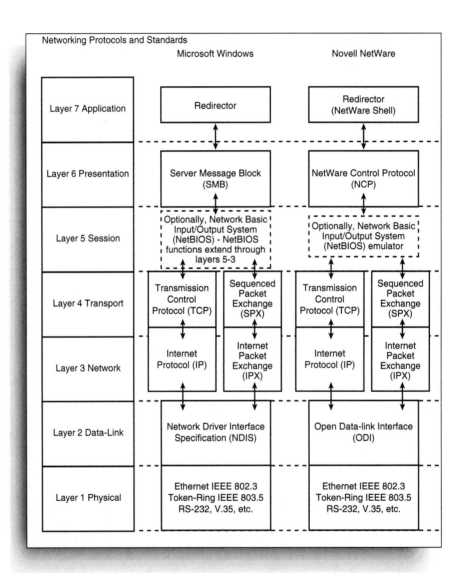

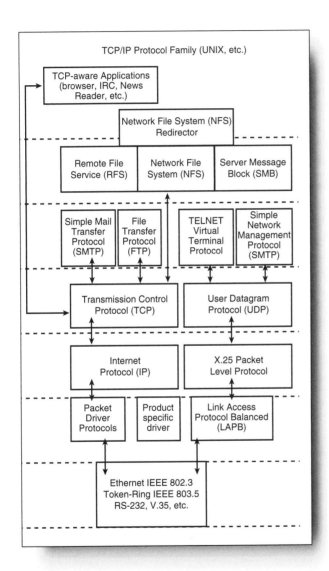

An application program interface (API) is actually a specification describing how application programs—ranging from word processing packages to graphics and spreadsheet programs—interact and request services from the disk or network operating system. The specification describes the *software interrupt* that a program issues to identify a request for service, along with the format of the data contained in the request.

SEE ALSO

➤ *Drive on over to Chapter 5, page 75, for a complete explanation of drivers and LAN adapters.*

Standard Applications

When an application program wants to access a file on a disk drive, it builds a block of data containing the parameters for the request. Under the Windows desktop operating system, standard applications put the data block's address into a specific register and generate an *interrupt 21 hexadecimal*. In response to the interrupt, the operating system reads the address register and then the data block. All modern "well-behaved" programs follow this process. Only older "ill-behaved" programs go around the Windows services to interrogate the disk-drive hardware directly. If you have any of these on your systems, my best advice is that you find a modern replacement.

If the desktop operating system has a redirector in place, the redirector examines the application's request to determine if it is directed toward a networked resource. For example, suppose the request from an application asks to read data from drive G:, and the redirector is programmed to recognize G: as a specific part of a specific server's networked drive. The redirector starts the request from an application on its trek out across the network.

Whenever you share resources, you face the potential of conflict. Let's say that two people are working on the same document called BUDGET.TXT. A single copy of the document resides on a file server's shared drive. If their word processing programs aren't equipped to interact with networking software in any way, it is possible that both people will be able to open the same file at the same time. In a typical word processing program, the act of opening the file means that the program reads the file and copies it to the local computer's memory. Let's say that the first person makes a change to the file and saves the file while the second person still has it open. The second person then makes a change and saves the file. The second person's save writes over the first person's save and, unless it was saved under a different file name, the first person's work is gone.

There are several ways around this problem. First, people could work on different copies of the file stored in different private subdirectories and then merge the changes manually. Second, they could coordinate their efforts so that they don't both open the same file at the same time. Finally, they could update to a version of word processing software capable of recognizing messages from the network operating system. For the most part, word processing programs marketed in the past few years can recognize when another application has a file open and inform anyone subsequently trying to open the file. Typically, the application offers the option of opening an in-use file in read-only mode, which prevents it from being saved under the same name.

Data Sharing

When you want to share data files among many people at the same time, matters get more difficult. Let's first consider the case in which files are shared like library books: one user at a time.

When an application program opens a data file, the program can set certain restrictions on the simultaneous use of the file by other application programs. Programmers can use one of several options when they design their applications. The program can open a file for exclusive use (denying any other application the ability to read or write to the file simultaneously), or the program can open the file in other modes that allow reading or writing (or both) by other applications under certain conditions. And finally, application programs can open data files under a condition called Deny None, which makes the file available to all applications for all functions at all times.

Modern applications use one of the SHARE modes to open a file. These are the sharing-mode options available to a programmer:

Option Number	Description
0	Compatibility
1	Deny Read/Write
2	Deny Write
3	Deny Read
4	Deny None

Programmers can open a file under any of these conditions. Option 2, Deny Write, is a common sharing mode for network operations because it allows one client PC to change the file while others can only read it. If all PCs need the ability to modify files, all programs must use option 4, and the programmers must use special techniques to avoid data corruption.

If an application is not designed to create shared data files, the programmer should write the code to open data files in a mode that denies all access to a second program trying to get into a file. This means that the files created by the application are available to stations on a network on a first-come-first-served one-at-a-time basis, like a book in a library.

Multiple Simultaneous Access

A database management system is the most common example of multiple simultaneous file access on a LAN. A database is made up of files containing records. Programs running in client PCs often must open several files at the same time in order to read records in each file. Simultaneously, programs on other PCs might have one of the same files open to write records. Obviously, if one station tries to read a record while another station is writing it, some kind of problem will occur.

Applications can lock a range of bytes in a file for exclusive use. For example, under Windows, if an application program issues a DOS 21 hex *interrupt* and a 5C hex function call (don't confuse this with the 5C hex *interrupt*, which calls NetBIOS), it can then tell DOS how many bytes to lock for exclusive use. When the operating system locks these bytes, no other program can write or read them. The operating system sends an error message back to any application that tries to access a locked data segment.

DBMS packages with their own programming languages let programmers use this data-locking function by providing an internal command called RLOCK. Typically, database programmers invoke the RLOCK command to tell the application program to lock one or more specific records before they are rewritten, but the DBMS converts this into a command telling the operating system to lock a range of bytes.

If you are a database programmer writing applications for a multiuser system, either you or the database program must tell the operating system which bytes to lock to prevent one application from reading a file while another application writes to it. If you have to remember to issue a command such as RLOCK, the program is said to have *explicit* record locking. If the DBMS is "smart" enough that it will automatically tell the operating system to lock a range of bytes while the program writes a record, the program is said to have *implicit* record locking.

In a multiuser system, you also have to do something about the application that tries to access a range of bytes when it is locked by another program. Some database management programs return a Record locked message to the application program that runs into locked bytes. The application programmer must anticipate getting this message and find a way to handle it.

The options for handling a Record locked message vary. A programmer might decide to build a loop that tells the application to wait a short time and try again, or he might instruct the program to abort the application or to send a message to the screen asking the user what to do. Some database programs automate this process by automatically retrying the access. This feature is usually combined with a limit on the amount of time the record can be locked.

So a real application, such as a networked database management system allowing several operators to access and update a warehouse inventory, must contain lines of code directing the operating system to lock a range of bytes in a file designated as a record or field while it is in use. The creator of the DBMS application also has to put in routines for responding to the `locked` signal from the operating system and for informing an operator who tries to change a field that it is already in use and cannot be modified. Opening files for shared or exclusive use and handling conflicts over simultaneous access to a given range of bytes in a file are problems faced by all people who write networked applications.

The most complex situation takes place when several applications have several files open at the same time. Because records in the different files are often indexed to each other in some way, you can get into a situation where two applications simultaneously lock data that both of them need to finish their tasks. This is called a *deadlock*, or "deadly embrace" in classic computer literature. Many techniques (such as time-outs) can break a deadlock, but all of them slow processing time.

Some database management programs don't use the operating system's file- and byte-locking options. They do the job for the operating system in a more elegant way that is also designed to avoid deadlocks. This type of application might leave a message in a special log file while it creates or changes a portion of a data file; when it is finished, it erases the message in the log file. Other applications check this log file. If one application (Application B) needs to read a record being written by another application (Application A), Application B waits. If the wait becomes too long, the person using Application B receives a message indicating which user has the record locked. At that point, it is up to the persons using the data to resolve the problem.

This log-file architecture is a more elegant method of sharing data, but it puts a greater load on the network and the server. Each application accesses the log file before every access to the data file. Applications writing to a data file write an entry in the log file before each data file access, and they erase the entry afterward. This results in more packets on the network and many more disk access requests for the server to satisfy than there are under an operating system's data protection method.

Beware of special vertical applications

Your most important software typically generates the biggest problems. Vertical applications are programs specialized for your business. They might keep the inventories and catalogs for your gift shop or car-repair business, track the rooms in your resort, or schedule deliveries to your manufacturing plant. For the most part, the creators of these vertical applications know more about the specific business than about writing software. Often, these neophyte but exuberant programmers do stupid things. In particular, they'll lock into the proprietary file handling services of an operating system like NetWare or a specific brand of UNIX. A programmer's indiscretion can wed you to that operating system for as long as you use the software. Therefore, you should examine all aspects of any vertical business application and make sure it is written for universal service.

Neither method of protecting data is perfect. You should know the advantages and drawbacks of both architectures. But now, at least, networks of PCs have mature methods that allow many people to use the same data at the same time.

The best advice for the average person acting as a network or database administrator is to choose application programs with good technical support options. You will often need to talk to an expert on the phone or in person to solve problems. The cost of LAN hardware, network software, and installation is just the opening gambit in the network game. You need good support to install, configure, and manage networked applications.

Using the Transport Layer

The layer of networking software under the redirector is called the Transport layer. It's the job of this software to package a service request that makes sense to all network servers running the same operating system. It does this by following a specific protocol. The Transport layer program addresses the packet to a specific function within the serving computer—not necessarily to a specific computer.

Novell developed a transport layer protocol called the Sequenced Packet Exchange (SPX), and Microsoft adopted a Transport layer specification called the Network Basic Input/Output System or NetBIOS. While these two protocols still see plenty of use on LANs, they're being nudged by another Transport layer protocol called the Transmission Control Protocol (TCP). The popularity of the Internet and the usefulness of TCP when it's linked to the Internet Protocol (IP) has made TCP/IP networking a big trend.

The Transport layer software, generally TCP or SPX in modern networks, uses a function called a *directory service* to determine the exact address for the data it's packaging. The Transport layer software has some way of identifying each service on the network. Figure 8.2 illustrates one type of naming service that Transport layer software might use. Note that networked devices such as file servers often have more than one service running internally (it's like having multiple apartments or office suites in a building).

TCP/IP isn't for LANs!

The TCP/IP protocol stack wasn't designed for the short "bursty" messages of local area networking. TCP/IP's packets are like 18-wheel armored tractor-trailer trucks designed to carry big payloads through riotous wide area networking territory. They're overkill for the short, clean, zippy LAN environment. Still, because of the popularity of the Internet and corporate intranets, managers are electing to use TCP/IP on LANs too. LANs have plenty of bandwidth, so the inefficiency created by the overhead of TCP/IP isn't a big issue. But be aware that if you choose to use TCP/IP networking on a LAN, you introduce problems of addressing and security that you don't have with LAN-only alternatives such as IPX.

FIGURE 8.2

FIGURE 8.2

A naming service should provide a detailed but flexible way of identifying services, resources, and users across a wide area network. In this example, the names combine geographical and corporate information.

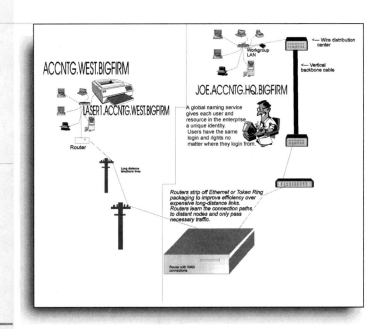

The clerk, the loading dock, and the truck

Before you start thinking this stuff is hard, consider this simple analogy. The Transport layer software acts like a shipping clerk for a company. A customer (an application program) drops off a package for delivery. The Transport layer/shipping clerk (like TCP or SPX) makes out a label addressed to the end user at the destination. This clerk typically inserts a note asking for acknowledgment of delivery from the end user. The Network layer protocol (like IP or IPX) performs the function of a loading dock supervisor who knows how to route a package from the loading dock to its destination. The Data-link layer software wraps the package for shipping if necessary, and the Physical layer hauls the package down the street. The Physical layer either drops the package on the receiving loading dock (Ethernet) or asks for a receipt (Token-Ring). Really, it's that easy!

In addition to packaging requests for services in an appropriately addressed packet, the Transport layer software also makes sure that the packet gets to its destination. In the previous chapter, you learned that Ethernet's datagrams don't provide assurance of delivery. The Network layer protocols (like IP and IPX) don't guarantee delivery either. It's typically up to the Transport layer software (SPX, NetBIOS, or TCP) to recognize a failed delivery and to initiate another try.

Applications for Transport

In the case of the Transport layer software, the standard API provides the redirector (and certain classes of application programs that make direct calls to the Transport layer software) with a way to send and receive requests to and from the network. For example, the NetBIOS API specifies the software interrupt 5C hex to request the data handling service of NetBIOS. An increasing number of applications—particularly in TCP networks—ignore the local operating system and directly ask the Transport layer software for services. On the contrary, email programs, web browsers, Internet Relay Chat, newsgroup readers, file transfer programs, and many other specialized applications make requests directly to TCP.

The Transport layer software (TCP or SPX) tracks the handling of packets going to a specific address, but the Network layer software figures out how to get to that address.

Riding the Network Layer

The Network layer software wraps the data package with more information that it needs to traverse the network. The IP protocol has a more robust wrapper than IPX, so IP packets are better equipped for routing across large networks.

The Network layer protocol also provides some way of identifying each functional node in a machine-readable form. The addressing scheme in IP is very complex and can accommodate many millions of nodes. Although the addressing scheme in IPX is more limited, it's also more automated, more flexible, and much easier to use, and it delivers fast performance.

Types of Servers

A network can have up to three generic types of servers: file servers, print servers, and communications servers. Any particular network might have several servers of various types. (Remember, I'm using the term *server* in a functional sense to refer to a device playing a role in the network.) Table 8.1 lists the types and subtypes of network servers.

TABLE 8.1   Types of network servers

File Servers	Print Servers	Communications Servers
Database servers	On a PC	Facsimile servers
CD-ROM servers	Special devices	Gateways to mainframes
		Electronic mail gateways
		IP network routers
		TCP/IP and Internet family servers
		DNS servers
		LDAP servers
		DHCP servers
		Web caching servers

Sometimes file, print, and communications services reside in one computer on the network, and sometimes the tasks are spread among many PCs. A multipurpose server can provide shared file access, communication links to a mainframe, and long-distance links between servers using X.25 technology. Figure 8.3 provides a generic view of the servers and client stations in a practical network.

FIGURE 8.3

PCs can act in multiple roles on a network. This diagram shows a network with three servers: a file server doubling as a print server, a communications server with a shared modem, and a remote print server. The communications server can also run standard applications as a personal computer, but there is always a trade-off when a computer simultaneously runs applications and provides network services.

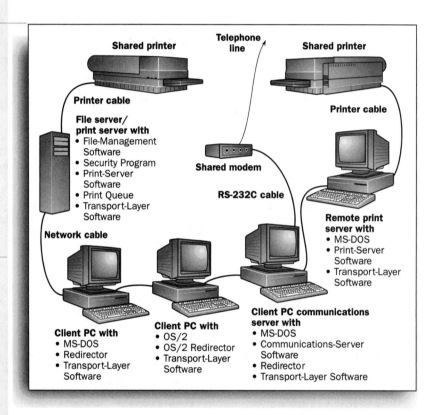

Companies like Microsoft and Sun design their network operating systems so that many PCs can act as servers of various types, even while people are using them to run standard applications. In a network using Novell's NetWare, however, the PCs acting as servers are typically dedicated to that task.

SEE ALSO

➤ We serve up information on print servers on page 38 and provide an overview in Chapter 4, page 43.
➤ The Internet servers are described in Chapter 12, page 309.

The File-Server Functions

A *file server* makes hard disk storage space (up to a gigabyte or more) available to the client PCs. The file server answers requests for data read and write actions, routed from application programs by the redirector software in each client PC, and mediates simultaneous requests for access to the same data.

Database servers, a subset of the file server category, include servers that make expensive hardware such as CD-ROM or optical disk drives available, as well as "back-end" database processors. These back-end database servers are the basis of the client/server computing model that has gained a great deal of popularity in recent years. The term *client/server* actually has several meanings. The oldest definition is simply a network technology that uses a dedicated server, as NetWare does. The opposite of this technology is a *peer-to-peer* network such as Windows 95/98. Two more recent definitions of client/server are based on differing network architectures: the database server architecture (mentioned earlier) that uses a back-end database processor, and the application server architecture.

The *database server architecture* is arranged so that the client PCs send requests for data to a program called a database *engine*, which runs a PC acting as a file server. Database engine vendors include Oracle, Gupta, Sybase, and Microsoft. In this architecture, the file server acts as a powerful database processor that executes special commands—often in IBM's Structured Query Language (SQL)—from database query programs running on networked PCs. The database processor receives simple requests for reports from the client stations and executes the complex code needed to extract and compile the information from a raw database. Because the database engine software runs a PC acting as a file server, the query programs don't have to pull files over the network cable for sorting and matching in the client PCs. This architecture reduces the communications load on the network but puts a heavy processing load on the PC that handles the database.

This architecture contrasts the older database technology that's still used by most programs, in which the database program running on each client draws the information across the network and sorts it locally on each desktop computer. While the older technology is much less efficient, it is also less complex and costs less up-front than running a database engine in the server.

Application server architecture is, in itself, a term with several meanings. As a client/server computing scheme, it means that one powerful PC runs some portion of the application, perhaps a database or a graphical processing program like X Windows, on request from programs running in client PCs. The two programs use a technique called *remote procedure calls* (RPCs) to communicate. RPCs are, in effect, prearranged shorthand requests for action.

IBM pioneered the database server and application server architectures through its development of an architecture called *Advanced Program to Program Communications* (APPC). IBM developed APPC so that PC programs could use mainframe programs and hardware in client/server roles. As the role of mainframes diminished, IBM moved APPC to *APPN (Advanced Peer-to-Peer Networking)*. So, the client/server technology that originated as a way to prolong the life of mainframe hardware has now become a way to sell high-end PC hardware and AS-400s.

A twist on the application server is the *distributed application*. In common usage, distributed applications are those that cross the boundaries between types of computer hardware and operating systems. The Open Software Federation, led by IBM, HP, and Digital, has established standards for the *Distributed Computing Environment* (DCE). DCE products provide standard program calls used between applications so they can share the available processing power. DCE includes security and administrative protocols that allow DCE programs to recognize and communicate with each other. DCE is a complex architecture, and there are many players in the game. Microsoft links into DCE with their *Object Linking and Embedding* (OLE) architecture, a set of programming tools designed to allow programs to share specific types of information modules called *objects*.

Another organization, the *Object Management Group*, has developed a set of specifications similar to DCE called the *Common Object Request Broker Architecture* (CORBA). These specifications accomplish about the same things as DCE, but they rely even more heavily on visual programming objects.

On the bottom line, the term client/server means many things to many people. Strategists at IBM, Microsoft, and Novell think client/server computing is an important part of their future, but each organization views the technology involved from a slightly different angle.

SEE ALSO

➤ *We get into network operating systems for file servers in Chapter 9, page 191.*

➤ *A lot more about AS/400-to-PC and mainframe-to-PC interactivity is on page 342.*

The Print-Server Functions

Computers acting as *print servers* make printers available for shared use—in some cases, up to five computers for each print server. The print server accepts print jobs from application programs running on the client stations and stores those jobs as files in a special subdirectory called a *print spool* on a hard disk drive. When the full print job arrives in the print spool, its file waits in a queue for the first available printer (or for a designated printer).

The drive that holds the print spool can be located on another PC acting as a file server, but this arrangement puts a lot of traffic on the network as print jobs move from the PC running the application, to the print server, to the spool on the file server, and eventually back to the print server for printing. In common practice, either the print-server function is located with the file-server software or the PC acting as a print server has its own hard disk.

The networking software that comes with Windows 95/98 allows any running networked PC to act as a file server, a print server, or both and still run application programs. Novell's NetWare lets you combine file- and print-server functions in the same PC or establish separate print servers. PCs acting as

NetWare file servers can't run typical desktop applications, but the print-server software can reside in a PC used to run application programs.

SEE ALSO

➤ *I describe more printing alternatives in Chapter 3, page 31.*

Advantages to Using Print Servers

The biggest advantage to designing a network with separate print servers is that you can arrange the geography of the network to suit the users. In contrast, if you combine the print-server and file-server functions, you must locate the shared printers close to the server hardware—primarily because of distance limitations on parallel-port connections. Because the PC acting as a file server for a robust network has many noisy hard disk drives, powerful fans, and probably a bulky uninterruptible power supply, it's usually consigned to a remote location—perhaps even behind a locked door for security. You'll have to plan carefully or have a lot of luck to find a location that's both suitable for the file-server hardware and convenient for people trying to retrieve finished print jobs.

Sharing printers through conveniently located personal workstations acting as print servers seems like a good way to overcome the problem of where to locate printers. While the idea of using a PC simultaneously as a print server and a personal workstation has appeal, it also has practical limitations. You can only slice a PC so many ways before the people at client stations and the person using the machine for local applications all receive slow service. Hardware interrupts generated by serial- and parallel-port activity and concurrent requests for access to the hard disk can slow down even the fastest PC when it operates as both a server and a personal workstation.

The decision of whether to make a print server part of a file server, part of a client PC, or a dedicated node hinges mainly on how much printing the client PCs will do. If your organization prints no more than 30 to 50 pages of plain text an hour, combining the print server and file server makes sense. But heavier printing loads and considerations about the printers' physical location might dictate using separate print servers or print servers combined with client workstations.

As the number of print jobs coming from the client stations builds, and as the complexity of application programs increases, only people running lightweight applications find it practical to contribute printer services to the network through their PCs. The common practice is to set up dedicated PCs as network print servers in convenient locations around the office. Note, however, that this architecture takes space and requires the full resources of a PC, complete with hard disk, monitor, and keyboard, for each print server.

Single-Purpose Print Servers

In late 1990, a new category of products showed up at *PC Magazine* LAN Labs. At first, we called them *Ethernet peripheral-sharing devices*. This mouthful of words describes their function, but it isn't a phrase likely to stick in the minds of buyers. After much brainstorming, we decided to call them what they are: *special-function servers*. The best example is the print server, but this class also includes CD-ROM servers and a few other specialized devices.

These products—from Castelle, Hewlett-Packard, Intel (see Figure 8.4), and Digital Products—attach to network cables and make printers available to the client PCs using Novell software without the need for any other hardware.

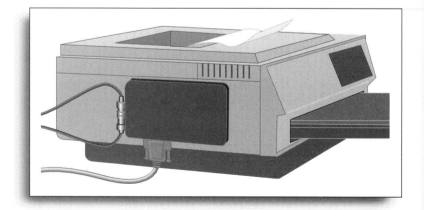

FIGURE 8.4

This print server for Novell and Ethernet allows users to locate printers anywhere along the network.

The processors in these devices use special software contained in read-only memory. They don't need attached monitors, drives, or keyboards. Special-function servers might use print-server software running on a NetWare file server to receive and store print jobs, but then they take those jobs from the queue and send them over the network cabling to the printer. This architecture moves the print job over the cable at least twice (something purists will moan about), but no one can deny the practicality and value of these special-function servers.

The Communications-Server Functions

The term *communications server* covers a variety of tasks. Communications servers can act as gateways to IP-based wide area networks such as the Internet or a corporate intranet. They can act as portals to mainframe computers, allowing client PCs to share a costly mainframe communications channel. They can also make pools of expensive high-speed modems available for sharing on a first-come-first-served basis.

Unlike print servers, the major consideration for communications servers isn't geography: You can set them anywhere you have a phone line. The major consideration is CPU power. While a print server buffers the print jobs going to the printers, communications servers must provide real-time connections between client PCs and communications channels. This puts a heavy load on the PC acting as a communications server.

Handling the hardware interrupts generated by the serial and parallel ports keeps the CPU in a communications server very busy. Few people will enjoy running application programs on a PC that simultaneously functions as a communications server. So in today's typical network, communications-server software usually runs on a separate PC dedicated to the task. Many companies use communications servers that are dedicated devices containing their own specialized communications processing hardware.

Fax Servers

Fax servers provide everyone on the network with the ability to share the hardware for incoming and outgoing facsimile transmissions. PCs acting as communications servers are usually dedicated to this task.

Fax servers are great at sharing modems for outgoing calls, but there are problems in handling incoming faxes. When the fax hits the server, where should it go? At one time, a person had to read every incoming fax, but the technology continued to improve, and there are now five good techniques for routing faxes internally: the fax server can "read" a line of text, read DTMF tones, recognize the incoming line, recognize the sending fax machine, or recognize distinctive rings.

- *Reading a line of text.* Routing incoming faxes by reading a line of text involves using OCR software to look for a specifically formatted line containing the name of an addressee. For this to work, callers must know how to format the fax.

- *Reading DTMF tones.* Devices that read DTMF tones allow the sender to generate touch tone signals to designate the recipient after the connection is made. This technique is useful because it can accommodate many recipients, but it requires special actions on the part of the sender.

- *Recognizing the incoming line.* If your fax server uses a multi-line adapter, it can route faxes to individuals or to workgroups based on the incoming line.

- *Recognizing the sending fax machine.* Recognizing the number, or *Customer Subscriber Identification* (CSID), of the sending fax machine is a useful trick because the sender doesn't need to take any special actions; remember, this technique limits the sender to a specific fax machine.

- *Recognizing distinctive rings.* Distinctive ringing is a useful option offered by your local telephone company. The telephone company sends calls directed to different phone numbers over the same incoming line using different ringing patterns. Just as some modems and fax machines can use distinctive ringing to determine when they should answer, some fax servers can use the distinctive ring to route incoming faxes to specific mailboxes. This technique doesn't require any knowledge or action on the part of the caller, and the caller can use any machine to place the call.

Finally, *Direct Inward Dial* is a technique that uses the signaling between the telephone company's central office and your private branch exchange telephone system to ring specific lines. The fax server interprets these incoming calls and properly routes the received documents.

The Structure of Server Software

Servers make possible the applications that provide the functional and economic rationale for installing a network; in addition, the ability to share information and the efficiencies provided by electronic mail or workgroup scheduling programs can justify a LAN. Of course, servers need special software—the LAN operating system—to handle the many tasks involved in sharing resources.

The sharing software in file, print, and communications servers comes in many different modules. Communications servers run software that translates between the network and whatever communications speeds, data alphabets, and protocols the external connections use. File-server software includes sophisticated queues for requests and usually some kind of disk cache. Disk caching loads large segments of the data from the hard disk into RAM to satisfy requests from fast memory instead of from the slower hard disk.

Servers have the same kinds of Transport layer software as workstations. The server also runs software that buffers and queues requests for service from the network stations. The server software typically includes some kind of security protection based on either a password attached to each resource or a table of rights assigned to each named user.

You can break file-server software down into three major elements:

- The *file-management system* writes and reads data on one or more hard disk drives.

- The *disk cache system* gathers incoming and outgoing data into a cache in RAM memory for faster handling than the physical capabilities of a hard disk would allow.

- The *access system* controls who may use the data and how multiple applications simultaneously access files.

The multitasking LAN operating systems (those that enable hundreds of nodes to access gigabytes of data on a single server) set the pace and direction of the industry and determine how people will connect to, across, and out of their network environments. Multitasking operating systems such as NetWare, Windows NT, and UNIX provide important options for flexible, secure, and reliable connections. A network of PCs running with one of these operating systems can shove minicomputers out the back door in many organizations.

File Management Functions

The basic function of the file management software is to move the heads of the hard disk drive and deliver data to the client stations through the network.

A technique called *elevator seeking* makes operation of the hard disks more efficient. The heads on a hard disk drive must move in and out on the spinning disk to read and write data. Each large movement takes milliseconds of time. The elevator-seeking software improves efficiency by queuing requests requiring head movement and moving them in an orderly fashion in the same direction. The order of the requests' arrival doesn't matter; each request is satisfied in the most logical fashion. This allows the drive heads to operate in a sweeping motion, from one edge of the disk to the other. Elevator seeking improves disk drive performance by significantly reducing disk head thrashing and by minimizing head seek time.

A *directory-hashing* technique indexes directory entries according to a mathematical formula for fastest retrieval. Two types of directory hashing expedite directory access. The first hashing algorithm indexes the volume directories, while the second indexes the files by volume and subdirectory. Directory hashing reduces the number of directory reads after the server starts operation. NetWare and other file systems take good advantage of directory hashing.

Server operating systems typically cache entire directory structures of volumes attached to the server. During initialization, the operating system reads entire volume directories into memory, and then it continually updates them. First the operating system updates the copy in server RAM; then it updates the physical volume, as time permits, between servicing user requests. The technique provides fast response, but it carries a potential danger: If a power failure or other problem takes down the server before the volume is updated, the file can be damaged.

Disk Caching

Disk caching, the process of using server RAM to hold the most recent and frequently requested blocks of data from server storage, greatly enhances retrieval times. Hard disk drives can retrieve data in times measured by hundredths of a second. Solid-state RAM can deliver the same data in thousandths of a second. When modern computers handle thousands of requests a second, people using client stations can perceive the difference a disk cache makes in delivering data to the screen.

Application programs typically request data in blocks of less than 1KB. Caching file systems, however, typically pick up at least 4KB of data surrounding the requested bytes and place them in RAM. Network administrators can often tune the caching software to use different sizes of data blocks.

Caching doesn't help speed processing of the initial requests for data, but when the responses to subsequent requests for related data can come from the cache, they move more quickly than when they come from the hard disk. In many operations, the cache *hit rate* (the number of data requests satisfied from the cache) will exceed 80 percent.

File caching also speeds up user writes to network files. Requested writes are cached in flagged file-cache blocks. These blocks are systematically written to disk between the handling of other user requests. But caching file-write actions is usually an option that network administrators must specifically turn on because a write cache has one significant drawback: If the hard disk or server system suffers a catastrophic failure or power outage, the data in cache waiting to be written is lost. You must balance the potential efficiency improvement in a busy network against the potential loss of data due to a malfunction.

High-Reliability File System Options

Fault tolerance, the capability to continue operation despite the failure of significant subsystems, is a relatively new factor in local area networking. As more users put their most valuable applications onto networks, fault tolerance has become increasingly important. Some network operating systems, notably the System Fault Tolerant (SFT) versions of NetWare, include capabilities to store data simultaneously on more than one drive for improved survivability.

Novell has offered SFT versions of NetWare for several years with such features as bad-block revectoring, disk mirroring, and disk duplexing. SFT NetWare is complex and significantly more expensive than the standard version.

In *bad-block revectoring*, a technique Novell refers to as *HotFix*, a small piece of software monitors the hard disk drive to detect malfunctions caused by a bad section of magnetic media on the drive. When it detects this problem, the software attempts to recover any available data and to revector the file address map to point to its new location. The software also marks the block of media as bad so that it isn't used again.

The *disk-mirroring* technique requires two disk drives: a primary and a secondary. Ideally, the secondary disk is identical to the primary one; if it is not exactly the same, it must at least be of the same type and larger than the primary disk (even though the extra space will not be utilized). All data copied to the primary disk is also sent to the "mirror" disk, but not necessarily to the same physical location. If the primary disk fails, the secondary disk immediately takes up the current task with no loss of data.

Another basic feature of disk mirroring is that data can be read from the mirror disk if a read error occurs on the primary disk. Read-after-write verification and HotFix are active on both disks. Therefore, the bad block on the primary disk will be marked, and the correct data from the mirror disk will be written to a good location on the primary disk. This completes a loop that allows full recovery from read and write errors.

Disk mirroring becomes *disk duplexing* through the addition of a completely separate hard disk controller card. This redundant configuration further improves reliability. Disk duplexing also benefits LAN throughput by allowing a technique called *split seeks*. When simultaneous multiple read requests occur, both drives receive and process them immediately, effectively doubling disk drive throughput and overall system performance. In the case of a single read request, the operating system looks at both disk drives to determine which can respond best. If both are equally occupied, NetWare sends the request to the drive whose current head position is closest to the desired data.

In summary, disk mirroring requires only one controller card and uses a second disk, which can immediately pick up a failed operation with no loss of data. Disk duplexing, which has a controller card for each drive, enhances system performance by sending simultaneous write and read requests to both disks through separate disk channels. It also allows continued operation if a disk controller fails. Disk mirroring and disk duplexing both provide additional levels of system survivability.

Clustering

While the high-reliability options in NetWare work very well, they typically require specialized hardware and redundant identical hardware. Microsoft led a consortium aimed at developing a technology known as *clustering*. The goal of clustering is to combine servers into self-support and self-healing groups. In concept, the servers in a cluster can be of different makes, models, and capabilities (the leading hardware vendors aren't likely to move too quickly toward interchangeability).

Beware of duplexing

While duplexing is good for improving reliability, you don't get something for nothing. The downside comes in the extra work the server's CPU must do to handle twice as many read/write requests. You need a high-quality disk drive controller that has its own on-board processor to make duplexing a practical approach.

Under the concept of "active/active clustering," every machine in the cluster is available to do real work, and each machine in the cluster is also available to recover the resources and workload of any other machine in the cluster. In theory, there is no need to have a spare server standing by waiting for a failure. Instead, the servers signal one another and take over for one another in the event of a failure. The take-over doesn't occur as quickly as it does under full hardware mirroring schemes, but it happens in seconds, and the system is very capable and affordable.

Security Systems

The concept of sharing resources and files carries a lot of appeal in terms of both economy and improved productivity. But too much sharing can become too much of a good thing. Server software must provide some way to differentiate the requests coming from different client stations and to determine whether each person or station has the right to receive the requested data or service. No one wants an unauthorized employee reading personnel or payroll records. You often need to limit the activity of network users to certain files to prevent both mischief and inadvertent damage.

A networking software package typically uses one of two types of file security plans. The first plan gives each shared resource on the network a network name; a single name can designate a whole shared drive, a subdirectory, or even a file. You can associate a password with a network name and limit the read/write/ create capabilities associated with that password. Although this scheme makes it easy to shift the shared resources, one user might have to keep track of several passwords, and security is easily compromised when password management is a constant headache.

The other security architecture uses the concept of groups: Each person belongs to one or more groups, and each group has specific access rights. This architecture, used by NetWare, makes each person responsible only for one personal password. The LAN administrator can easily move people into and out of groups as they change jobs or leave the organization.

The biggest security holes are human!

Networking software can supply elaborate security schemes, but they are only as good as your administrative security practices. You have to enforce proper password handling practices, provide physical protection for resources, and foster an awareness of security. The most dangerous threats aren't from destructive hackers, but from disgruntled employees and competitors. Typically, you do not know that network intrusion is happening until you suffer a catastrophic blow in some other part of your business. Don't count on software to do administrative security work!

Both security architectures typically enable an administrator to grant or deny individuals or groups of users the ability to read, write, create, delete, search, and modify files. For example, you might want to give data-entry clerks only the ability to modify accounting files in order to prevent people from copying your financial files for their own purposes. A few operating systems even include a capability called "execute-only." This function allows a person only to run a program, which can't be copied or accessed in any other way. Appropriate use of various security options safeguards your important information.

The encryption of passwords, both when stored on-disk and during transmission, is an important feature in high-security applications. Whereas previously a technician could easily attach a network analyzer to the cable and capture passwords and data files as they crossed the network, network operating systems now include encrypted passwords to thwart the success of anyone who might tap into the cable.

A final note for the security-conscious: Consider the physical security for any server. Put servers behind locked doors and protect them with passwords.

The Network Operating System Is a System

Network operating systems contain many pieces and parts. Often, you can select options and configurations—such as Transport layer software or application program interfaces—that are uniquely suited to your organization. But such interactive systems need careful management. In the next chapter, I'll outline the most popular network operating systems and emphasize their practical capabilities and limitations.

Using the Network Operating Systems

Industry trends

Client/server computing

Networking protocols

Novell's Family of Products

Microsoft's Strategy

The power of UNIX

What server features?

Novell's name game

Novell grasped onto the Internet like a drowning sailor grabbing a life vest. The company insisted on the name IntranetWare for the primary version of the 4.0 release. However, it seems that even the Internet can be a little overboard; the company is coming back to the NetWare product name.

This chapter provides detailed overviews of the best-selling and most technologically advanced network operating systems. It describes Novell's NetWare and Microsoft's Windows in their various flavors and tips a hat to the networking in UNIX. This chapter primarily tells you about the operating systems and their features. The following two chapters extend the discussion into the role of these operating systems in making connections to wide area networks in general and specifically to the Internet and corporate intranets. Let's begin with a quick look at industry trends and the impact of competition on the various LAN operating systems.

Industry Trends and Evolution

You should know a few things about the current state of the networking industry:

- The major LAN operating systems are all fast enough for practically any organization's needs. Speed is only a minor factor in selecting a network operating system.

- Operating systems are becoming increasingly compatible and interoperable. They gain interoperability through modularity. You can customize a network operating system to meet your needs.

- NetWare still has the largest market share of installed file servers.

- Microsoft's Windows NT is a worthy challenger to NetWare, and NT servers now do many jobs on networks that once were all Novell.

The size of the market and the potential for profit make for hot competition among LAN operating system vendors. Novell, which once enjoyed as much as 70% of the market share in PC-based networks, has lost sales momentum but offers very capable products.

In 1989, network operating system companies fueled the growth of networks by announcing and delivering products conforming to open standards rather than proprietary protocols. AT&T,

Digital, and 3-Com led the industry in providing interoperable products for open standards. Rather than try to lock in and control each account with unique communications standards, they lured buyers with software that worked according to nationally and internationally accepted standards.

During the 1990s, the companies in this market have continued to provide buyers with increased compatibility and interoperability. This trend has gone so far that now companies not only support open standards, they also deliver software for each other's proprietary protocols. For a couple of years, Microsoft adopted Novell's IPX protocols as the default networking protocol for Windows NT. Now Microsoft and Novell have joined the UNIX crowd in making TCP/IP a default in the latest versions of their networking systems.

In the practical sense, support for multiple protocols means that an administrator can configure a networked PC so that the DOS F: drive is a UNIX file server, the G: drive is a NetWare file server, and the H: drive is a Windows NT server. The person using this PC needn't know anything about any of these operating systems to access the data on each server. This capability is available today, but the pieces and parts must be carefully integrated so that they mesh without binding.

Improved interoperability and flexibility are prime marketing and technology features for networking software companies. Just as you can mix and match Ethernet adapters from different vendors, you can combine elements of network operating systems and linking servers running different operating systems on the same network, all of them supplying services to the same clients.

Performance and Other Important Factors

We learned a lot about network performance in our years of testing at PC Magazine LAN Labs, but we have also learned that some other important factors are more difficult to measure. To the average user, reliability, technical support, compatibility, and management features are more important than throughput. In terms of speed, all the operating systems described in this chapter perform well enough to meet almost anyone's computing needs.

It's not all or nuthin'!

In networking, you don't have to make a choice and stay wed forever. For example, it might be smart to run your important line-of-business file servers under NetWare. Novell offers excellent options for improved server reliability. But, at the same time, you could choose to run your communications servers under Windows NT because many vendors offer security and remote connection products for NT. You can mix and match software, hardware, and protocols across the LAN to suit your needs.

Under a heavy network load equaling the activity of 100 client PCs, a typical file server delivers a 50K file to a client PC in 1.4 seconds—about the same performance a laptop computer's hard disk supplies. Under a lighter network load, you get better file retrieval times from these systems than you can from the hard disk found on most laptops.

Another conclusion I've drawn from our testing is that a PC acting as a file server is an interactive and relatively homogeneous system, which makes it difficult to comment on the importance of one part of the system without commenting on other system parameters. For example, with today's drives, disk controllers, software, and LAN adapters, after you get to a 200MHz Pentium, the speed and type of processor used in a machine acting as a file server don't seem to make much difference. The picture changes, however, when you take advantage of a modern network operating system's capability to run network management, communications, or database server programs in the same PC that is acting as a file server. These server-based applications can rapidly bog down the server's processor.

Modern file servers do much more than simply provide networked PCs with multiple simultaneous access to shared files and subdirectories. They have become the hosts for database engines that provide simple responses to complex queries from application programs. They also host other types of client/server applications such as messaging engines like Microsoft's Messaging API. Today's servers communicate with uninterruptable power supplies and take appropriate actions when the power goes out. In addition, they run network management and monitoring programs and even provide the portals for wide area networking connections such as the Internet and corporate intranets.

Client/Server Computing

A hot buzzword in the LAN operating-system market is *client/server computing*. In the client/server architecture, certain disk-intensive tasks, such as database and message services, stay

The server in a nutshell

We'll get into server options later in this chapter, but my bottom-line advice for office-type networks is this: Buy the fastest and biggest SCSI hard disk drive system you can afford. Install it in a motherboard with a minimum of a Pentium 133 processor, three usable PCI slots (after the video, memory, and PCI hard disk controller are in), at least 48MB of RAM, and a power supply with at least a 300-watt rating. Buy an uninterruptable power supply to match. That configuration will meet 75% of your needs.

on the file server. This technique lowers network traffic congestion but increases the load on the server's processor.

SEE ALSO

➤ *See all of Chapter 8, starting on page 161, for more information on LAN software functions and client/server computing.*

As you load more jobs onto the file server, it requires more RAM and processing power. As you gain power in the server, you can add more features in the LAN operating systems—and so the cycle repeats itself. New software, usually chasing the power of the latest hardware, increases the importance of network operating systems in a growing web of computer interconnections.

Don't forget to include an uninterruptable power supply for the server.

Networking Protocols

Networks depend on *protocols*—agreements describing how things work—to handle data reliably and efficiently. Although network protocols are invisible to users, the protocol architecture is one of the most important pieces you must choose when you plan and build a LAN or WAN. Except for single-vendor networks where protocols such as IBM's SNA and Digital's DECnet prevail, your decision will probably come down to using Novell's SPX/IPX (*Sequenced Packet Exchange/Internet Packet Exchange*) or the TCP/IP (*Transmission Control Protocol/Internet Protocol*) suite. Figure 9.1 shows how application data is encapsulated in TCP/IP packets.

SEE ALSO

➤ *The TCP/IP suite is an important part of Chapters 10 and 12, starting on pages 247 and 309, respectively.*

One of many great ideas to fall to the ax of reality is the single-protocol, keep-it-simple network. Most organizations with more than a few dozen networked computers have a mix of computer and network operating systems that has evolved in response to unforeseen mergers and reorganizations rather than careful planning. As networks become increasingly heterogeneous, the job of networking and managing the different systems gets tougher. Although there are tried-and-proven standards, managing one of these hybrid networks is still a complicated process.

FIGURE 9.1

The various layers of networking software each wrap the payload of data from an application or the keyboard in an envelope with a specialized format. This diagram shows program data going into a TCP packet, the TCP packet going into an IP packet, and the IP packet (containing all the other packets) going into an Ethernet packet or frame. It's a highly structured process and not as streamlined as it could be, but the structure ensures interoperability.

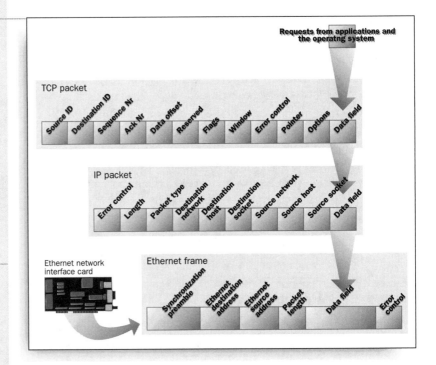

Novell's huge share of the networking market has given SPX/IPX a large installed base. Since the 1980's, Novell NetWare has based all network Transport layer communications on the SPX/IPX protocols. NetWare's success and power have drawn many other manufacturers to SPX/IPX, so you can buy everything from sophisticated analyzers to special communications programs for these protocols.

Like other network communications protocols, SPX/IPX is not a single protocol but a suite of standard procedures for connecting computers. In practice, each set of protocols formats a message or *packet* with specific characteristics such as addressing, receipt, or routing information. Packets are often nested three to four layers deep, so there may be a packet within a packet within a packet, each having a specific function.

The IPX part of the protocol is responsible for addressing the packets between the NetWare nodes, but it doesn't account or receipt for them. When it is used, SPX provides a receipt for the data at its destination and tallies the receipts at the sending side. A few applications needing guaranteed delivery, such as network file transfers, can address their blocks of data through SPX. But most applications, particularly those that can monitor the success of communications for themselves, use IPX because it's more efficient and introduces less overhead into the network.

Novell's IPX is fast and efficient, particularly with the relatively small data packets (in the range of 512 bytes) usually requested by Windows applications. But small data packets aren't desirable on wide area networks with slower, expensive internetwork links because they add overhead.

Until late 1994, Microsoft's networking products used a networking protocol called NetBIOS to carry data between LAN adapters. Although NetBIOS is fast across small networks, the NetBIOS packets don't carry enough information for routing across inter-LAN links. Consequently, later versions of Windows NT and the networking capabilities in Windows 95 use Microsoft's implementation of Novell's IPX as a primary networking protocol. Microsoft's products also work well with TCP/IP, but IPX is more efficient than TCP/IP on local networks. Windows NT now defaults to TCP/IP as its initial protocol suite.

The TCP/IP protocol is an open standard that was developed by the U.S. Department of Defense (DoD) to link thousands of dissimilar computers. The DoD's Defense Advanced Research Projects Agency (DARPA) developed a standard set of nonproprietary protocols that could provide communications between computers connected to a large WAN. Like SPX/IPX, TCP/IP is not a single protocol but a suite of protocols designed to control communications services. Unlike SPX/IPX, TCP/IP is designed to provide communications between different types of computers in a truly heterogeneous network.

The IP portion of the TCP/IP protocol handles the addressing between network nodes. Both IPX and IP provide the delivery mechanism for sending and receiving data. Like IPX, IP cannot guarantee the delivery of an application's data. A very simple—but important—benefit of IP is its capability to carry larger

Small pipes...big blocks

Long distance networks need streams of big blocks of data to be efficient. That design principle flies in the face of the Asynchronous Transfer Mode (ATM) system that emerged in the mid 1990s. The next chapter gets into ATM, but for now you should know that IPX packets are small and well suited to bursty LAN traffic. IP packets are big and designed for efficient use of expensive long distance links. You run into significant problems when you try to shove big IP packets into tiny ATM cells.

To IP or not to IP?

"So," as your mother used to say, "Just because all the other kids jumped off a cliff you're going to jump off a cliff?" Novell made IPX popular, but is abandoning IPX for IP. Microsoft wanted to be compatible with Novell and adopted IPX, but now is moving to IP as a default. However, IPX is faster, more secure, and much easier to use on local area networks than IP. So why are they going to IP as a default? It's mostly Internet marketing hype. In later chapters I'll show you a couple of good ways to stick with safe and easy-to-use IPX while still giving every user appropriate access to Internet and intranet goodies. Don't jump off the TCP/IP LAN cliff without knowing what's below.

blocks of data across an internetwork link for greater efficiency. An IP packet can grow to 65,535 8-bit bytes—more than a hundred times the size of an IPX packet. That's like the difference between carrying your furniture across country on a motorcycle or in an 18-wheeler.

TCP packets encapsulate IP packets and provide the connection information services. TCP also provides the delivery guarantee that IP lacks. Unlike SPX, which is used very little in NetWare LANs, TCP is used by most applications in the TCP/IP environment because its creators anticipated running over less reliable connections.

TCP improves efficiency by a technique called *windowing*. It can transmit a number of packets while watching for acknowledgments of all previously sent packets. It doesn't just send a packet and wait for a reply. The number of packets in the window varies with the degree of transmission success. NetWare includes a similar feature called *packet burst*, which uses the same general principle; however, packet burst is part of the higher-level NetWare Core Protocol, not of SPX or IPX.

TCP/IP's most significant advantage over SPX/IPX is its capability to network millions of heterogeneous computers over a global network. The Internet, which currently includes many millions of networked computers, is the best example of TCP/IP's robustness across different networks and computers. Unlike SPX/IPX, which uses a broadcast technique to keep track of all the computers and services on the network, IP version 4, the currently deployed version, relies on a series of unique 32-bit addresses. Every node on a TCP/IP network must have an unique address, and someone must keep track of the assignments in any organization.

This quick look at the SPX/IPX and TCP/IP protocol suites highlights their differences and drawbacks. In practice, SPX/IPX is a proven standard for PC-based LANs or WANs connected by high-speed, reliable communications devices. TCP/IP is the preferred protocol for connecting disparate computer systems over extended networks that have lower throughput and reliability. Figure 9.2 illustrates some of the concepts discussed in this chapter and in the preceding chapter, including multilayered software, database engines, and remote procedure calls.

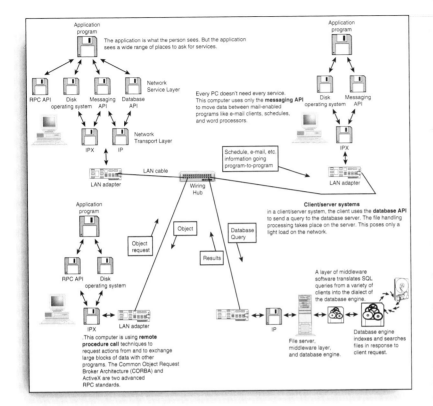

FIGURE 9.2

Networking software has many components. This diagram illustrates how some protocols and services work together to efficiently share resources across a LAN.

If you use only PCs running DOS and Windows with a few Macs or OS/2 PCs on a LAN, you are certainly better off sticking with NetWare and SPX/IPX as your network communications protocol suite. SPX/IPX does not rely on manually assigned, independent network addresses and is much easier to install and manage than TCP/IP on a LAN or WAN. Novell also offers several solutions, including NetWare NFS and NetWare for SAA, that enable you to connect to other operating systems and computers such as mainframe and midrange systems over IPX.

SEE ALSO

➤ *For more information on links to mainframes, see Chapter 13, starting on page 329.*

Interoperability is always a potential problem

In 1997 ZD Labs uncovered a significant interoperability problem between TCP software delivered by Sun Microsystems and TCP software from Microsoft. These software products had been in field use for years. These folks should have known what they were doing, but the designers interpreted the standard differently. The Sun- and Microsoft-equipped computers could exchange TCP data, but with about half the normal efficiency. People lived with slow throughput and attributed it to anything but different TCP timing sequences programmed into the software.

Novell has taken great pains to enhance SPX/IPX services and to offer optional products for flexibility. Novell's SPX/IPX support is flexible and customer-driven, but TCP/IP is supported by a committee and by companies with many different—and possibly incompatible—interpretations of the standard. It's difficult for a customer with a TCP/IP problem to find out who to call for help.

The most appealing feature of TCP/IP is its capability to connect all your systems together. Almost every combination of computer hardware and operating system has a driver available for the TCP/IP network protocol. If a particular company does not include a driver for TCP/IP, a third-party vendor probably makes one. SPX/IPX is widely, but not as universally, available.

Another important factor to consider is the type of software you are using. As a rule, application software dictates operating system. If the software that runs your company does not work with a certain protocol stack, you are going to have to be flexible in your decisions. Most applications do not care about the protocol you are using, but certain network management utilities require a particular network driver to gather information.

Network communication protocols are becoming a commodity. Thanks to network interface card standards such as NDIS and ODI, it's relatively easy to load software conforming to both protocol architectures in one PC, so they aren't mutually exclusive. Figure 9.3 illustrates how two protocol stacks can load over the same network adapter. When you are building a network, you need to decide on the protocol that offers the best performance and flexibility with the least amount of intervention and network maintenance. Although hundreds of programs are available from third parties that enable you to connect all your different computer systems using almost any network protocol, it's best, if possible, to use the same protocol on your entire network.

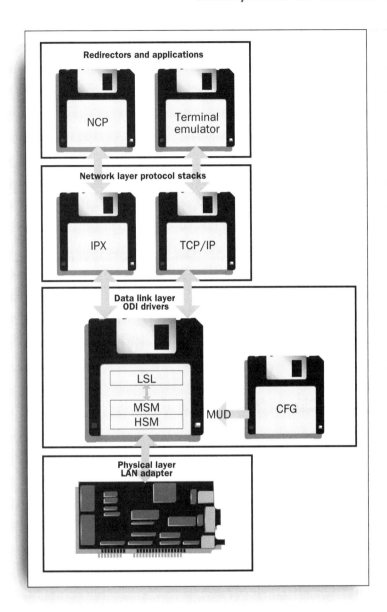

FIGURE 9.3
Two protocol stacks load over
the same network adapter.

Two protocol stacks, working within the same operating system, can share the same LAN adapter. In this case, NetWare's NetWare Core Protocol (NCP) redirector sends requests to IPX for transmission across the network. At the same time, a

TCP-aware application, like terminal emulation software, passes data to TCP and then IP for packaging and addressing. The Link Support Layer (LSL) takes the data from both network layer software, joins with the elements of various software and configuration libraries specific to the physical adapter, and packages the data for the adapter. Two protocol stacks, working within the same operating system, can share the same LAN adapter. In this case, NetWare's *NetWare Core Protocol* (NCP) redirector sends requests to IPX for transmission across the network. At the same time, a TCP-aware application, such as terminal emulation software, passes data to TCP and then IP for packaging and addressing. The *Link Support Layer* (LSL) takes the data from both network layer software, joins with the elements of various software and configuration libraries specific to the physical adapter, and packages the data for the adapter.

With such factors as interoperability, compatibility, and manageability in mind, let's turn to the specific operating systems you can buy today. We'll start with the winner of many acquisition decisions, Novell's NetWare.

The NetWare Family

In 1982, in a small office by the steel plant in Orem, Utah, Ray Noorda, Judith Clarke, Craig Burton, and programmers from a company called Superset, foresaw what PC networking could become. At the time, their competition was from companies, such as Corvus Systems, that were mainly interested in selling hard disks, but from the beginning Novell has been directed toward providing software for integrated computing systems.

When times were tough and financial backers put pressure on Noorda to turn a quick profit, he kept Novell headed toward the longer-term goals of providing software, systems tools, and support.

While Noorda was at its head, Novell's product strategy was clear and consistent: Market an operating system that offers good features and performance, and do everything possible to create the environment it needs to run. Novell is primarily a software company, but it has entered the hardware market several times to develop new products or drive down hardware prices through competition. Novell has never overtly used the "account control" strategy (raised to a fine art by IBM) to capture business. Instead, it has gone to great lengths to build outside support and even to stimulate competition. Its philosophy of "NetWare Open Systems" is in step with the current trend toward standards. Unfortunately, after Noorda left, Novell floundered because of weak leadership. The company turned away from the value added resellers and the relatively small systems that had built its success and tried to attack the market for large enterprise systems using different sales channels. Although Novell could have become the leader of the "Anything But Microsoft" movement in 1996-97, it was off on a crusade trying to scale corporate ramparts.

The NetWare product family set four milestones for PC-based network operating systems.

- Novell was the first company to introduce a network operating system for true file sharing, as opposed to simply writing private, unshared files to a shared hard disk.

- Novell led the way to hardware independence by providing NetWare with the capability to run on more than 30 brands of networks and over 100 network adapters.

- Novell reached companies needing reliability with *System Fault Tolerant* (SFT) NetWare. SFT NetWare ensures data integrity by including the *Transaction Tracking System* (TTS), disk mirroring, and disk duplexing.

- Novell introduced *Open Protocol Technology* (OPT). By providing a protocol-independent architecture for all NetWare services, NetWare supports heterogeneous connectivity.

The Product Family

NetWare 2.X, previously known as Advanced NetWare 286, provided support for medium-sized networks (up to 100 users) and for internetwork routing services. Although it is still installed on servers around the world, Novell no longer directly supports the NetWare 2.X series. With NetWare 3.X, previously known as NetWare 386, Novell provided the industry with the widely used platform for building networked applications, while it also incorporated all the features of previous NetWare versions. NetWare 2.X and 3.X share features such as high-performance disk caching (with elevator seeking and other techniques), strong security, and the capability to use a wide variety of network adapters.

The NetWare 4.X series of products is designed for large enterprise networks that contain hundreds of network resources including file servers, clients, network printers, remote access servers, and other equipment. In earlier versions of NetWare, Novell relied on a database called the NetWare Bindery to keep track of all the network users and resources on each server. The bindery was adequate if you had only one or two servers and limited resources to keep track of, but if you had hundreds of network servers, you had to keep track of hundreds of bindery databases. To make it easier to track network resources, Novell replaced the bindery with the *Novell Directory Services* (NDS). Like the bindery, NDS keeps track of all the network users, groups, and printers, but it distributes this information across all the file servers in the network. This database enables users to connect to all the resources on the network by using a single login command and lets the network administrators manage all the network users and servers from a central location. The best way to think of NDS is as a DOS directory tree. Each resource is represented as an individual subdirectory or file on the directory tree.

Novell made NetWare 4.X the core of several attempts to ride the rocket of Internet interest. Novell's IntranetWare bundles NetWare 4.X with various services needed for IP networking. The product includes Web and FTP servers, a multiprotocol router, and several other intranet-type utilities. However, although IntranetWare enables you to connect your network to the Internet, it doesn't provide any security. A later product called BorderManager is Novell's attempt to fill the holes in, or borders between, the LAN and the intranet/Internet connections. Initially released on NetWare 4.11, BorderManager includes a firewall, caching proxy server, *Virtual Private Network* (VPN), and remote access server. BorderManager also comes with a copy of IntranetWare, which provides you with all the intranet services, including the web server, and the powerful NetWare OS. BorderManager plus IntranetWare make for a total solution for local networking and internetworking.

SEE ALSO

➤ For more on routing, see "Routers," page 259.

Basic Security

NetWare has an excellent security system that offers many options. The primary security structure assigns people to groups, each of which has specific rights. Of course, a group can consist of one person or hundreds of people. This structure works well in organizations of any size and is particularly useful in companies that have high personnel turnover or where people move between jobs. The network administrator can easily add a person to or delete a person from a group, such as accounts payable, and be certain of effective security. Additionally, administrators can restrict the days and even the times when users can log onto the network. Forced periodic password changes require all users to adopt new passwords at selected time intervals.

The only drawback of NetWare's security system is that it requires you to create and update the data identifying groups, rights, and users on every file server separately. In large multi-server networks, this becomes an endless task for network administrators. Novell's response to this problem was the introduction of the Novell's Directory Services. Let's look at the basic features of Novell's major LAN products and then discuss NDS.

NetWare Features

In NetWare 3.X, Novell provided the industry with a powerful platform for building client/server applications. NetWare 3.X is very fast; what's more, it doesn't degrade under heavy processing loads, and it provides huge amounts of storage. The NetWare 4.X series built on many features of 3.X. The 3.X family is still popular and has not yet been abandoned by Novell.

The following sections give you an overview of the features of 3.X and then use it to discuss some fundamental features that carry over to all modern NetWare operating systems.

Specifications

NetWare is a true 32-bit network operating system designed for use on Intel 80486 and Pentium processors. If NetWare detects the presence of a 486 or Pentium processor, it takes advantage of that chip's advanced features by executing longer instructions (more commands per CPU cycle). The file system in NetWare continues all the old tricks of elevator seeking, I/O queuing, and disk caching that it gained from previous versions of NetWare, but it adds huge capacity. Sporting a maximum disk space of 32 terabytes (1TB = 1,000,000MB), NetWare can handle the largest organization's data load. Volumes can span multiple drives, and you can have files as big as 4GB (gigabytes). That means a single data file may be spread across several hard disks, and your application will never know the difference.

The maturity of the NetWare line shows in the way it reports error messages. When I mistakenly left the cable from a NetWare server disconnected and tried to start the operating system, it responded with an onscreen message saying, "The network cable is not connected to the computer." That's a pretty clear error message! Another time, a NetWare server sent me a special message reporting that it was receiving an unusual number of bad packets from one of the client stations. When I inspected the network connection, I saw a small crack in the cable connector. These are good examples of how NetWare helps a network administrator succeed.

NetWare includes two nice security enhancements: security auditing and encrypted backups. A security auditing function keeps a nonmodifiable audit trail of all security changes occurring on the server. Moreover, as NetWare backs up files over the network, the data is sent and stored in encrypted form and is unencrypted only when it returns to the server after a restore.

NLMs

NetWare Loadable Modules (NLMs) are applications—often developed by companies other than Novell—that run in the file server. This category includes simple programs such as drivers for micro channel cards, complex but familiar products like SNA and electronic mail gateways or network backup services, and products for network management, security, and workgroup productivity. Figure 9.4 shows a NetWare server monitor screen with a list of the active NLMs.

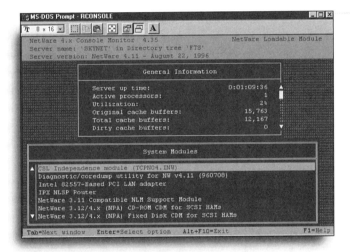

FIGURE **9.4**

This NetWare console monitor screen shows various NetWare Loadable Modules (NLMs), including a router and drivers for SCSI and LAN adapters, running in a NetWare server.

NLMs enable the powerful server to replace the dedicated network machines you might be using today as SNA gateways, electronic mail gateways, and communications servers—but not without some risk.

Although NLMs offer great functionality, they run in the same machine and at the same time as the file-server software. If the file-server hardware malfunctions, you lose all the functions it contains. (In today's most common network configuration, with separate PCs acting as different kinds of servers, if the file server goes down, you can still use SNA gateways and some other services operating on separate machines on the network.) What's more, if some task requires it, an NLM can access the kernel of the NetWare operating system. If the NLM crashes, it can potentially bring down the file server.

The remote-console NLM enables system administrators to monitor server information from their workstations. This feature is a network administrator's dream. An administrator can sit at any workstation and monitor any server on the network. In addition, the administrator's computer acts as though it is actually the server console, enabling an administrator to load and unload NLMs and completely control the server. An NLM called Aconsole allows dial-in modem access to the management functions.

The print-services NLM, shown in Figure 9.5, provides the spooling and queuing of print jobs for up to eight printers. It also enables authorized users to access and manipulate print jobs. The print-services NLM supports printers attached to local workstations and manages up to 16 printers on the network. This flexibility enables organizations to do high-volume printing at the most convenient and secure locations. Novell has a new printing scheme for the NetWare 4.x family. It is discussed later in this chapter.

FIGURE 9.5

NetWare's pserver monitor provides a central point for information and control of networked printers.

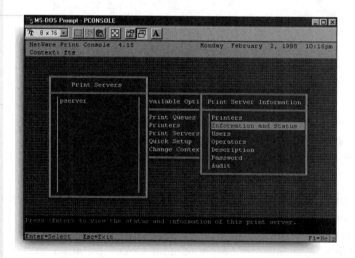

To keep just anyone from adding an NLM to the server, Novell includes the Secure Console option, restricting anyone but the system administrator from adding NLMs or server applications. Another feature that makes the system manager's life simpler is the new Workgroup Manager classification. As the name implies, a person with this description has supervisor privileges for the users assigned to a particular workgroup.

With add-on NLMs, NetWare also supports *Network File System* (NFS), a file-server program widely used in the UNIX world. In addition, it offers better support for Macintosh computers acting as clients to the NetWare server. Servers running the optional NFS and Macintosh NLMs can store files from UNIX and Macintosh computers in their native formats.

Functions

Another useful general feature of NetWare is *Dynamic Resource Configuration* (DRC). System administrators and users alike benefit from this artificial intelligence-type feature. NetWare automatically allocates specific amounts of memory for directory caching and routing buffers. The operating system itself determines the optimal values and adjusts them on the fly.

Novell's Multiple Name Spaces feature enables NetWare to handle files from different operating systems. NetWare associates different filenames with the same file if it is to be used by different operating systems. For example, a Microsoft Excel file used by both the Windows and Apple versions of Excel would have two file entries on the server.

NetWare provides data security with file-salvaging and encryption features. One file-salvaging option automatically purges all deleted files, and another maintains all deleted files until NetWare runs out of disk space. When NetWare needs more disk space, it purges on a first-deleted basis, and the system manager can purge all recoverable files at any time. NetWare preserves security by enabling only those users with proper authorization to undelete a file. In addition to encrypting passwords on the server, NetWare 3.X encrypts them on the wire, preventing network analyzers from reading what the client PC sends to the server.

The system also includes NetWare Management Agent for NetVIEW. This group of NLMs enables a NetWare server with a Token-Ring adapter installed to forward NetVIEW-specific alerts to an IBM host running NetVIEW, which is an IBM network maintenance program.

The Multiprotocol Router

NetWare 3.X introduced a capability that can be invaluable to any manager of a modern network—the capacity to establish a multiprotocol router in the server. *Routers* are devices that move traffic between otherwise independent LAN segments, based on the address of the destination station and on other information they read inside packets created by networking software conforming to protocols such as IPX, IP, NetBIOS, or AppleTalk. Multiprotocol routers are often standalone devices with their own processing capabilities and price tags running to many thousands of dollars. However, each copy of NetWare provides the capability to establish a multiprotocol router in the NetWare file server.

For example, assume you have two LAN segments using Novell's IPX over Token-Ring, another segment using IP over Ethernet, and a fourth segment using IPX over Ethernet. In this example, each LAN segment has its own file and print servers for its client PCs (note that they could be NetWare servers, but they don't have to be). However, the IPX over Ethernet LAN segment also has a PC that acts as a gateway to a mainframe computer, and some nodes on all the LAN segments occasionally need to access the mainframe through that gateway. If you equip one NetWare server with two Token-Ring adapters, and two Ethernet adapters with appropriate drivers for each LAN segment, you can run a multiprotocol router NLM that moves packets as needed between all the LAN segments. Client PCs can run mainframe terminal emulation software compatible with the shared gateway software and use the services of the gateway through the server acting as a router.

A NetWare server can even route among LocalTalk, EtherTalk, and TokenTalk in the same server, providing connectivity to several normally isolated LANs. LocalTalk is Apple's network hardware, whereas EtherTalk and TokenTalk are versions of AppleTalk that run over Ethernet and Token-Ring cabling. As the size of modern networks increases, so does their need to interconnect. Novell's multiprotocol router is an important tool in the LAN-to-LAN connectivity of modern organizations.

Packet Burst

One of the most useful and interesting networking features introduced in NetWare 3.X and carried into NetWare 4.X is *Packet Burst* mode. The Packet Burst software, which is implemented in the BNETX.COM file on a client PC and in PBURST.NLM on the server, enables your network to go beyond NetWare's 512-byte packet limit so that it can use expensive long-distance communications circuits more efficiently.

IPX is a datagram protocol that sends packets without acknowledgment. Novell's Packet Burst software enables a client PC to create IPX packets of up to 64K and to send those packets back-to-back without waiting for acknowledgment. This type of transmission makes the most efficient use of an expensive long distance, low-speed circuit. If the application needs guaranteed delivery, then either application has to supply it, or it can use SPX.

The amount of throughput you gain using Burst mode rather than the traditional NetWare transmission scheme depends on factors such as how much data the client PCs write versus how much they read, the size of the files, and how applications handle the data. Writing is a one-way task, whereas reading demands a response, but if an application handles data in only small blocks, nothing the underlying network software does is of benefit. You see a bigger cumulative improvement as you move bigger files.

The improvement figures range from as much as an ideal 400% gain to around 100% in typical applications. Clearly, by doubling your throughput you can avoid investing several thousand dollars a month in a higher-speed leased line, so it's a prudent step. Interestingly, Novell reports throughput gains of up to 50% using Burst mode on regular Ethernet and Token-Ring systems, due to reduced overhead, but any gain you might see varies widely. You don't have to use the Burst mode software in all the client PCs, just those that benefit from it. Burst and non-burst clients can communicate with burst-equipped servers.

NetWare 4.X

"Where is SYSCON?" The absence of SYSCON, the comfortable management utility used by tens of thousands of NetWare administrators, underlines the difference between NetWare 4.X and its predecessors. NetWare 4.X isn't an upgrade to Novell's popular NetWare 3.X. It wraps the core NetWare file and print services with a new architecture aimed at the multiserver market. New utilities, which enable a new naming technology, replace SYSCON. Figure 9.6 shows the NetWare 4.X naming structure.

FIGURE 9.6

Novell Directory Services (NDS) is a powerful feature. It eliminates the server-by-server management of users and enables any user to log in to all authorized resources from anywhere with a single password. However, the price you pay is a fairly rigid naming scheme that isn't easy to change. Mergers, acquisitions, and expansions are bad news for a manager running NDS because it's difficult to trim or add branches of the network naming tree.

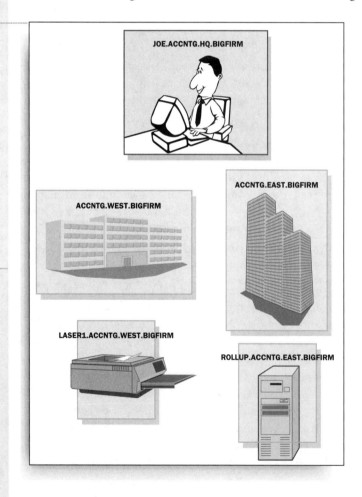

Here is my advice: If you have six active NetWare 3.X file servers, it's time to consider the change to NetWare 4.X. If you have a dozen servers, the management benefits of 4.X are persuasive, but if you have only a few servers, are happy with SYSCON, and have your login scripts working the way you want, you don't have much reason to upgrade. However, if you decide to run IP on your local area network, you need to upgrade to IntranetWare BorderManager—introducing IP is a big step in terms of system management and overhead.

The major architectural changes to NetWare 4.X begin with a naming service that globally positions each user and resource in the network. In practical terms, this means each user logs in only once rather than log in to every server. NetWare 4.X includes file data compression, so your server's drives can hold nearly twice as much data—a feature that can offset the price of the software by enabling you to avoid a hard disk upgrade. On the client side, the new NetWare shell, VLM.EXE, handles global naming requirements. VLM.EXE can look like NETX, so it works with NetWare 2.X and 3.X servers. A much-needed innovation enables you to load and unload the client software under Windows. The client software comes with drivers for approximately 150 adapters and runs over Microsoft's NDIS if you have a rare adapter that doesn't use Novell's ODI. The client software also includes Novell's Burst mode client support, which improves throughput in some applications by streaming data without waiting for acknowledgment.

You can install the software in less than 15 minutes, including the time it takes to read the documentation. During our evaluation, the upgrade utility built a 4.X server over our existing 3.12 server and kept the 3.12 user and resource names. You need a backup to restore the data files after an upgrade, so be certain your restore function works before you start the upgrade. If you select file compression, 4.X immediately gives you more disk space; the amount you gain depends upon the nature of your files.

The software installation is quick, but properly naming the server during setup can take days of study. The NetWare Directory Services (NDS) replaces the server-by-server management process of earlier NetWare with a global naming scheme in

Upgrade or else!

Novell is serious about pushing users to upgrade to versions 4.0 and 5.0 of NetWare. In fact, upgrades and support for NetWare 3.x have gone up in price while NetWare 4.x has become more economical. Novell is going to force you to NetWare 4.x and beyond, whether you like it or not.

Netware upgrade printer setup problem

NetWare 4.x includes a migration utility that takes your NetWare 3.x system and upgrades it to NetWare 4.x. In my experience, it works pretty well, except that it usually misses your printer setups. Be sure to document your printer assignments and rights before you start an upgrade.

which all servers know the rights of all users. When you answer the naming questions on any server you should have the whole structure in mind and understand how this particular server relates to all the others.

Planning the NDS naming structure is like planning the layout for all the directories and subdirectories on a hard disk drive before you load the data. NDS uses the same kind of root and tree organization, and you can make as many layers of branches as you need, but the top-level directories are key. The structure should have enough layers so that you can add servers in a logical sequence, but you must limit the number of layers to reduce complexity. For example, the name LASER.ACCOUNTING. 4THFLOOR might work for an organization that will never extend the network beyond one building, but another organization might need a more specific name such as LASER. ACCNTG.4THFLOOR.NEWYORK.NAMERICA. COMPANY.BIGFIRM for the same resource. Fortunately, NDS lets you designate aliases that represent the longer identification, so the same printer might be known by the alias NYLASER in this large organization's accounting departments around the world.

Novell provides two utilities, NetSync and Dsmerge, to help maintain the NDS structure. NetSync enables you to synchronize the bindery information on your NetWare 3.1X servers to the objects in NetWare 4.1's NDS. To enable you to manage all your NetWare 3.1X servers, NetWare 4.1 uses a bindery emulation utility. Your NetWare 3.1X servers still use the bindery, but you can view and manage them as objects from a NetWare 4.1 client.

You use Dsmerge to make changes to your NDS tree structure. For example, if a department moves to a new location, you can use the Dsmerge utility to move the department to its new location in the directory tree.

The global nature of the NDS drives other changes. For example, the servers recognize time zone changes when they update the time. Also, the NDS traffic is encrypted with a sophisticated public key encryption standard to keep security tight.

SEE ALSO

➤ *For more on Ethernet, see the section "Ethernet the Elder" on page 133.*

Adopting NetWare 4.X is a strategic corporate decision. Installers and administrators need training to learn how to set up and support the system, and changing the naming service causes turmoil. Novell has announced other strategic options for 4.X, including the capacity to run *NetWare Loadable Modules* (NLMs) on PCs, wiring hubs, and other devices across the network, and an imaging service for handling large image files. NetWare 4.X has memory management and protection features that make it more efficient at running NLMs. Adopting 4.X is a big step, but if you have a big network, the product has a lot of appeal. Table 9.1 lists some of the differences between NetWare 4.X and NetWare 3.12.

TABLE 9.1   **NetWare comparison**

Version 4.X	Version 3.12
Global naming	Server-by-server naming
Active security	Not available
Imaging option	Not available
Expanded Windows	Basic Windows
Packet Burst mode	Optional

Novell Distributed Print Services

You can't ignore the basics. You save corporate dollars by lining your enterprise telephone systems to the Internet, and you can enhance enterprise productivity by establishing an intranet, but you're a bum if people can't print across a LAN. Novell pays attention to the basics, and the *Novell Distributed Print Services* (NDPS) does things correctly. A very complex product, NDPS essentially combines the functions of the printer, print queue, print server, and spooler. With NDPS you can configure all your printers from a single location by using the NetWare Administrator utility. NDPS is also tied into NDS, so you have strong security and centralized management. The only drawback to the NDPS is a somewhat difficult installation, a long wait for truly NDPS-complaint printers, and the lack of client software for Windows NT. However, with a price tag of only $49.95 per site, it is more than worth using.

A matter of frames

In a network of NetWare 3.x and 4.x servers, there is a tricky incompatibility in the underlying Ethernet frames coming from a 4.X server. The drivers in early versions of NetWare conformed to an Ethernet protocol that has since changed. Unlike Netware 2.X and early versions of 3.X, version 4.X conforms to the current IEEE 802.2 standards. If you want the 4.X server to be compatible with earlier NetWare, you must make sure a "frame=" line in `AUTOEXEC.NCF` loads the 802.3 drivers. As an example, for one of 3-Com's popular lines of adapters, the line would be `Load 3c5x9 Frame=Ethernet 802.3`. If you don't know about it, this is a frustrating problem, but it's easy to solve.

NDPS consists of both server and client software. You must install the server software on a NetWare 4.1X server. Before you can install the software, you have to install the latest service pack from Novell. Fortunately, the CD includes the service pack for you. Unfortunately, it takes about 20 minutes to install all the software and printer drivers, so you'll want to set aside an hour or two.

The jobs of the print queue, print server, and spooler have been replaced with a single NDS object called an *agent*. In the past you had to use two or three different utilities to manage these components, but with NDPS you can do it with one. The agent represents a single printer attached to your network via a parallel or serial connection to a file server or a direct LAN link. The agent communicates with a NLM called the *broker*. The broker's job is to provide notification, advertise available printers, and store printer drivers. The broker also eliminates the need for *Service Advertisement Protocol* (SAP) packets to be constantly sent to all your network printers. This feature alone can greatly reduce unwanted network traffic.

SEE ALSO

➤ *For more on network printing and alternatives, see Chapter 3, starting on page 31.*

➤ *For information on print servers, see the section "The Print Server Functions," on page 179.*

To communicate with the printer, NDPS uses an NLM called a *gateway*. It's up to printer vendors like Hewlett-Packard and Epson to work with Novell to develop NDPS gateways. The gateways translate proprietary printer protocols into NDPS information. For example, the Hewlett-Packard gateway can communicate with any printer with a JetDirect card installed. It can also provide information such as the amount of toner in the printer and provide warnings about a paper jam or other problem. The amount of information you can monitor is based on the type of printer you have. Novell hopes that vendors will deliver NDPS-compliant networked printers that embed NDPS technology in the hardware and don't require a gateway NLM.

The best feature of NDPS is the time it can save administrators when they are installing and troubleshooting network printers.

With NDPS, you can install a network printer from a single location and make that printer available to all the users on the network. The clients run the NDPS Printer Manager software to see the available printers and monitor them.

The Printer Manager enables you to search for a specific printer to meet your needs. For example, you can search for a printer in accounting that provides color on legal size paper. After Printer Manager finds the printer, it automatically downloads the drivers to your client PC.

The notification utility provides proactive and completed information. You can configure NDPS to notify you of a problem, such as a paper jam or an out-of-paper condition, and also when the job is completed. The notifications can be sent to a pop-up screen, email, or, if you have GroupWise, a pager.

If you have any printers attached to a NetWare 4.1X, or higher, file server, NDPS is definitely worth the time and effort to install. As gateways and NDPS printers become available, the dream of a plug-and-play network printer will finally be realized.

Novell and the Internet

In this section of the chapter, I stopped short of examining Novell's IntranetWare and BorderManager. These are important products, but you've got to get the fundamentals down before you can hope to go off and surf the Net.

VINES

Banyan System's *VINES* (VIrtual NEtworking Software) is a network operating system that broke new ground but now is all but buried by Microsoft. The VINES system is actually a series of applications running over a special version of AT&T's UNIX operating system, but the UNIX layer is hidden by VINES and is not available for other application programs. A PC running VINES typically performs all server functions, including acting as a communications server. This concentration of functions makes the system's multiprocessor capabilities particularly important.

The technical specifications for VINES put it in competition with NetWare 4.X and Windows NT, but both Novell and Microsoft have more aggressive expansion and development plans in place than Banyan does. VINES' main claim to fame has been its capability to connect widely separated file servers efficiently through a variety of long-distance communications alternatives. For this reason, VINES finds its best acceptance in large network installations. However, Novell's NetWare 4.X is aimed directly at the same market.

Banyan pioneered the use of global naming services, a valuable feature for networks with many file servers that has been emulated by Novell and Microsoft. Banyan calls its naming service StreetTalk. StreetTalk provides a way of naming resources and users located on various servers and nodes across the network. The VINES software enables you to assign each resource a name in the form "Item@Group@Organization" and a password. Every server maintains and updates a universal *Access Rights List* (ARL) containing the StreetTalk names of the resources and the users authorized to access each resource. The administrator doesn't have to log on to each server and configure resources and user rights; one step does it all. This technique makes it easy to establish a high level of resource security and reduces the administrator's workload.

VINES also includes a feature called StreetTalk Directory Assistance (STDA). STDA replicates directory information on multiple servers throughout the network so that users can find network resources faster. This feature is most useful for extremely large networks that have multiple servers.

One feature that sets VINES apart from the popular Novell and Microsoft LAN operating systems is the fact that StreetTalk enables users to access gateway services, mail systems, print queues, fax gateways, and host gateways with a single password. Another advantage Banyan has over the competition is its experience in client/server computing. VINES offered SQL database operations on the server years before other products did.

Banyan is also committed to supporting industry standards. In cooperation with Microsoft, Banyan has given VINES the capability to work with SMB, NDIS, NetBIOS, and Windows NT APIs. Because VINES can work with this acronym-laden list of interfaces, companies writing application software for networks have a common development environment that lets them master one technique for communicating between nodes on the network. Consequently there's a larger potential market for their products.

The VINES operating system uses a specially designed version of UNIX V to run on computers that have multiple processors. Unlike other multiprocessor operating systems that assign specific types of tasks to specific processors, VINES divides tasks evenly among the processors by finely parsing the stream of work and assigning tasks to the available processors on a first-free-first-tasked basis. VINES can assign tasks to as many as eight processors in a single PC.

VINES provides an all-in-one-box solution for connecting to remote servers and transferring data to other servers, SNA gateways, async services, database servers, and mail servers. Banyan also offers a host of communications products aimed at minicomputers and mainframes. These include products for server-to-server communication within the LAN, over a wide area network, or through an X.25 network, as well as products for 3270/SNA terminal emulation, email, and remote network management.

As a communications server, a computer running VINES has a variety of ways of connecting to IBM mainframes. For example, Banyan's 3174 Emulation/Token-Ring product enables a VINES server to communicate with an IBM computer using the SNA communications protocol over a Token-Ring network, or through an IBM 3174 controller or 3745/372X communications processor. This feature enables people to use a single IBM Token-Ring network for both PC-to-host and PC-to-server traffic and provides greater throughput when accessing the host.

Additional Token-Ring support comes through a feature called *source-level routing*. This technique enables VINES servers or clients to communicate across IBM Token-Ring bridges to remote VINES servers, so users gain flexibility in configuring

Token-Ring networks. Another feature, Token-Ring bridge emulation, puts the bridge function inside the server and eliminates the need for dedicated PCs operating as Token-Ring bridges; however, this places some added load on the server's processor.

Overall, Banyan's VINES has lost out to Windows NT. NetWare and Windows NT provide faster throughput than VINES file servers for PCs running typical applications, and NT servers are much more flexible than VINES.

Microsoft's Networking Strategy: Networking Everywhere

A psychologist coined the term "Aha! Phenomenon" to describe what takes place when developments click together and you see things from a new perspective. Microsoft's plan for networking is a set of developments that should set your "Aha! Phenomenon" in motion. The primary insight you'll discover is that networking is now everywhere in Microsoft's products, and nothing in the computing world will ever be the same. Microsoft started this trend in late 1992 by introducing a product called Windows for Workgroups. Windows for Workgroups was an advanced version of Windows that included both client and server software in every package. In the same time frame, a product called LAN Manager was supposed to carry the high-end server role for Microsoft. Windows for Workgroups and LAN Manager both had their ups and downs, but they became the root stock for the successful integration of networking into the lower-level versions of Windows and Windows NT. Now networking is part of everything, and other companies that make network operating systems, including Novell, must adapt, evolve, or die. Figure 9.7 shows how easy it is to connect to a networked drive.

Starting with Windows 95, Microsoft's Windows comes with peer-to-peer networking built in. With this product, any Windows PC can be a server or a client for any other Windows or DOS PC.

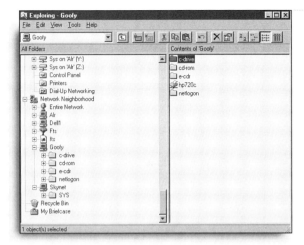

FIGURE 9.7

The Network Neighborhood icon in the various versions of Windows shows you the available network resources and enables you to click on your selection.

No matter how much or how little you like Microsoft, you can't dispute the importance and popularity of Windows. In May 1992 Microsoft's monthly shipments of Windows began to surpass those of DOS, and the curve of Windows use shoots practically straight up. Windows comes bundled with, and usually installed on, all the best-selling brands of PCs. Practically all new software development for PCs is being done under Windows.

Improving Windows Networking

Microsoft continues to improve the networking built into the Windows 95/98 family. Aside from the invisible aspects of file and printer sharing, the network component of Windows that many people use daily is dial-up networking, or *Remote Access Services* (RAS). The RAS client enables you to connect to the Internet, another RAS server, Novell's NetWare Connect, or almost any remote-access server on the market. The folks at Microsoft know that RAS is a powerful marketing tool and have added several new features to RAS with Windows 98. The most important new features include *Point to Point Tunneling Protocol* (PPTP), *Multilink PPP* (MP), a powerful scripting language, and a RAS server.

SEE ALSO

➤ *Topics like PPP and PPTP are handled in more detail in Chapter 12, starting on page 309.*

In a nutshell, PPTP enables you to use the Internet to establish your own private network. PPTP works by encapsulating other protocols, such as IPX and even NetBEUI, into an IP packet that is sent across the Internet. This keeps your data secure and enables you to use the existing pipelines that the Internet provides. For example, you could set up a private network between two networks in different cities and pay only for each city's connection to an Internet service provider.

The only drawback is that you must connect to a remote access server that works with PPTP. Fortunately, several popular products work with PPTP, including the Shiva LANRover, RAS, and Total Control Hub.

The MP enables you to aggregate or combine multiple ISDN or analog modem connections to increase your connection to the server. For example, with the MP feature, you can use two 28.8Kbps analog modems to establish a 57.6Kbps connection to the Internet. MP also enables you to combine ISDN channels to connect at speeds of 128Kbps or faster. As with PPTP, MP works only if the server you are connecting to supports it, and most of them do. PPTP and MP capabilities are in both Windows NT 4.x0 and Windows 98.

The scripting utility in Windows 98 enables you to automate connection tasks, such as sending a username and password. You can also write more detailed scripts for automatically sending and receiving files and launching applications. The scripting tool is useful for users who need to connect to online services.

The RAS server in Windows 98 enables remote PCs to dial in to your desktop and access files. Note that unlike the RAS server that comes with NT, the RAS initially shipped with Windows 98 does not work with PPTP and MP connections.

Windows NT

Windows NT (New Technology) is a separate branch of the Windows family. Windows NT has full multithreaded and multitasking capabilities that Windows lacks. This means the computer can do several tasks, including communications, at one time without faltering. The Windows NT server package also delivers better security than Windows. Both Windows and Windows NT make extensive use of 32-bit operations to quickly move data that's inside the computer.

The single biggest advantage of Windows NT is the increased speed gained from Microsoft's *NT File System* (NTFS), which is a departure from the original *File Allocation Table* (FAT)-based system developed for floppy disks more than ten years ago. At that time, hard disks for PCs were rare. In the early 1980s, their increasing popularity necessitated patches to DOS that did not manage large amounts of data efficiently. Like NetWare, Windows NT can handle gigabyte-size files and heavy traffic loads.

Developers can use the WIN32 System Developer's Kit to write applications for both Windows and Windows NT. The SDK enables developers to create a single program that will run on both Windows 95/98 and Windows NT. Under Windows 95 and 98, these products can use a 32-bit flat memory model that enables developers to move data in bigger and more efficient blocks and take advantage of the 32-bit registers in Pentium processors.

One unique attribute of Windows NT is designed to appeal to government and corporate users by providing data security meeting the U.S. government's C2 rating. But this architecture means Windows NT must maintain total control and cannot allow applications to take shortcuts by communicating directly with the hardware. This consideration also limits the compatibility of any application or driver that is not written according to specific guidelines.

Windows NT can use symmetrical multiprocessing—that is, it can allocate tasks to two or more CPUs simultaneously—on hardware from NCR and other companies, and it includes TCP/IP network drivers.

The biggest drawback of Windows NT for large corporate installations has been its lack of an enterprisewide naming service. Interestingly, both Novell and Microsoft are working to plug this hole in Windows NT. The *Distributed File System* (DFS) from NT 4 has been updated and incorporated into

Windows NT has wide support

One of the smartest things Microsoft did with Windows NT was to help a variety of hardware companies create versions of Windows NT for their own processors and systems. Therefore, you can find companies such as Digital, Tandem, and IBM offering Windows NT for their specialized systems. The existence of widespread support for Windows NT also increases the comfort level that network and corporate managers have with it.

Windows NT feels like home

The big advantage of Windows NT is that it is so familiar. Neophyte network managers aren't as intimidated by Windows NT as they are by NetWare because they've used Windows. This familiarity has motivated many vendors to develop a wide variety of utility and service programs, such as Internet routers and firewalls, for Windows NT.

Microsoft's new Active Directory. Active Directory is a multi-level enterprisewide naming service similar to Novell's NDS and actually inspired by the same manager who led the development of Banyan's StreetTalk. Using Windows NT 5's new management console, *Microsoft Management Console* (MMC), you can browse the directory and see network resources such as file servers and disk volumes, much as you can using Novell's NDS browser and NDS. Simultaneously, Novell has extended NDS to Windows NT. If you decide to use NDS on your network, you can add software to the Windows NT servers that integrates them into Novell's system.

Windows Features

Microsoft made a smart move by bundling network communications software for Novell's IPX protocol into all versions of Windows. The IPX protocol and ODI drivers are options you can load either during installation or at a later time. As the screen in Figure 9.8 shows, under Windows you can simultaneously log in to other Windows PCs and to NetWare servers.

FIGURE 9.8

Through this utility program, you can map a drive letter, such as I:, to a NetWare resource such as the SYS subdirectory on a server named "A1r."

In effect, present users of NetWare can add the functions of Windows networking without losing the dedicated NetWare features. You can have both the shared links between applications offered by Windows networking and the elaborate server management, communications, and routing features of the higher-powered NetWare server software at the same time. Some users on the network can elect to make disk drives, shared printers, or CD-ROM drives available through Windows while everyone continues to use the dedicated server for primary file operations.

If you don't want to contribute or use shared drives under Windows, you don't have to. But if you want to take advantage of available resources, they simply appear as more disk drive letters or LPT ports. The drag-and-drop file transfer feature is also available on all networked and local drives.

If invisible and ubiquitous networking is your goal, you have to provide nearly automatic installation. The Windows networking software has the unique capability to recognize and automatically load drivers for nearly 200 makes and models of LAN adapters. If the adapter can be totally configured by software, as many products from Intel, 3-Com, Madge, SMC, and other vendors can, the software takes care of everything. If the adapter has jumpers or switches, the software asks you to confirm the default settings or enter new ones. You only get truly automatic and seamless network installations in PCs equipped with fully programmable or on-the-motherboard LAN adapters, but the software gives you hints about IRQ and memory address combinations even for hardware-detectable adapters.

If anything, Microsoft might have made it a little too easy to stop sharing a subdirectory, drive, or printer. Although warnings caution you if other PCs are attached to a shared drive, with a few mouse clicks you can prevent someone from saving a file.

If you elect to load NetWare, you use the standard NetWare Map utility to select the resources that show up on NetWare servers. Of course, you have to avoid disk drive letters already used or potentially used by Windows for shared drives.

Administrative Resources

Windows NT includes several administrative utilities that help users access shared resources and help the administrator regulate users. These menus conform to IBM's Systems Application Architecture, which means they are highly graphic; thus, many people find it easier to work their way through them with a mouse than with a keyboard. You can control all the resources and make all the connections in a network using the menus, but in case you like to use batch files to control things, Windows NT has a command language, too.

The early popularity of IBM's now-defunct PC LAN networking software and of the related MS-Net products marketed by other companies led to the industry's adoption of the MS-Net command language. This language contains commands such as Net Share, which makes a resource available, and Net Use, which links a workstation to the available resource. It also includes a concept called *Sharenames*. A Sharename is a handy way to refer to a resource. For example, it enables you to share files by calling them Accounts rather than SERVER1\D:\DBMS\ACCNTG\PAYABLE\ JUNE, or something similar. Although most of the time you establish links between the server and clients using graphical tools, you can, if you want, use a command-language syntax with Windows NT.

Windows NT's centralized management features make administering large networks much easier. Network managers can logically group a set of servers as one domain and administer the domain as a single server; thus, managers can change users' rights, passwords, and time restrictions for all servers at once rather than for each server individually. Managers can also safely delegate certain types of management tasks, such as disk backup or print-queue management. Additionally, a complete set of security utilities gives managers fine control over end-user access to the system. Through the Remote Administration facility, network managers can do all these things from any Windows workstation.

SEE ALSO

➤ *You'll find more information on system management in Chapter 16, starting on page 399.*

Other management tools include a network auditing facility, network statistics and error logging, and automatic event scheduling.

- The network auditing facility enables managers to monitor and use any network resource.

- Windows NT logs error messages and network performance statistics that may be useful in fine-tuning the server. It includes a self-tuning memory-management facility like the one in NetWare. This artificially intelligent feature dynamically reallocates memory buffers, enabling the server to give the fastest possible response.

- Performing certain tasks at a specific time each day or month can be time-consuming and monotonous. This is where auto-scheduling comes in. This feature can send messages and run programs at preset intervals, freeing the administrator for more thought-intensive tasks.

Windows NT supports diskless workstations better than NetWare does. Unlike NetWare, Windows NT enables each computer to have its own AUTOEXEC.BAT file, which gives system administrators more flexibility for configuring the users on the network. In addition, each user can have a unique logon batch file. Conversely, NetWare's logon scripts offer more functionality than normal DOS batch files.

Auto-reconnect is a great convenience for users. If the network goes down, the auto-reconnect feature establishes the network connection when the server comes back up. As long as a workstation wasn't expecting something from the server at the moment of failure, its user won't know the server has been down. This feature saves people the effort of logging on again. In many cases, application programs don't even know the server was down.

Windows NT now offers built-in fault tolerance, including drive duplexing, disk mirroring, and a new file-replication system. These features match any offering on the market. File replication enables administrators to automatically duplicate specified files across servers at predefined intervals. NTFS is similar to NetWare's HotFix: It manages bad disk space and reroutes the data to other sectors.

Windows NT protects the server from power failures with an *uninterruptable power supply* (UPS). The program communicates with the UPS through a standard RS-232 serial port. When the power goes out, the UPS signals Windows NT, which in turn sends a warning to everyone on the LAN. If the battery drops below 10 percent remaining life before power is restored, the server is shut down safely.

Windows NT does an excellent job of handling shared printers through the Print Manager. Microsoft's system designers obviously learned from some of the problems people had experienced with shared printing under early versions of MS-Net. Windows NT print-job-management capabilities include standard functions such as prioritizing and managing jobs in the print queue. You can also control form feeds and set the system to hunt for available printers for certain kinds of jobs. In addition, Windows NT includes a PostScript despooler that makes it easy to use networked printers for desktop publishing. The Print Manager does not let anyone without the proper security level modify a print job.

Another interesting sharing feature enables serial devices like modems, scanners, and printers to be pooled and shared across the LAN. Thus, these serial devices can be addressed by an application program as if they were attached to a local serial port.

You can administer a Windows NT server from the server itself or from any workstation running NT on the network. If your network has more than one Windows NT server, you can create a separate NT management session for each server on the management workstation.

Windows NT has good capabilities for monitoring and troubleshooting network operations. A display screen called Net Statistics reports data such as the number of I/O actions, active sessions, and network errors, and even the average response time. Windows NT sends automatic messages to the administrator when certain problems arise, such as a malfunctioning printer or an excessive number of bad password attempts. A feature called the Alerter can forward alert messages to another user on the network.

The network administrator also has several tracking and recording tools. The Audit Trail service keeps track of who has used server resources and what kinds of actions they've taken. You can set up the audit log to record when users open files and access I/O ports. A real-time report on the active sessions that is available to the administrator shows who is connected to the server, how long the connection has been up, and how long the connection has been idle. To disconnect a user or free up resources, an administrator can force a session to close.

Digital and AT&T

I can't discuss serious network operating systems without describing the approaches taken by two important companies: Digital Equipment Corp. and AT&T. Digital has introduced or sponsored many networking concepts, most notably Ethernet.

AT&T and its spinoff, Lucent Technologies, don't have a big share of the LAN software market, but many important architectures and products, including UNIX, have come from its laboratories, and it is a leader in the design of the basic components for LAN and WAN hardware. Lucent provides a wide range of services and is an important integrator and installer of complete network solutions.

Digital's Networking History

Digital Equipment Corp. got its start in the 1950s in an old textile mill in Maynard, Massachusetts. Founder and CEO Kenneth Olsen saw a need for computers that could do things other than the accounting and payroll functions prevalent at the time. Olsen had a vision of computers that would be affordable to engineers and scientists and would not require a sterile environment to operate.

From its first minicomputer, the PDP-1, to its present-day VAX series of superminis, Digital has come a long way. The PDP-1, announced in 1959, was the first of its kind. It came with an unheard-of innovation, a CRT integrated into the console. The system was housed in a cabinet about the size of a refrigerator but required only normal office power and air conditioning.

The VAX 11/780 computer was introduced in October 1977 and was Digital's attempt to compete with the king of the hill—IBM. The idea was to provide a more powerful computer that would give current Digital users a way to migrate upward without junking their existing investment in software and peripherals. The VAX 11/780 offered a "compatibility" mode in which software written for the PDP-11 series of minicomputers would run without modification. It also contained a compatible bus structure that would accommodate existing peripherals.

In May 1980 Digital made another significant announcement: Along with Xerox and Intel, it introduced the plans for Ethernet to the world. Ethernet provides a fast and economical way to connect computers in offices and across campuses. This capability let Digital set its sights squarely on becoming the largest computer company ever.

Along with the release of the first VAX computer, Digital also came out with its Virtual Memory System, or VMS. This operating system was written to take full advantage of the VAX hardware's 32-bit architecture. The VAX 11/780 with VMS was a true multitasking/multiuser, hardware/software system.

When it introduced the VAX 11/780, Digital also announced a networking product called DECnet, which became the basis of all Digital networks. DECnet is a network architecture implemented primarily in software that enables multiple computers to link by using any of several kinds of connections and to share resources such as large disks and printers.

The original DECnet was designed for parallel interfaces and was intended to connect computers located within 20 to 30 feet of each other. Serial interfaces were available for longer distances, but they were much slower than the parallel connections. With Digital's announcement of its Ethernet plans in 1980, DECnet took on new significance: The DECnet protocol layers fit nicely over the Ethernet cable and signaling scheme. Today, DECnet over Ethernet cabling is still installed in many locations. Digital's customers represent a huge base of Ethernet connections, which they use to link minicomputers and PCs in integrated networks.

Digital recognizes that integrated multivendor systems are the rule today. In mid-1989, it began selling a full line of completely IBM-compatible PCs. Perhaps more importantly, the present system architecture has room for many non-Digital products. Technical support people from Digital have been to Novell's schools and can help you install NetWare, Novell's LAN operating system, on a VAX. The folks from Digital now know many ways to integrate PCs and VAX computers and to link networks of these computers to IBM mainframes.

Digital and UNIX

The people at Digital Equipment Corp. once had very ambivalent feelings toward UNIX. Throughout the 1970s and much of the 1980s, a lot of Digital's hardware ran versions of AT&T's UNIX operating system rather than Digital's competing VMS. Now, seeking a more flexible stance, the people at Digital offer an implementation of UNIX, Ultrix, for their hardware. In mid-1991, Digital released a version of Microsoft's LAN Manager called Pathworks for Ultrix, and now Digital fully supports Windows NT.

Digital also includes support for electronic mail programs, including the Simple Message Transport Protocol and Digital's VAXmail. The client package also has TCP/IP capabilities, so applications and utilities using TCP/IP will work across the network to Ultrix software that also includes TCP/IP.

As some of the strongest proponents of Microsoft Windows, Digital's people believe in graphical user interfaces. Their Pathworks for DOS package includes a VT-320 terminal emulator designed to run under Windows. They have a version of the X Windows System called PC DEC Windows, which enables a person using a PC to execute and display an Ultrix DECwindows application in one window and a VMS DECwindows application in another.

People with networks of Digital's computers are likely to continue expanding the use of Digital's products while simultaneously linking them to other networking systems. Pathworks for Ultrix provides an excellent way to link PCs to Digital's RISC and VAX hardware.

UNIX Networking

UNIX is a multitasking operating system that enjoys widespread popularity. On one end of the spectrum, UNIX runs on high-powered desktop computers called graphic workstations, used for computer-aided design work. By contrast, many organizations use UNIX running on a computer with a stripped-down

PC as a very low-cost way to provide multiuser accounting and database services. Low-cost terminals connect to the computer running UNIX and run special UNIX application software in the shared processor.

These high- and low-level activities in the UNIX market leave a lot of room in the middle, which will probably be occupied by UNIX computers acting as file, print, and communications servers for networks of PCs.

The history of UNIX involves both Digital and AT&T. For many years AT&T was the only company that could sell long-distance telephone service and high-speed communications circuits in the United States. Starting in the 1960s, the switches and control units AT&T used to deliver these services became computerized. As AT&T's engineers and computer scientists worked with the telephone switching systems, they determined that a program-development environment would make their efforts more productive. That's how the UNIX operating system was born.

Initially, AT&T turned to companies such as Digital Equipment Corp. for computer hardware. The UNIX operating system was written for one of Digital's early machines, the DEC PDP-7. The initial work on UNIX was done in 1969 and 1970, primarily by Dennis Ritchie and Ken Thompson at AT&T Bell Labs. In 1973, the UNIX system was completely rewritten using the newly developed C programming language. AT&T made the operating system available at no cost to colleges and universities because the Federal Communications Commission prohibited them from selling computer products. This gave UNIX a strong technical base, and computer scientists' early exposure to UNIX has certainly contributed to its large and growing market.

Improvements to AT&T's UNIX made at the University of California at Berkeley brought network support, support for many peripherals, and software-development tools. Specifically, the *Berkeley Standard Distribution* (BSD) version of UNIX added an implementation of the TCP/IP protocols. In UNIX System V, Release 3.0, AT&T added networking capabilities and a high-level multitasking feature called Streams.

The increasing momentum of the UNIX bandwagon has convinced many companies to offer application software that can run on a larger UNIX-based minicomputer system as well as on DOS-based PCs. One example is the Informix database package, which enables you to create data tables on a terminal through the minicomputer's multiuser operating system and update them from a PC. Common file areas can be created that look like DOS files to the PC and like UNIX-type files to terminals attached to the host. This feature provides a means of creating a true distributed database system.

Similarly, there are several ways to turn a computer running UNIX into a server for a network of PCs. An early favorite was a program called *Network File System* (NFS), first offered by Sun Microsystems. NFS gives client PCs running a program called PC NFS simultaneous multiple access to data files stored on a computer using the UNIX filing system. Many companies marketing UNIX products license NFS from Sun. AT&T included a similar program called *Remote File Service* (RFS) in AT&T UNIX System V, Release 3 and later releases, but RFS has never gained the acceptance of NFS for PC networking.

In 1993, AT&T sold its proprietary interests in UNIX to a division of Novell. Novell then entered its "lost in the desert" period when leadership, product development, and particularly product marketing were all lacking. The company eventually sold its interest in the original UNIX to the *Santa Cruz Operation* (SCO), but by that time the leadership of the UNIX community had migrated to Sun Microsystems.

The major problem with UNIX continues to be that there are so many versions of it. SunSoft's Solaris, IBM's AIX, Hewlett-Packard's UX, Digital's UNIX, and SCO Open Server all loudly compete for attention. Berkeley Software Design, Inc., doesn't market as much as the others but sells an excellent operating system. But the biggest market share, at least in Internet operations, goes to a more-or-less shareware operating system package called Linux. It's difficult to build a cadre of product developers, re-sellers, or supporters when loyalties are divided so many ways.

Generally, Windows NT has advantages at the workgroup level, where most users use computers with Intel processors. Yet for high-power, enterprise-level servers, UNIX has at least a perceived edge over NT because it provides better scalability, availability, and systems management functions. Needless to say, Microsoft is determinedly nibbling away at that edge. Many system designers choose UNIX-based computer systems for line-of-business applications that use Oracle databases.

Liking Linux

UNIX mixes, too!

Generally, the comments earlier in the chapter about the capability to mix operating systems across the LAN apply to UNIX, too. UNIX servers often have special roles in business applications. A blend of NetWare servers for file and print, Windows NT servers for communications, and UNIX servers for database applications actually makes sense, but only if you have a good network administrator or a good value-added reseller to support you.

Linux, a UNIX operating system, is a multiuser system that offers full preemptive multitasking features. Linux is available as a shareware product and as a shareware-plus-paid-support product. In other words, you can start using it for nothing, but if you want upgrades and special drivers, you have to pay something.

Linux supports all the important UNIX tools, protocols, and applications, including TCP/IP and popular editors and email clients. It's an excellent networking tool, and it's a good choice for your networked Internet or intranet activities. Because Linux is covered by the Free Software Foundation's Public License, the authors are required to make its source code available for free. Commercial Linux versions, from companies such as Redhat Software and Caldera Inc., come on CD-ROM and include development tools, program libraries, network management, very good web servers, and other Internet-related features that are well worth the still modest price.

By itself, Linux is tough to use. If you've lived with UNIX for years, you'll like Linux, but mere mortals need help. There is a graphical user system called the X Window System for Linux. The X Window Project Consortium includes IBM, DEC, MIT, and other computing leaders. The version of X Windows that comes with Linux is called XFree86.

X Windows separates the base system and the windowing system. The base X server runs the software that provides the graphical user interface. The actual objects you see on the X desktop, including everything from icons to toolbars to buttons to menus, come from a program called a *window manager*. The most popular window manager is called fvwm. Other window managers include mwm (the Motif manager) and olwm (Sun Microsystems' Open Look interface), but fvwm has captured a large share of the market.

You find more hardware compatibility problems with UNIX in general than you do with either Windows or NetWare. You find a smaller selection of LAN adapters and, in particular, video adapters that run under any particular brand of UNIX.

Sun Microsystems has relied on its own hardware for a long time. However, the company would be silly to ignore all the hardware that is based on Intel chips. Sun's Solaris Server is an excellent operating system offering complete file and print services for Windows, Macintosh, and NetWare clients. Solaris is an excellent common ground for applications and basic services.

Generally, Linux and Solaris are each an excellent basis for networked applications ranging from web servers to database engines. The entry cost for Linux is low, but don't forget to count the cost for either a UNIX-experienced technician or someone with a lot of determination, time, and energy.

It's lin-iks

I didn't make up these UNIX names, such as fvwm. They have their roots in the exquisitely arcane command and utility names concocted by university students in the early days of UNIX. By the way, Linux is pronounced as if it's spelled lin-iks. Pronouncing it "line-uks" marks you as truly unknowing.

Choosing Server Hardware

Throughout this chapter, I've provided information on the amount of processing power and memory needed to run the various network operating systems. Several companies, including Compaq Computer Corp. and Dell, market a class of computers designed specifically to act as file servers. These machines typically have room for many hard disks and ports to connect printers and plotters. The newest feature of these specialized servers is their capability to make multiple CPUs available to the network operating system. These "super servers" typically carry a significantly higher price tag than machines with slightly more humble, but still very substantial, capabilities.

SEE ALSO

➤ *There is good information on LAN adapters for servers and features such as I2O in "Intelligent I/O," page 84.*

Very few organizations need super servers today. A properly configured computer with a Pentium processor operating at 133MHz or better can act as a file and print server for 100 to 200 client PCs running typical office applications. I recommend splitting the job of servicing client PCs between several servers rather than putting all your processing power in one cabinet. The separate-PC approach has some significant advantages in terms of system reliability and performance. In my opinion, the best approach is to build your network modularly. Use separate computers acting as servers to deliver the capacity and throughput you need where you need it. Modern networking software products make it easier than it used to be to manage separate servers, and the advantages of reliability and scalability inherent in a modular approach are considerable.

It's easy to tick off the elements of a good multipurpose server: the biggest and fastest hard disk system you can afford, a fast data bus, four to six usable expansion slots, enough RAM for the size of the drive and the number of users, and a sufficiently powerful CPU. The most important element is a fast hard disk drive. Modern disk-caching software can overcome the negative impact of a slow drive on subsequent requests for the same or related data, but common functions such as loading application programs from the server ask for the data only once, and they get the best service from a fast hard disk drive.

Obtaining good support for the hardware is another key element in the successful operation of a network. The leading hardware companies offer at least a one-year warranty on parts and labor for their systems. Consider buying from companies that provide on-site support for your server.

SEE ALSO

➤ *Chapter 8 contains more information on the specific types and functions of servers in the section "Types of Servers," page 175.*

RAIDs and SLEDs

When discussing serious server hardware, the contention is between advocates of *redundant arrays of inexpensive disks* (RAIDs) and *single large expensive drives* (SLEDs). Arrays combine multiple drives into one unit that can move data into storage in a parallel bit stream, provide varying degrees of added reliability depending on the number of drives and the sophistication of the controller, and achieve highly efficient read and write actions. However, single large drives are fast, very reliable, and getting less expensive every day. To provide a high degree of reliability through redundancy, it is possible to mirror large hard-disk drives within the same server or even in separate servers.

RAID Systems

RAID technology was first described in 1987 by Patterson, Gibson, and Katz of the University of California at Berkeley. In the most basic sense, RAID is a very flexible solution that enables you to add lots of disk capacity to your server without any performance loss. It also provides fault tolerance. Since its introduction, RAID has become very popular. Some form of it is used in almost every server in medium-to-large networks.

RAID relies on a series of configurations, called *levels*, to determine how the drives connect together and how your data is protected. Although everyone in the industry agrees on six RAID levels (0 to 5), many vendors invent their own levels, such as 7, 10, and 35. Eventually these new RAID levels may become mainstream. Today, though, most network administrators stick with the most common RAID levels: 0, 1, 3, and 5.

- *RAID level 0* is a misnomer because it doesn't provide any redundancy. RAID level 0 simply stripes, or spans, your data across all the drives in your RAID system. You may already be familiar with RAID level 0 if you have ever used NetWare or Windows NT to span a volume across two or more drives.

  Striping or spanning is useful if you want to add disk capacity to your server without adding a new volume name. RAID level 0 is also fast. But, if one drive fails in the RAID array, the entire system goes down.

- *RAID level 1* provides a strong level of redundancy. Level 1 uses disk mirroring to make a full copy of your data on a second drive. If one drive fails, the second one takes over, and the end user never knows the difference. However, if corrupt data is written to one drive, it is also copied to the mirrored drive.

The advantage of RAID level 1 is that it gives immediate access to data if a drive fails. The disadvantage is primarily financial. Most network administrators can't afford to mirror all their disk space, especially if it reaches into the hundreds-of-gigabytes range. Standard disk mirroring requires two times the number of drives, and three-way mirroring requires three times the number of drives. Even with the cost of hard disks dropping, mirroring is feasible only for the most important data, and even this level of protection can be foiled.

- *RAID level 3* introduces a concept known as *parity*, or error-correcting information, to provide redundancy for your disk subsystem. Level 3 dedicates a single drive in the array to act as the parity drive. Information is striped across the remaining drives, usually one byte at a time. The parity drive keeps track of all the information on the striped drive and can re-create that information if a drive fails. In other words, RAID level 1 relies on redundancy. But RAID level 3 introduces the capability to re-create data. If the parity drive fails, though, you must replace it quickly because it means you have lost your redundancy. Level 3 is somewhat expensive because it requires you to dedicate an entire drive to parity. Because it writes data in bytes, level 3 is especially good for applications that send and receive large chunks of data, such as graphics and multimedia.

- *RAID level 5* doesn't use a single drive for parity but instead stripes the parity information across all the drives in the array. RAID 5 is the most redundant of the striping levels, because if a single drive fails, all the parity information on the other drives can work together to rebuild it.

Unlike level 3, level 5 writes data to the drive at the block level and is better suited for multiple small transactions. RAID level 5 is great for most networks, which tend to send data such as email, word processing documents, spreadsheets, and database information across the LAN. RAID level 5 is also fairly inexpensive because you don't have to dedicate an entire drive to parity information.

Nothing can protect against every contingency, but RAID is a smart investment.

SLED Alternatives

To add confusion to the issue of RAIDs versus SLEDs, you may think you have an array when you actually have a single large drive team instead. If you elect to configure an array so that each drive can independently seek, you forfeit the reliability of the array but gain faster responses to read requests. You can also set up several SLEDs to perform split disk seeks. Because disk systems can receive a four-to-one, or better, ratio of read-to-write requests from typical PC applications, anything you can do to improve the servicing of read requests directly improves network performance. Many companies, including Compaq, Dell, and IBM, offer disk arrays. It's also relatively simple to add an array through a SCSI adapter and cable.

As a tip, if you have an active database file that exceeds 100MB, you can often improve performance by using the capability of an operating system such as NetWare to span several drives as a single volume. Several small, fast drives can respond separately and quickly to read and write requests on the same very large file.

Cache Much?

The subject of disk controllers with built-in caching is another area of confusion and contention in the server world. Modern server software does an excellent job of caching both reads and writes. There aren't many technical or practical reasons to pay more for a caching controller that simply caches the data that comes from or goes to the cache in RAM. The main theoretical advantage of a caching controller is that it is on the disk-drive side of the data bus; if the bus is a bottleneck, a caching controller can help.

Slots and Watts

As soon as the drive and disk cache are providing fast access to stored data, it's important to avoid a bottleneck where the network meets the server. Because a single modern networked PC can pump data onto the cable at a rate exceeding 4Mb per second, it doesn't take many active nodes to saturate the media-access control system of Ethernet or Token-Ring. The best way to avoid cable saturation is to split the network and use multiple LAN adapters in the node that is the center of traffic—that is, the server.

NetWare and Windows NT can route data between four active LAN adapters in the server, so the PC acting as the server needs plenty of expansion slots. Considering the potential need for four LAN adapters, a communications adapter, an internal modem for trouble calls, and perhaps a separate adapter for a file backup device, it isn't unreasonable to ask for six free expansion slots in a fully functional PC that you intend to use as a server. On a high-performance server, at least four of those slots should be PCI.

In addition to the slots, you need a power supply that can deliver the current needed (particularly on the +5 volt line) and that has enough connectors for the storage devices you want to install. A server should have a power supply rated for at least 300 watts, and supplies of more than 400 watts are available. In addition to the amount of power, you might also need to know how many connectors for peripherals such as CD-ROM drives and tape drives each power supply has.

Finally, even the best PC power supply can't run your server if no power is coming from the wall socket or if the main AC lines are subject to voltage surges and sags. You should equip every computer acting as a server with an uninterruptable power supply. All the operating systems I've described in this chapter have the capability to exchange signals with a UPS and gracefully shut down before the UPS runs out of battery power.

As a practical estimate, four Ethernet LAN adapters can deliver an aggregate of up to 30Mb per second of data to a server. Each adapter has to unload fast and get back to the busy job of servicing the cable, so the ideal server needs an internal bus that can move data in 32-bit-wide blocks and yield control to bus-mastering adapters.

How Much RAM Is Enough?

How much RAM is enough? The answer depends on what you want to do.

As a rule of thumb, a NetWare file server with a 2GB hard disk drive needs a minimum of about 16MB of RAM. By comparison, Microsoft's Windows NT needs a minimum of 32MB, but 64MB is better. Network operating systems allocate all remaining memory for disk caching. The amount of memory actually used for caching depends on how people and applications use the server. In real NetWare or Windows NT installations with large hard disk drives, you should plan on installing 32–64MB of RAM as a minimum.

The picture changes dramatically if you want to run a program in the server like the ORACLE Server for NetWare or Microsoft's SQL Server. The ORACLE program, a NetWare Loadable Module, needs 9MB of RAM to run, but the maximum amount of memory it requires depends on how the applications are written and on the number of active users. The SQL Server can address up to 28MB of RAM. Obviously, even a 32MB system can be restrictive if you have many active users on a database server. Applications such as web servers and firewalls have their own relatively large RAM requirements.

CPU Power

Finally, after clearing out all other potential bottlenecks, such as hard disk drives and LAN adapter cards, the server workload falls on the CPU. The functions of a file server operating system don't put much of a burden on the file server's CPU, but when you run a few server-based applications such as network management programs, UPS monitors, and communications programs, it doesn't take long to overload the CPU. Although there are many servers efficiently running 80486 processors under heavy loads, the modest cost of buying a Pentium with at least a 133MHz clock speed is a good investment in future growth.

Error Correction Code Memory

In many ads for computers sold as servers, you'll see a line about *error correction code* (ECC) memory. You probably assumed that ECC was good, but did you ever ask why? Did you ever ask how you use this ECC stuff or how much it costs?

On the bottom line, ECC memory detects and corrects data errors on the fly and tells you about them later. The detection part is easy, but the correction part is tricky because it involves deriving the correct data from the incorrect data through the interpretation of a stored checksum. In 486-based computers, ECC probably costs more than it is worth, but in Pentium-based machines it is a tremendous, and practically free, benefit. And— just so we don't sound biased toward Intel—ECC also provides value in computers powered by several models of processors from Digital, IBM, PowerPC, and Sun.

As more Windows NT and NetWare servers use Pentium, Alpha, PowerPC, and SPARC processors, the presence of ECC becomes an important factor in deciding which server to buy. ECC is particularly valuable when it is linked to a management system for reporting errors, but it's useful in any computer that uses large blocks of RAM and a fast processor.

How Big Is the Problem?

Vendors of computer systems agree that the types of data storage errors caught and corrected by ECC—those in memory and on tape—are not the biggest source of malfunctions in servers. Hard disk drives top every vendor's list of server problem spots, followed by power and cabling problems that are often external to the computer. However, many memory problems can be caught and fixed on the fly, so it is useful to include some circuitry to handle them. In servers, the major causes of memory problems stem from different timing characteristics within memory chips. Differences measured in less than a microsecond can lead to broken bytes.

I asked experts in computer architecture and design at Compaq, Distributed Processing Technology, Digital Equipment Corporation, Hewlett-Packard, and IBM about the scope of the problems ECC can solve. In general, they responded that the more you use the computer, the more you need ECC. The industry typically offers DRAM (Dynamic Random Access Memory) chips that experience one error in a million hours of operation. According to Don Smelser, a consulting computer hardware engineer at Digital Equipment Corporation, "If you have a PC with 4MB of memory, that's about 100,000 operational hours between failures. If you run it only twelve hours a day, you could go for decades and never have an error. Now let's say you have a server with 256MB of memory, representing perhaps 500 DRAM chips, that runs 24 hours a day. That's an error every three months or so."

Of course, average failure rates operate over a normal curve, and your computer may be anything but normal. Every flip of a bit is a new spin of the wheel. If you are betting your business on your server, you want the intervals between downtime measured in terms of years, not months. If you need reliability at this level, you need ECC. So far, so good. But now, what is it?

Old and New Error Checking Systems

ECC is rooted in mathematics—polynomials to be exact. As each data word (typically an 8-bit or longer block) passes into storage, a processor mathematically derives an ECC code from the contents of the data word and tacks the code onto the end of the word. Then, when the word is read from storage, the processor checks the appended ECC code against a newly computed sum. The type of processor and the ECC formula it uses depend on whether the storage is on tape, on disk, in cache, or in RAM.

If you're familiar with parity checking you'll recognize the concept of computing a sum from the data word to catch an error. Parity checking systems typically count the number of ones in a byte and then tack on one bit, either a zero or a one, so that a count of the total number of ones, including the parity bit, comes out even. Anyone who has set up a serial port knows that odd parity (adding a bit so that the sum of all the ones is odd) is also an option in those systems. In communications software and in other products such as tape backup software, a parity error generates a retry. Computer memory has no way to retry the access, so the parity detector is connected to the processor's *nonmaskable interrupt* (NMI) pin, which halts the processor. An incorrect parity sum in memory generates the dreaded NMI error, and everything stops. By the way, there are many other causes of NMI errors; not all are memory errors.

Of course halting the system because there's an indication of a parity error isn't acceptable when businesses run their critical applications from network servers. Also, the relatively simple parity system can be fooled by an error that changes, for example, a one to a zero and a zero to a one in the same byte because the parity comes out the same even though the data word is wrong.

ECC computations address both of these problems. First, they find and correct errors without halting the system. Second, the ECC processor does binary addition of specific bits in the data word and repeats the process using different bit positions, as shown in Figure 9.9. The resulting ECC addition to the data word is longer than a single parity bit (the exact length depends upon the length of the data word and the size of the errors you want to catch), and it contains much more information. The ECC processor computes the ECC value of a newly read data word and loads both the new and the old ECC value stored with the word into a few gates that make up a device called a *comparator*. The comparator should come up with a match, represented by a string of zeros. If the result contains any ones, the positions of the ones tell the processor which segment of the word to correct and how to correct it.

The capability to both detect and correct errors in data words makes ECC a valuable feature in a server used in networks that are critical to a company's business. Price-conscious shoppers never get ECC because the extra chips and processors it requires raise the cost of the systems. But value-conscious buyers, particularly those evaluating systems with high-end processors in the Pentium, Alpha, and PowerPC class, should keep ECC high on their checklists. Selecting ECC up-front could prevent a costly processor halt in the years to come.

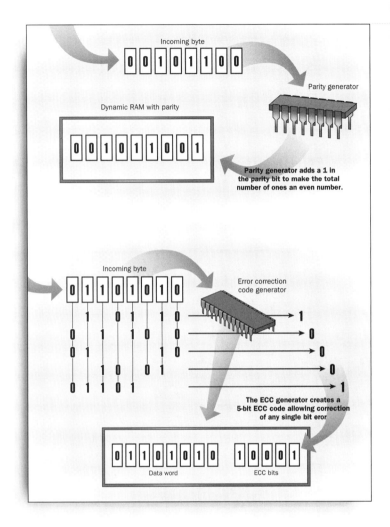

FIGURE 9.9
ECC's error checking is far more sophisicated than simple parity checking.

Summing Up Servers

So what is a server? Obviously, it is a computer that has enough of the major elements such as expansion slots, RAM, storage, and watts to meet your needs. Your definition of "enough" depends completely on how you want to use the network. If you have 2 to 20 PCs storing files on a server, you'll get enough of everything from a PC in the $2,000 to $4,000 price range—depending primarily on what hard disk subsystem you want. But if you need gigabytes of storage with backup subsystems on a database server, expect to spend as much as $8,000 and up for your hardware.

LAN Portals

In the first chapter I introduced the idea that information is the raw material, inventory, and processed product of many modern organizations. Computer networks are the production line, the warehouse, and even the retail point of sale for the information products generated by many businesses. These networks act as local, regional, and even international distribution systems for modern commerce. They form a commercial infrastructure for businesses, countries, and multinational economies.

If local area networks are like the in-house production lines of manufacturing plants, then computer networks using leased telephone lines, *metropolitan-area networks* (MANs), and *wide-area networks* (WANs) are the equivalent of the various roadways, ranging from driveways and access roads to expressways. Other analogies from the transportation infrastructure, such as toll roads and private roadways, can be applied to the communications infrastructure too. Like those transportation roadways, MANs, WANs, and private networks have different capacities, economies, and even regulatory problems.

Some organizations own their own rail lines and private roadways, while others use public and commercial transportation services. Similarly, some organizations own their MAN and WAN facilities, while others lease these specialized services from commercial suppliers. The suppliers include long-haul carriers like AT&T, Sprint, and MCI, specialized companies such as UUNET, and others such as the local telephone exchange and cable television companies.

The Internet and corporate intranets are nothing more than shopping centers, libraries, town halls, sign boards, and strip malls built next to roadways. The question of whether the shopping centers caused the road building or the road building made shopping centers possible takes you in a big circle, but at least both happened in the same time and space. The power of the Internet and the World Wide Web comes from small things like the capability to create instant and endless cross-references and the ease of putting up billboards. The technology of the Internet isn't that special. It's pure and simple networking, but the scale and utility is pretty sensational.

When managers of smokestack industries leave the control of transportation systems totally to specialists, they risk inefficiency and unpleasant surprises. Because computer communications systems are so important to the operation of many modern companies, these systems also call for the attention of high-level management. Unfortunately, well-designed networks aren't highly visible, and generally networks are cloaked in technical jargon, but they are critically important and expensive to run. Managers of organizations that rely on computer networks need a generalized understanding of these networks to supervise information-system professionals effectively. This chapter deals primarily with the portals of LAN-to-LAN internetworking— because even the Internet is a series of pipes between LANs. The next chapter describes the alternatives for LAN links. Then, following that, we'll get down to the nitty-gritty of IP networking, intranets, and Internet access.

Fat Cables

Local area networks have a wide bandwidth; they can pass millions of bits of data per second. The concept is easy to understand if you picture a LAN as a fat cable that can move a lot of data quickly. Because the signals needed to represent the 0s and 1s on a fast LAN are closely spaced, the equipment cannot tolerate signal degradation or noise in the data stream.

Unfortunately, copper cables accumulate electrical noise as they travel over longer distances, and the pulses of electricity or light representing the data bits lose their sharpness and strength as they travel through copper or fiber-optic cables. Induced noise and signal degradation are the two primary factors that limit the fat LAN cable's coverage to several kilometers under the best conditions.

Typically, longer communications links must move data more slowly because of induced noise and degraded signals. Multiplexers, repeaters, and other special equipment enable the transmission of data at high speed over long distances, but this kind of equipment is expensive, so the combination of signaling speed and distance work together to increase costs. You can buy and install your own cable to run data at 10Mbps (megabits per second) for less than $1 per foot at distances of several thousand feet. But you have to pay about $12,000 per year to lease a 1.5Mbps link from New York to San Francisco, and the equipment to interface your computers to the leased line may cost you several thousand dollars more up front.

Still, many organizations need to move a lot of data over distances greater than a few thousand feet, so managers need to learn the techniques of extending and linking LANs. The techniques you use to link LAN segments depend upon the distance and speed you need, the network communications protocols you use, and your business philosophy regarding leasing versus owning facilities.

Extending and Segmenting the Network

The first category of products I'll describe—repeaters, bridges, and routers—enables you to extend and segment your network's fat, or high-speed cable. They act as portals on the LAN. They open to an outside world and, depending on their sophistication and design, regulate the flow of traffic and even break down or bundle up loads in appropriate form for the highway.

You can easily understand why you might want to extend the LAN cable; you might need to span 40 stories in an office building or two miles of a college campus. Devices called *repeaters* enable you to extend your network cable to several thousand feet by retiming and regenerating packets or frames so they can continue over such distances.

The reasons for segmenting a LAN may be less clear. Workers in all organizations interact in groups based on common interests. Most communications follow specific paths and take place within these workgroups; however, people also need ways to communicate between workgroups. The simplest scheme is to put all the people in all the workgroups on the same cable and let them communicate and interact as business requires. But this arrangement quickly consumes the cable's resources. It doesn't make sense to clog the LAN cable serving the accounting department with all the traffic generated in the engineering department simply because engineers sometimes need to share budget programs with accountants. Organizations with busy networks need a device that can link workgroup LANs while exercising discretion over which traffic passes between the various workgroups.

The first kind of discretionary portal device is known as a *bridge*. Unlike a repeater, which passes all data between cable segments, a bridge links cable systems while passing only certain specified traffic between them. A *router* is a more complex linking device that has a greater capability to examine and direct the traffic it carries. Figure 10.1 shows the basic concept behind each of these three LAN-linking devices.

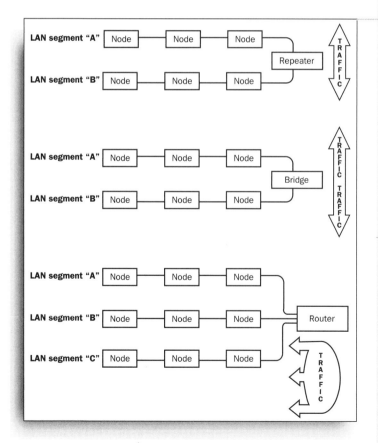

FIGURE 10.1

In simple terms, a repeater moves all traffic in both directions between LAN segments without discrimination. Its main function is to extend the network. A bridge only passes traffic specifically addressed to a node on the other side. A bridge extends and segments the network. A router reads more detailed addressing information and makes decisions based on current information it has about the network.

Each of these devices functions at a different layer of the ISO's OSI model. The repeater looks only at packets or frames generated by adapters operating at the Physical layer. Bridges use the specific station addresses generated by firmware in the Data-link layer. Routers use information provided by software following specific Network layer protocols. As Table 10.1 shows, a fourth type of device, the LAN gateway, operates at higher layers of the OSI model to translate data formats and open sessions between application programs. LAN gateways are described in more depth in Chapter 14, "Telephone Modems."

TABLE 10.1   Linking devices in the network layers

Layer	Functions	Linking Device
7 Application	Applications move files, emulate terminals, and generate other traffic.	Gateway
6 Presentation	Programs format data and convert characters.	Gateway
5 Session	Programs negotiate and establish connections between modes.	Gateway
4 Transport	Programs ensure end-to-end delivery.	None
3 Network	Programs route packets across multiple interLAN links.	Router
2 Data-link	Firmware transfers packets or frames.	Bridge
1 Physical	Firmware sequences packets or frames for transmission.	Repeater

Although the names, concepts, and uses of bridges and routers are relatively simple, selecting one of these products involves consideration of enough options to keep a committee busy for a long time. I'm going to give you the classic descriptions of these devices and a number of explanations and examples. But companies keep bringing out products that go beyond the classic descriptions. The concepts are clear, but their practical application can make the classic definitions fuzzy in real installations.

Repeaters

The differences among the products you can use to extend your local area network cable are sometimes subtle, but they are all based on the concept of the multiple layers of communications protocols. Typically people refer to the ISO's OSI model, but Digital Equipment Corp. and IBM have communications models and network equipment that don't exactly fit the OSI model.

A repeater is typically a humble little box, about the size of a modem, that connects two segments of network cable, retimes and regenerates the digital signals on the cable, and sends them on their way again. These functions are typical of those described in the Physical layer of the OSI model, so it's common to say that a repeater is a Physical layer device.

The actions of a repeater enable you to increase the geographical coverage of your LAN. For example, the Ethernet standard specifies that a signal may travel over a maximum cable length of 500 meters for a single segment, but with repeaters interconnecting five segments, a signal on an Ethernet network could reach a maximum distance of 2,500 meters of cable. The slightly different IEEE 802.3 standard allows for up to four repeaters connecting five cable segments, to a maximum of 3,000 meters (1.8 miles), with a total cumulative delay of 950 nanoseconds introduced by the transmission media.

Often, repeaters interconnect cable segments that use different physical media such as thin Ethernet coaxial cables and fiber-optic cables. Similarly, repeaters for Token-Ring networks can translate between electrical signals on shielded or unshielded twisted-pair wiring and light pulses on fiber-optic cabling. In modern installations you can often find repeater modules housed in the central wiring hubs of 10BASE-T and fiber-optic cable systems. But repeaters don't provide a feature called *traffic isolation*. They dutifully send every bit of data appearing on either cable segment through to the other side, even if the data consists of malformed packets from a malfunctioning Ethernet adapter or packets not destined for use off the local LAN segment.

Modern repeaters have features such as light-emitting diodes to

Hubs are repeaters, but...

Technically, wiring hubs are repeaters. However, when you mention the word "repeater" to most networking folks, they think of a 2-port device designed specifically to extend a network cable beyond normal distances and not a multi-port hub.

Switches are bridges, but...

Yes, it's true: switches are technically bridges. But, just as people don't think of hubs as repeaters, they also don't think of switches when they think of bridges. They typically think of a bridge as a connection device between one slow WAN port and one fast LAN port. It's also true that bridges are less popular than routers today, and bridging services for specific protocols typically show up in routers. However, if you have an all-IPX LAN or perhaps a LAN blending AppleTalk and IPX, you can save money and a lot of work by using simple bridges rather than routers. If you want Internet access on an IPX LAN, consider using an IPX-to-IP gateway, described later in this chapter, rather than installing IP and routers on the whole network.

Bridges don't know subnetworks

A bridge does its work by consulting a table it builds of Ethernet or Token-Ring node MAC addresses. MAC addresses are assigned to adapters at the factory, so the distribution of addresses on the LAN is totally random. The bridge simply notes which station addresses appear on which connection and, after the address table is built, handles traffic accordingly. This approach doesn't require any action from the network administrator. In contrast, routers want nodes grouped according to an addressing scheme such as IP. That's a lot more work initially, but the scheme offers more elegant traffic handling.

display network operation, and they are available in a variety of physical configurations including stand-alone or rack-mount. Costs are generally a few hundred dollars, but you pay more for fiber optic cable connections.

Bridges

Repeaters always link elements of a local area network; bridges can link local cable segments, but can also link the fat cable of a LAN to networks of thinner media such as leased telephone lines. The two main purposes of a bridge are to extend the network and to segment traffic. Like repeaters, bridges can send packets and frames between various types of media. But unlike repeaters, bridges forward traffic from one cable system only if it is addressed to devices on the other cable system; in this way, they limit the nonessential traffic on both systems. A bridge reads the destination address (typically the address programmed into the destination node's Ethernet adapter) of the network packet and determines whether the address is on the same segment of network cable as the originating station. If the destination station is on the other side of the bridge, the bridge sequences the packet into the traffic on that cable segment.

The functions of bridges are associated with the *media-access control* (MAC) sublayer of the Data-link layer (layer 2) in the OSI model. For example, bridges can read the station address of an Ethernet packet or of a Token-Ring frame to determine the destination of the message, but they cannot look deeper inside the packet or frame to read NetBIOS or TCP/IP addresses. Thus, they're often called MAC-layer bridges.

As Figure 10.2 illustrates, bridges are categorized as *local* or *remote*. Local bridges link fat cable segments on a local network. Remote bridges link fat local cables to thin long-distance cables to connect physically separated networks. The important point is that you need only one local bridge to link two physically close cable segments, but you need two remote bridges to link two cable segments over a long interconnecting span of media.

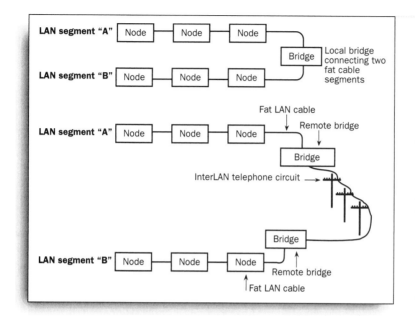

FIGURE 10.2

A local bridge directly connects two LAN segments. Remote bridges operate in pairs, connecting the LAN cable segments using an intermediary interLAN link such as a leased telephone line.

How Bridges Learn

As with many aspects of internetworking, the operation of bridges is reasonably simple to generalize: Bridges only relay messages from one cable destined for a station on the other cable. But if you ask, "How does it know?" you uncover a pretty complex subject.

The simplest bridges use a routing table, created by the network manager and contained in software, to decide whether to pass or hold data messages. But people move their computers and change their offices and jobs frequently. Making someone update the routing table in the network bridges every time a computer is moved down the hall creates too much administrative over-head, so bridges typically have software with a learning algo-rithm.

Bridges learn about the stations on the network by sending out a broadcast message that creates a reply from all stations. The bridge listens to all traffic on the attached cable segments and checks the source addresses of all packets and the locations of the sending stations. The routing software builds a table of the stations and cable segments and then decides when to forward messages and when to drop them.

The job of building an address table is relatively simple when a bridge links only two segments of a network, but it becomes much more complex as networks grow. For example, consider the case of a company with networks on the first, third, and fifth floors of a building. These networks can be connected in one of two ways: in a *cascade* or through a *backbone*. If the segments are cascaded, the first-floor LAN is bridged to the third-floor LAN, and the third-floor LAN is bridged to the fifth-floor LAN. The cascaded bridge topology loads the intermediate LAN segment with traffic destined for the third LAN segment. The cascade arrangement requires only two bridges, but today it isn't considered a good design. A good conservative design uses a backbone to isolate LAN segments.

The backbone bridge topology links bridges dedicated to the various LAN segments through a separate backbone cable. The backbone cable is often a fiber-optic link, which allows for relatively great distances. Figure 10.3 illustrates the cascade and bridge topologies. A less common *star topology*, not shown in the diagram, uses a single multiport bridge to link multiple cables and is typically used with lighter traffic loads.

It's possible, either through error, through a desire for redundancy, or through independent connections to some common point like a mainframe computer, for the first- and fifth-floor LAN segments to become connected by a redundant path. In theory, the bridges can then recirculate packets and an overload condition called a *broadcast storm* may result. Network designers have developed several intelligent algorithms to detect multiple paths and shut them down.

Logical Algorithms for Bridges

Software operating in each bridge determines the most efficient path between network segments and adopts it as the primary route. If the primary route fails, the bridges use the next-best alternative path. This redundancy is particularly valuable when long-distance circuits that are subject to interruption connect network segments.

Bridges provide good info!

Bridges can be important elements in network-management systems. Because bridges read the destination and source of every packet, they can collect statistics and report on and control traffic conditions exceeding specific criteria.

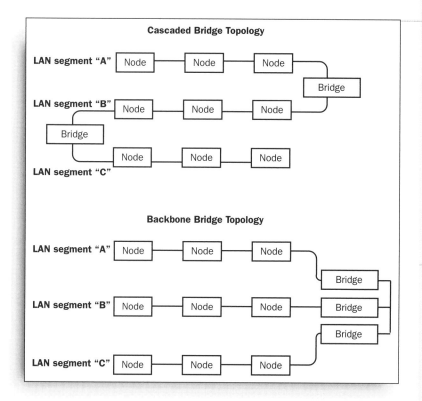

FIGURE 10.3

The cascade bridge topology requires fewer routers and less connecting equipment than the backbone bridge topology. But the cascade topology must move all data from LAN segment A through segment B to get to segment C and isn't considered a good design. The backbone topology reduces the overall traffic load because it can discriminate between types of traffic going to various segments. It isolates LAN segments, improving efficiency and reliability.

The software in all the bridges on the LAN must follow one of several logical algorithms to decide which path to use. The IEEE 802.1 Network Management Committee has adopted a standard for a technique called the *Spanning Tree Algorithm* that was originally developed by Digital Equipment Corp. and Vitalink Communications Corp. Products with this algorithm are used primarily by local bridges; the technique isn't economical for use over leased telephone circuits connecting remote bridges. The logic in the Spanning Tree Algorithm enables you to link two LAN spans with two bridges for reliability, while avoiding the problems of multiple packets being broadcast by both bridges.

A category of products called *remote bridges* uses different techniques called *source routing* and *protocol-transparent routing*. Source routing is a technique used mostly on Token-Ring networks and backed primarily by IBM. In the source-routing system, the source node sends test frames over the network until they arrive at the destination station. Each network bridge along the way adds its own address. The destination station sends the test frames it receives back to the source station. Finally, the source station uses that information to determine the fastest path and sends the entire message over that path.

The source-routing technique ensures that messages take the fastest path and balances traffic on long-distance links, but it generates network traffic and requires a lot of processing at the nodes.

The protocol-transparent routing technique puts the workload on the bridges. Each bridge maintains a map of the entire network and forwards each packet to the correct network segment. If the bridge hasn't yet learned the location of the destination station, it forwards the packet to all the LAN segments until the destination replies. This is known as *forward-if-not-local* logic. Routers use the opposite, *forward-only-if-known-remote* logic.

The IEEE 802.1 Network Management Committee and the 802.5 Token-Ring Committee have developed ways to use both source routing and protocol-transparent routing on the same network.

No Translation Services

Like repeaters, bridges can only link similar networks, but bridges and repeaters concentrate on different similarities. A bridge doesn't deal with the Physical layer hardware and drivers handled by repeaters. You can use a repeater to link one Ethernet network to another Ethernet network, despite the type of cabling they use, because the Ethernet packets and the media-access control protocols are the same. But bridges can link LAN segments using completely different LAN adapters and media-access protocols as long as the networks use the same communications protocol; for instance, NetBIOS to NetBIOS, IPX to IPX, or DECnet to DECnet.

The State of Bridges Today

You don't hear as much about bridges today as you do about routers, but a lot of bridging goes on. Bridges can run inside PCs or they can be specialized dedicated boxes. In fact, when you put several LAN adapters inside a server running Windows or NetWare, you typically are bridging the LAN segments attached to each adapter.

Many companies, including Bay Networks and 3-Com Corporation, offer bridges that have their own processors and don't need a PC. These devices, often about the size of a modem, vary widely in price depending upon the connections and protocols involved. There is also an active market in wireless bridges for building-to-building connections. However, the trend today is to include bridging capabilities within routers.

Routers

Just as bridges improve on the functionality of repeaters, so routers improve on bridges. Routers read the more complex network addressing information in the packet or token and may add more information to get the packet through the network. For example, a router might wrap an Ethernet packet in an "envelope" of data containing routing and transmission information for transmission through an X.25 packet-switched network. When the envelope of data comes out the other end of the X.25 network, the receiving router strips off the X.25 data, re-addresses the Ethernet packet back, and sequences it on the attached LAN segment.

Routers make very smart interconnections between the elements of complex networks. Routers can choose among redundant paths between LAN segments, and can link LAN segments using completely different data-packaging and media-access schemes. Primarily because of their complexity, however, routers move data more slowly than bridges. They also require a complex addressing scheme—typically IP—to identify networks and sub-networks.

Bridging plus routing

Slightly improved throughput is one reason why many routers retain bridging capabilities. The other reason that routers use bridging is that some protocols, such as AppleTalk, don't contain enough destination information to allow true routing. It's common to read a specification saying that a particular router routes IP, but bridges AppleTalk. That's a useful capability if you have some Macintosh computers working directly with an AppleTalk printer.

The media versus the protocol

Let's do a quick review: repeaters and bridges link identical MAC layer systems—such as Ethernet to Ethernet—but don't care a thing about higher-level protocols such as SPX/IPX or TCP/IP. Bridges are more discriminating. However, if you want to link dissimilar physical LANs, such as Ethernet to Token-Ring or ATM, you have to route because repeaters and bridges don't have MAC layer packets to work with. That means you must use a routable protocol, such as IP.

Routers work at the Network layer (layer 3) of the OSI model. Unlike bridges, routers don't know the exact location of each node. Instead, a router knows only about subnetwork addresses. It reads the information contained in each packet or frame, uses complex network addressing procedures to determine the appropriate destination, and then repackages and retransmits the data. The router doesn't care what kinds of hardware the LAN segments use, but they must run software conforming to the same Network layer protocol. Some of the products sold by vendors include routers for DECnet, IP, IPX, and XNS.

Some companies, including Cisco Systems, 3-Com, and Bay Networks, sell multiprotocol routers that enable you to combine routable protocols such as IP and DECnet while they bridge IPX and AppleTalk in the same network.

Routers aren't transparent as bridges are. They take a lot of setup and management. Typically, you won't consider dealing with the complexities of routers for segmentation until you have a LAN of 20 or more nodes. The addressing scheme used by routers enables administrators to break the network into subnetworks. This architecture can accommodate many different topologies including a highly reliable ring of leased circuits, such as the one shown in Figure 10.4. Routers receive only specifically addressed packets or frames from originating stations or from other routers. They don't read every packet or frame on every attached LAN segment as a bridge does. Because they don't pass or even handle every packet or frame, routers act as a safety barrier between network segments. Bad data packets or broadcast storms simply don't make it through the router.

Routers play a vital role in connecting LANs to the Internet, intranets, and any other outside network. When you connect to the Internet from your LAN, you are actually connecting your LAN to your Internet Service Provider's (ISP's) LAN. Further Internet connections go to the LANs of other companies or ISPs. A router is the portal between your LAN and the connection to the ISP's LAN. The router only sends the LAN traffic addressed to distant nodes across the Internet connection and, in theory, it only allows desired packets into the LAN. However, in

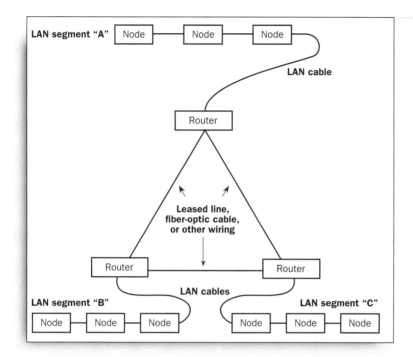

FIGURE 10.4

Routers in a large interLAN network can use the interconnecting circuits as alternative routes for traffic. If the circuit between LAN segment A and segment B breaks down, the routers can send traffic around the long way to retain connectivity.

fact routers don't discriminate well enough to defend against a determined intrusion attempt. So, a router is typically paired with a device called a *firewall* that has better blocking capabilities.

When it relays a packet between LAN segments, a router decides what path the data packet will follow by determining the number of hops between internetwork segments. Usually the router software chooses the route that requires the fewest hops. A router that always picks the shortest route typically uses a routing table a programmer has created for a specific network. This kind of device, known as a *static router*, works fine in many networking systems.

Some administrators want to give the router more options. A category of devicescalled *dynamic routers* can examine factors—such as the cost of sending traffic over specific links and the amount of traffic on specific links—and decide to send packets or frames over an alternate route. Of course, the more thinking a router does before it forwards a packet or frame, the longer it takes to get the data to its destination. The throughput you get from a local router depends upon the complexity of its routing tables and the CPU power available to run its software. The throughput of remote routers is typically limited by the speed of the media linking them together.

SEE ALSO

➤ *The details of IP addressing are in the section "The Heaven and Hell of IP," on page 317.*

➤ *For information on DECnet and other "mainframe" protocols, see Chapter 13, page 329.*

Data Compression and Routers

As I explain later in this chapter, you might pay thousands of dollars a month to lease a circuit to link LAN segments. The cost is driven by the speed at which you want to send data across the link. Therefore, it makes sense to invest in equipment at both ends of the link that can use the expensive circuit most efficiently.

Because routers strip off the LAN MAC-layer address information before they send a packet from one LAN to another, they reduce the total number of bits going across the interLAN communications link. The remote router at the receiving end restores the correct MAC-layer address back onto the packet before moving the data into its local LAN segment. Because of this action, routers send information across the interLAN circuit more efficiently than bridges.

As an example, the Ethernet MAC-layer address is 18 bytes. A request for a file sent by an application might be just a few bytes. Because most packets on a LAN of Windows-based PCs are very small, the address can constitute over 50% of many packets. Simply removing the MAC-layer address can reduce the percentage of transmitted data significantly. Additionally, router companies include compression algorithms that can compress certain kinds of data to improve throughput by as much as a factor of four. Generally, you benefit if you use routers from the same vendor across a dedicated link. Routers from different vendors can work together, but routers from the same vendor often get better compression or management because they have features beyond the minimum standards for interoperability.

Least-cost routing is important!

We'll deal with network links in more depth in the next chapter, but I want to emphasize the importance of a router feature called *least-cost routing*. Routers have the capability to know which circuits cost the least and when and to use them first. The costs of LAN-to-LAN circuits are complex, but the amounts that are spent and that can be saved are large.

RIP and OSPF

Routers use specific protocols to communicate across a LAN or WAN. The most common inter-router protocols are the *Routing Information Protocol* (RIP) and *Open Shortest Path First* (OSPF). *RIP version 1* (RIPI) is one of the oldest routing protocols and is implemented by almost every router vendor you'll encounter. RIP also works with both IPX and IP protocols, unlike OSPF, which is for IP routing only.

RIP is a distance vector routing protocol, which means it represents the routing information in terms of the cost of reaching the specified destination. For example, RIP represents circuit priorities using numbers between 1 and 15. You use this scale to establish the order of use of links. In effect, the priority listing tells the router to use specific paths, if available, before using others. You must create these rankings based on your own weighting of the speed, reliability, and cost of all available alternative connections. After you establish the priorities, this information is stored in a RIP routing table. The routing table includes information such as the IP address of the destination, the IP address of the next router in the destination path, and the cost of the route. RIPII is an enhanced version of RIP. The biggest advantage of RIPII is that it sends the subnet information in the network packet.

The biggest drawback to a RIP router is the broadcast traffic it generates. In order to keep the routing tables up to date, each router periodically transmits its entire routing table to all the other routers on the network. Although this alone is not a major detriment to network efficiency, the routers also transmit a route response packet every 30 seconds. The router uses the broadcast to see whether the other routers are communicating and to make sure nothing has changed. All this broadcasting can generate traffic on the wide area network and can even cause some routers to initiate a call on a dial-up circuit, such as ISDN, only to pass the RIP packets. Special configurations prevent this, but also prevent RIP from being passed over a WAN.

OSPF is a link state routing protocol, which means that every router on the network keeps its own database of the network layout and a table describing the adjacent routers and their connections. OSPF was designed to improve on RIP, and although it does, not all products from all router vendors work with OSPF, so you may have to stick with the RIP protocol. In the most basic sense, the OSPF routing technique works as its name implies. If you have multiple routed connections to a site, OSPF attempts to use the shortest connection to that site. If the shortest connection is down or busy, it tries the next shortest one, and so on. OSPF routers learn the shortest paths by using the "Hello Protocol" to find all the other routers on the network. Fortunately, the protocol is only sent across the link when a new router is added or changes, so you don't have unnecessary traffic. However, if your routers don't work with broadcast, and the Hello Protocol can't be sent or received, you have to manually configure the routers with the connection information.

Another difference between OSPF and RIP is that OSPF operates directly above IP, while RIP uses UDP as its transport. Another advantage of OSPF routers is that the link state information they send to their counterparts is only transmitted infrequently. Likewise, the routers only send link state and route information to the next router in the chain, not to all the routers in the network. The next router's job, in turn, is to tell its neighbor until the information is propagated throughout the network.

Besides creating less broadcast traffic, OSPF also works well with larger intranets that include WAN links. Because RIP uses only 15 numbers to represent cost, the algorithm is only designed for a maximum of 15 routes. Although that might seem like a lot, as intranets grow you might need to connect more routers together to establish a single connection.

The State of the Router Art

Routers have evolved and changed more than any other networking hardware—and they aren't done yet. From 1996-1998, router prices dropped a trailing zero while features soared. The $10,000 router of 1996 took someone skilled in an arcane programming language a full day to set up. Today's $1000 router can be a plug-n-play device—although there is plenty of room for customization. Important router features include the following:

- *Automatic configuration of ISDN ports.* Smart modern routers remove most or all the pain of establishing ISDN connections.

- *Management through a web browser.* Today's smart router is a little web server. As soon as you assign it an IP address, you can point your browser at that address and see screens of configuration information and options.

- *Blocking the trash traffic.* Some messages broadcast on the network (such as server status messages conforming to NetWare's Service Advertisement Protocol) are relevant to the users in only one location. They're legitimate broadcasts, but a smart router doesn't get routed over the WAN link. That's especially important over a dial-up ISDN that might be billed by the minute.

- *Flexible and redundant connections.* Routers should have slots for a variety of wide area networking options, including ISDN, Switched 56, X.25, and frame relay. A redundant connection provides a backup in case the primary connection fails.

- *Security and recognition features.* Modern routers can recognize callers using several different techniques. Authentication schemes offered by different vendors include the *Challenge Handshake Authentication Protocol* (CHAP) and the *Remote Authentication Dial-In User Service*, or RADIUS. RADIUS is a centralized network-authentication standard developed by Livingston Enterprises. The RADIUS system requires a separate server on the LAN, but it's very effective.

- *A variety of compression schemes.* Ascend and Microsoft each have excellent data compression schemes and a compression scheme known as Hi/fn, which was developed by a company known as Stac, has wide acceptance. However, unless your router is using permanently connected leased lines, you don't always know what brand of router is on the other end of the line. A good router should be able to compress data going across the line if the device on the other end has that capability.

- *Easy upgrades.* Modern routers have their instructions in *programmable read-only memory* (flash ROM). This is a real necessity for fast upgrades.

- *Quality of service features.* Routers have to implement an important set of features that provides quality of service for specific types of data. The *Resource Reservation Protocol* (RSVP) and new features in the sixth release of the Internet Protocol specification (IPv6) make quality of service real. Your router should include these capabilities.

- *IP Address translation and gateway.* A feature called *Network Address Translation* (NAT) enables you to connect an entire LAN to the Internet via a single-IP-address ISP account. This means that you can make up your own IP addresses inside the LAN while only the router conforms to the rigid Internet addressing scheme. A feature called an optional IP-to-IPX gateway (described later in the chapter) provides Internet access for IPX-based LANs.

Modern routers are jacks of many trades. They sort, package, direct, and defend. The proper selection and operation of a router is critical to the success of any widespread multiprotocol network.

Gateways

If you have to link very different kinds of networks, such as a network of IBM mainframe computers and a network of PCs, you might elect to use a device called a *gateway*. Gateways function at the high end of the OSI model; they totally repackage and sometimes even convert the data going between the two networks. Routers add addressing information to the packets or frames they move and don't change the content of the message. Gateway programs often do change the format of the message to make it conform to the application program at the receiving end.

PC-to-mainframe gateways are widely used, but the most common LAN-to-LAN gateways are those used by the electronic mail systems. These gateway programs move email messages from the format and coding of one program, sometimes through an intermediate common format, into the format of the receiving program.

Gateways also provide an interface between IPX-based LANs and the IP protocols of the Internet. IPX-to-IP gateways provide a centralized and secure way to connect IPX-based LANs to IP networks. An IPX-to-IP gateway can use a single IP address for the entire IPX network. This gateway service eliminates the configuration and maintenance headaches introduced by assigning IP addresses to all client PCs. IPX/IP gateways are easy to use and offer management features that let you control users' access privileges, so you can designate when and where your employees may roam on the Internet.

You can purchase IPX-to-IP gateways as either specialized turnkey boxes, as a function of a router, or as software packages that run in servers. IP/IPX gateways are available from Bay Networks, Cisco Systems, and other companies.

The primary benefit of these gateways is that they avoid IP addressing problems. But an equal benefit is the security they provide. An IPX-to-IP gateway simply does not allow IP traffic across the gateway barrier IPX LAN. Attacks from the IP WAN simply don't have a point of entry.

The IPX-to-IP gateways require some special software on the client side. A piece of software emulates the TCP services addressed by Internet applications such as browsers. A Microsoft specification called *Windows Sockets* or *Winsock* dictates how these interfaces work. The Winsock software routes requests from an Internet application to the gateway. If it's not already connected, the gateway dials up the ISP and sends the client's requests to the Internet. The people using the applications don't see any difference.

The WAN connection determines the load-carrying capacity of an IP/IPX gateway—up to a point. Initially, throughput is related to the amount of bandwidth between the gateway and the

ISP. These gateways particularly benefit ISDN connections. With a 128Kbps connection, one of these devices can carry the load of 2-3 dozen clients—but of course everything depends on what those clients are doing. Fortunately, you can parallel these gateway devices or dedicate one to each network segment, so you can smoothly and economically increase your IPX/IP load carrying capacity.

SEE ALSO

➤ *See Chapter 13, starting on page 329 for routers through gateways and into mainframes.*

WAITS

In a *PC Magazine* article published in the middle of 1990, I christened a new category of products called *Wide Area Information Transfer Systems* or WAITS. WAITS programs use PCs to move files economically and efficiently between LANs. They can be viewed as a type of gateway, primarily because they are applications and completely insensitive to any underlying protocols.

Automated, unattended operation is key to the WAITS concept. Typically, PCs running WAITS software contact each other and move information at scheduled times, although most give you the option of simply moving files when these PCs are ready. They usually connect over dial-up telephone lines because they don't need high data rates, but they can use any interconnecting circuits.

The XcelleNet Wide Area Network Management System, marketed by XcelleNet, is certainly the most sophisticated WAITS product. XcelleNet uses a multitasking master station to interrogate and control remote nodes running under any of several other operating systems. For really big operations, several XcelleNet master stations in the same location can coordinate their operations across the LAN.

WAITS products can solve the interLAN communications problems of many people who only need to move files between networks and don't need more sophisticated computing capabilities involving multiple layers of protocols. These products are inexpensive to install and invisible to the people who benefit from receiving the latest updated data with very little fuss or recurring expense.

Summary

In this chapter we've dealt with the portals of LAN-to-LAN systems. But the portals have no function without connecting circuits. In the next chapter we'll look at the many extensive and often confusing connection options.

Fast WAN Links

The Linking Media

The previous chapter described the logic and devices used to move frames and packets between LAN segments—the LAN portals. If the LAN segments are within a few thousand feet, bridges and routers can use fiber-optic cable to link them together. But many organizations need to link LANs separated by thousands of miles. In these cases, the speed must downshift and considerations such as cost become very important.

Selecting a method of linking LANs is all about costs. Remember that it is difficult and expensive to send data quickly over long distances. In all the decisions you make regarding linked LANs, you have to balance throughput against distance and cost. Because the cost of the internetwork segment is typically the driving factor in the equation, it's smart to pay more for network hardware that makes the best use of the long-distance media.

The internetwork media available to link LAN segments includes telephone lines, satellite networks, microwave radio, fiber-optic networks, and perhaps cable television coaxial systems. These devices connect to your LANs through portal devices—typically routers.

SEE ALSO

➤ For more about routers and other LAN portals, see the section "Extending and Segmenting the Network" on page 250.

Telephone Line Systems

Stated a little simplistically, there are two types of telephone lines: those going to the public dial network (dial-up lines) and those leased for long-term dedicated use. When you dial a long distance telephone number, the computers in the telephone switches route your call and set up a temporary dedicated connection. Leased lines provide a full-time dedicated connection that does not pass through the system of switches.

As usual, real products blur the simple definitions by offering, for example, circuits in the dial-up network that virtually appear to be dedicated lines. These *virtual private networks* (VPNs), offered by AT&T, MCI, Sprint, and other long distance companies, enable the telephone carriers to make optimal use of the switched telephone system while providing users with service equivalent to full-time leased lines.

You can use standard dial-up telephone lines to link LANs. Using the latest high-speed modems meeting the V.pcm signaling standard and V.42bis data-compression standard, you can move electronic mail messages at a respectable throughput of well over 80Kbps (kilobits per second) or better over a standard dial-up telephone line. Another type of dial-up connection, ISDN, can move data at 128Kbps.

Competition in the long distance telephone industry within the United States has driven down the price of dialed long distance service, so making dialed calls to link LANs on a temporary basis is a practical alternative for many organizations. In the United States, it is often practical and economical to dial up a link between two routers or bridges for several hours a day to update databases or application programs on LANs. But in many other countries, calling long distance is still expensive, and in some cases the circuits can't pass high-speed data effectively.

SEE ALSO

➤ *The section "Modem Basics" on page 350 has more information on dial-up modems.*

Leasing Lines

Selling leased telephone lines has been an important business for the long distance telephone industry since the 1930s, but in the United States the process became more complex after the Bell Telephone System's Divestiture and the Federal Communications Commission's Computer II decision. Computer II and the Divestiture decree opened the industry to competition. The result is that in many parts of the United States competition for connectivity is at every level. You can typically choose from among 2-4 wireless telephone carriers, a dozen long distance carriers, and even two or more local exchange carriers.

In the United States, a person who wants to lease a single full-period telephone line across state boundaries might have to coordinate the efforts of three different companies to get the long distance circuit, the "tail" circuit from the long distance vendor's equipment to the customer's premises, and the necessary terminating equipment. Even with this need for coordination, it is often possible to install a leased line within a few days, or a few weeks at the most, after the companies get their service orders. In some parts of the country, however, the engineering studies required for these installations can lead to delays of many weeks.

People in countries outside the United States can often get the complete long distance service package from one vendor—typically a government monopoly—but in many cases they have to wait months for the service to appear.

Leased lines for digital data transmission are available in various grades of service. The grade of service relates to how fast you want to move data over the line. Leased data lines are specially configured or "conditioned" for data transmission in several speed ranges.

In the United States, companies selling long distance services are often called *interexchange carriers* because their circuits carry service between the major telephone exchanges. The companies that sell the service between buildings and homes and the exchanges are called the *local carriers*. In countries outside North America, there is often no differentiation between these carriers. AT&T is a regulated interexchange carrier whose rates or "tariffs" are subject to the supervision of the Federal Communications Commission. Other long distance carriers, such as MCI and Sprint, do not have to file a schedule of public tariffs, but their rates are almost always competitive with AT&T's published tariff rates.

T1 Service

You can lease point-to-point circuits certified for data rates ranging from 2,500 bits per second (bps) to over 45 megabits per second (Mbps). The basic unit of measure for data service, used both by engineers to specify service and by salespeople to price service, is the *T1 channel*. A T1 channel can carry 1.544 megabits of data per second, and conforms to certain technical characteristics for signaling and termination of the circuits.

You can establish your own circuits following the T1 channel specifications to move data across a campus or within a large building, but network designers and managers typically think of T1 as a service traversing hundreds or thousands of miles over leased long distance facilities. AT&T and other carriers charge about $5,000 per month for a dedicated T1 circuit spanning 1,000 miles. A T1 line only 500 miles long still costs about $3,000 a month, but T1 service over 2,000 miles costs about $8,000, or somewhat less than twice the price of the 1,000-mile service. Generally, the formula is cost = base monthly rate + (monthly charge per mile × the number of miles).

If your organization needs even faster service, it isn't cheap. What is termed a *T3 link*, providing 45Mbps service, costs over $50,000 per month on a 1,000-mile path.

In addition to the leased-line charge, you may also pay several hundred dollars a month for the connection from the interexchange carrier to your facilities and for the termination equipment.

You can use the entire capacity of a T1 circuit to link two LAN segments, but the terminating equipment typically gives you the option of breaking the circuit into several parts. For planning purposes, a channel for one voice conversation takes 64Kbps (kilobits per second). So if you lease a T1 circuit between different branches of your organization, you could, for example, use 768Kb of the 1.544Mb capacity to carry 12 voice connections between the PBX telephone systems at each end and still have another 768Kbps available to link the LAN segments through a router or bridge at each end.

As a footnote: Because AT&T encodes certain supervisory information in the data stream, that company has typically provided 56Kbps service to its customers although it is evolving to 64Kbps service. You should also know that equipment is available from several companies to compress a voice conversation into a 32Kbps or even 16Kbps channel, making the space on the T1 link even more economical for voice as well as data transmission. Even 8Kbps voice channels are available, but the voice quality is clearly inferior to that of the faster 16Kbps or 32Kbps services, and few organizations find this voice compression option desirable.

As the demands of your organization change, even on an hourly basis, you can adjust the amount of T1 capacity you allocate to voice and data traffic. There are some problems with shifting between voice and data because the two services have different error and delay tolerances, but many organizations find it efficient to balance their use of T1 channels between voice and data.

Fractional T1

A packaging scheme called *fractional T1* makes it economical to lease circuits for data-communications service slower than the full 1.544Mbps T1 channel. The basic rate of service for fractional T1 is a channel speed of 64Kbps. Interexchange carriers commonly sell fractional T1 service at rates of 384, 512, and 768Kbps. A 1,000-mile 512Kbps service costs about $2,000 per month, plus the fees for terminating circuits and equipment.

Reliability

Redundancy provides reliability. Experienced network administrators know that long distance links are the major cause of internetwork outages. Routers, bridges, and other network devices seldom fail, but the leased long distance circuits linking them often do. You typically don't have to pay the fee for the circuit during the malfunction, but this is little consolation for people who can't move the data that is the lifeblood of their business.

If you buy a couple of full or fractional T1 circuits from different interexchange carriers, your network routers can automatically use whatever links are available in the event of a failure. Some routers even use the dial-up telephone lines to back up the leased lines. The data transmission rate over the remaining or alternative route might be slower than the primary route, but slow internetwork connectivity is far better than no connectivity.

T1 = Primary Rate ISDN

I'll get into ISDN a little later in the chapter, but it's worth noting here that a service called Primary Rate ISDN provides about the same service as a T1, but it's often offered at lower tariffs. The reason has more to do with arcane tariff practices than technology, but today many people buy a "pri" (rhymes with "eye") rather than a classic T1 service.

Connecting to High-Speed Channels

When you connect a remote bridge or router to a high-speed T1 or fractional T1 communications channel, an adapter board in the bridge or router changes the network traffic into a stream of data meeting one of several standards for connection and signaling. The output might follow the EIA RS-232, RS-449, or CCITT V.35 standards. Somehow, you need to connect that output to a device called a *multiplexer* that interfaces with the high-speed communications line.

The job of a multiplexer is to subdivide the available single fast communications channel into multiple channels of voice and slower data communications. Companies such as Network Equipment Technologies, Newbridge Networks, StrataCom, Timeplex, and Verilink Corp. provide multiplexer equipment. The Micom Marathon 5K shown in Figure 11.1 combines the capabilities of a multiplexer with other LAN connectivity products in one box.

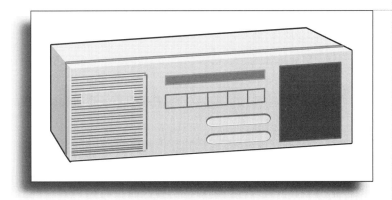

FIGURE 11.1

The Marathon 5K from Micom Communications Corp. is an example of a product that defies typical definitions. It is a high-quality statistical multiplexer that can mix voice, data, and fax signals on a single fractional T1 circuit. You can insert optional bridge or router modules into the same chassis to make it a router/multiplexer combination.

You may hear people talk about a *channel service unit* (CSU), the side of the equipment connected to the communications channel, and a *data service unit* (DSU), the side of the equipment connected to the bridge or router. As Figure 11.2 shows, the DSU converts all the incoming data into the proper format for transmission over the T1 or fractional T1 circuit, while the CSU terminates the high-speed circuit and keeps the signals in phase and properly timed. Some bridge products contain a DSU, so all you need is an inexpensive CSU.

FIGURE 11.2

This diagram shows a complex and a simple termination for a T1 or fractional T1 circuit. The top diagram shows a system mixing voice and LAN data on the same T1 link through the services of a multiplexer. The bottom diagram shows a router with a built-in DSU connecting directly to the CSU used to terminate the T1 or fractional T1 circuit.

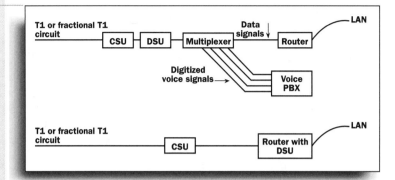

The cost of typical DSU/CSU equipment starts at about $800 and climbs to many times that amount for sophisticated multiplexers with numerous network-management and reporting functions.

It is important to remember a few facts about T1 circuits:

- T1 is a way of packaging service in increments of 1.544Mbps.

- T1 service is provided by many kinds of companies, but primarily by the long distance or "interexchange" carriers.

- Fractional T1 delivers service in 64Kbps increments.

ISDN

Leased lines are great for high-volume full-time connections. But a dialed-up connection scheme called ISDN is an excellent alternative to or substitute for full-time connections. The *Integrated Services Digital Network* (ISDN) uses standard telephone wires to move data down the hall, across town, or across the country. ISDN is more than just circuits; the ISDN specification also covers what kinds of signaling travel over those circuits.

ISDN has been a decade in arriving. The local exchange carriers that had to install ISDN faced unforeseen problems in training their installers, buying new software for their network switches, and finding the correct tariff schedules. ISDN is still not available in many cities in the US, although it has wide availability in Japan and Western Europe.

The availability and pricing of ISDN varies from town to town. Your local telephone company is your source for ISDN service, so you have to know the status of the service in every town where you or your company operates.

ISDN Technology

This international Integrated Services Digital Network program sets standards for the complete digitization of the telephone systems in Western Europe, Japan, and North America. The plan calls for converting the present analog signaling circuits and systems to digital circuits and systems circulating 0s and 1s rather than analog voice frequencies.

This isn't as radical as it sounds. Modern phone systems are already mostly digital. When you press the keys on a touch-tone phone, you program a sophisticated computer in the telephone company's central office and tell it to connect your phone to the desired destination. Your local telephone company's central office computer communicates digitally with computers from other companies, both nationally and internationally, to move your voice.

Digital computer-based telephone switches are the rule in most communities in North America. Many organizations have *Private Branch Exchanges* (PBX)—business telephone systems that convert analog voice signals to digital 0s and 1s right in the telephone. Many of us use all-digital phone systems already.

Because you've come so far in this book, you should be quick to ask, "If digital switches are so common, why do I have to use a modem to change my PC's digital signals to analog tones for the telephone lines?" The answer is that modern telephone systems are only modern up to the dial central office. From the dial central office to homes and businesses, they drop back to technology that Alexander Graham Bell would recognize. This local wiring, the "local loop," was designed for analog telephones and signals. Special line cards in the dial central office's telephone switch translate between the digital signals in the switch and the analog signals in the phone line. You must convert your PC's new-technology digital signals into old-technology audio tones with a modem so they can be converted back to digital signals, in a different form, at the switch.

SEE ALSO

➤ *This isn't unlike the parallel-to-serial conversion described for LAN adapters in all of Chapter 5, "Working with Network Adaptors," starting on page 75.*

Advertisements from long distance telephone carriers aside, most of the noise you hear on a telephone call comes from the analog local loops on each end. Make these local loops digital and the noise disappears. Of course, digital square waves get clipped and distorted, but you can fix digital signal problems by regenerating the signals at intermediate stops. Analog noise is additive throughout the system.

Using digital local loops means you need digital phones at each end. Does that mean you have to throw out your existing phones to use ISDN? No, it's not necessary. Today, most ISDN adapters provide a connection called a *Plain Old Telephone Service* (POTS) port to integrate an old-style analog phone into ISDN service. Even on a digital local loop, your PC still needs a modem-like adapter to use ISDN. The unique signaling scheme and voltage levels of ISDN create the need for a digital-to-digital ISDN *terminal adapter* (TA) in each PC.

When you make the local loops digital, you eliminate the bandwidth problems that necessitate sophisticated and high-priced computer-controlled modems to move data at anything over 300bps. Using data compression and sophisticated signaling techniques, modern modems advertise throughputs of over 56KBps over dial-up lines, but not on every line and not with all data. If you make the local loop digital, you can easily send over 140Kbps over the telephone lines.

Sometimes it's easy to make the local loops digital, and sometimes it's very hard. If the premise (home or office) is within 6 to 10 miles of the dial central office, as it would be in most cities

Modems are old stuff

It's strange, but true. The new modem you bought to connect to your computer takes the digital data stream from your computer's serial port and converts it to analog tones. Those tones go over the analog line to the telephone company's central office somewhere in your neighborhood. At the central office, the tones are converted back to digital and they traverse the entire country or world digitally. At the destination, perhaps for only a few hundred feet, they go back to analog form and connect to another modem. Among other things, ISDN's main task is simply to convert the last mile of the connection to digital signaling.

AC power for the phone

When your phone or its ISDN interface is an active digital device, it needs a source of local power. If you don't have a back-up power source for the phone, when the lights go out, so does the phone service. Buy your ISDN interface an uninterruptable power supply (UPS) or risk losing telephone service with the power service.

and towns, copper cables link the premise and the central office. Copper cables can carry high-speed data, but devices called *loading coils*, commonly installed to minimize distortion of the analog signals, make it impossible to send digital signals over the copper cables. Converting the cabling for digital signaling can be as easy as clipping off the loading coils.

For premises farther from the dial central office, engineers have used other techniques, including radio repeaters, to carry the voice signals. These repeaters don't have digital capabilities, so they don't pass ISDN, but they're expensive to replace.

For these and other reasons, ISDN grew first in the cities and in new suburban communities installing telephone systems for the first time. Because the initial market for ISDN services has come from companies in cities with an existing analog infrastructure, the availability of service and the demand for service have not grown smoothly. In many cases organizations have not been able to get ISDN service or to get accurate billing information.

Who Is Calling?

What does ISDN offer the average telephone user besides higher-quality voice calls? The answer the telephone industry loves to demonstrate is that it gives you the capability to know who is calling before you answer the phone.

Because an ISDN telephone call is digital, the phones and switches can pass a lot of information about the call. A key ISDN buzzword is ICLID or *incoming call ID*. The ICLID message goes from the calling phone's ISDN switch to the called phone. ISDN telephone sets typically have an LCD panel showing the number of the calling phone. With a small amount of internal memory augmentation and your own programming, the phone can display the calling person's name, ring differently for calls from certain people, and route incoming calls to other numbers or services based on who is calling.

The next step in the application of this technology is to route the originating number of an incoming call to a local computer, which then displays the credit record, buying history, or other

---

ISDN costs what?

Often nobody knows what ISDN service costs. Typically, it's billed like any familiar dial-up service. You pay an installation charge, a basic monthly service charge, and a charge based on the number of minutes each call is connected. But in some states there is practically no per-minute charge and in other states it varies according to time of day. Knowing the per-minute charge you'll pay is critically important in evaluating the trade-off between ISDN service and leased line service.

caller-related information before you answer the call. This technique can save valuable minutes in order-taking or other heavy call-handling situations.

Let Computers Talk

The best use of ISDN is in serving as the pipe that links LANs. These LANs can be in homes and offices, in the facilities of Internet Service Providers, and in the computer centers of information content providers. The applications that use these communications links include Internet browsers and utilities, electronic mail systems, database applications, and even humble printer sharing.

SEE ALSO

➤ *For more on the general uses of LANs and LAN options, see Chapter 2, starting on page 17.*

The designers of ISDN developed a standard dividing the available bandwidth into three data channels. Two of the channels move data at 64Kbps, although many long distance ISDN calls are actually carried at 56Kbps per channel because that is the data rate of the interexchange carriers. The third channel operates at 16Kbps and provides a path for telephones to send requests to the ISDN switch while moving data from applications at full speed on the data channels.

The D channel was designed for signaling (to indicate the line is busy, for instance), and its bandwidth is usually not available to you. However, some phone companies allow you to use the D channel as a continuous connection to the Internet. Because the D channel has low throughput, it works well for sending and receiving relatively small amounts of data at regular intervals, such as email or stock quotes. The primary advantage of such a service is that you can get small amounts of data without placing an ISDN call, which often incurs per-minute charges.

These services are illustrated in Figure 11.3.

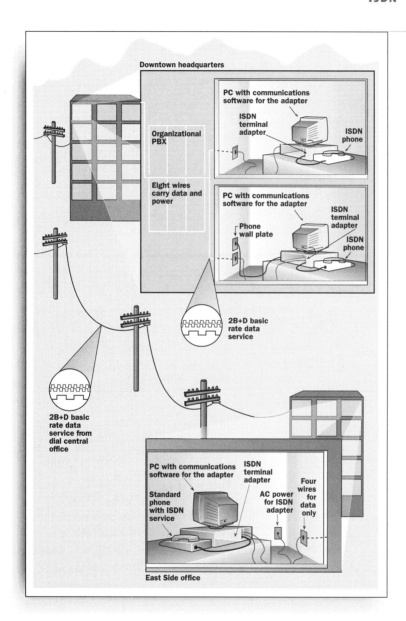

FIGURE 11.3

ISDN carries voice and data over standard telephone lines digitally. Several different rates of service, each combining 19.2Kbps and 64Kbps signaling, can link subscriber locations and the central telephone equipment. PCs with ISDN terminal adapters and routers can combine voice and data on the same desktop.

A computer looks at the ISDN line as a wide-open pipe for the transfer of data at nearly 150Kbps through compression. People who are used to reading about 10a and 100Mbps Ethernet might assume that ISDN is slow in comparison, but LAN schemes such as Ethernet and Token-Ring use sophisticated media-access protocols to control the access of each node to the cable. LAN nodes must wait, retry, repeat, and perform many overhead tasks to share the cable. These actions cut the overall LAN throughput of even the fastest computer to hundreds of kilobits per second rather than megabits.

Suddenly the ISDN pipe doesn't look so thin. You can move a lot of data quickly over a high-quality ISDN circuit because other nodes don't share or contend for its service. It's certainly faster than a dialed-up connection with even a so-called 56Kbps modem.

Companies such as Motorola and 3-Com have modem-like PC adapters for ISDN. Similarly, 3-Com, Cisco, Ascend, and many other vendors make a variety of routers for ISDN dialed-up connections.

Getting ISDN

Getting and configuring an ISDN line from your local phone company can be a frustrating experience. There are dozens of configuration options on an ISDN line, and if one of them is wrong, your line may not work with your equipment. Most ISDN devices come with ISDN line-ordering instructions in the box or with forms to fax to the phone company. Vendors and phone companies have worked to make the process simpler through *ISDN Ordering Codes* (IOC) and EZ-ISDN, which specify sets of voice and data service parameters.

Microsoft offers a service to help you order ISDN service. Point your browser at www.microsoft.com/windows/getisdn. You'll find a nice set of frequently asked questions and specifications. If you jump to the order page, click on your location, and enter your phone number, the server sends back a page with your local ISDN service providers, installation costs, monthly fees, and service options.

Pulling It Together

At this point, we've covered the portals between the LANs and the most important inter-LAN circuit alternatives: leased lines and ISDN. We have a few more connection alternatives to investigate, but let's pause and put it all together. Let's examine how a typical organization connects to remote offices and to the Internet. Use Figure 11.4 as a reference. This organization has a home office LAN with a fiber optic backbone between segments. A single multiport router is the portal between the LAN and WAN links. This device has internal CSU/DSU interfaces for the outside circuits. In this example, traffic moves between the central office and the branch office more than four hours a day, so a leased line is more economical than using ISDN.

People on the home office LAN generate packets going to the branch office LAN in several different ways. Email messages go between email servers on each LAN. Users can send files to or read files from the branch office file server. Applications at the home office can even be set to print specific reports on printers in the remote location. When any node on the home office LAN generates traffic destined for the branch office, the router picks it up and sends it across the WAN link to the branch office router. If the traffic isn't on a routable protocol, then the router box can use bridging techniques rather than routing to move the packets. Alternatively, the router can package the non-routable packets, such as AppleTalk or IPX, inside of IP and send them that way.

SEE ALSO

➤ *We package the discussion of routing protocols in Chapter 12, starting on page 309.*

The next chapter shows you how the home office network can have its own corporate web server as the basis of a corporate intranet. This intranet can extend beyond the corporation or enterprise and link to suppliers, accountants, shippers, and other business partners.

In this example, the folks in the home office can also generate traffic for the Internet. They can use browsers, file transfer programs, and many other Internet utilities. The router detects the intended destination of these packets and sends them out a link to the *Internet Service Provider* (ISP) of choice. In a real system, there would probably be a little more security at the LAN/WAN portal than you see here, but that's for the next chapter too. The link to the ISP connects to the ISP's router and that router is part of a LAN at the ISP's operating location. The ISP has special purpose web and web caching servers that respond to most of the requests for service coming from the ISP's subscribers. The ISP also has a high-speed pipe into a central point of Internet connectivity—probably an Internet *Network Access Point* (NAP).

That's how it more or less looks in the real world. Now, let's look at some other alternatives for circuit connections.

Alternative Connection Schemes

All kinds of businesses are moving in to improve data delivery speeds with the new technologies. The telephone companies that today provide data services via a two-way copper path to the home—once the only game in town—are under siege. The Telecommunications Act of 1996 opened the regional phone companies to competition even for local dial-tone service. Jumping into the mix with phone companies are cable operators and satellite services, Internet service providers, alternative local phone service providers (called *competitive access providers*—CAPs or CLECs), wireless data companies, and even utility companies offering high-speed data services. Many of these companies use technologies called digital subscriber line and cable modems.

Digital subscriber line (DSL) and cable modems are technologically very different but conceptually similar. Both provide dedicated multimegabit connections, so your service is always on, unlike ISDN or analog dial-up connections. Also unlike ISDN, these services connect from the customer premise to specialized equipment at the communications company's central office. The communications companies must build large backbone systems to further the connections. DSL is supposed to use existing copper telephone lines, but it has significant limitations.

DSL is an all-digital service, and it promises to deliver data at speeds ranging from 1.5Mbps to 8Mbps or better. You may also hear about *ADSL* (asymmetric digital subscriber line), *HDSL* (high-bit-rate digital subscriber line), *RADSL* (rate-adaptive digital subscriber line), and maybe even other variations. These signaling techniques vary, but the idea is that the link is faster in one direction than in the other. The reverse channel speeds range from 64Kbps to 1Mbps. The differences between the competing technologies don't matter much to you, because you'll probably get all the equipment and service from a local telephone company or another service provider. As Figure 11.4 shows, the providers of DSL service can integrate data and voice on their systems.

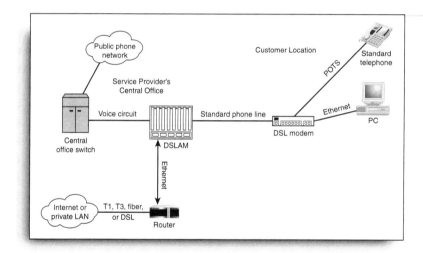

FIGURE 11.4

Because most DSL providers are voice telephone companies, they like to use a single DSL connection for both data and voice. A device called a Digital Subscriber Line Access Multiplexer (DSLAM) combines data and voice at the Central Office onto a single DSL connection.

As with cable modems, large-scale implementation of DSL requires a substantial investment in new equipment. The telephone companies have managed to put a positive spin on new DSL technologies, creating the impression that they are deeply committed to providing fast data services in the near future. But gauged against the phone companies' success in promoting ISDN as a high-speed service, the prospects for a fast DSL rollout don't look promising.

DSL has promise as a campus-wide system. It is practical for companies to buy DSL modems and use them on their own campuses or building wiring systems. Similarly, it is possible to lease copper lines from local telephone companies to use for cable modem connections stretching a little over a mile. It's beginning to look as if DSL will be more successful in businesses while cable modems will be more successful as an Internet access technology for homes.

Cable television companies and cable modem equipment vendors talk about cable modems and their claimed 27Mbps throughput. But few cable operators talk about the costs of making their systems bidirectional or routing the data onward after they've collected it. In the next five to seven years, you're much more likely to see fast cable downloads with analog telephone modem uploads than to get real two-way cable modem service. And unless you're very lucky and happen to live or work in the correct place, you won't be able to get cable modem service soon.

If you are fortunate enough to live in just the correct spot and can get cable modem or DSL service, what do you do with it? The cable modem or DSL connection is typically a LAN adapter in a PC. In their initial forms, they don't connect to a LAN wiring hub and accept data from only one MAC address. I suggest that you load a piece of software called a *proxy server* in the PC connected to the cable modem or DSL service. The proxy server pulls down previously used or requested web pages and keeps them updated on a local server. That server can provide the stored pages to clients on a locally attached LAN. This is the best technique for using a cable modem connection. Proxy servers are covered in more depth in Chapter 12.

Satellite Communications

The interexchange carriers, such as AT&T, MCI, and U.S. Sprint, use ground-based copper and fiber-optic circuits for nearly all their connections. But rather than leasing long distance circuits from the telephone carriers, many organizations, including companies such as K-Mart Corp. and Wal-Mart

Stores, use their own private satellite radio systems to carry data between their widely separated enterprises. Chrysler Corp. has one of the largest private satellite networks in the world, linking over 6,000 locations. In effect, you could create your own corporate intranet using only satellite links.

Companies such as Alascom, AT&T, Comsat World Systems, Contel ASC, and GTE Spacenet Corp. offer a wide variety of satellite services for private industry and governments, ranging from on-call emergency backup services to point-to-point data services, at rates from 19.2Kbps to multiple T1 rates.

There are two configurations for satellite systems: those that appear to move across the sky and those that don't. The largest government and commercial communications satellites are typically in a geosynchronous orbit around the earth's equator, so from the ground they appear to be stationary in the sky. But several companies are in the process of launching large constellations of satellites in near-earth orbit. These satellites move across the sky, but so many are in orbit that more than one is always in view.

Whether it is geosynchronous or in near-earth orbit, each satellite has a number of transponders that relay communications signals. A transponder takes in a weak signal broadcast from an earth station, cleans it up and amplifies it, and rebroadcasts the signal back to Earth. Because of the geosynchronous satellite's 23,300-mile (35,810-kilometer) vantage point, its rebroadcast signal can cover most of Europe, North America, or South America—depending upon the antennas used on both the satellite and ground sides of the link. The near-earth orbit satellites have a space-borne backbone network that links the satellites, but gives global coverage.

This large area of coverage is one of several potential advantages that leased satellite communications circuits have over terrestrial leased circuits. Satellite communications companies don't charge for their circuits according to distance as the terrestrial companies do. The people in the industry say that satellite circuits use "distance-insensitive" pricing, while prices for terrestrial circuits are "distance-sensitive." The satellite companies charge for access to the transponder and possibly add charges based on the amount of bandwidth, a measure of the data transmission rate you use. You should note that leased terrestrial links are typically usage-insensitive; you pay the same monthly charge for the terrestrial lines regardless of how much or how little data you move through them.

The general rule of thumb is that satellite links can't compete on a cost basis with leased terrestrial links under distances of 500 miles. At distances over 500 miles, the satellite links become increasingly competitive with leased lines.

Another advantage of satellite service for many organizations is ease of installation. You don't have to worry about the coordination between the interexchange carrier and the local carrier or the time needed to install service. For satellite communications, a *very small aperture terminal* (VSAT) with an antenna size of 1.2 to 2.8 meters can be installed on a rooftop or in a parking lot within a few hours. Obviously, such systems are also relatively portable and enable you to avoid telephone-line installation charges for temporary operating locations.

Moreover, satellite services offer reliability that terrestrial services can't match. The signal paths to and from the satellite are unaffected by all but the heaviest precipitation, and as long as your earth station is operational, natural disasters can't take out your circuits. Even the terrestrial carriers use satellite circuits to back up their copper-wire and fiber-optic links.

So if you need to link a LAN in your organization's Chicago headquarters to LANs in branch offices in London and Houston, you could equip each location with a small earth-station antenna and radio system on the roof or in the parking lot, bring a wire from the earth station into the building, connect it to the network's remote bridge or router, and let the packets or frames fly through space.

Reality is a little more complex than the concept. There are two significant drawbacks to using a satellite to link LANs: relatively slow throughput and, for geosynchronous satellites, a factor called *satellite delay*.

Typically the low-cost VSATs can transmit only at 19.2Kbps, so they are a slow link between LANs. This speed is fast enough for many kinds of applications, but some jobs need faster interLAN links. If you want faster service from a satellite, even up to multiple T1 speeds, you need a larger and more expensive antenna. The exact size of the antenna depends on the distance from the satellite's position on the equator and other factors, such as the surrounding radio-frequency environment, but T1 service typically requires a 3- to 4-meter antenna, and the installation might require special permits and planning.

Because of the distance from Earth to a geosynchronous satellite and back again, it takes 0.27 seconds for the signal to make the round trip, even at the speed of light. This satellite delay can be significant to people using certain kinds of applications over interLAN circuits. The delay of near-Earth satellites is less, but other factors such as the effectiveness of the backbone interconnections come into play. Satellite circuits are fine for automated updates performed by email systems, file transfers done by database or accounting programs, and other program-to-program tasks. They work well to push data—everything from stock quotations to program patches and updates—to a wide audience. They also work well to broadcast web pages and requested files. But if someone is entering keystrokes into a program and trying to receive immediate replies, the slow speed of typical satellite circuits and the delay imposed by the extraterrestrial signal paths probably limit the acceptability of this transmission alternative.

Because of the need to conserve the power and resources of the satellite transponder, geosynchronous satellite links typically operate in a star topology similar to the one shown in Figure 11.5. In this configuration, the transponder receives a number of incoming signals, combines them, and beams them back toward Earth in one economical data stream. One earth station serves as a hub, exchanging data with a number of smaller stations situated almost anywhere within the signal footprint of the geosynchronous satellite.

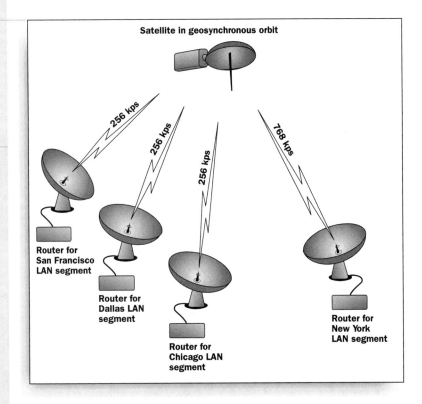

Satellite in geosynchronous orbit

256 kps

256 kps

256 kps

768 kps

Router for
San Francisco
LAN segment

Router for
Dallas LAN
segment

Router for
Chicago LAN
segment

Router for
New York
LAN segment

The hub station has a larger antenna than the others, so it can receive the signal from the distant geosynchronous satellite with less noise and handle a fat data stream with an acceptable level of errors. Many cities have satellite "parks," like New York's Teleport, where several companies share a few large antennae. When several organizations share a single large earth station, they also share the burdens of installation cost and maintenance problems. In theory, the shorter distance path to the low-earth orbit satellite makes it possible to have stronger signals and much smaller antennas.

Satellite circuits aren't a perfect interLAN solution for every organization, but they offer unique features and geographic flexibility that no other service can match.

MANs and FDDI

So far, in this chapter I've described how you can lease high-speed services in 64Kbps increments from terrestrial carriers and satellite carriers. But other companies sell the circuits to interconnect your facilities within metropolitan areas. For planning purposes, you can think of a metropolitan area as a circle with a 100-kilometer (62-mile) circumference.

As I've explained before, there is the technically ideal way to link LANs and there are the practical alternatives. The IEEE 802.6 committee has developed a standard—the technically ideal solution—for *metropolitan-area networks* or MANs. But organizations as diverse as railroads and cable television companies can also sell you local circuits to link your LANs.

The IEEE 802.6 committee's work describes a standard called the *Distributed Queue Dual Bus* (DQDB). The DQDB topology includes two parallel runs of cable (typically fiber-optic cable) linking each node (typically a router for a LAN segment) on the system. This dual-cable system provides high reliability and high signaling rates, typically in the vicinity of 100Mbps. Each ring of cable is independent and moves small 48-byte packets around the ring from node to node; this packet size is specified in other draft standards, specifically *Asynchronous Transfer Mode* (ATM) systems.

The DQDB system allocates system capacity to each node in 125-microsecond segments. The IEEE 802.6 MAN is designed to be a metropolitan utility serving a large number of organizations across a large area. In the United States, IEEE 802.6 MANs are typically installed and run by the local telephone companies.

Commercial companies and organizations such as universities can also elect a campus or community-wide system called the *Fiber Distributed Data Interface* (FDDI). In the grand scheme, FDDI networks act as traffic-gathering points to feed the larger DQDB network. FDDI systems have a sustained throughput of about 80Mbps and are limited to smaller areas than DQDB. FDDI operates over distances limited to about 100 kilometers of cable in each ring, and the nodes can't be farther than 2.5 kilo-meters apart. FDDI systems can be economically installed using existing equipment by organizations that need them, or by companies that want to sell a service to anyone in the extended neighborhood.

The FDDI architecture uses two rings of fiber—the primary ring and secondary ring—to carry data, as shown in Figure 11.6. The rings are in a physical hub topology similar to that described in the IEEE 802.5 token-ring architecture. All nodes attach to the primary ring, but because the secondary ring is designed primarily to provide a backup connection in case of primary ring failure, some nodes—called *Class B stations*—might not attach to the secondary ring for reasons of economy.

FIGURE 11.6

The FDDI hub topology uses a primary ring for data and a secondary ring as a backup. In this simplified diagram, one node is not on the secondary ring and cannot benefit from its redundancy. On the other hand, a node with a single connection has a low cost for installation and equipment.

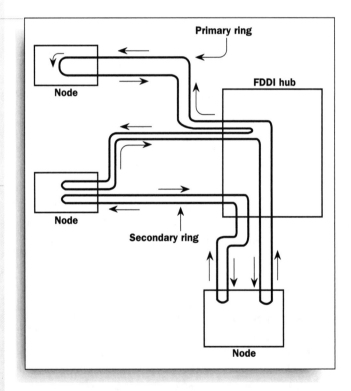

Some organizations, such as Advanced Micro Devices (AMD), promote using FDDI to deliver data to desktops rather than limiting it to internetwork links. Gigabit Ethernet uses some of the data packaging techniques of FDDI, but combines them with the CSMA media-access control scheme of traditional Ethernet. Gigabit Ethernet is displacing FDDI in many installations because it's a more familiar technology.

FDDI is an excellent technology for metropolitan network coverage. The capability of fiber-optic cable to ignore electrical interference and to be relatively inert makes it possible to pull cable in all sorts of unlikely places. Railroads and power utility companies have FDDI fiber optic cables along their rights-of-way, while innovative companies are pulling glass fiber through the steam pipes under major office buildings and, in Chicago, in the abandoned tunnels under the city, once used to cart coal to building basements.

Other Carriers

If your organization needs to connect LANs in a metropolitan area, you might look for communications circuits from unlikely carriers. Many cable television companies have installed two-way coaxial cables and can carry data at high speed. Railroads often have excess microwave radio or fiber-optic channels installed along their routes. Power utility companies can offer circuits on their fiber. I've even seen television stations with excess capacity on their private microwave systems. These organizations and others might be able to sell you a service that can link your LANs.

Specialized companies in many metropolitan areas offer circuits for MAN connectivity. For example, Metropolitan Fiber Systems sells fiber-optic MAN circuits in Baltimore, Boston, Chicago, Houston, Los Angeles, Minneapolis, New York, San Francisco, and other cities. Bay Area Teleport sells circuits—primarily carried over microwave radio—throughout central California. The Teleport Communications Group offers fiber-optic service throughout the New York City commercial area.

Finally, you can be your own carrier within a metropolitan area, particularly if you have at least one office with a top-down view of the skyline. Several companies, including Amp, Microwave Networks, and Motorola Microwave sell microwave radios operating at 2.3GHz and at 23GHz that you can literally set on a desktop and point out the window toward the distant LAN. These products can only span line-of-sight distances, for a maximum of 3 to 5 miles, but they can provide throughput of 1.544Mbps, and because you can typically buy the equipment for less than $10,000 per set, there are no monthly leased-line charges.

X.25 and Frame Relay: Versatile and Efficient

You should be aware of a protocol called X.25, which defines how communications devices such as bridges and routers package and route data over a connecting circuit. You can use X.25 data packaging and routing over any of the terrestrial, satellite, or ISDN communications circuits I've described. You can use the data-packaging and data-handling aspects of X.25 over any type of point-to-point circuits, but the protocol is better known for its packet-switching capabilities.

Packet switching is one of three major switching classes. The others are *circuit switching* and *message* or *store-and-forward switching*. You use circuit switching every time you make a telephone call. The lines the call traverses are dedicated to you and the person you called, and they remain fixed until you hang up. These lines are unavailable to anyone else, even when neither party is talking. In store-and-forward switching, the complete message, like a Western Union telegram, is sent from switch to switch. When the message reaches the destination switch, it is printed out and delivered.

Packet switching breaks messages into small bundles or packets (for instance, 128 characters). These packets are sent out as they are built in a *packet assembler/disassembler* or PAD. A PAD may be nothing more than a special kind of adapter board with its own processing capability and software. A PAD can reside in a PC, and Hayes even built a PAD into its V-Series of Smartmodems. The packets coming from a PAD are interleaved on a circuit with packets from other sources to make maximum use of the available bandwidth.

To make matters confusing, several different packet-switching protocols are used both in LANs and in wide area networks. These include protocols as diverse as IBM's *Systems Network Architecture* (SNA), Token-Ring, and FDDI. The most widely used, internationally agreed-upon protocol for packet switching is X.25. The X.25 standard was first adopted as an international standard in 1976 and has been revised and updated every four years since then.

The protocol for X.25 details a specific exchange of packets required to pass information. These packets have structured contents and precede the passing of information. A *call request packet* is sent to the requested host, which can grant permission for the exchange by issuing a *call accepted packet*. The call is set up and information exchanged in the form of packets that contain addressing information. Of course, these packets also contain the actual data that the sender wishes to transmit. The call is ended when a *call clear packet* is sent and a *clear confirmation packet* is received in acknowledgement. Each of the packets in this exchange has a specified structure, and each field is defined. Special *reset* and *restart packets* add to the robustness of X.25. These, along with other prescribed packets such as the *diagnostic packet*, make X.25 extremely versatile and easy to use.

X.25: Good and Stubborn

The X.25 protocol describes a method of encapsulating and handling packets with high reliability. Like token ring, X.25 focuses on making reliable connections. It's an elegant system designed for worldwide multipoint connectivity.

Several companies, such as AT&T, MCI, and Sprint, manage networks of special computerized switches spread across the nation and across the world that connect together with high-speed data-communications lines and use X.25. These companies sell their networks' data-handling and transmission capabilities to subscribers under several pricing schemes. Outside the United States, national telephone companies in many countries offer X.25 services, sometimes at lower rates than leased lines or dial-up lines.

Because these networks use software conforming to the X.25 protocols to ensure the accuracy of the data they carry, and because they can offer other associated services, they are called *value-added networks* or VANs.

Because X.25 packet-switched VANs route each packet to any destination on the fly, they have the capability to link thousands of locations simultaneously. You see this best in online services such as CompuServe, where people calling in from locations around the world simultaneously communicate with the central database computers.

When you use X.25 VANs to link LANs, you gain error-free simultaneous connections to multiple locations. This capability should make X.25 VANs almost perfect for LAN-to-LAN connections. Artists often depict an X.25 network as a "cloud" with connections in and out. They use the cloud to obscure the complexity of the computers inside the VAN and their interconnections. Two types of connections go into the "cloud." The first is a high-speed leased line that can carry data at 56 or 64Kbps, at 1.544Mbps or faster, from the computer to the cloud, using full X.25 protocols. This connection can go to a host computer, but typically today it goes to a router. The other type of connection is a dial-up telephone line—either ISDN and analog.

TCP goes through a "Did you get what I sent?" exchange to make sure every packet arrives. X.25 does essentially the same thing, although at a lower level. Therefore, a lot of X.25 packets consist of TCP confirmations to packets that X.25 already confirmed, at least at the X.25 network level, so you waste bandwidth carrying the overhead. Although the X.25 confirmation is redundant to the higher TCP confirmation, the additional X.25 packet information is needed for the VAN routing.

The other problem with using X.25 VANs to link LANs comes from the traditional use of VANs to make one too many

---

X.25's paradox

It's strange to note that X.25's reliability is, in fact, its major drawback. The design philosophy of modern networks puts the responsibility for guaranteed delivery of data on higher-level protocols. Maybe this is the influence of the Ethernet datagram that makes a best effort at delivery and then quits, but it is the way things have evolved. Both TCP and X.25 have built-in error correction.

connections. In the past, multiple clients used VANs to get to one host. The fee structure and programming of the networks reflect and perpetuate this scheme, but this isn't the best structure for LAN-to-LAN connections.

Because of the limitations on speed and on connection options, X.25 networks in the United States have been pushed aside by Frame Relay networks. Frame Relay has many of the advantages of X.25, but less overhead.

Public Versus Private X.25 Networks

X.25 packet-switching networks provide effective solutions for many applications. For example, X.25 works well where high reliability and low delay are required, and where multiple users need to connect to multiple hosts for short periods of time.

A perfect example of an X.25 network application is the processing of credit-card charges you see in stores daily. The electronic transaction from the card reader is frequently carried over an X.25 network. Short messages (which include your account number, store identification, and the amount of the charge) can go to the proper clearing house or bank. Receipts of the transaction flow to several points. The X.25 network enables this to occur without the use of costly, dedicated connections from each store to each bank that issues credit cards.

Packet-switching services can be obtained by building private networks or through the use of public data networks. As the name implies, a private network is one in which network resources are usually dedicated to a small number of applications or a restricted set of users, as in a corporate network. In other words, you buy your own switches and lease line and act as your own carrier. The network resources include the access circuits, the network interfaces between the user and the packet switches, the *packet-switching nodes* (PSNs) and the trunk circuits that connect them, and the control systems for the network.

Private network access is typically handled through dedicated circuits. With public data networks, network resources are owned by third-party companies and leased on a usage basis to many users, serving many applications. Access to public networks is typically through dial-up circuits.

The decision to use a private or public network is primarily based on economics and, to some extent, on desired network performance. From a performance perspective, public networks are sufficient for many uses, but specific applications may require a specialized customized network. In these cases, a private network provides the flexibility to incorporate the necessary performance capabilities.

In public networks, costs to a user are determined by the amount of time the user is connected and by the number of packets the user sends and receives. Although various cost algorithms are employed, generally the more you use, the more you pay. In private networks, user costs are driven by the initial capital investment and network operations costs.

Frame Relay

The X.25 protocol is a conservative design that numbers, acknowledges, and supervises every packet and even asks network switches to retransmit packets that don't make the trip across the network. This conservative approach protects data, but requires a lot of expensive computing and communicating resources within the network to do all the extra work involved. A less careful, but less burdensome, protocol called *Frame Relay* has moved into the WAN market so forcefully that, in the United States, almost all new WAN connections use Frame Relay rather than X.25.

The Frame Relay protocol design takes advantage of the fact that modern networks build reliability into higher-level software and that modern transmission systems are generally reliable. So it reduces the protective overhead and allows more throughput at lower cost without unacceptable data loss.

The Frame Relay concept transfers some of the responsibilities of the switches in the X.25 network to the terminal equipment on each end. If there is a problem with a packet—for example, if bits are lost or if a node is so congested that it receives more

About the money

In a nutshell, leased lines (such as T1 and fractional T1 services) are distance-sensitive, but not usage-sensitive. You pay by the mile no matter how much or how little you use the lines. ISDN lines are usually usage-sensitive. You typically pay by the minute for ISDN; however, ISDN tariff structures vary wildly from region to region. X.25 and Frame Relay services typically have a flat rate for a specific level of service, so they are both distance and usage insensitive. However, it's important to correctly figure your needed level of service.

packets than it can process—the Frame Relay network discards the data and expects the terminal equipment to take corrective action. Typically, this involves retransmitting the data that failed to make it across the network. Because LAN protocols such as TCP or SPX have their own error control that is redundant with the error control in X.25, they fit nicely into the Frame Relay architecture.

But on the downside, the end-to-end recovery scheme can be costly because it increases traffic on the network. If Frame Relay packets are discarded because of congestion, retransmitting the data can merely aggravate the problem. So even though the terminal equipment can recover discarded blocks, it's still important to minimize frame discards.

Because LAN traffic tends to flow in bursts, the probability of occasional congestion is high (unless the user puts extra capacity into both the lines and the switches and pays more than necessary for network costs), so it's important for a Frame Relay network to have excellent congestion management features. The Frame Relay standards include several nonmandatory suggestions about how the network can signal congestion and how the LAN portal devices should react. Because these suggestions aren't mandatory, companies can field devices that conform to the Frame Relay protocols but don't have congestion control capabilities.

Two important Frame Relay congestion control systems involve using the *discard eligibility* (DE) bit in the Frame Relay format and establishing an estimated rate of traffic called the *committed information rate* (CIR).

Setting the DE bit to a binary 1 marks the frame as eligible for early elimination in the event of congestion. The DE bit could be set by a LAN portal device on lower-priority traffic or traffic that can withstand a few seconds of delay, such as electronic mail. Marking potential sacrificial frames with the DE bit provides a good way to let higher-priority traffic pass.

The committed information rate represents an estimate of the normal amount of traffic coming from a node in a busy period. In a commercial network, the higher the CIR, the higher the monthly cost. In private networks, the CIR is still an important budgeting and management tool. The network measures the traffic coming from each node. If the load is less than the CIR, it passes the frames untouched if possible; however, if the load exceeds the CIR, the network sets the DE bit on the excess frames. If the network experiences congestion, frames that exceed their own CIR are eliminated before those that don't have the DE bit set. Because congestion control is so important, I strongly suggest you select products that provide DE and CIR capabilities along with other forms of node-to-node communications.

ATM

The newest (and therefore to lovers of status technology, the hottest) technology for linking LANs is called *Asynchronous Transfer Mode* (ATM). ATM is a packet-switching technology like X.25 and Frame Relay, but with a few twists.

The chief advantage of ATM is its capability to create a seamless and fast network reaching from the desktop out across limitless wide areas. In its full splendor, ATM would do away with routers, allocated bandwidth, and contention for the communications media. Believers in ATM include the world's largest telecommunications and computing corporations, but who really needs ATM and what makes it necessary?

The answer is that the only people who need ATM are in organizations that need to deliver synchronized video and sound. These few folks are the only ones who can really see the grandeur of ATM. This category includes movie and entertainment players such as Time-Warner and Viacom International, who want to deliver on-demand video and sound to your home.

Organizations that only need to move a lot of computer data pay a penalty for ATM's overhead. For data that doesn't demand millisecond synchronization, there are better and more efficient transmission technologies, such as the proven and widely available Frame Relay. My advice is, wait and then wait some more before applauding ATM.

In some ways ATM benefits from the related Frame Relay technology, but in other ways it's a throwback. Good connections and smarter software at the higher levels enable Frame Relay packets to move data reliably and more efficiently than X.25. Every vendor of wide area packet-switching services from CompuServe to Wiltel, Sprint, AT&T, and MCI can provide Frame Relay subscriber service at DS-1 (1.544Mbps) and European standard E1 (2.048Mbps) speeds. Service at DS-3 (44.736Mbps) rates is available, but is not as widely used.

The advantage of Frame Relay is that it makes the best use of the available bandwidth by packaging the data in variable-length packets for transmission across the network. It is commonly accepted that variable-length packets suit the bursty nature of computer data transmissions.

On all types of communications links, the engineering goal is always to bundle the data into big packets that have little overhead. Reducing the data bits that provide routing, error-checking, timing, and other information provides the most efficient throughput and lowest communications channel cost.

Packet-switched architectures that use large packets have two problems: First, the packet switches must buffer packets of different sizes. This juggling act requires sophisticated software that consumes processing power and memory, so the cost of the switch goes up. Second, as big packets make their way through the switch they hold up other packets. In technospeak, these switches have a high *latency*; that is, there can be irregular gaps of several milliseconds between the arrival of packets in a stream. If you are running a time-sensitive application like videoconferencing, unsynchronized packets can make lips move without sound and images jerk on the screen.

Two switched-circuit services are related to, predecessors of, and today sometimes carriers of ATM: *Switched Multimegabit Data Service* (SMDS) and *Broadband ISDN* (BISDN). SMDS is a LAN-bridging service, weakly marketed by local telephone companies, that provides transmission at DS-1 or DS-3 rates. Beautifully designed to use copper or fiber-optic cabling, it was integrated into the IEEE 802.6 specification for metropolitan area networks.

Never heard of SMDS? The telephone companies were supposed to market it to meet your data needs, but they failed to work out the long-distance side of the connections. A few cutting-edge companies use SMDS in metropolitan networks, but competing technologies, such as the privately owned fiber-optic loops available in Chicago and other cities, offer higher speed and excellent economy in metropolitan settings.

Broadband ISDN is that shy and never-blooming perennial, the Integrated Services Digital Network, piped over fiber-optic cable at 155Mbps. ATM was first described within the BISDN architecture and BISDN serves as a carrier for ATM packets.

Some of the hot data communications ideas that preceded ATM, such as Frame Relay, are designed to squeeze the best value out of the communications channel. Technologies like SMDS and BISDN, which have been very slow to take hold in the market, enhance the channel by adding intelligence to the fabric of the network. So far, that approach hasn't hit it big because people favor adding intelligence to the ends of the network, at prices they can control. It remains to be seen whether ATM will fare any better.

ATM Facts and Fallacies

If you listen to the cheerleading for ATM, you'll hear that ATM gives you a high-speed, scalable architecture that works from desktop to WAN without all the sticky protocol changes and transmission techniques commonly used today. You'll also hear that the small packets ATM uses provide low latency, so sound and picture arrive together. All these benefits are real.

Another theoretical advantage of switched technologies such as X.25, Frame Relay, and ATM is that they facilitate multipoint networks. Technologists call these *meshed* networks, meaning that traffic flows through all levels. But in the real world, despite the reengineering of corporations, traffic flow is typically still centralized or hierarchical. The advantage of meshed-network communications is lost on most organizations moving computer data today.

If you listen well to the ATM boosters, you'll notice that ATM is always mentioned in the same breath as high speed and broad bandwidth. There's an unspoken assumption that ATM somehow creates high speed, which isn't true. ATM is associated with high-speed signaling primarily because the protocol is simple and flexible enough to work over a broad range of speeds. But you never get something for nothing. Even with ATM, high speed costs more and ATM imposes significant overhead costs of its own.

The unrelenting fact of physics is that costs escalate dramatically as you increase signaling speed, distance, or both. ATM doesn't change that equation; however, it does enable companies with the largest networks to pay less for their switches, to use their wide-bandwidth fiber-optic links, and to manage their entire networks—from desktop to distant desktop—as single end-to-end entities. All this means that these carriers can increase margins, or lower prices, while selling more services.

ATM's cell-switching technology appeals to today's telephone companies because ATM can handle both data and voice on the same network, something X.25 and Frame Relay cannot do. In fact, the design of the ATM cell was driven by requirements imposed by voice telephone transmission. ATM gives these carriers an intelligent network to resell. Sprint Corp. was the first to make ATM services commercially available, and other carriers such as AT&T, MCI, and Wiltel weren't far behind.

ATM Overhead

If you're going to pay many tens of thousands of dollars a month for a fast digital service, you'll want to squeeze every bit of data through that channel you can, so let's look at the efficiency of different transmission techniques.

The X.25 and Frame Relay packet-switched architectures follow a protocol called the *Link Access Procedure Balanced* (LAPB) that is built on the well-known *High Level Data Link Control* (HDLC). Generally, the user data—the useful cargo in the frame—can occupy as many as 4,096 bytes, but the default is 128 bytes. If you add about four bytes for address- and control-field overhead in Frame Relay, the resulting packet has as little as .08% and an average of just 3% overhead.

The ATM packet totals 53 bytes, of which 5 bytes, or a little more than 9%, are overhead. In some cases, timing added by the ATM adaptive layer can raise the overhead to 13%. So the smaller ATM packets use at least 6% more of the communications channel than do Frame Relay packets to move the same data. To put this into perspective, 6% of a DS-3 channel is 2.68Mbps, or about forty 64Kbps channels in ATM overhead.

Admittedly, this analysis is simplistic—other factors are involved—but it's generally accurate and conservative. To the end user or network manager, the major advantage of ATM is its low latency (its small packets can move through a congested switch with minimal delay), but that single advantage can cost you a lot of wasted bandwidth and a lot of money.

ATM Fever

ATM started out hot. Several companies developed and marketed ATM adapters for Sun workstations and even for standard PCs. But ATM to the desktop ran into good old Ethernet and stopped dead. At 100Mbps, Fast Ethernet is fast enough even for applications demanding the lowest latency. Ethernet switching and good network segmentation techniques eliminate delay problems.

Similarly, ATM ran into Fast Ethernet on campus backbones. Now the major application for ATM seems to be in the very large backbone systems of wide area network carriers. In this arena, ATM meshes with SONET and other technologies to provide a smooth infrastructure.

ATM-to-the-desktop might not be dead. Microsoft and Novell have included special ATM-friendly software in their latest operating systems, but this might be opening the door for opportunity long after it knocked.

Interestingly, IBM has taken a strong pro-ATM position. But if you look a little deeper you see that the company is offering ATM as an upgrade to its Token-Ring loyalists. The company is shipping products that use ATM at 25Mbps over unshielded twisted-pair wire. For IBM, this is a smart move because it provides an upgrade to Token-Ring users while leveraging a potentially useful new technology.

Ask Yourself About ATM

Is ATM for you? Ask yourself some simple questions:

- *Do I need to deliver voice or synchronized voice and video in real time?* If not, first investigate Ethernet switching or 100Mbps Ethernet systems.

- *Do I need to send data more than two or three miles, but still keep it within the United States?* If you need to move data only a few miles, look at microwave or fiber-optic cable options. If you need to go outside the United States, look at leased lines or Frame Relay public data network options because ATM will be accepted even more slowly outside the United States.

- *Do I need to deliver data to many locations or is my need point-to-point?* If your enterprise-network is a pyramid with few interconnections, circuit-switched services such as Switched 56, Switched T-1, or SMDS will probably be more cost effective than pure ATM.

- *Do I have a budget of tens of thousands of dollars for a testbed?* If not, look at Ethernet switches.

- *Am I willing to commit myself to one vendor for several years?* Compatibility is an issue. If you like to mix and match vendors, stick with more mature technologies.

If you answered yes to each of these questions, you may be ready to climb on the leading edge of ATM. But despite the clamor it has generated, at present only a few corporations reap great benefits from ATM technology.

Linking LANs: A New Frontier

The Internet is a rocket marking the spot where technologies meet. It happens to be the most obvious manifestation of a change in the way we conduct commerce, education, and social interaction. But the technologies the Internet uses, particularly the long distance LAN-to-LAN links, aren't unique to the Internet. You can weave the same technologies together into pubic and private systems with many uses. In this chapter you have met the transportation portions of the Internet and intranets. It is all about linking LANs. The next chapter provides details on what goes on just above the Transport Layers.

The Protocols of the Internet

In the late 1970s, the terminal on my desk was attached to a computer that could exchange messages over a connection to the Defense Advanced Research Projects Agency Network, called ARPAnet. At that time, this network linked more than 600 universities, companies, and government agencies for the purpose of sharing information. Frankly, a lot of the network traffic—particularly after dark—was either game playing or personal messages from college students; but even that proved useful because it helped stress and test the network in many ways and also trained a generation of technophiles to love getting online. In the 1980s, the Department of Defense turned to more secure networks, and sponsorship for the Internet (as it came to be called) moved to the National Science Foundation. Commercial uses of the Internet have grown so much and the system now evolves so quickly that trying to create a map of the Internet is like trying to paint a moving train.

The New Internet

The basic components of the Internet are the same devices described in the last two chapters: communications lines and routers. An Internet server installation can be as simple as the one shown in Figure 12.1, consisting of a UNIX, Windows NT, or NetWare-based computer with some terminals and a router connected to a leased line. Multiply that several million times, and you've got something pretty big.

Looking at the Internet from the inside out, let's start with the backbone and work our way out to the end users. In the U.S., the major long-distance carriers like AT&T, Sprint, MCI, and IBM have multiple backbone circuits running up and down and across the country. Typically, each of these circuits has a capacity of more than 600 megabits per second. These carriers and others have agreed to interconnect their circuits in large banks of routers called *Network Access Points* (*NAP*s) in Washington D.C., Pennsauken, New Jersey, Chicago, and San Francisco. The major carriers connect to each other at least at those four points.

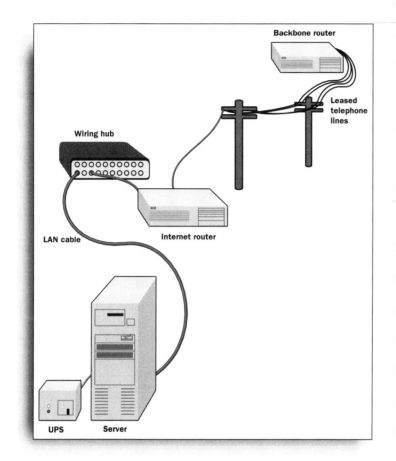

Backbone router

Leased telephone lines

Wiring hub

LAN cable

Internet router

UPS   **Server**

FIGURE 12.1

An Internet host might be nothing more than a computer running UNIX attached to a router over an Ethernet cable. If you add more computers to the cable, the same computer can provide Internet access for an entire organization. The other side of the router connects to a leased line that travels to a backbone router at an ISP.

Carriers of all sizes can also connect at what are called *Metropolitan Area Exchange* (*MAE*) systems. There is an MAE in San Jose (it has to be called MAE-West). Other MAE locations are MAE-LA, MAE-Dallas, MAE-Houston, MAE-Chicago, and MAE-East in Washington, D.C. Together, the NAPs and MAEs constitute the primary interconnection points of the Internet.

This combination of competing but cooperative carriers that interconnect at various points gives the network excellent reliability and flexibility. If something happens to one of the NAPs or MAEs, alternative routes fulfill the function of the component that's down. To date, the only major outages have resulted from incorrect router programming that propagated through major portions of the backbone.

It's all linking LANs

The term *MAE* used to stand for Metropolitan Area Ethernet–a clear sign that the MAEs and NAPs are a bunch of routers with Ethernet LAN backbones between them. They changed the term for clarity, but the technology of the Internet, and of internetworking in general, is about linking LANs.

Carriers of all sizes have connections to the Internet backbone, but there is a clear hierarchy. The big carriers connect to one another, and the smaller carriers connect through the big ones. Some major carriers sell Internet access service to individuals and private corporations, acting as *Internet service provider* or *ISPs*, but others simply function as a "carrier's carrier"—operating at the highest levels without directly serving end users. There are several thousand active ISPs in North America. Some are very small, with perhaps a few hundred customers, and some have 3–4 million customers.

SEE ALSO

➤ *To be exact, routers are covered in the section "Routers," on page 259.*

➤ *I discuss the details of leased line wideband systems on page 273.*

The Role of the ISP

The job of the ISP is to aggregate data and to collect money for doing it. The ISP aggregates the data going to and from individual subscribers for economical transmission on larger pipes. The ISP also typically aggregates and subdivides information sources from the Internet to better serve local customers. Figure 12.2 shows a typical ISP's LAN and servers. Today's powerful servers with multiple Pentium processors can handle very heavy loads. The bigger ISPs might use hardware like IBM's AS/400 computers, in which cases the specific functions of the specific servers might reside together on one piece of hardware. However, this diagram depicts a fairly typical installation.

This Internet = your intranet

Figure 12.2 shows what functions reside on a LAN belonging to a typical ISP. Using the latest versions of NetWare or Windows NT, it's fairly easy to duplicate these functions in your own organization. The web server can hold your corporate "write-once-read-many" documents, the newsgroup server can carry discussions about projects, and the proxy server can carry only the specific Internet web pages you want employees to access. This corporate intranet uses Internet web technology, with or without the real Internet, to extend information to employees and business associates.

Internet servers can hold databases that perform many different functions. The three most popular general functions are electronic mail, newsgroups, and special server programs.

An email server gathers messages from other servers anywhere on the Internet and holds the mail queue until users log on and download it. Electronic mail systems on the Internet conform to either the Post Office Protocol version 3 (POP3) or the Internet Messaging Access Protocol version 4 (IMAP4). IMAP4 servers are rapidly replacing POP3 servers.

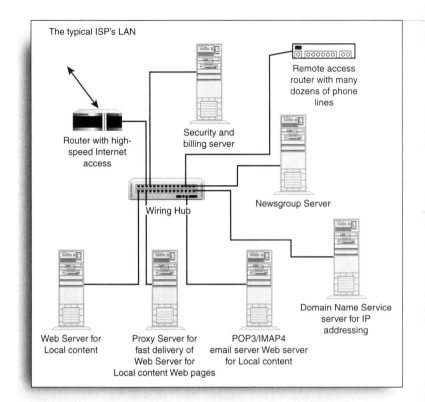

The typical ISP's LAN

Router with high-speed Internet access

Security and billing server

Remote access router with many dozens of phone lines

Wiring Hub

Newsgroup Server

Web Server for Local content

Proxy Server for fast delivery of Web Server for Local content Web pages

POP3/IMAP4 email server Web server for Local content

Domain Name Service server for IP addressing

FIGURE 12.2

The typical ISP has a LAN with a couple of routers, several servers, and many communications links. Subscribers can call in or have full-period leased line connections to the ISP. If a corporation sets up this same kind of system for the use of its employees and business partners, with or without an Internet connection, it is called an *intranet*.

An IMAP4 server is more sophisticated and flexible than a POP3 mail server. IMAP servers can archive messages in folders, but POP servers don't retain messages after they're delivered. IMAP also has better integration with the *Multipurpose Internet Mail Extensions (MIME)* protocol used to attach files. The major benefits of IMAP servers include the ability to read only the headers in the message without having to download all attached files and the ability to log into the server from different computers (perhaps at work and at home) and have the same current mail file.

Newsgroups are special interest groups whose files reside on servers across the network. They provide a discussion forum in which messages are archived and arranged in message threads by subject and date. Newsgroups often deal with very technical and far-out subjects. But there are newsgroups for practically every interest in the world, and many people spend most of their online time simply browsing newsgroups in search of the interesting, arcane, or peculiar.

Figure 12.3 shows a newsgroup reader. A newsgroup reader utility uses the *Network News Transport Protocol (NNTP)* to interact with a newsgroup server. Today, newsgroup readers are often tightly linked to browsers, but you can always elect to use a separate reader.

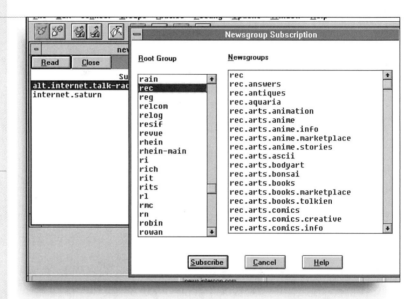

FIGURE 12.3

Newsgroup reader software provides a way to browse through the newsgroups made available by your Internet service provider. Your service provider typically copies hundreds of megabytes of text daily so that it is available to you with a fast response.

SEE ALSO

➤ *We dip deeper into applications that deliver email in the section "Electronic Mail Programs for Productivity," on page 429.*

Caching the Web

A web-caching proxy server is an important part of your ISP's service, but it can be even more important to you on your corporate intranet. In general, a *proxy* is something that stands in place of another thing; in the case of a web-caching proxy server, it is a specialized server that pulls HTML-encoded pages from web sites for client computers. Then, when a client asks for the pages, the pages come from the proxy server's disk drive storage cache.

Proxy server software is available from Microsoft, Novell, and other companies. In an ISP's installation, the proxy service is hidden behind complex IP addressing schemes. Because of this addressing, the subscribers' browsers operate normally, and it appears to the subscribers that web pages are coming from the original web site. In fact, the pages come from the ISP's mirrored web server. This proxy action, or *mirroring*, provides fast service to subscribers and significantly reduces the size and cost of the circuit the ISP must have into the Internet.

On your intranet, the web-caching proxy server cruises the web and checks web pages that you and other users on your LAN have previously visited and that have been cached on the server. If a page has been modified, it stores the new version on a local drive in the server. It can also use certain guidelines to hit links on that page to pull down related pages. Note that, unlike on an ISP's mirrored web site, the browsers on your intranet have to be specially configured to use a web-caching proxy server. Typically, you tell each client's browser to use the proxy server by checking one box in the configuration menu.

Installing a web-caching proxy server on your network benefits your organization in several ways. First, your users get their web pages fast. Second, you can reduce or at least control the growth of the size and cost of your link to the Internet. The proxy server uses the Internet link on a level and constant basis. Without a proxy server, your users would crowd the link at certain times of the day, forcing you to increase capacity, but they would leave it idle at other times. Finally, and this is of critical importance, if you also install a software service called URL filtering on your router connected to the Internet, you can use the filtering to prevent anyone in your organization from accessing web sites that some might find objectionable.

The proxy server has great persistence and patience. It can examine and store thousands of web pages, and when any local user on the LAN asks for a specific stored page, the page flies out of a local drive or cache without Internet transmission delays. The proxy server makes efficient use of any Internet connection, so you can save money by sharing one connection

You need a policy on appropriate use!

If your LAN gives employees or members of your organization access to the Internet, you can have a liability for inappropriate use of that access. In other words, if somebody pulls down material from the Internet that somebody else finds offensive, the offended person can win a judgment against you. You should publish a policy on appropriate use of the Internet and make reasonable attempts to enforce that policy. Installing a web-caching proxy server and URL filtering server creates a system that will deliver only web sites appropriate to your business. This system protects you from liability, improves overall productivity by reducing random web surfing, and helps to guard against intrusion from the outside.

among many users and squeeze the maximum benefit from that one connection. Although a proxy server doesn't have the sophisticated flexibility of a specialized firewall, it is an impermeable barrier between your network and the outside. A full firewall, described later in this chapter, protects from invasion through the Internet but has more flexibility than the typical proxy server. Adding a proxy server is one of the smartest things you can do for your corporate network.

SEE ALSO

➤ *A web-caching proxy server is simply a specific kind of communications server, which I describe in the section "The Communications-Server Functions," on page 182.*

Into the Processes of the Internet

As we go deeper into the functions of your intranet and its links to the Internet, you'll find a set of well-defined structures, procedures, and terms. The guardianship of Internet terms has passed through several hands, but it now resides with the Internet Architecture Board (IAB). The IAB is made up of the Internet Engineering Task Force (IETF) and the Internet Research Task Force (IRTF). The IAB develops and describes the procedures and processes used to run the Internet in a series of *Requests for Comments* (*RFCs*) and *Standards* (*STDs*). The RFCs form an extensive library describing the evolution of the Internet technology. In many cases, RFCs don't make it to the STD phase, but the exchange in the RFCs is frequently interesting and informative. The STDs contain the accepted descriptions of how the protocols work.

Point your browser at `http://sunsite.auc.dk/RFC` for a full library of RFCs and STDs. If that link doesn't work, search for RFC2000 using any Internet search service. RFC2000 contains links to other RFCs and STDs and should lead you to a library.

The Internet Protocol (IP) stands above all other technologies and techniques defined in the RFCs and STDs of the IETF. It is the core technology for moving packets across the Internet or an intranet, and improvements in IP ripple into many other areas.

The Heaven and Hell of IP

Addressing is the heaven and hell of IP. IP's address scheme makes it practical to put tens of millions of nodes on a huge network like the Internet. That's heavenly. But, on the long downside, IP's addressing scheme also necessitates that if you adopt IP for your LAN, you'll have to worry about assigning an IP address to every networked device. Every computer, hub, print server, or router and every other networked device needs a unique address. Then, you'll have to change the address of any device that moves to a different LAN segment and hope that you have enough addresses to cover the network.

Address Basics

IP uses a numeric address to define each node on a network. IP version 4 relies on an address method that comprises a series of four numbers separated by periods, called *octets*. A typical IP 4 address might look like this:

204.195.130.166

Imagine the drudgery of tracking all the node addresses on a large network. Imagine manually entering the addresses for hundreds of nodes and hoping all the while that no one ever changes jobs within the company and takes his or her computer along.

The numbers are called octets because in binary form they have eight bits. These eight bits have a total of 256 combinations, so each octet can represent a number between 0 and 255.

The developers of the present IP addressing scheme attempted to distribute addresses fairly and economically by allocating blocks of addresses to organizations of different size. They established three classes of addresses. The first octet in an IP address indicates the class of the address. For example, if the first octet is a number from 1 to 127, the address is a Class A address; if the first octet is 128 to 191, it's a Class B address; if the first octet is 192 to 223, it's a Class C address.

A little personal TCP/IP history

I had a good seat to watch the birth of TCP/IP. The Defense Advanced Research Projects Agency (DARPA) is a small organization with a huge impact. In the mid-1970s, DARPA saw the need to link dissimilar computers across the nation. Contracts were awarded to develop a standard set of nonproprietary protocols that would provide easy communications between dissimilar computers connected in a multinode network. The TCP/IP protocols evolved from work done at MIT with the participation of several companies and using healthy rounds of industry comments. In 1980, DARPA installed the first TCP/IP modules on computers in its networks. It mandated that all computers attached to the growing nationwide ARPAnet network had to use TCP/IP by January 1983. DARPA and other organizations, such as the Defense Communications Agency, contracted with several companies to deliver TCP/IP modules for the computers and operating systems commonly used by the government. This seed money was well spent because it motivated these and many other companies to use their own funds to get onto the TCP/IP bandwagon. The Defense Communications Agency began a program of testing and certifying software for compliance with the DoD's TCP/IP standard. My role? I helped to find the money and oversaw the contracts for that testing. A small role, but the farther away in time it gets, the bigger it seems.

Generally, the remaining octets determine the network address and addresses for specific network nodes. This might seem complicated enough, but there's more. While the first octet determines which class an address is in, the use of the other octets varies according to the type of address:

- In a Class A address, only the first octet is used to designate the network address; the last three octets describe unique addresses for the network nodes. So while there are only 254 Class A network addresses available, each Class A address can have approximately 17 million unique nodes. As you might guess, governments and big institutions got the Class A addresses.

- Class B addresses use the first two octets to designate the network address and the last two to create unique node addresses. Because there are more number spaces, more Class B addresses are available, but each one can only have 65,000 unique addresses.

- Class C addresses use the first three octets for the network address and only the last octet for node addresses. Therefore, a lot of Class C addresses are available, but each one can accommodate only 254 nodes.

In practical fact, Class A addresses are impossible to obtain, and Class B addresses are scarce. Although a lot of Class C addresses are still available, you might need more than one if your organization's network has a lot of nodes.

Usable blocks of IP addresses have become scarce because of the inefficiencies in the class system. If a small company with only a dozen nodes needs to connect to the Internet, the only option is to give it a Class C address. This assignment gives the company control of more than two hundred node addresses that no one else can use.

You can still get a Class C assignment for your organization, but it is becomingly increasingly difficult. You have to show a real need. And if one Class C block isn't enough for all your nodes, you can try for multiple blocks, but the hassle increases.

Roll Your Own Addresses

Your first good alternative is to make up your own internal IP address scheme and never connect to the official Internet. With a self-fabricated address scheme, you can connect your branch offices with TCP/IP across leased lines, establish an intranet, send web pages, and use all of the TCP/IP services. But you can't connect directly to the global Internet. Then again, not having a direct Internet connection might not be a bad thing. You'll avoid the risk of attack from the Internet and the risk of people wasting time or engendering lawsuits with inappropriate Internet content. Certain reserved address blocks, such as the entire Class A block beginning with 10.X.X.X, are intended for this purpose and are never used over the Internet. If you are going to make up your own addresses, use these.

If you absolutely must have an Internet connection with a conforming addressing scheme, your best bet today is to go to an Internet service provider to get a sub-block of addresses from those that are assigned to the ISP. The benefit of this arrangement is that the addresses will be unique and routable over the Internet. In addition, getting addresses from the ISP doesn't waste addresses in the overall pool, and the addresses are also available to you immediately when you contract for service.

The downside of getting your IP addresses from an ISP is that you become tightly linked to that service provider. This ISP has its addresses installed in every router, PC, networked printer, and managed device on your network. If this ISP decides to raise its rates and you want to change to another ISP, you'll find that changing is a big job. However, as you'll learn later, software that conforms to a protocol called DHCP can help.

The approach that makes the most sense today is to use a non-assigned IP addressing scheme inside your network—regardless of its size—and then to connect to the Internet through any or all of several different devices that have conforming addresses assigned by an ISP. If you ever decide to part ways with the ISP, it's easy to change a few addresses on some portal devices.

Devices you can use as a buffer between a network with non-conforming IP addressing and the Internet include a web-caching proxy server, an IP/IP gateway, and a router with a service called *network address translation* (*NAT*). In fact, although I can say that these devices are very different in terms of operation, in terms of real products, they are merging into one device. It's probably easier to call this device a router with gateway services, but it certainly does a lot more than a router of 1997 could do.

The web-caching proxy server described earlier presents itself to the Internet as a single IP address and makes connections on behalf of the users behind it. IP/IP gateways, which are practically identical to the IPX/IP gateways described in Chapter 13, do an excellent job of greeting the Internet with an assigned IP address while handling requests from unassigned nodes on the other side. Network address translation is a feature offered by many products. In function, it's exactly the same as an IP/IP gateway, although products marketed as gateways often have more management features than a device that simply offers NAT. Microsoft offers a Windows NT application level proxy server with NAT, and Novell markets a comprehensive package as part of its BorderManager product family.

DHCP to the Rescue

Setting up an IP addressing scheme for a corporate network is an imposing challenge. However, there is software to help. The way you avoid the manual part of the IP addressing challenge is to use a server program that conforms to the *Dynamic Host Configuration Protocol* (*DHCP*). DHCP also helps if you use an ISP-assigned addressing scheme inside your network and then decide to switch ISPs.

DHCP is, in effect, a leasing service. A DHCP server answers requests for service from client devices when they enter the network. The server makes a temporary assignment of an IP address to a node. You can configure the server to assign addresses randomly, or you can make assignments based on user names or on the MAC addresses of the LAN adapters.

Security is better without IP

Just because they didn't write on the walls, don't assume that you haven't had visitors! It's estimated that the majority of corporate networks are often penetrated by people who don't have permission to do what they are doing. These people are typically very careful about leaving evidence behind because they want information on your company or business. If you have a conforming IP scheme, you make it easier for Internet invaders. Using IPX on your internal network or using a non-conforming IP scheme and hiding behind a gateway erects a high barrier against this method of entry.

Many nodes on the network, particularly routers and print servers, need static IP addresses to do their jobs, so they won't be clients for dynamic IP addressing. Either they'll have permanently assigned addresses, or they'll be DHCP clients with permanent assignments. Nodes that use IP-based management software, like some wiring hubs and remote access servers, should have static node addresses assigned manually. But the majority of the nodes on your network can have on-the-fly DHCP assignments. You typically tell the client software, like the Windows TCP/IP client, to request DHCP service in the same menu where you would otherwise enter an IP address. The DHCP server software doesn't tax the processor heavily, so it can run on a computer doing other jobs such as file and print services.

Names Humans Understand

The IP addressing scheme is critical to big routed networks, and computers make good use of the detailed numeric IP addresses. But those detailed numbers don't mean anything to people. People want to express things in words with clearly associated meanings. The Internet uses a system of *domains* to divide and name all of its resources. The structure of names has evolved into five worldwide generic domains (COM, ORG, NET, EDU, and INT), two U.S.-only generic domains (MIL and GOV), and country-code domains (such as, US for the United States, AU for Australia, and so on).

An organization called the InterNIC, a cooperative activity between the National Science Foundation, AT&T, and Network Solutions, Inc. registers domain names and IP addresses. Go to www.internic.net for the latest information on domain name policies.

Generally, the policy has been to charge a registration fee of $100 for a new domain name and to charge an annual maintenance fee of $50. But you should understand that these fees buy a service beyond simple registration. The InterNIC maintains the master list of domain names and provides Internet servers with that list. That list is the primary step in making the naming service work.

Tell Me My Name

The *Domain Name System* (*DNS*) constitutes a worldwide distributed database that tracks and gives meaning to Internet domains and host names. Nameserver machines handle chunks of the database called zones, which correspond to the domain or domains within their responsibility. Clients run down a ladder of nameservers to find the IP address of a single node. Figure 12.4 shows you how the distributed and hierarchical DNS process works.

Traditionally, Internet host information for zones is stored in look-up table files on nameserver machines. Under this system, when an administrator needs to move or change a name, the system administrator must edit the files by hand and then instruct the nameserver software to reload the zones.

DHCP allows you to assign or lease IP addresses to network devices, and DNS allows you to assign user-friendly names to IP addresses. Unfortunately, the two servers don't know about each other. For example, when the Windows NT DHCP server leases an IP address to a client PC, it doesn't send a name for that address to the Windows NT DNS server. Because of this, in most cases you assign DNS names only to devices that have static IP addresses, not DHCP-assigned leased addresses.

FIGURE 12.4

Finding a name in the DNS process involves several layers of queries, but it's the best way to spread the work. The segmentation of the database keeps the work of making the frequent changes of individual node names at the lowest level. The highest level names remain under control of the InterNIC to avoid conflicts.

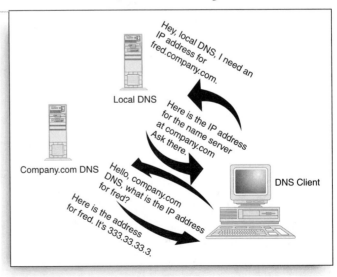

Make DNS Dynamic

A process called dynamic addressing or Dynamic DNS can update DHCP and DNS servers with information. DDNS is available in Windows NT version 5.0 and in products from other companies like Quadritek and Cisco.

The most obvious application of Dynamic DNS is to update with DHCP. It would be particularly useful to link dynamically assigned IP addresses to specific DNS names. For example, if the big boss is out traveling and logs in from a PC at a branch office, that PC will probably have an IP address assigned at login by DHCP. The DNS can link that IP address to the domain name boss.company.com so that other devices on the network can send notices to that PC or take other specific actions without first having to be loaded with the IP address of the machine the boss is using that day.

Dynamic DNS can coordinate static host names for an ISP's dialup subscribers. Many people would like to keep the same host name for their home computer, but ISPs typically randomly assign IP addresses with DHCP when you connect. If an ISP uses a centralized authentication server, such as RADIUS, or identifies the callers by incoming caller ID, the system can coordinate the IP address with specific host names in the DNS.

Dynamic DNS?

I have to note that the term *Dynamic DNS* (*DDNS*) is being used pretty broadly by several companies. It generally means providing a link between DHCP and DNS, but it also means better automation of the DNS information entry process. Check RFC2136 and RFC2137 for current information.

What's WINS?

Microsoft has a proprietary addressing tool called *Windows Internet Name Service* (*WINS*). WINS is on the way out, but it will probably hang around in networks for several years. So in case you run across a WINS network, I'll give you a quick description of what is happening.

The early Windows networks were based on *Network Basic Input/Output System* (*NetBIOS*) names. NetBIOS is a session-level interface used by network applications to communicate over NetBIOS-compatible transport software, including TCP/IP transport software. It establishes logical names for all the devices on the network. Whenever a new device with a new name is added to the network, the global NetBIOS database is updated to reflect the change.

However, NetBIOS names don't function well in a WAN environment linked by routers. NetBIOS computer names on one side of the network are invisible to the users browsing for resources on the other side. Interestingly, NetBIOS clients can usually link to NetBIOS servers across routers if the path name of the server is accurately typed into the client. This drive mapping can be saved for automatic re-use, but that isn't a good fix across the board. To overcome NetBIOS mapping problems, network administrators have relied on text files called LMHOSTS, which contain information that maps the NetBIOS name of a device to its IP address. These files had to be located on each side of a routed connection, and anytime you made a change to one, you had to update all of the others.

WINS replaces the need for LMHOSTS files because it's essentially a NetBIOS name server. Like DNS, WINS servers use a replicated database to hold the NetBIOS device names and their correlated IP addresses. When a Windows-client PC attaches to the network, its NetBIOS name and leased or static IP address are automatically added to the WINS server database.

It appears that Microsoft is giving up on WINS in new releases of Windows NT. But it's still a good practical service.

SEE ALSO

➤ *We describe more of the history of NetBIOS in the section "Microsoft's Networking Strategy: Networking Everywhere," on page 220.*

Heavy Security

Let's assume that you need a conforming IP network addressing scheme. It's true that NAT and gateway services can slow down Internet access and bring some of their own problems in using services like the File Transfer Protocol (FTP). If you have a conforming IP internal network, you need more than a simple router to keep out the snoops and deviants who are a part of modern life (including life on the Internet).

The principle device you'll use is called a *firewall*. Like gateway services, NAT services, and proxy services, firewall functions are being rolled into routers. But there are some good arguments for keeping the firewall as a separate device.

The firewall is a hardware or software product that is the foundation of your Internet security strategy. A firewall inspects all data coming in and out of the network using techniques that compare the data with a security profile you create.

As Figure 12.5 shows, the firewall uses three separate LAN adapters to connect three LAN segments. One connection goes only to the Internet access router. Another connection goes to the high-security internal business network. The third connection is to a *perimeter network*, which carries the servers that require access to the Internet. In this way, the file transfer, newsgroup, FTP, web, email, and other servers can connect to the Internet without acting as an inadvertent pathway into your corporate network. The firewall uses various techniques to check the appropriateness of communications among remote networks and among dial-in users.

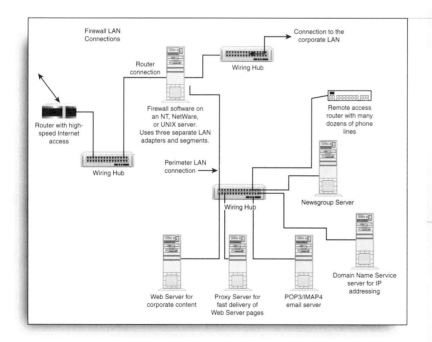

FIGURE 12.5

A good firewall system includes a perimeter LAN with "sacrificial" servers. While the firewall makes every effort to protect the Internet and intranet servers on the perimeter LAN, the amount and type of traffic they exchange with the Internet makes them vulnerable. You can set much tighter restrictions on the traffic on the LAN segment going to and from the enterprise business network.

The firewall intercepts packets when they come in as IP packets. You can set up a firewall to reject all incoming traffic except that from certain addresses or to restrict access according to time of day, application, origin, and other factors. As firewall software evolves, firewalls will look more deeply into the applications payload of the packets. They'll look for inappropriate requests for access and data and make increasingly sophisticated judgments about network traffic.

Internet Tools

The real secret to the success of the Internet and the World Wide Web lies in a common and ubiquitous set of tools. Older computer systems from companies such as IBM and HP had graphics and data transfer capabilities to equal those used on the web, but those tools and protocols were more-or-less proprietary. But today, the tools used on the web are everywhere. You can find a browser for every combination of computer hardware and operating system software. The ubiquitous and standardized nature of the browser makes the underlying hardware and software unimportant to the user.

The TCP/IP suite includes its own set of tools, now more than a decade old, which allows you to perform some basic tasks. The File Transfer Protocol (FTP) provides a way for you to go out and find files and bring them back to your system. Figure 12.6 shows an FTP session. Telnet is a program that lets you connect to a host computer across the Internet (which isn't much different from a terminal connection to a minicomputer). A little more sophisticated is the newsreader, a generic program that allows you to read specific newsgroups. Telnet and FTP are basic tools of the trade based on teletypewriter technology, but the interesting technologies on the Internet—the technologies that will have the greatest impact on the rest of the convergent technologies—make it easier to find and display data.

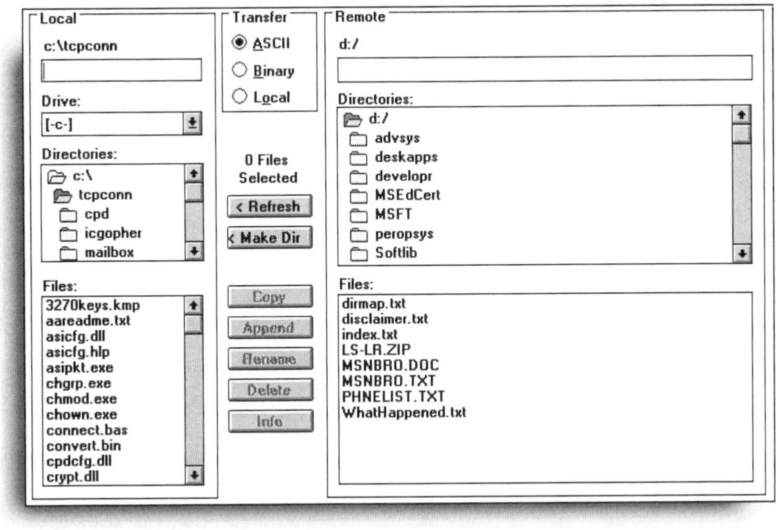

Local	Transfer	Remote
c:\tcpconn	● ASCII	d:/
	○ Binary	
Drive:	○ Local	Directories:
[-c-]		📂 d:/
Directories:	0 Files	📁 advsys
📂 c:\	Selected	📁 deskapps
📂 tcpconn		📁 developr
📁 cpd	< Refresh	📁 MSEdCert
📁 icgopher		📁 MSFT
📁 mailbox	< Make Dir	📁 peropsys
		📁 Softlib

Files:
3270keys.kmp
aareadme.txt
asicfg.dll
asicfg.hlp
asipkt.exe
chgrp.exe
chmod.exe
chown.exe
connect.bas
convert.bin
cpdcfg.dll
crypt.dll

Copy
Append
Rename
Delete
Info

Files:
dirmap.txt
disclaimer.txt
index.txt
LS-LR.ZIP
MSNBRO.DOC
MSNBRO.TXT
PHNELIST.TXT
WhatHappened.txt

FIGURE 12.6

The FTP utility isn't much to look at, but its basic commands allow you to pull down files from servers throughout the Internet. All TCP/IP software packages include the FTP utility.

The aspect of Internet services that most people are aware of is the *World Wide Web* (*WWW*). The web uses an evolution of a concept called *hypertext* to good advantage. The idea for hypertext has been around for quite a while, but it was terribly hard to make it work in **print**. If this were an electronic hypertext document, you would be able to click (or touch or blink at or otherwise indicate) the bold word **print**, and you would branch into a discussion of printing. Hypertext links between subjects can become very complex; while they're the very devil for writers or designers to create, they are extremely useful to readers. A few hypertext books have been published, with tabbed pages leading to linked subject matter, but creating—and using—this kind of document has to be a labor of love. Creating hypertext documents on a computer also requires a lot of detailed work, but at least it's practical.

The *Hypertext Markup Language* (*HTML*) and the *Hypertext Transfer Protocol* (*HTTP*) have made it easy for diverse Internet sites to share all kinds of information. Web browsers use HTTP to create queries for web servers. The queries return in the form of text, diagrams, and illustrations described according to

HTML. The browsers interpret HTML and create the display screens. Many word processors and other programs have the ability to create HTML code from documents you create. So it's easy to create web pages.

But the use of Internet technologies does not have to be limited to a worldwide information platform. Increasingly, organizations are realizing that the same technologies that can stand up to the beating of the Internet can also be used to create a powerful corporate information and collaboration system—an intranet.

Linking PCs to Mainframe Systems

The computer industry is buzzing with the word *downsizing*. It refers to the process of replacing large centralized computer installations with networks of PCs. But despite the trend toward downsizing in the development of new applications and systems, organizations have billions of dollars invested in proven programs running on centralized mainframe and minicomputer systems. Replacing these programs is not cost-effective, and certain scientific and engineering applications will require the power of a mainframe for years to come. Mainframes and minicomputers are going to be around for quite a while, and increasingly, people will want to use PCs to interact with them.

In this chapter I'll describe how to link PCs—and particularly networked PCs—to dissimilar computer systems. I'll provide specifics on the alternative ways you can connect PCs to IBM mainframe computers.

Mainframe and Minicomputer Systems

A mainframe computer system lives up to its label as a "system" with a lot of different interacting parts. Many different pieces of hardware and software must play together in a successful mainframe installation. The system must have at least one central processor, but it isn't unusual for several processors to operate together to share the processing load and to provide backup processing in case one device fails. Such a system might include gigabytes of online data storage and even more storage using tape and other archive systems.

Minicomputer systems are more difficult to define. Only a few years ago, you could safely define a minicomputer as a computer with more than one megabyte of memory. Today, the PCs many people use on their desktops have more processing power and memory than the million dollar minicomputer of a decade ago. Since the 1970s, mainframes were designed to communicate with people through devices called *terminals* that have screens and keyboards. While the terminals include their own processors, memory, and sophisticated video capabilities, they aren't PCs, and they don't run application programs. The mainframe applications, which are often written to serve many users simultaneously, run in the mainframe's central processing unit. One

"Legacy" means "cash cow"

If it isn't broke, don't fix it! If a company has an important line of business applications running on mainframe or minicomputers, why change? Some ambitious MIS managers have used the "Fear of the Year 2000" problem (which focuses on programs that don't understand dates beyond 1999) to force upgrades. But for the most part, smart managers will leave working systems alone. They call them *legacy* systems, but that often means "low-overhead" to managers with budget responsibilities.

terminal can typically have several programs or sessions running on the mainframe at the same time.

Manufacturers offer a variety of connection alternatives for terminals. IBM provides ways for terminals to connect to the central computer system over coaxial cables, through modems, and as part of a local area network.

IBM and the BUNCH

In the 1970s and early 1980s, there were many mainframe and minicomputer companies. The "BUNCH"—Burroughs, Univac, NCR, Control Data, and Honeywell—gave IBM a run for its money. Digital Equipment Corp. established itself as the major vendor of minicomputers. Other companies such as Amdahl and Telex cloned pieces and parts of the IBM mainframe systems.

Today, Digital and a few other survivors market servers running Windows NT and UNIX. Unisys, built on the structure of Burroughs and Sperry, continues to have success in certain mainframe market areas, but most PC-to-central-computer products are designed for IBM mainframes.

IBM 3270

Any explanation of how to hook PCs to IBM mainframe computers has to deal with a lot of IBM equipment numbers and describe the IBM network architecture schemes. IBM's major line of terminals, printers, and other communications devices falls into the general category of the "3270 family" of equipment. Each type of device has a specific model number, many of which begin with the digits 327. They're all designed to work in conjunction to orchestrate access to the mainframe's computing power for users of both PCs and other equipment. Well over 2 million 3270-family terminals were in use in 1990.

IBM's Systems Network Architecture (SNA) is the company's grand scheme for connecting its myriad 3270-family products. It includes a flexible suite of network protocols that can be configured in several ways. Here's how the 3270 family of products fits into various SNA setups.

In a classic 3270 system, each 3278 or 3279 terminal connects to a 3174 or 3274 terminal cluster controller through coaxial cable.

The cluster controller acts as a concentrator by gathering messages from the terminals for more efficient transmission to the mainframe.

Groups of cluster controllers attach via a telecommunications line (which can run a few hundred feet locally or even across the country, through leased telephone lines and modems) to another larger device called a communications controller or a front-end processor (FEP). The common IBM front-end processors are models 3705 and 3725. Other companies, such as ITT Courier, Lee Data, and Memorex Telex, make products that are "plug compatible" and compete with IBM's 3270 devices.

In a relatively recent evolution of the classic plan, IBM gave the 3174 terminal controller, the 3725 FEP, the 3745 communications controller, and other devices the ability to become nodes on a LAN. First the company focused on Token-Ring networking, but later it created options for Ethernet. This architecture requires relatively expensive adapters and more memory on the 3270 hardware. Because the IBM Token-Ring Interface Coupler mainframe hardware has the acronym TIC, this architecture is usually called a "tick" or "tick connection."

SEE ALSO

➤ For more information on the basics of Ethernet networking, see the section "Ethernet the Elder," on page 133.

➤ For more information on Token-Ring networking, see the section "Token-Ring: The IBM Way," on page 149.

PUs and LUs

In IBM's SNA connection scheme, each terminal or printer connected to the controller is called a *physical unit*, or PU. Different kinds of PUs have different capabilities. The front-end processor expects to send certain kinds of data to and get specific kinds of responses from each type of PU.

Each PU holds one or more *logical units*, or LUs, which address and interact with the host in an SNA network. It is actually the LU—typically a program—that does the work that's transmitted over the communications link. IBM's Virtual Telecommunications Access Method (VTAM) software, which runs in the mainframe, works with the Network Control Program (NCP) in the front-end processor to recognize, configure, and communicate with the LUs.

During operation, the 3278/9 terminals send messages called scan codes to the cluster controller each time a key is pressed. The cluster controller echoes the keystrokes back to the terminal so that they are confirmed and displayed on the screen. Data from the mainframe host steps through the front-end processor to the cluster controller and then into a display buffer in the terminal.

Data coming to the terminal for screen presentation is handled in blocks called fields; these can vary in length from a few characters to a whole screen. The size and characteristics of a field depend on what the terminal finds in the display buffer. Characteristics like blinking, reverse video, seven-color displays, and underlining are defined by modified characters containing extended-attribute bytes. These bytes give different meanings to incoming characters to let them represent functions not ordinarily handled in the 8-bit data alphabet the 3270 terminals use.

Easy Transfers

Simple file transfers between a PC and a mainframe are often performed using an IBM editing utility called IND$FILE on the mainframe. This method of moving data is effective, but slow. Companies like Attachmate and Wall Data sell software for both the PC and the host that speeds file transfers between them.

Making mainframe data easily available to PC applications is another task for paired PC/host software. Companies as diverse as Lotus Development Corp. and Martin Marietta market software for the PC that extracts data from mainframe systems for PC applications.

One Screen for All and All Screens for One

Today, people have PCs on their desktops. Personal computers offer a flexibility and responsiveness the mainframe systems can't touch, but many people with PCs also need access to mainframe systems. People from system programmers to administrative assistants make good use of multiple mainframe sessions. Some people continually monitor mail systems (such as IBM's once highly popular PROFS) in one session, while using a scheduling program in a second session and a major mainframe application in a third. People developing applications often have multiple

Very little new under the sun

Today's browser and HTML encoding is nothing more than an open-standard terminal emulation language. It reached an acceptance level greater than any single proprietary terminal language, leading to the ubiquitous browser being available for practically any combination of hardware and operating system, but it is built on the bones of all earlier terminal emulation languages. Similarly, modern "thing clients" and "network computers" seem a lot like terminals by a new name.

sessions active so that they can receive error messages and simulate several users.

People don't want screens and keyboards for both terminals and PCs on their desktops, though, and there are many ways application programs running in a PC can use information distilled by a mainframe application. So the logical thing to do is to make the PC act like a terminal. Some of the most successful and long-lived PC add-on products give PCs the capability to serve as terminals for IBM mainframes.

Before a PC and an IBM mainframe can communicate and exchange data, some major obstacles must be circumvented. For example, the PC's keyboard doesn't have as many keys as a 3270 terminal does, and the terminal has several special graphics characters that aren't in the PC's screen repertoire. The PC also lacks an appropriate communications interface, and it uses the ASCII data alphabet instead of IBM's standard mainframe alphabet, the Extended Binary Coded Decimal Interchange Code (EBCDIC).

Currently, there are three basic ways to overcome these difficulties: by adding a plug-in card combined with software or hardware that makes the PC act like a 3270 terminal when it is attached to a cluster controller; by connecting a protocol converter between the PC and the mainframe that translates the mainframe's data into a form usable by the PC; or by using a network to link the PC and the mainframe.

Connecting the PC to a 3174 or 3274 terminal cluster controller through coaxial cable is a popular technique because it is simple and requires no action at the mainframe end. The technique of using a separate computer called a protocol converter to interface the PC and the mainframe has lost its appeal because it is expensive and because today's powerful PCs can handle the terminal-emulation tasks very well. Given the subject of this book, you can guess that I'll focus on using a LAN to link PCs and mainframes.

SEE ALSO

➤ *We coil up all the information on coaxial cables in the section "Cables for Network Connections," page 106.*

Regardless of the connection scheme, these terminal-emulation products let you touch a key to toggle between a local Windows application program and a screen showing a mainframe process. You don't even have to consider finding desk space for both a PC and a mainframe terminal.

Terminal-Emulation Functions and Features

The terminal-emulation portions of the various products on the market differ mainly in the variety of IBM terminals they ape. Some products act like simple character-mode terminals, while others let the PC, driven by mainframe programs, display excellent color graphics screens. All of them give you the option to remap the PC's keyboard so that various keystroke combinations send the messages expected from the special function keys on IBM terminals.

A PC acting as a terminal operates in one of several modes. A *control unit terminal* (CUT) can have a single session with the mainframe. In the DFT (Distributed Function Terminal) mode, the 3270 terminal can have up to five concurrent sessions with the mainframe. IBM has another related mode it calls MLT (Multiple Logical Terminal) that allows multiple sessions with CUT-mode terminals through IBM's 3174 terminal cluster controller.

An *application program interface*, or API, looks for input from other programs. When an API is available, people who write applications such as accounting, inventory, and communications programs can use simple commands to move data through the network to the mainframe and to interact with mainframe applications. The API converts the relatively simple commands that have been written in C or some other high-level programming language into the complex actions needed to move, verify, and store data.

IBM has defined several APIs for use with mainframe applications. Some of them require software running on both the PC and the mainframe, but others work locally in the PC. For instance, IBM's 3270-PC API and the High-Level-Language Application Program Interface (HLLAPI) run only on the PC; Advanced Program-to-Program Communications (APPC) requires software on both the PC and the mainframe, but it allows for a high degree of integration between PC and mainframe applications.

These products also have the capability of recording and replaying *macros*, sets of recorded keystrokes that are stored and always ready to replay. Macros make it easy to use applications that normally require many keystrokes to start. The programs can memorize the keystrokes you use and store them as a macro that you can easily initiate. Attachmate Corp.'s facility for creating macros is particularly handy because you can easily create a macro that will pause, wait for keyboard input, and then continue. This is useful for entering a date, a password, or some other piece of information.

3270 Under Windows

The topic might sound dry, but products providing 3270 terminal emulation under Windows are exciting to see because they display the full activities of several mainframe programs simultaneously in small windows you can easily read.

Under Microsoft Windows, 3270 terminal emulators can shrink the window displaying a 3270 session almost to postage-stamp size and still provide a usable and readable display. This enables you to monitor the activity in as many mainframe sessions as you're likely to have and still use other local applications.

The *dynamic data exchange* (DDE) capability of Windows allows different applications to share data. The techniques used are called *hotspot* and *hotlink*. Under the hotspot technique, you can control mainframe applications with your mouse. The terminal-emulation program understands cursor movements and mouse inputs over screen elements generated by the host. In other words, you can double-click your mouse on a screen element generated by the host application or mainframe communications software, and the Windows terminal-emulation software will tell the host to take a corresponding action. Under the hotlinks scheme, a specially written application can accept messages in predefined areas of a display generated by the host computer. For example, Microsoft Excel can hotlink to the host display session and react to the information displayed on the screen.

Another way applications can share data is through the Microsoft Windows Clipboard. All the products in this market include an edit feature, with which the user can copy portions of the host display to the Clipboard in Windows and then paste the same data to another application's Windows session. This differs from DDE in that using the Clipboard requires user intervention in order to move the data between applications.

The graphical interface also helps reduce problems associated with remapping the PC keyboard to emulate the much larger 3270 keyboard. Onscreen keyboard maps make it easy to realign the keyboard and to use the mouse instead of keystrokes to select special "keys."

The Coaxial Terminal Connection

The coaxial adapter card architecture, pioneered by DCA and now offered by a dozen companies, supplies each PC with a direct coaxial attachment (common to IBM 3270 terminals) for the mainframe's terminal cluster controller. The PC runs software that makes it act like an IBM terminal, and the mainframe regards it as such. Data is transmitted via standard IBM 3270 cables. The terminal-emulation software in the PC not only lets you transfer files between the PC and the mainframe, but it also typically lets you toggle between mainframe sessions and DOS programs.

Because this type of architecture calls for a dedicated port for each PC on the mainframe's terminal cluster controller—whether or not it is active—connecting a large number of PCs via this method becomes expensive. The performance (measured in terms of throughput and response time) is good, and the installation easy, but the costs for mainframe hardware are high. Additionally, the 3270 coaxial adapter is, like a LAN adapter, another device that you must integrate into each PC; it takes an expansion slot, an interrupt, and some portion of RAM.

LAN Connections

If you use a LAN to connect to a mainframe, you avoid the expense of putting a 3270 coax adapter in every PC, the problems of installing such adapters, and the cost of buying additional terminal cluster controllers for the PCs. There are two distinctly different ways of using a LAN to connect to a mainframe: a direct connection and a gateway. The gateway connection scheme includes several options.

Coax is still good

If your building has coaxial cable connections for 3270 terminals, they'll work with your PC 3270 adapters. If you don't use coax, use unshielded twisted-pair wire. Many companies make plug-in devices to connect between UTP and coax.

Older gateways used a relatively slow SNA synchronous data link control (SDLC) connection operating at 19.2 kilobits per second (Kbps). Today, over a Token-Ring or Ethernet network between the gateway and the mainframe, you can create a link that operates at speeds up to 16 megabits per second (Mbps).

The throughput over the shared 19.2-Kbps SDLC line adequately supports a dozen or more PCs acting as terminals. Gateways with LAN links to the mainframe can handle a hundred or more PCs acting as terminals. While the overhead created by gateway activity on a typical network is negligible, if the PCs do more than terminal emulation—for example, if they exchange files or engage in program-to-program communications—the throughput over the shared link quickly becomes a limiting factor. You can install more gateways on the network to divide the load, but that requires a greater cash outlay for PCs and possibly mainframe hardware. It also means adding to the network manager's workload.

The LAN gateway alternative significantly reduces the cost of mainframe hardware needed for multiple PC-to-mainframe installations. One PC, usually dedicated to the task, acts as the gateway—a specific type of communications server. This is the only machine that connects directly to the mainframe. The mainframe regards this gateway as a terminal cluster controller and talks to it over one of a variety of communications links.

A LAN gateway product consists of a special card that fits into the gateway station's interface bus, software that runs in the gateway station and links the card to the LAN, and terminal-emulation software that runs on each PC on the LAN. The emulation software and gateway software communicate through the network's communications services software.

Both Novell and Microsoft offer gateway products for mainframe connections. You can use IPX, NetBIOS, or IP to carry encapsulated data between the client PC and the gateway. These communications servers work from node to node and are totally separate from the file-server software. You can set up and use a LAN gateway on a network that doesn't even have a file server. Just be sure the gateway product you choose supports the communications services of your network.

In a LAN gateway configuration, the networked client PCs run terminal-emulation software and share the single mainframe connection through the gateway. If you use the network for other tasks, like file sharing and printer sharing, the per-PC cost of attaching to a mainframe can be very low. The primary cost factors are the prices of the gateway computer, the gateway and terminal-emulation software, and the connection scheme you choose.

SEE ALSO

➤ *In the section "The Heaven and Hell of IP," on page 317, I describe how sophisticated gateways translate between IP and IPX and between IP systems conforming to IETF addressing specifications and those that don't.*

Other Gateway Connections

Today, a typical gateway uses a relatively slow SDLC link to connect to the mainframe hardware suite. But you should consider two other gateway-to-mainframe connection schemes: Token-Ring (IEEE 802.5) and IBM 3299 multiplex. Figure 13.1 will help you understand the network-to-mainframe connection alternatives.

The Token-Ring gateway (often called an 802.5 gateway, with reference to the IEEE standard) links the gateway PC and mainframe over a Token-Ring network. The mainframe element is TIC-equipped, and the PC gateway houses one or more network adapter cards, which connect the gateway to the network stations over Ethernet or Token-Ring. Another LAN adapter card in the gateway PC makes the Token-Ring connection to the TIC. You might establish a "PC Token-Ring to mainframe Token-Ring" gateway to reduce the number of physical units polled by the mainframe.

Several companies market gateways that emulate IBM 3299 multiplexers. The real IBM 3299 multiplexer is designed to make it easier to connect a group of terminals to a mainframe over several thousand feet of cable. The multiplexer combines the data from eight coaxial cables onto one cable to reduce the cost of wiring.

Each of IBM's 3174 terminal cluster controllers has one of its four primary channels configured for an IBM 3299 connection. You can economically upgrade controllers with a microcode change to give 3299 service.

FIGURE 13.1

PCs acting as 3270 terminals can connect to the mainframe through an SDLC gateway, a Token-Ring gateway, or a direct Token-Ring connection. A large mainframe installation might include all these attachment schemes.

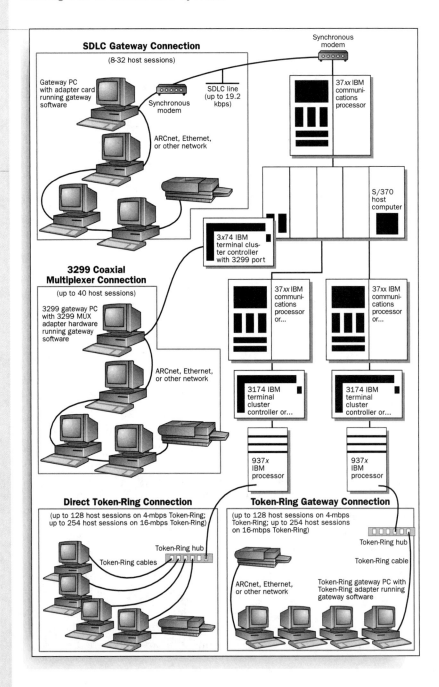

SDLC Gateway Connection

(8-32 host sessions)

Synchronous modem

Gateway PC with adapter card running gateway software

Synchronous modem

SDLC line (up to 19.2 kbps)

37xx IBM communications processor

ARCnet, Ethernet, or other network

S/370 host computer

3x74 IBM terminal cluster controller with 3299 port

3299 Coaxial Multiplexer Connection

(up to 40 host sessions)

3299 gateway PC with 3299 MUX adapter hardware running gateway software

ARCnet, Ethernet, or other network

37xx IBM communications processor or...

37xx IBM communications processor or...

3174 IBM terminal cluster controller or...

3174 IBM terminal cluster controller or...

937x IBM processor

937x IBM processor

Direct Token-Ring Connection

(up to 128 host sessions on 4-mbps Token-Ring; up to 254 host sessions on 16-mbps Token-Ring)

Token-Ring hub

Token-Ring cables

Token-Ring Gateway Connection

(up to 128 host sessions on 4-mbps Token-Ring; up to 254 host sessions on 16-mbps Token-Ring)

Token-Ring hub

Token-Ring cable

ARCnet, Ethernet, or other network

Token-Ring gateway PC with Token-Ring adapter running gateway software

When a gateway PC on a network emulates a 3299 with appropriate software and a special coaxial adapter card, it uses a high-speed connection to the IBM 3174. The gateway can distribute up to 40 simultaneous mainframe sessions to its attached PCs running terminal-emulation software. The 3299 gateway architecture provides throughput at least as good as the Token-Ring connection, with the potential for significantly lower cost.

You can look for many options in gateway systems, including pooled sessions, sessions divided by groups of users, security controls, and trace/dump utilities. Several companies have good management packages, with varying abilities to audit and retire unused mainframe sessions and to control the use of resources.

Installing any LAN gateway requires collaboration between the LAN system administrator and folks with special skills on the mainframe end: the system programmers. People on both sides of the link must set numerous electrical and software parameters to ensure effective terminal operation and file transfer through the gateway.

TIC Trick

The method of PC-to-mainframe connection that IBM's sales force most frequently recommends is a direct Token-Ring connection. The TIC endows IBM mainframe equipment—including the 3174 terminal cluster controller, several front-end processors, the AS/400 processor, and the 9370 mainframe—with the ability to connect to an IBM Token-Ring network directly. Because PCs can also connect directly to a Token-Ring network, PCs and mainframes can interact as peers on the same network as long as each machine runs the appropriate software. This eliminates the need for gateways, dedicated coaxial-cable connections, and slow-speed communications channels.

The TIC generates fast response times. Tests show that you can initiate a file transfer from the mainframe to your PC and receive a 50KB file through the network in one second. The throughput rates measured for Token-Ring connection were, in some cases, 80 times as fast as those recorded when the same hardware was connected through an SNA SDLC LAN gateway.

With the Token-Ring connection, graphics screens sent by the mainframe seem to snap into place as soon as you press Enter.

TIC equipment is not available for older versions of IBM's terminal cluster controllers or front-end processors. If you want to use the TIC architecture, you might have to upgrade to new mainframe communications equipment.

Using the direct Token-Ring connection requires close coordination between the people managing PCs and the people living with the mainframes. The system programmers tending the mainframe must explicitly define each SNA physical unit (that is, each connected PC) in the mainframe software. This means you have to coordinate the addition and deletion of PCs with the mainframe system programmers and wait until they make the changes to their software before the PCs can be serviced.

Finally, if you use a network gateway to connect PCs and mainframes, only one physical unit is defined; that unit distributes many logical units or sessions to the connected PCs. You can add networked PCs in back of a gateway at any time, and they can immediately use 3270 SNA sessions. If you have been in this business for more than a few years, you know that configuration freedom was one of the driving factors behind the popularity of PCs. While the TIC option might appear simple, it can make management more complex.

PC-to-mainframe products for Token-Ring connections are solely software-based. Because Token-Ring adapter cards supply the electrical connections to the mainframe, the PC-to-TIC products consist of 3270 terminal-emulation programs, various utilities, application programming interfaces, and driver software that carries data to and from the Token-Ring adapter cards.

Linking to IBM's AS/400 Family

IBM's AS/400 family of minicomputers offers flexibility and a large time-tested library of software for many businesses. In its standard configuration, the AS/400 connects to separate IBM 5250-series terminals over a specialized dual coaxial cable called *twin-ax*. However, unshielded twisted-pair wire in new installations is replacing the actual coaxial cable.

People sitting at these terminals run programs in the shared processor and memory of the AS/400. Eventually, almost all organizations using AS/400s will want to link PCs to the minicomputer. If you have only a few PCs, you can install a special adapter in each PC for the AS/400 twin-ax cables, load 5250 terminal emulation, and switch between running local applications and running software on the AS/400. AS/400 port connections are expensive, though; but because many PCs in offices are networked, it makes sense to use the network connection to get to the AS/400.

There are several good ways to link a LAN running Novell NetWare, for example, to an AS/400, and there are also a lot of things to consider. Your options include a direct network attachment over either Token-Ring or Ethernet, direct attachment of each PC to the AS/400, or attachment through either of two types of gateways. Then you can choose to use IBM's software with any of the attachment schemes, or you can buy third-party software. In all, it's a situation with a lot of options.

First, you can do things the "IBM way." IBM would like you to buy a Token-Ring adapter for your AS/400 and then run 5250 terminal-emulation software on each PC that works over Token-Ring. If you want to take the Token-Ring attachment route, your present Ethernet LAN doesn't present a problem; you can establish a router in a NetWare server to combine the Ethernet links to the PCs with a Token-Ring link to the AS/400. The primary advantage of the AS/400 Token-Ring connection scheme is that it doesn't require the addition of expensive twin-ax ports on the AS/400.

You can, of course, equip each networked PC with a twin-ax adapter, load 5250 terminal-emulation software, and make a direct connection to the AS/400 from each PC. Because you can attach up to seven terminals or PCs acting as terminals to each AS/400 twin-ax port, you can daisy-chain the wiring to keep costs down. However, choosing this alternative means that you'll have two cables (a LAN cable and an AS/400 twin-ax cable) going to each PC, and that you'll have to have enough AS/400 twin-ax ports to service all the PCs that could ever be on at the same time.

A LAN gateway holds down costs and lets you share the twin-ax port connections. You set up a single PC on the LAN as a gateway to the AS/400. This gateway machine can be an older recycled PC. A single twin-ax adapter in the gateway PC is the only connection to one port on the AS/400, so the gateway can access seven AS/400 connections that it distributes to networked PCs on a first-come, first-served basis. You can put as many as three twin-ax adapters in the gateway, so it can give access to 21 PCs simultaneously across the LAN.

The choice between these attachment schemes is a matter of economics:

- *How many free twin-ax ports have you already bought and paid for on the AS/400?* If you have a lot of ports standing idle, the direct attachment or gateway approaches become more appealing.
- *Do you have a spare PC you can use as a gateway?* If so, that reduces costs.
- *Is it more economical to add a Token-Ring adapter to the AS/400 than it is to buy more twin-ax ports and an individual twin-ax board for each PC?*
- *Is it more economical to add a Token-Ring adapter to the AS/400 and establish a Token-Ring link to a router than it is to establish a gateway between the Ethernet LAN and twin-ax ports?*
- You only have to do some simple addition to come up with the numbers for each attachment alternative.

TCP/IP Online

In a typical TCP/IP network, a cabling and signaling scheme like Ethernet provides the basic links between dissimilar machines. Ethernet adapters are available for practically every type of computer data bus. The cable delivers data wrapped in an Ethernet packet to each machine. Computers with different operating systems and architectures that strip away the Ethernet packet do not know what to do with data they receive from foreign machines unless they find further instructions. TCP/IP provides those instructions. The packets receive standardized handling when they arrive, regardless of the operating environment on the receiving side.

The TCP/IP module used by each machine must be customized for the computer and its operating system but standardized for the network. TCP/IP modules are available for hundreds of mainframe and minicomputer systems and for all PC networks.

There are two ways networked PCs can connect to mainframes using TCP/IP. The first involves loading a TCP/IP software module into every machine on the network. The second configuration uses one machine as a gateway to the TCP/IP network or higher-powered computer.

If your network has a great deal of interaction between different types of machines, it makes sense to give every PC its own TCP/IP module. The small penalties you pay for putting the software on every machine are greater RAM use and increased network overhead.

As the power of the average computer on an office desktop increases, it becomes increasingly practical to use more than one network communications protocol stack in the PC. It is often useful to load a TCP/IP protocol stack in the PC along with some other network protocol stack, such as the IPX used with Novell NetWare.

Setting up a TCP/IP gateway is the best solution for a homogeneous network of PCs that sometimes need access to a specific TCP/IP network or machine. The PCs on this kind of network do most of their work together using whatever PC-to-PC communications protocol the network provides. PC applications needing TCP/IP services send data through the gateway. The gateway translates between the PCs' network-protocol environment and the TCP/IP environment. The TCP/IP software typically runs on a machine dedicated to the gateway task.

The TCP or Transmission Control Protocol portion of TCP/IP comes into operation once the packet is delivered to the correct Internet address and application port. Software packages that follow the TCP standard run on each machine, establish a connection to one another, and manage the communications exchanges. A data-delivery system like Ethernet makes no promises about successfully delivering a packet; neither IP nor UDP knows anything about recovering packets that aren't successfully delivered. But TCP structures and buffers the data flow, looks for responses, and takes action to replace missing data blocks. This concept of data management is called *reliable stream* service.

Programs supporting the FTP protocol give users the ability to log on to dissimilar machines across a network, use a standard command to list available directories and files, and exchange files with the remote machine. FTP can perform some simple data-translation tasks, like converting data between the standard ASCII alphabet and IBM's EBCDIC. FTP is controlled either through responses to command-line prompts or by commands passed from an application program.

The Simple Mail Transfer Protocol (SMTP) lives up to its name. Programs supporting this protocol do little more than follow a strictly defined script used to enter and retrieve email messages. Several companies market SMTP programs for different kinds of computers. The real advantage of this protocol is that the commands that save and retrieve email messages are the same regardless of what machine acts as the host.

The Telnet protocol describes the operation of a communications program that knows how to call for services from the TCP and IP software. The main purpose of software that implements the Telnet protocol is usually to convert the computer it runs on into a minicomputer terminal. Most of the companies include at least a DEC VT-100 terminal emulator in their Telnet packages. Some companies let you run special versions of popular terminal-emulation programs like Walker Richer and Quinn's Reflection on top of their Telnet software. This combination provides sophisticated emulation of Hewlett-Packard and other terminals.

The newest trend in mainframe connectivity is to use the ubiquitous browser to control applications running on the mainframe. Instead of using PC terminal software emulating a specific terminal (such as an IBM 3270), the mainframe is set up to act, in effect, as a web server. Each menu or report of the application program becomes an HTML screen. This method of linking to a mainframe blends the best of the newest and oldest networking technologies.

SEE ALSO
➤ *The section "Software in the Client PC," on page 163, describes encapsulation and the functions of the software layers.*

Telephone Modems

What does a modem do and why? Modems are very valuable communications tools, but they're also cantankerous and difficult to use. The purpose of this chapter is to tell you all about modems and to describe how you can best make them work for you. As modems for standard, dial-up telephone lines make faster connections, they've begun to challenge traditional, leased telephone lines as a way to link LANs. This chapter describes the latest developments in modem technology, provides hints on buying and using modems, and discusses some of the things to look for in modem communications software. Finally, it delves into the modem network remote access products that are so important in extending the network beyond the corporate office.

Modem Basics

Because the dial-up telephone system was designed to pass the sounds of voices, it can't pass the electrical on-and-off signals computers use. The only way to pass computer data over conventional voice telephone lines is to convert it to audio tones that the lines can carry. Simply stated, a modem converts between audio tones on the telephone line and a serial data stream, typically connected to an RS-232 port. If you take the other approach and make the telephone lines compatible with digital data, then you have an ISDN system.

SEE ALSO

➤ *For more about ISDN systems, refer to the section "ISDN," on page 278.*

Interestingly, the signals that your analog modem generates stop just a few miles down the road. Typically, you are within a 6-mile cable run from your telephone company's local central office. The telephone switch inside that central office is a computer. It's usually a fully redundant computer system that responds to the commands from your "terminal" (your telephone dial) and takes complex actions to give you a connection.

As a part of the activity of that switch, the analog signal is translated to a digital data stream. From that point on, the entire system of worldwide switch-to-switch telephone trunks is digital. It's only the last-mile connection that is analog. And it's only because of the last mile that you need an analog modem. Figure 14.1 depicts the analog-to-digital-to-analog translation.

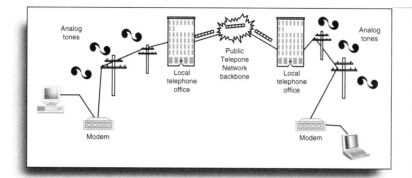

FIGURE **14.1**

Analog modems move their data to the local telephone company's central office. At that point, the data is translated from analog to digital and it travels in digital form across the public telephone network. At the destination, it is typically translated from digital back to analog for delivery on that local loop. However, large organizations now typically have their own digital connections, a fact that has significant implications for faster modems.

Note that in many cases today, if the destination receives more than a dozen or so calls simultaneously, the local loop to destination is a digital line. This digital end connection is the critical factor in the introduction of the so-called "56K" modems. We'll deal with those later in this chapter.

In order to pass data in both directions at the same time, modem signaling schemes split the channel according to the frequency and phase of the signals. One modem uses an "originate" signal set and the other uses an "answer" signal set. Typically, the answering modem sends its signal out first when it picks up the line. This initial signal causes the calling modem to send its own tone set, and the two modems then negotiate a connection.

Sophisticated modems perform several actions during this negotiation phase, including adding electronic adaptation to account for different telephone line conditions and to determine the fastest possible signaling rate the two modems can use. Unfortunately, although the procedures for these negotiations are set by international standards, people who design modems implement those procedures differently. Independent work leads to incompatibility, so whenever a new batch of modems emerges, vendors must spend several months working together to improve

Will ISDN kill off modems?

ISDN is a two-decade-old plan for digitizing the telephone structure. Aren't analog modems going to die off any day now? Frankly, no. At least not in the United States. The analog infrastructure is firmly entrenched. Perhaps after yet another decade of fiddling with local tariffs and access lines, ISDN might become a substantial part of the local loop market—if everything else stands still. But cable modems, wireless access, digital subscriber line services, and competitive local carriers will not stand still. It's more likely that in a decade other services will have brushed ISDN aside, but there will still be a sizeable amount of traffic carried on analog modems.

What's all that noise?

The sounds of modems negotiating a connection are familiar in modern offices. With a little experience, you can tell whether you're going to get a good connection within the first few seconds of the modems' exchange. The modem that answers the phone starts first. It sends out an answer tone and the calling modem replies. From that point on, a sophisticated four-part exchange of heavily modulated and complex patterns helps each modem determine the capabilities of the device on the other end and the quality of the line in between. The exchange consists of start-up, probing/ranging, equalizer and echo canceler training, and final training. During this exchange, each modem tries to configure for optimum transmission speed, error control, and compression.

interoperability. The warning is clear: If you are buying modems for your company or organization, you'll typically get better performance and reliability if you buy all of your modems from a single vendor. Standards are standards, but a lot of modem programming is a matter of style.

Getting Modems Up to Speed

People want to move data quickly and reliably over telephone lines, but generally the lines don't cooperate. Modems convert the electrical signals from a computer into audio tones, but the bandwidth of the telephone line limits how fast the audio tones can change frequency to represent the zeros and ones of computer data. As modems developed, the drive for greater speed focused on two aspects of their operation: the way modems signal and what they say when they signal.

In the United States, early 300-baud and 1,200bps (bits per second) modems used the Bell 103 and 212A modulation schemes, respectively. Other countries settled on similar signaling conventions described in the CCITT V.21 and V.22 standards. The former uses 0–300bps, full-duplex modem transmission; the latter, 600bps and 1,200bps, half-duplex (two-way) modem transmission with a reverse channel of up to 75bps. These early standards became the root of modem evolution around the world.

Modems have evolved on a regular and predictable schedule. On the average, technological developments double modem signaling speed every 18 months. The industry doesn't deliver a new species of modem that often, but the time lapse between modem products correlates closely to the newest product's gain in speed.

Lack of competition and the dearth of inexpensive modem chip sets were the major reasons for the relatively high cost of modem products in the 1970s and early 1980s. In the mid-1980s, Rockwell and other manufacturers made a modem chip that not only encompassed the V.22bis, 2,400bps protocol but was also downward-compatible with the Bell and CCITT protocols for 300bps and 1,200bps. The availability and compatibility of such modem chips led to the introduction of a multitude of low-cost, high-quality 2,400bps modems.

The combination of actions by the U.S. Federal Communications Commission that allowed the attachment of non-Bell System equipment to the telephone lines and the market pull of the PC industry spurred the evolutionary process in the 1980s. In 1987 vendors such as Hayes Microcomputer Systems began offering modems with a 9,600bps proprietary signaling scheme and data compression for under $1,000. In the same time frame, that company offered a modem with full-duplex, CCITT V.32, 9,600bps signaling in the $2,000 price range.

In 1990, modem companies fielded affordable modems with V.32, 9,600bps signaling and a new compression and error control scheme called V.42bis. The V.42bis compression scheme offers as much as a four times improvement in throughput, depending on the compressibility of the data, so although they still signaled at 9.6Kbps (kilobits per second)Kbps over the phone line, under ideal conditions these products could move data at speeds as high as 38.4Kbps. In practice, throughput of 20 to 25Kbps was common when two modems used V.32-style, 9,600bps signaling and V.42bis compression to move compressible data such as spreadsheet files and some graphics files.

In late 1991, modem companies started delivering products that conform to a revised signaling standard called V.32bis. Modems that follow the V.32bis standard offer faster 14,400bps signaling over telephone lines and smoother fallback to more choices of speeds than V.32 models do. V.32 modems try to connect at 9,600bps; if they experience errors, they drop back to 2,400bps. The V.32bis modems do a more extensive analysis of the connection to immediately determine the best usable signaling speed, either 14.4, 9.6, 7.2, 4.8, or 2.4Kbps.

In 1994, the CCITT (now part of ITU) approved a new modem standard called V.34. Because the standard took so long to emerge, a few companies fielded modems using an interim standard called V.Fast Class or V.FC. However, these modems did not provide a full implementation of the standard.

The V.34 modems push against a principle of physics called Shannon's Limit. In simple terms, this law says that the maximum signaling speed is governed by the bandwidth and the ratio of signal to noise on the line. Because the bandwidth of dialed-up telephone lines is set by technical standards and federal law regulates the modem output signal level, line noise effectively governs throughput. The V.34 modems should be able to signal as quickly as ideal lines theoretically allow.

At first, the modem designers thought that the telephone systems of North America would allow signaling at a maximum rate of 19.2Kbps. But reexamination of the systems showed that fiber-optic cable and new equipment provide for a signaling rate of at least 28.8Kbps. Modern V.34 modems try to start signaling together at 33.6Kbps and then move down.

In theory, the combination of V.34 signaling at 33.6 or 28.8Kbps and V.42bis error control and compression could move highly compressible application data across the wire at an effective speed of over a megabit per second. As is true for so many top-end speeds, however, you only get something close to the theoretical maximum under ideal conditions on a closed track, and with a professional driver. As I'll explain later in this chapter, both the telephone lines and the PC hardware work against optimal performance.

The 56K Modem

The latest evolution in modem technology is the V.pcm standard. The pcm acronym stands for *pulse code modulation*, a scheme that broke the previous speed barriers, at least in one direction. It took more than a year of inconvenience, uncertainty, and partial steps to get to V.pcm.

SEE ALSO
➤ Modern V.pcm modems are very useful for the type of WAN connections described in Chapter 11, starting on page 271.

For several years, we were told that 33.6Kbps was the end of the line for modems. Two things limit a modem's maximum speed. First, the frequency response of a telephone line is fairly limited, so modems must use a narrow range of audio frequencies to move the data back and forth. Second, the audio-to-digital conversion process performed at the telephone company's central switching facility introduces a small amount of noise into the audio signal.

In 1997, U.S. Robotics (since purchased and molded into 3-Com) rolled out a modem technology called the x2. A few months later, Rockwell fielded a chip set that many companies used to deploy a competing product called K56Flex. Both of these products were widely known as "56 kilobit" modems, but neither one was. The FCC regulations controlling the amount of audio power going into the telephone lines keep the "56K" modems throttled back to a maximum of about 53 kilobits. The typical connection rate is about 45Kbps on the downlink from the Internet service provider or corporate office to the distant caller. The path from the caller to the ISP or office is a V.34 modem with typical connection speeds of 19–22Kbps.

The 56K modem developers found a loophole in Shannon's Limit by routing the data via a digital line from the telephone company's central switch to a server at an ISP or corporate office. By taking advantage of the high quality no-noise line provided by the host-side digital connection, they achieve higher overall download speeds. All other things being equal, the shorter and cleaner the line to the telephone company's switch, the better the connection speed will be.

The vast majority of lines coming into ISPs or into corporate access servers are digital T1 or ISDN PRI (Primary Rate Interface) lines. Generally these digital lines are preferred because they provide cleaner connections than analog lines do and they are more economical to order. A single T1 or ISDN PRI line can accommodate up to 24 users at once, and the lines are often cheaper than the equivalent number of analog lines.

Problems arise when you factor in some of the tricks the telephone company plays to get the most out of its lines. Many phone lines are multiplexed together using a device called a *Subscriber Line Concentrator*, or SLC. The SLC combines 24 or more analog phone lines into one digital signal for transmission over a pair of copper wires.

The problem is that many older central switches can't directly connect to an SLC line. At these locations, the SLC line is converted back to analog form, and each analog line is individually connected to the central office switch. Digital phone switches—the majority of switches in use today—re-convert the analog phone signal to digital format once more for connection over the phone company's digital network.

The bottom line is this: If your phone line is on a nondigitally connected SLC, you're out of luck; V.pcm modems simply do not work on these lines. In some areas, you may be able to convince your phone company to bypass the SLC and give you a dedicated nonmultiplexed line, but those lines are in short supply. Laptop users looking for near-ISDN speeds from their hotel rooms will be equally disappointed. That's because V.pcm technology won't work behind most office or hotel PBX systems unless the PBX is attached to the telephone company's central office through a T1 or ISDN PRI line.

Most modern PBX systems are digital, so they convert each extension's analog signal into digital form. If you place a call on an outbound analog line, the PBX reconverts the digital signal into analog form, causing the same multiple-conversion problem.

When it works, V.pcm provides near-ISDN speeds at a fraction of the cost. Several modem vendors offer dial-up test centers you can use with any modem to test your line. We have found that if you have two lines into the same house, installed at different times, one might work at full speed with V.pcm even if the other doesn't work.

Voice over Data Modems

For a while around 1996–1997, the idea of combining voice and data functions on the same analog phone line took hold in the industry. The concept is called *simultaneous voice/data* or SV/D. Technical support people, in particular, saw SV/D as a great way to be able to talk to a customer while also uploading a software patch or taking other actions inside the computer to cure a problem. Like so many other great ideas in search of a problem, the SV/D modem never reached the greatness of its designers' dreams. Standards do conflict, and buyers can never be sure that modems will be compatible. However, some useful voice capabilities remain in modem products in the market.

Generally, voice+data modems offer one or more of these features:

- *Autodialer:* If you use it with a personal information management program, the autodialer function of a modem is valuable. Under the command of an application, the modem dials the phone, but doesn't attempt to make a data connection. Traditional modems can dial the phone, but your software then has to send sophisticated instructions to get them to not try to send data.

- *Speakerphone:* Could be a headset or handset connected to your computer. The modem has an input/output jack or some other way to connect to your sound card, or, like the Creative Labs Phone Blaster cards, the modem is a combined sound/modem card. You can then use the microphone and speakers you already have for your phone.

- *Voice mail:* Some modems include sophisticated voice mail capabilities with separate voice mailboxes and the capability to give callers a menu of choices.

- *Caller ID:* This service transmits the telephone number of the calling party to you between the first and second rings. If the modem vendor includes the correct software, the caller ID information pops up on your computer screen.

- *Incoming call auto-detect:* Listens for the CNG tone sent by a calling fax machine and attempts to distinguish between incoming fax and voice calls.

- *Simultaneous voice/data* (SVD): This is the dream that never came true. This capability enables users to send data over voice lines during a voice call or at least shift back and forth between voice and data within a single call.

It's pretty clear that SVD is another casualty of the Internet. The techniques for combining voice and data over IP networks have more momentum than SVD. But other modem features such as integrating a sophisticated answering machine can be valuable, particularly in a small business environment.

ROM du Jour: Choosing Modems with Programmable ROMs

The most complex modem products use programmable digital signal processors, so they are what the programming in their ROMs tells them to be. This fact has important implications for anyone buying these modems. Shop with an eye on the nameplate as well as the price and performance figures—you should choose a product from a company that will be in business long enough to refine their ROM programming.

It's true that most ROM updates make small changes that impact only a few users. One such example would be a ROM change that merely enables a modem to recognize the busy signal or dial tone generated by a specific brand of PBX. Some changes certainly have a wider impact, however. My advice is straightforward: first, check the company's upgrade policy before you buy; and second, if you have trouble with one of these modems, contact your dealer or the company to see whether they've made any ROM changes to control the problem. The ROM tells the modem how to do its work, so don't hesitate to ask for new instructions if you think you need them.

Getting It Right: Error Control and Data Compression

As signaling speed increases, it's important to maintain—and ideally, to improve—accuracy. As communications systems have evolved, this has been accomplished through the development of error control techniques in both modems and communications software.

The Microcom Network Protocols (MNP) 2 through 4 became the industry's de facto standards for hardware error control. The CCITT caught up with the modem industry in 1988 when it issued the V.42 error control standard. V.42 includes two protocols: The primary one is the Link Access Procedure for Modems (LAPM); the secondary protocol is functionally equivalent to MNP 4.

The desire for greater speed has also led to data compression. During data compression, a program (either communications software or modem firmware) running at one end of the link examines data that's ready for transmission, looking for redundant elements. During transmission, it uses a short data string to replace commonly used characters and redundant data strings.

Microcom's introduction of the MNP 5 protocol for data compression was followed in 1989 by CCITT's release of the V.42bis standard for asynchronous data compression using the Lempel Ziv compression algorithm. This algorithm offers a significant improvement over the MNP 5 protocol, both in data compression capability and in real-time compensation.

The V.42bis data compression scheme represents the state of the art in single-pass, adaptive compression techniques. It is always better to compress files before transmission using a multipass program such as ARC, Lharc, or PKZIP that examines the contents of a file and uses the best compression technique than it is to rely solely on V.42bis compression. V.42bis provides good throughput when no pretransmission compression technique is available, however. Unlike the older MNP 5 compression system still used by many modems (and typically offered as a fallback to the primary compression scheme in V.42bis), V.42bis compression does not slow the transmission of already-compressed files.

Both error control and data compression protocols are independent of modulation protocols; that is why you can find MNP, V.42, and V.42bis capabilities in most new modems. Table 14.1 describes the signaling, error control, and data compression standards that apply to modem communications. As you can see, modems and communications programs can conform to a bewildering combination of signaling protocols, error control schemes, data compression schemes, and file transfer protocols. Note also that functions are often redundant—it isn't unusual to use modems that provide error control on the modem-to-modem link in conjunction with software that provides error control over the entire link.

TABLE 1.1   Standards for modem communications

Modem Signaling Protocols	Description
Bell 103	An almost obsolete standard for signaling at 300 baud
V.21	An international 300bps signaling standard that is similar to Bell 103
Bell 212	A standard developed by the Bell Operating Companies for operations at 1,200bps
V.22	An international standard for 1,200bps operation that is similar to Bell 212
CCITT V.22bis	An international standard for modem signaling at 2,400bps
CCITT V.32	An international standard for modem signaling at 9,600bps, with a fallback to V.22bis rates
CCITT V.32bis	An international standard for modem signaling at a maximum rate of 14.4Kbps with a fallback to 12, 9.6, 7.2, or 4.8Kbps
CCITT V.FC	An interim standard for signaling at a rate of 19.2Kbps over dial-up telephone lines
ITU V.34	An international standard for signaling at a maximum rate of 28.8 to 33.6Kbps
Error Control Protocols	An international standard for signaling at speeds theoretically as fast as 56Kbps, but typically 40–50Kbps in the download channel from the service provider to the user. The upload channel follows V.34 standards. The systems relies upon a digital connection from the telephone company to the ISP or corporate office.
Microcom Network Protocol (MNP) Level 4	A widely adopted scheme for discovering errors in a stream of data and requesting transmission of an appropriate block
Microcom Network Protocol (MNP) Level 10	A system used primarily in Microcom modems for rigorous control, as in cellular telephone modem connections, for example
CCITT V.42	A standard scheme for discovering errors in a stream of data and requesting retransmission of an appropriate block; includes the LAP-M and MNP Level protocols

Modem Signaling Protocols	Description
Microcom Network Protocol (MNP) Level 5	A widely adopted compression scheme, riding over MNP Level 4 error control, that is often able to give a 3:1 compression advantage; does not work well with precompressed files
CCITT V.42bis	A standard data compression scheme able to give as much as a 4:1 commpression advantage on certain types of files; requires V.42 error control, and is compatible with file pre-compression techniques

Handling the Data

Both V.42 and MNP error control modems segment data streams into packets. Each outgoing packet includes a 16-bit (optionally, 32-bit for V.42 and V.pcm modems) cyclical redundancy check (CRC), which is a statistical analysis of the packet's contents. The receiving modem performs the same statistical analysis on the incoming packet that the sending modem performed as the packet went out; if it cannot match the CRC, it asks the sending modem to retransmit the frame.

With no error correction, data is sent with a start bit, 8 data bits, and a stop bit. This means that it takes 10 bits to send a single byte in asynchronous mode, and that a 2,400bps modem can send only 240bps. With V.42 or MNP error control employed, you can achieve about 22% more throughput, including packet overhead.

Most popular communications software, such as Kermit, XModem, YModem, and ZModem, offers error control and data compression schemes. These protocols operate only during file transfers, while the MNP 5 and V.42bis firmware in modems work all the time.

Communications software packages that include their own error control do not provide optimal performance with modems that are already using MNP or V.42 error control connections. To take full advantage of MNP or V.42 error correction, select the software's no-error-correction option when transferring files. YModem-G sends 1,000 bytes per block without software acknowledgment. Using YModem-G, it is common to see throughputs above 270 bytes per second using V.22bis modems with MNP or V.42 error handling.

Data compression provides the potential for even larger savings during file transfers. For both MNP 5 and V.42bis operations, the data throughput speed varies according to the type of data being transmitted, but both ASCII and binary data are compressed. V.42bis offers a potentially better compression algorithm, and is more robust in the way it dynamically adjusts the compression scheme for the data flow.

Most modems on the market today include Microcom's MNP Class 5 data compression protocol. MNP 5 uses two types of data compression algorithms to move certain kinds of files up to twice as fast as they would normally traverse a communications line were they transmitted without any software or hardware compression protocols in place. These two techniques are *Huffman encoding* and *run-length encoding*.

Huffman encoding takes advantage of the simple fact that some ASCII characters appear more frequently than others. In a typical data communications session without compression, each character is encoded using a 7- or 8-bit code. Software following the Huffman encoding strategy sends the most frequently used letters in 4-bit groups; less frequently used characters are encoded by as many as 11 bits. Although less frequently-used characters can require more bits than uncompressed characters, you still save time with Huffman encoding because the more frequently repeated characters are sent in fewer bits.

When a file is transmitted, the compression software includes information on the length of the encoded character and then the encoded character itself. Because some characters are repeated so often, the data stream containing these common characters is much shorter after compression than it would be using more typical ASCII encoding.

The second type of compression used in MNP 5, run-length encoding, takes advantage of the easy identification of a string of repetitive characters, including nonprinting characters such as line feeds, carriage returns, and spaces. When MNP 5 sees at least three of the same characters in a row, it uses run-length encoding. It sends those characters and a count indicating the number of times those characters repeat. Effective handling of repetitive characters provides excellent compression for certain types of files, such as spreadsheets, that use many repeated non-printing characters for formatting.

Modern modems enable you to disable MNP 5, an important feature when you're downloading compressed files from bulletin boards or transmitting files that have been previously compressed with programs such as PKZIP or Lharc. If the MNP 5 protocol on the modem link is active when you're dealing with previously compressed files, it actually slows the throughput.

MNP 5 software provides data compression and error handling on the entire link, including the segment between each PC's serial port and the attached modem. Nonetheless, other file transfer protocols such as XModem and ZModem, which include their own compression and error control, have proven more popular than MNP 5 because they also automate the task of transferring files.

Microcom enhanced its data compression technique with the introduction of MNP 7, which encodes characters according to the frequency of character pairs. MNP 5 provides a 2-to-1 compression ratio for some types of files; MNP 7's compression ratio for similar files is 3 to 1. This means that, when sending exactly the correct kind of compressible data file, a modem with a modulation rate of 50Kbps can provide a throughput of up to 150Kbps, if it is connected to a high-speed serial port. Still, the Lempel Ziv algorithm used in V.42bis is more efficient than MNP 7 with certain types of files.

SEE ALSO

➤ *The routers described in the aptly named section, "Routers," on page 259, make good use of standard compression techniques.*

➤ *Compression reduces the costs of the wideband circuits described in Chapter 11, starting on page 271.*

For some applications, the V.42bis protocol is clearly superior to MNP 5. Both V.42bis and MNP 5 provide data buffering, which enables your computer port speed to be faster than the signaling rate used between the modems. Modern modems enable you to configure the modem to communicate with the PC at speeds of up to 115.2Kbps. To take full advantage of the improved throughput of data compression protocols you have to set the serial port link between the PC and the modem to a speed higher than the connection speed between the modems.

If you're transmitting a file previously compressed with an efficient program like PKZIP or Lharc, V.42bis is significantly faster than MNP 5. MNP 5 protocol on the modem link actually slows the throughput by constantly searching for ways to compress the already compressed file.

Performance Limitations

The more products push the performance envelope, the more they need a controlled environment. Modern modems require nearly perfect telephone lines and specially configured serial port connections to reach throughputs near 1Mbps when moving a highly compressible file. Typical throughput for text files between same-brand modems hovers at around 30–60Kbps.

The conditions a modem faces on any dialed telephone call vary widely. Interestingly, some of the worst conditions can occur on calls that are considered local rather than long distance. Local "tail" circuits seldom receive the maintenance given to long distance circuits, so calls within a city or regional area may traverse some of the worst telephone lines. The noise and distortion on a circuit can affect the speed of the connection the modems negotiate and their capability to move data without errors. Error control schemes can catch errors and request retransmission of the bad blocks, but that takes time and reduces effective throughput.

Although most people anticipate hostile telephone lines, the limitations built into the PC's serial port often present a surprise bottleneck. You can lose data coming from a fast modem to a PC if you don't have modern hardware, and many communications programs deliberately slow the system's throughput for reasons that were once sound but are now possibly obsolete.

Improving Throughput

Because of data compression, the throughput between two modems can be much faster than the signaling rate indicates. Modems signaling at 20Kbps may be moving files with an effective throughput of 30Kbps or even more; however, if you are running your PC's serial port at a slower speed, you don't benefit from the increased throughput.

When you configure modems for faster port speed, you must send a setup string to the modem to disable a feature called the BPS Rate Adjust. When this feature is on, it links the port speed to the modem carrier speed. After turning it off, you must also set the Serial Port Flow Control parameter to enable bidirectional control of the RS-232 Clear to Send (CTS) and Request to Send (RTS) lines.

The internal programming in some modems operates using MNP 5 or V.42bis as a factory default condition, but other modems must be programmed to use these protocols. It's good practice to send a complete setup string to any modem every time it dials. For most modems that follow the Hayes AT commands, the setup string `AT\J0\G0\Q3\N2\VI%C1` disables BPS adjust, disables XON/X-OFF flow control, enables bidirectional RTS/CTS, forces a link with MNP error control, shows you the status of the MNP connection, and enables MNP 5 data compression. The setup string `AT&K3&Q5S46=138WI&R0S48=128` works to initialize Hayes V.42bis modems for the same conditions using a V.42bis connection. Not all V.42bis modems are the same, however. You might have to work with the modem vendor to get the setup string exactly right if it doesn't work out of the box.

Don't forget, you must also set your communications software for the correct port speed and for RTS/CTS flow control. After you have the serial port, modem, and communications software initialized for optimum performance, your data is sent and received faster and more reliably.

About the UART

Most serial cards have an 8250 (8-bit) or 16450 (16-bit) UART (Universal Asynchronous Receiver-Transmitter)—both versions operate the same way. When we tested modems, we discovered that the UART can be the weak link in the communications chain.

The UART controls the flow of data through the serial I/O port—it moves data between the serial port and the CPU's parallel data bus. Normally, when a byte arrives at the PC from the modem, the UART signals the CPU with an interrupt. If the CPU is already answering a higher-priority interrupt, the CPU may not immediately respond to the incoming interrupt, which causes the next inbound byte to overwrite the current one. For most asynchronous file-transfer operations, this results in a checksum error, which demands that the entire data packet be retransmitted.

The 16550AFN UART, a direct replacement for the other chips, solves the overrun problem by creating a first-in, first-out (FIFO) buffer stack. This lets the UART save incoming data until the CPU is ready to process it, but to initiate buffer operations, the 16550AFN needs communications software that can control its FIFO buffer.

At the highest speed of a V.34bis modem, data travels from the modem to the PC at a rate of about 10 characters per millisecond. The buffer in the 16550AFN can hold 16 characters (about 1 millisecond worth of data) provided your communications software turns the buffer on—many of us use programs a year or two old that do not activate the buffer. This 16-character buffer provides enough holding space to enable the UART to survive short periods of inattention from the CPU without losing data. Unfortunately, older UART chips, like the 8250 and 16450, don't have this first-in, first-out buffering.

But sometimes the CPU ignores the UART for more than a few milliseconds. Communications software writers have learned, for example, that some disk drive controllers block interrupts from reaching the CPU for as long as 20 to 40 milliseconds while they access a disk sector. With interrupts blocked, the data can't move from the UART to the CPU, so it is overwritten and lost. Modem error control programs can't prevent these losses because they happen in the PC. For these reasons, communications program designers rely on hardware handshaking—controlling clear-to-send signals on the RS-232 line—to slow the data flow from the modem to the PC. Typically, communications programs tell the modem to stop sending data to the PC whenever they move data to disk or perform other functions that might result in blocked interrupts.

You didn't buy an expensive new modem to have a communications program slow the data flow, so you must make sure your PC has modern serial port hardware that your communications software can use to get the best possible data flow from a high-speed modem.

USB for Modem Connection

The votes aren't all in yet, but it appears that Universal Serial Bus connections are just the thing to use as an interface to fast modems. With its 12Mbps capability, USB can handle the fastest ISDN and modem connections, even using full compression. Watch for values in USB modems, but make sure that your computer and operating system are both fully equipped for USB before you buy.

SEE ALSO

➤ *For more information on USB, please refer to the section "USB: The Universal Serial Bus," on page 82.*

External Versus Internal Modems

Almost all modem vendors market internal modems that plug into a slot in your PC. Except for their physical configuration, internal and external modems aren't much different. Every organization should have some of each type to meet specific users' needs.

Internal modems offer some significant advantages: Primarily, they come with their own UART and a built-in method of controlling the flow of data between the UART and the modem. The makers of fast modems typically put a 16550AFN UART on the internal modem to reduce overflow problems. Also, because the internal modem combines the serial port and modem in one device, you don't have to hassle with the proper configuration of an RS-232 connecting cable, the modem doesn't occupy desktop space, and you don't have to find a free AC wall plug for it. Because they don't have cabinets and power supplies, internal modems are typically a little less expensive than their external kin. They're cheaper to produce, too, so manufacturers can usually afford to throw in a communications software package. Finally, you can assign most internal modems to COM3 or COM4 to save an existing serial port. On the other hand, the few internal modems that are limited to the alternatives of COM1 or COM2 can be difficult to install if the PC in question already has those ports wired into the motherboard. To use an internal modem at one of these port designations, you usually have to run a special program or move jumpers to turn off the internal COM port.

Many people like external modems because the lights installed on the front panel of most models show what is happening. A quick glance at the carrier detect, read data, and terminal ready lights tells you whether the circuit is still up and functioning. In addition, it's easy to move external modems between PCs, but changing internal modems is a project.

Electrically, PC Card modems are similar to internal bus modems. Amazingly, they pack a UART, data pump, line transceiver, and all the other necessary parts inside a creditcard-sized package. Also, the PC card is handy for resetting a hung modem—you can just pull it out and slide it in again. Note that Windows 95 prefers that you stop the PC card device, using the icon on the toolbar, before physically removing the device.

Preparing Your Modem for Action

Modems for standard telephone lines typically have two RJ-11 telephone jacks, one for a telephone and one for the line that plugs into the wall jack. A few have their RJ-11 jacks wired straight through so you can use either jack for either connection, but in this configuration picking up the phone while the modem is connected can inject noise into the circuit. Other products designate the telephone and line jacks and provide for orderly

---

Pull the card!

PC Card devices draw their power from the computer's battery. A modem draws as much as seven watts while in use, but only about one watt in sleep mode. In rough numbers, modem operation can take 10–30% percent of your laptop's total power, so using a modem can significantly reduce your battery's life. Pull the card out of the slot if you're running on batteries and don't immediately need a modem.

switching between the two devices through a software command or manual switch.

The major setup task for many modems involves determining which commands you must embed in a setup string and send to the modem so it knows which error control and data compression protocols to use, which speed to use on the modem and serial links, and which type of flow control to use on those links. The configurations for a few modems are explicitly included in the setup menus of the most popular communications programs and in Windows dial-up networking.

The Hayes Standard AT command set enables you to configure any modem for specific operations: You can set the speaker volume, turn it on or off, change the flow control between your PC and modem, or dial telephone numbers. The AT command set also enables you to tell the modem whether to use dial tone or pulse, which kind of telephone line (2- or 4-wire) to use, when to answer automatically, and how many rings to allow before answering. For modems with both error control and data compression, the instruction set is extended to control the way the modem negotiates its protocols, as well as specific parameters within the protocols. Most implementations of the Hayes AT command set also enable you to change your modem configuration on the fly and store the change for future use.

Using Modems Under Windows

Microsoft did a good thing for modem communications by bundling the drivers and setup strings for dozens of modems in Windows. Windows makes these setup strings and communications port control services available to applications in Windows Dial-Up Networking. Programmers can write applications that conform to the Windows application program interface and avoid the hassles of trying to account for different kinds of modems and connections. Microsoft calls the specification *UniModem*. The modern Unimodem specification provides for interfaces to voice devices and provides ties to other Windows services. You're likely to hear the term *Unimodem* used in conjunction with specific modem drivers that conform to the Microsoft specification.

During the initial setup of Windows, the operating system attempts to determine the brand and type of modem attached to each of the computer's serial ports. If the modem is a new one that isn't in the Windows library, the manufacturer supplies a Windows driver on a diskette. If you misplaced the diskette, you can usually download the file from the modem manufacturer's web site. Windows does a surprisingly good job of identifying modems. If you want to add or change a modem after Windows is installed, simply click on the Modems icon in the Windows control panel.

International Road Warriors

I've focused on North American telephone communications systems, primarily because outside of North America the situation is very confused. If you're an international road warrior, you face some unique problems starting with a few that are simply mechanical. For example, about 35 types of telephone jacks are in use around the world if you include variations such as the old Swiss 3-prong and the new Swiss 4-prong. Other challenges come from standards or equipment that are even more arcane. For example, several countries put intermittent pulse tones on the local loop from the central office to trigger metering equipment in the customer's premise. These tones might be optional and might be filtered by a PBX, but they also might interrupt your modem. The best advice I can give you is to phone ahead and ask about modem connections wherever you might be going.

Sharing Telephone Lines

Many people today work in small or home offices with a limited number of telephone lines, but still need the capabilities of voice, data, and fax operation. A product I call a line manager enables you to share a phone line among several devices with a minimum amount of hassle.

The line manager looks like a small modem. It connects to the telephone line and to the voice telephone instrument, to a modem, and to a fax machine. In operation, the line manager answers the ringing telephone line, listens for a while, and then decides how to route the call. But if you're thinking "it can't really be that simple," you're correct! It's what happens during the listening period that makes the difference.

The least complex type of line manager shares a voice telephone and a fax machine on a single line. Many new fax machines aimed at the small and home office markets have this feature along with an answering machine capability. These devices work by listening for the calling (CNG) tone generated by a fax machine when it originates a call. If the line manager hears the CNG tone, it generates a ring to the fax machine. If it doesn't hear the CNG after 3 to 4 seconds, it concludes that the incoming call is a voice call and rings the telephone. Because a person listening as the call goes through might interpret silence as an incomplete call and hang up, the line manager supplies a ringing tone to the caller while it listens for the CNG tone.

You can also use one of these relatively simple devices if you want to share a modem and a fax machine on the same line. Because calling data modems are silent, like calling people, you can attach your modem to the fax line manager port that's designed for a telephone instrument, and it rings the modem and completes the call after it decides that the incoming call is not a fax. However, make sure modem callers set their software to expect 7 to 10 rings before an answer.

The situation becomes much more complex if you want to share a line between an answering modem and a voice telephone instrument. Unlike fax machines, calling modems and calling people are both silent, so the fax line manager can't differentiate between them. The usual technique is to have the calling modem dial extra digits—usually a number 4 on the tone pad—just after the line manager answers. The line manager is programmed to look for these tones and to respond by connecting to the answering modem. This technique is tricky because calls to different places and calls placed at different times of day take different periods of time to connect; you have to experiment with the number of commas you put in the dialing string to create a pause, and with the number of times you send the digit 4.

Alternatively, you can program the calling and answering modems to use each other's tones, so that the calling modem originates a set of answer tones. This technique isn't as sensitive to the time needed to complete a call, but the modem commands are more complex. With either technique, you'll have to program the communications software so that the modem makes some noise if you want the line manager to differentiate between voice and modem callers.

A word of caution: All line managers are not compatible with all modems. The modem looks for a ring signal that is a sine wave with a 90-volt amplitude and 20Hz frequency. Most line managers try to emulate the sine wave by generating a digital signal, but some modems don't respond. If your modem doesn't respond to the line manager's ring, return the line manager for another model; it's not the modem's fault.

Communications Software

Dennis Hayes delivered his first modem designed specifically for a personal computer years before IBM shipped the first PC. Yet despite more than a decade spent refining the bonds between modems and communications software, unless you've had a lot of rehearsal or experience you still stand only about a fifty-fifty chance of successfully transferring a file between two PCs on the first try using sophisticated V.34 modems.

There are three types of communications software products: general purpose, network remote access, and front-end access. Network remote access programs fall into two categories: remote node and remote control. Modem remote control packages enable one computer to substitute its keyboard and screen for the keyboard and screen of another computer for remote control operation. Remote node systems give the calling computer new disk drive letters and, within limits, access to network applications. Front-end access packages are specifically designed to access a single special-purpose information service such as NEXIS or many investment services. However, today the ubiquitous browser has taken over the role of these special purpose

programs in almost all cases. There are a few high-value investment and arcane research databases with their own front-end
software, but their days are numbered.

General Purpose Telecommunications Programs

One interesting category of communications software products
consists of the general-purpose telecommunications packages.
These are "Swiss army knife" programs that do a lot of jobs well.
You can use them to establish PC-to-PC communications, to
dial into systems such as mini- or mainframe computers, and to
dial into the few remaining ASCII-based information services.

The most widely available general-purpose communications program is the HyperTerminal program included in Windows. Most
other general purpose programs offer a host of similar features
implemented in a similar way. Pull-down menus, dialing directories, and a variety of file transfer protocols grace virtually all of
them.

In simplest terms, a telecommunications program turns your PC
into a communications terminal that has a screen and a keyboard. The program sends the characters typed on the keyboard
out the serial port and displays the characters received from the
serial port on the screen. Each of these seemingly simple tasks
has unique complicating factors.

Inside the PC, the communications software must activate and
manage the functions of the UART as it converts between the
parallel data stream used inside the computer and the serial data
stream used for connections to the outside world. Typically, the
software does this through hardware for the RS-232C signaling
and cable connection scheme.

The data flowing in and out of the serial port requires careful
control. PCs typically use either hardware or software methods
of flow control with modems. Software flow control relies on
sending special characters called XON and XOFF in the data
stream that signal the modem or the PC to stop sending data
so the receiving device can catch up. Hardware flow control
depends upon changing voltage levels on certain wires in the

Upgrade your HyperTerminal

If you use general-purpose
communications software,
download HyperTerminal
Private Edition from
www.hilgraeve.com.
This slick and easy-to-use
update adds important features
and is a free upgrade designed
to draw your attention to
Hilgraeve's other programs.

RS-232 cabling scheme—typically Request to Send and Clear to Send—which signal a PC's availability to receive data. I recommend using hardware flow control, because software flow control schemes can be fooled by characters embedded in the streams of data PC users send when they transfer compiled program files or precompressed data files.

On the incoming side, the communications software also controls the display of received data on the screen. Some computers, particularly mainframe and minicomputer systems such as those delivered by Digital Equipment Corporation and IBM, expect special purpose terminals on the other end of the communications link. These machines control the position of the cursor and the display of the characters on the screen through special codes they transmit in the serial data stream. A portion of the communications software called the *terminal emulation package* gives a PC the capability to respond to control codes and to generate special keyboard codes just as a terminal does.

The quality of terminal emulators varies widely. Although all general purpose communications programs have some terminal emulation capabilities, there are also programs that specialize primarily in terminal emulation functions. General purpose programs typically make PCs respond to a code set specified by the American National Standards Institute (ANSI) and to the commands designed for Digital Equipment Corporation's VT-100 and VT-220 series of terminals.

File Transfers

When PCs link with each other, with information services, or with mini- or mainframe computers, they are often used to send and receive files. A file may be moved from storage into the data communications stream in one of two ways: The first technique is to dump an ASCII file out of the port one character at a time, hoping that some program at the other end will catch it in a buffer which it will then write to disk. The second technique is to set up a file transfer process between the programs on both ends that moves all types of files, including non-ASCII files, in blocks with control over errors introduced in the communications stream and possibly even with data compression. Because these file transfer programs are relatively complex, using statistical analysis techniques to spot errors and compress data, they follow specific protocols, often published and updated by one individual. The common protocols used for error-controlled file transfers include XModem, YModem, Kermit, and ZModem. Some information services have also published their own file transfer protocols, such as CompuServe-B.

The universal problem with protocols is that their implementations in programs generally aren't as smooth as their descriptions on paper. When different programmers write code to implement the same protocol, they often come up with programs that don't work together. Additionally, in an effort to improve performance and flexibility, all the protocols have developed options, and programmers often differ on which options should be active in the default setup. The bottom line is that file transfer software can be tricky to use. The different implementations and menu options lead to frustration as often as they do to satisfaction.

Additional Program Features

Although controlling the data flow, controlling the screen, and transferring files are the flour, milk, and butter of communications programs, there are many ways to ice the finished cake. All communications packages provide some way to hold frequently called telephone numbers and to associate data such as port speed, file transfer protocol, login name, password, and other details with each number.

Every package also provides some way to write scripts to automate the communications sessions. These scripting languages range from simple lists of statements resembling DOS.BAT files to complex programming languages.

Some programs automate the scripting process, recording your keystrokes and the other system's replies during a manual data exchange, and then creating a script to accomplish the same task. Although many people never use the scripting capabilities of their communications packages, some write sophisticated scripts to automate the activities of an entire workgroup or organization.

When Computers and Telephones Meet

A telephone is a client device for the telephone system in just the same way that a PC is a client device for a LAN. This observation has led to a least three waves of attempts to combine telephones and PCs into a single device. In the early 1990's, several companies released products that attempted to combine data communications and telephone call control in a single box. The best known was the TeleCompaq from Compaq computers. These early attempts at integration were great ideas, but the sophisticated call controls that these systems needed for success were slow to come from the telephone companies.

The second wave of computer and telephone integration—and so far the most successful—added automation to the outbound and inbound call centers that power many businesses. When you have a group of people on the phone taking reservations or orders all day, that's a call center. When someone calls you at 6:00 p.m. to get you to subscribe to the newspaper, they're calling from a call center. Automating call centers is a big business. Your organization might or might not take reservations all day, but you can probably use more automated calling in other places.

The third wave of computer-telephony integration is in the integration of Internet access into telephones—particularly wireless phones. Wireless telephones are probably the best example of successful "thin client" technology. Thin client systems control the cost of computing. We'll deal with them in the next chapter.

The Bones of CTI

Your PC itself can't do everything in the modern office, but it should be the place from which you can do everything. You should be able to handle your documents, links to Internet and intranet information services, your email, video conferences, phone calls, voice mail, fax, and all other actions from the keyboard and screen. This doesn't mean that the software for all those functions runs in the PC, only that you can get at what you need from the PC through consistent and integrated interfaces.

Harry Newton, editor-in-chief of Computer Telephony Magazine, describes CTI as "connecting a computer (a single workstation or file server) on a LAN to a telephone switch and having the computer issue commands to the switch to move calls around." Although this is a good explanation of what CTI does, it's fairly basic. In essence, CTI is a way to connect your phone system to your network and enable callers access to all kinds of server-based information by speaking or by touching numbers on the keypad. Likewise, through services such as Caller ID, employees can use CTI to gather information about callers, especially if they're repeat callers. CTI is fairly inexpensive and can save your company a lot of money.

There are two basic kinds of CTI systems for your network: the standalone system and the private-branch-exchange (PBX)/server-based system. If you have no PBX, you can use a stand-alone PC and a multiline voice card, such as the cards in the large family offered by Dialogic, to handle your incoming and outgoing calls. Multiport call processing cards are available in two- and four-port configurations, and you can install multiple cards in a single PC. (See the diagram CTI Setup, on p. 641.) Each card may require separate memory, I/O, and IRQ addresses, however, and you may be limited to four cards per PC. If you have more than seven or eight phone lines, then you probably already have a PBX, so you might want to consider the second option. The PBX/server option usually requires a proprietary card installed in your file server or dedicated PC. Novell and AT&T have developed a proprietary standard called TSAPI (Telephony Services Application Programming Interface), which utilizes a serial cable connection between the phone switch and the file server. The NetWare file server runs a series of NLMs (NetWare Loadable Modules) that communicate between the client PCs and the switch or PBX. To perform tasks such as forwarding calls, checking voice mail, and setting up conference calls, these NLMs enable software running on the client PCs to control the switch directly. Unfortunately, not all PBXs are alike. You need to make sure that your PBX works with the TSAPI specification. Microsoft offers a competing specification called TAPI.

Novell's NetWare Telephony Services Architecture (NTSA) defines a physical link between a LAN server and the PBX, which maintains an arm's-length relationship that's more comfortable to the PBX vendors. In this scheme, applications running in each PC interact with the PBX just as they do with printers or other networked devices. The telephone stays on the desk, but you can control it from your keyboard. Microsoft's integration is tighter, but Novell's structure makes it less daunting to install the system and to develop applications for the PC and PBX. Figure 14.2 illustrates how LANs and telephone systems meet.

FIGURE 14.2

Computer Telephony systems integrate LANs with telephone systems, often through a special interface linking the local telephone switch (called a private branch exchange or PBX) with a LAN server. Special purpose servers can execute call-handling, fax-on-demand, and other programs for specialized telephony applications. Less sophisticated computer telephony systems integrate the desktop telephone and PC with or without a LAN.

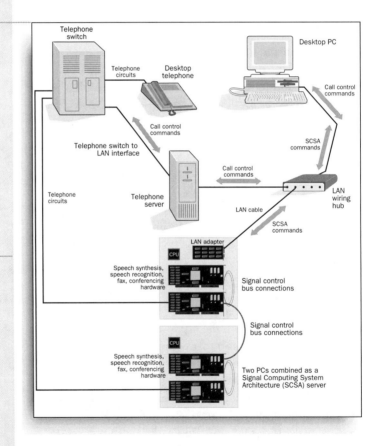

Dialogic Corporation's Signal Computing System Architecture (SCSA) adds smart voice capabilities to both the LAN and the PBX. SCSA is a specification for hardware that talks and listens so you can use software available from several companies to build interoperable speech recognition and voice synthesis applications. SCSA is compatible with TAPI, but initially developers worked under Novell's NTSA because it has a bigger market. Many SCSA voice products are designed to slide into a NetWare server.

It's not very difficult to set up the hardware for a CTI call-processing system on your network, but what can you do with it? Well, in addition to basic voice mail and conference calls, you can write CTI applications. The two most popular types of CTI applications are what are called IVR (Interactive Voice Response) and call center. IVR is usually more popular and less expensive, while a call-center application is important if your company uses operators to sell a product.

The best example of IVR (or information pull) is when you call a phone number and receive a voice menu. These menus can be nested several deep, and some are so complicated that it's easy for the caller to get lost. Although these IVR menus may seem annoying, think of all of the money they can save. Companies such as Pronexus and Voysys offer packages that simplify writing your own online IVR applications. These programs range in price from $400 to $2,000, based upon the number of phone lines you have.

Although we call them applications, most of these IVR products are really Visual Basic database extensions, which plug into your Visual Basic application and provide menus and other tools for writing IVR programs. They are extremely easy to use and even provide sample scripts. In fact, even if you don't know Visual Basic, you should be able to write your own simple IVR applications. These products usually include canned voice files, or you can use a sound card to record your own menu responses.

When a caller connects to an IVR system and requests information such as an account balance, the IVR software sends a request to a database and reads the response back to the caller.

You can set up IVR systems that salespeople use to check inventory or that customers call to check an order's status. All you need is a Visual Basic application and a simple database.

Call-center applications, by contrast, deal with information coming in, not going out. A good example is when the CTI computer answers a call and uses Caller ID or a PIN number to identify the caller. It then displays the caller's account information onscreen as the company operator answers the phone (this is also called "screen pop"). Right away the operator has all the necessary information about the caller. This saves the operator the trouble of asking for the caller's name and account number. Call centers with hundreds of people on line are complex systems, but smaller offices can benefit from many aspects of computer and telephone integration.

Internet in Your Phone

I'm cautious about falling in love with new toys and technologies. But the integration of the Internet into portable telephone technology is something I believe in. Clearly, I'm talking about special categories of applications specially designed for the smaller screen and different needs of the mobile telephone user. The same technology has significant uses in private internets. People doing deliveries, real estate agents, and anyone on the road can benefit from specialized corporate information delivered to a portable telephone.

The range of technologies behind mobile Internet access capabilities reads like an alphabet soup of acronyms. Advances that enable data to be used over cellular phone networks such as Cellular Digital Packet Data (CDPD) are coming into the limelight. At the same time, data services are becoming an integral part of the new wave of Personal Communications Services (PCS) handsets that are being introduced in the United States after years of use in European and Asian markets.

By using CDPD, for example, certain cellular phones can send small email messages or retrieve specialized bits of web code that are developed especially for a tiny browser inside the phone.

Although factors such as more powerful phones, less expensive service, and sophisticated handheld computers are driving the acceptance of these devices by mobile users, broadband technologies such as Local Multipoint Distribution Service (LMDS) and Multichannel Multipoint Distribution System (MMDS) are now entering the picture. Unlike narrowband technologies, these technologies typically assume a stationery target, but the target can be portable within a limited range. They are delivering far more data than cellular, CPD, or PCS.

For example, one Internet service provider has begun deploying Internet access with LMDS technology that can deliver information at 500Kbps, four times the speed of ISDN. The service requires a special card inside the PC as well as a transmitter the size of a ping-pong paddle that connects to the window of the home or office. An MMDS ISP has begun to offer service at either 10 or 27Mbps, depending upon the market. The service requires a roof-mounted satellite dish that must have line-of-sight access to the point of presence, which is mounted on a high point. For example, in New York City, that transmitter is located on top of the Empire State Building.

A Major Use for Modems

Certainly, Internet access is the primary use of modems today. But the other major use of modems is for remote access to a corporate or enterprise network. We'll describe the details of remote access in Chapter 15.

Network Remote Access

Time, money, lifestyle, and legislation influence the logic behind the use of remote access products as much as technology does. As any corporate manager who deals with issues of benefits or legality can testify, these forces are often in conflict. But technology and practicality achieve harmony when it comes to remote LAN access products. Giving employees remote access to networks from their homes or hotels improves productivity, reduces costs, and makes it easier for U.S. companies to conform to the Clean Air Act, the Family and Medical Leave Act, and to many related state and local regulations.

Studies show that employees produce more and are happier when they can telecommute. In addition, telecommuting allows companies to reduce costs for everything from office space to furniture and utilities, so it also makes good business sense. Apparently Congress thinks telecommuting is a good idea, too. The Clean Air Act of 1990 includes provisions that kicked in during late 1993 and surprised senior managers in many companies. The Act decrees that organizations that have more than 100 employees and are located in specific metropolitan areas designated by the Environmental Protection Agency must take action to reduce travel to the worksite by 25 percent during peak commute hours.

Similarly, the Family and Medical Leave Act of 1994 provides for up to 12 weeks of unpaid leave each year for specific family and medical reasons. However, because it could benefit both the employer and the employee to get some work done during those weeks of leave, the act also provides for options like telecommuting.

Remote Connection Options

I practice what I preach

Just to provide perspective, let me say that I'm a full-time employee of a major New York publisher, and I live and work on an island off the coast of Florida. I have ISDN for Internet access and video teleconferencing, and an airport is 30 minutes away. Remote access is critically important, but I'm happy to report that it works well.

In a number of ways, users can gain control of information stored on their office PCs from across the building, on the road, or on the other side of the world. Accessing the data or applications stored on a PC or a corporate network from another PC over some type of communication link is known as *remote access*.

Road warriors and remote workers of all kinds need remote access to keep in touch with the main office as part of their daily activities. But more and more stationary desk dwellers also want to be able to work from home after hours or in the event of foul weather, and they want to be able to access their office data and applications quickly and easily.

Many products can connect to your network and provide simultaneous access for remote callers. Often, new installations of remote access services use standalone turn-key network devices called *access servers*. The phrase *turn-key* is supposed to imply easy, painless installation, but that isn't necessarily so; the so-called turn-key products can have their own sets of problems. If you want to hold down costs, you can roll your own remote access server using software from Microsoft or Novell in a PC running Windows or NetWare. The other common alternative is to run remote access software in a networked PC, making it into an access server.

Today, remote access is accomplished through two techniques called *remote control* and *remote node*. Remote control allows a remote client PC to take over another PC (called the host) over an analog dial-up, LAN, or Internet connection. The host can be either a standalone desktop PC or a PC on a network. The remote client takes control of the host PC's CPU, screen, and keyboard and then runs applications on the host or transfers files between the host and client. But nothing is ever quite that easy: Many applications first make a remote node connection and then use remote control across the remote node link to run special applications.

Because the host does most of the processing, remote control is great for accessing large network databases and executing applications that your remote client lacks the power or local storage space to run.

Remote node, by comparison, treats the remote client as an extension of the LAN. Connected over a dial-up connection, remote-node clients communicate as if they were PCs connected to the office network. Log-on and drive mappings are the same, and most of the processing takes place on the remote client, with transactions and files being sent via modem, ISDN line, or Internet link.

Blending remote node and remote control

The bottom line is that the available software and remote access servers make it easier to set up an access server for remote node connection. This is a connection to the corporate LAN or intranet. After that connection is made, the user can elect to create a remote control session with a specially designated remote control server. This technique is particularly useful for running applications that search a large database. The PC on the LAN does the searching through its high-speed connection, but only a small amount of data crosses the communications link to the remote user.

A remote-node connection is especially suited to interactive applications such as email or for pulling files from the network to the remote PC. In a remote-node scenario, multiple users generally share a single point of connection to the network, making management and security more practical than with remote control.

A cross between the two techniques is called *remote control over remote node*. This technique is increasingly common. Remote control over remote node offers users the functionality of remote control, but over a centralized point of entry. This helps to cut down on the necessity for every office PC to have a modem, and it provides strict security access to the network. Figure 15.1 shows the operation of remote mode and remote control systems.

SEE ALSO

➤ *To learn more about analog modems and ISDN services, see page 278.*

FIGURE 15.1

Remote control systems execute programs on the called PC, so the calling PC doesn't need a lot of processing power or memory. Remote node systems execute all programs (including the network communications software) on the calling PC. Remote node operation requires higher speed connections, but V.34 and V.pcm modems or ISDN links are adequate.

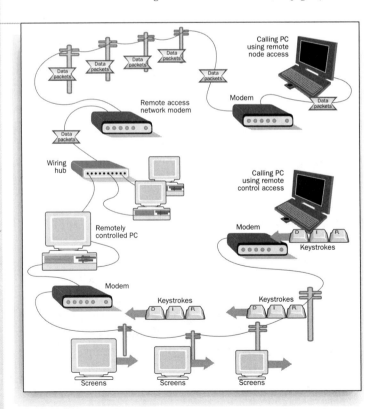

Modem Remote Control Programs

Whether you want to use the files from your office PC at home or provide technical support to a user in another location, remote-computing packages can give you access and control. No matter how many files you manage to fit onto a portable's hard disk, time and again you'll need a file that resides on your office network; having a remote control program installed can be a great relief.

Remote control uses software, modems, and the phone lines to connect two PCs and make them behave like one machine, even when a great distance separates them. The computer whose files and programs are accessed is called the host, and the one that takes control of the host's operations is the remote. While you sit at the remote, it's as if you were also seated at the host: the host's keyboard and screen become an extension of your own. If another user is actually at the host site, you may feel like a flight instructor who's giving lessons in a plane equipped with dual controls; you can see everything the student does, and the student can observe your maneuvers and learn by watching.

Remote access to a LAN is one of the most common functions for a remote-computing program. But probably the most valuable function is troubleshooting. If you're a tech support person, you can monitor, control, and troubleshoot software through remote control without traveling to the customer's site.

Perhaps the easiest way to exchange data among LANs is through remote control of a networked PC. Applying modem remote control software to a LAN-to-LAN scenario means that someone working at a networked PC in city A could use normal dial-up telephone lines to call a modem attached to a networked PC in city B. Once they were connected, the modem remote control software running in both PCs would provide an efficient way for the person in city A to make entries in a database, use electronic mail, or copy data files from the city B networks.

A remotely controlled PC allows employees calling from any location, even a non-networked one, to access the full power of the network. The caller can run programs, use printers, access a mainframe computer through a gateway, and otherwise act as a full member of the network. Remote control programs include good security, but they cannot protect against ill-behaved software or human error. Modem remote control programs do not care what network operating system or network adapter cards you use. Therefore, these packages allow people to span different LAN operating systems easily.

While this type of remote control connection is effective, at some level of activity it becomes uneconomical to dedicate individual networked PCs to receiving dial-in calls. When remote control of a networked PC becomes frequent, it is wise to establish a separate remote control server system to handle many incoming calls simultaneously. If you want callers to be able to run applications off your network, an access server running remote control software is the optimum choice. Such servers sometimes have multiple CPUs in one cabinet, or if the load isn't too heavy, they can be running software in multiple Windows NT or UNIX sessions on a single CPU.

Remote control programs and devices have some special techniques to reduce the traffic going over the line. The features used to improve remote control performance include wallpaper suppression, screen sizing, and color scaling.

- *Wallpaper suppression* speeds performance by disabling the background graphical wallpaper on the host's Windows screen, thereby avoiding the transmission of a large, relatively useless bitmap across a slow modem connection.

- *Screen sizing* solves the problem of hosts and clients with different screen resolutions by fitting the host display into the remote screen so you don't have to scroll around. This feature sounds great in theory, but you'll sometimes find it's pretty tough to read screens that have been scaled down. Incompatible screen sizing is the most common problem in remote control sessions.

- *Color scaling* is a technique that lets you choose a reduced number of colors for your remote control session.

- *File transfer* is another popular function of remote control.

Among the standard features you'll find are drag-and-drop copying; delta-file transfer, in which only changed portions of a file are transferred; long filename support; and directory synchronization, in which the software makes sure the most up-to-date files are on both machines. Other useful file-transfer features include virus protection during copy, file transfer recovery in the event the link is broken, and file compression for added speed. Another useful remote utility, printer redirection, lets you print files stored on the host to a printer on the remote client.

- *Role reversal* is a feature that's available in some products to add some value for training and technical support. This allows the host and client to change occupations without having to disconnect from one another. Moreover, these vendors offer connections from multiple clients or to multiple hosts simultaneously.

Modern products attempt to capitalize on Windows 95's look and feel, with features like drag-and-drop file transfer and multitasking and support for Windows 95 Dial-Up Networking, TAPI (Telephony API), and Unimodem.

- *Windows 95 Dial-Up Networking*, a remote-node utility included with Windows 95, lets you dial into any Windows NT Server running the built-in Remote Access Service (RAS) or to any other remote-node server, such as Shiva's LanRover.

- *TAPI* is a programming interface for creating interactions between your PC and communications devices; it lets multiple applications use the same modem simultaneously.

- *Unimodem* is Windows 95's universal modem driver interface specification. If you've already installed and configured your modem in Windows 95 and your remote control package supports Unimodem, you won't have to reconfigure the modem during the remote control package installation.

The Remote Node Connections

Until the Windows graphical user interface caught on, the modem remote control method of making a remote connection to a LAN was always more efficient than remote node. In the remote node, the calling computer runs all the networking software, including the normal networking software and protocols, with driver programs that send network requests out the serial communications port. That port connects to a modem or ISDN adapter and then to a remote access server on the distant LAN. The remote client computer has a full set of redirected disk drive letters, but the remote client connection must push many layers of messages—carrying different network packets and acknowledgments—across the relatively slow telephone line.

Remote control is faster than remote client if the screens are simple, but the multipixel changes that take place in a Windows graphics screen every time you click a mouse take several seconds to traverse even a fast modem link. So the time needed to pass images of dense graphics screens like those used in Windows reduces the efficiency of the remote control approach when compared to something like that of the remote node. Additionally, companies like Shiva Corp. have come up with ways to reduce the amount of network traffic moving over modems and telephone lines, which significantly reduces the amount of time needed to move data under the remote client arrangement.

The people who create the software for remote client operation use special techniques to reduce data traffic. For example, they use routines to create shorthand tokens for certain repetitive elements of the NetWare Core Protocol packet within the IPX packet. This reduces overhead and improves throughput significantly.

Modem connections operate with only a few percent of the signaling speed of network connections. So while the disk drive letters and printer names look the same on a PC connected either through a remote node or through the LAN, they don't work the same.

Using a remote node product complicates the network administrator's job because the calling PCs may need careful customization to conserve disk space. It also becomes more difficult to update software when network utilities are spread across a large group of traveling machines.

Security and Protocols

Many managers quake when they think about opening their network to outside access. They fear hackers, viruses, and other threats. All quality remote access products offer password protection, and most have features such as call-back. Using call-back, an authorized user initiates a call into the system. Once the system recognizes the user, it hangs up and calls back to a number on a pre-authorized list. Modern access servers integrate with Novell's bindery of names and privileges so the administrator has only one list to keep straight.

Another way to protect your resources is to limit access based on time of day and even network protocols. For example, you can allow a user to access the server only if he is using the IPX protocol, not TCP/IP, so he can't surf the Internet via the company's expensive leased-line links. In addition, remote node servers typically have call accounting systems to track how long a user is connected and how much data he transfers so you can either bill him for access or monitor his usage.

In addition to keeping people out, it's also useful to have a record of who did what and when. Remote access servers typically provide some type of management that will allow you to see if a port is operational and in use and which users have logged into the system. Some will even give you statistics on the quality of the dial-up telephone line. Other information you can gather includes failed connection attempts, network packet errors, and the speed of the connection.

SEE ALSO

> *Other types of statistical reporting and management control are covered in Chapter 16, starting on page 339.*

Be careful what you pull across!

It pays to carefully configure the calling PC so that all the large files it needs are on its own hard drive. You want to push and pull only necessary files through the modem. This means that login programs, utilities like Novell's MAP.EXE, virus protection programs, and anything else you might normally pull from the file server should reside on the calling PC.

Security begins with good administration

It's worth repeating that the biggest security threat comes from sloppy password protection and poor general administration—not technical trickery. However, every company, particularly every publicly traded company, has information that is worth something to somebody. Good electronic security should back up your administrative security practices.

PPP Power

Because remote access is so important, there are a number of protocols for security and control. The Internet Engineering Task Force developed the *Point-to-Point Protocol* (PPP) as a primary means of authenticating and controlling remote access sessions. PPP is a data link protocol designed specifically for dial-up access over modem, ISDN, and similar digital circuits.

PPP encapsulates IP or IPX packets in specialized Network Control Protocol packets. The protocol provides for password protection using the Password Authentication Protocol (PAP) and the Challenge Handshake Authentication Protocol (CHAP). While PPP, PAP, and CHAP sound imposing, the good news is that software to perform these functions is built into Windows and is widely available for Macintosh and UNIX clients. After you authenticate yourself to your desktop operating system, features of that operating system automatically authenticate you to the remote access server.

However, for the best level of security, you can call on a separate authentication server to verify that callers are who they claim to be and to keep a log of who called, when, and for how long. Livingston Enterprises of Pleasanton, CA, has won widespread support for its RADIUS (Remote Access Dial-In User Service) protocol, which combines authentication with authorization and accounting functions. UNIX binaries and source code are available directly from Livingston. RADIUS is supported by a range of devices, including remote access systems and firewalls from Cisco Systems, Ascend Communications, Bay Networks, Shiva Corp., U.S. Robotics, and Raptor Systems.

The RADIUS server can manage a large number of remote users accessing the network through multiple portals on the network. Remote access servers communicate with the RADIUS server to access a single database on users, the types of access methods allowed, and any logon restrictions. The RADIUS server can also pass parameters to the access server, such as the IP address to assign to the caller and the maximum allowed connection time. And the server collects accounting information such as the amount of data sent and received and the length of time online.

The latest implementations of RADIUS can use naming services such as Novell Directory Services (NDS) so that the network administrator has only one list of users and resources to maintain.

PPP is the heart of several other useful remote access protocols. The Multilink PPP protocol (abbreviated MP, MPPP, or MLPPP) bridges two or more serial ports or ISDN B channels for higher-speed operation. For example, using ISDN's Basic Rate service (BRI), you can obtain 128Kbps with Multilink PPP. Again, MP is now a standard part of Windows and popular communications software for Macintosh and UNIX computers.

Tunneling Through the Internet

So far, I've talked about remote access using dial-up circuits such as analog modems and ISDN. These remote access connections seem safe because you can control the identity of the phone numbers, the passwords, and the actions of individual users. However, this system often requires callers to pay for long-distance calls and certainly requires the corporate host to have many dedicated connections to a telephone company central office.

But the Internet and corporate intranets represent huge resources of connections just waiting to be used. Internet service providers can offer Internet access through local calls in most cities. Can an individual sitting in a house, hotel room, or remote office dial into the Internet and use it to get into a corporate LAN? The answer is yes. But if you are not careful, you can open the corporate LAN to intrusion.

Remote node systems can call into the Internet or a private corporate intranet and use a technology called Virtual Private Networking (VPNs) to gain secure LAN access. You have two options for using a VPN: You can build your own, or you can use a service available from most any large long-distance carriers.

Double the speed isn't twice as good

I worked hard to get an early version of MP to work so I could get a 128 Kb ISDN connection to the Internet. Overall, the results were disappointing. Internet servers and local ISPs typically cause bigger bottlenecks than a 64Kb connection. My experience is that trying to set up parallel analog modem connections isn't worth the hassle for most web surfing.

The easiest way to create your own VPN on a standard Internet connection is to use a network firewall. Basically, a firewall inspects each packet coming in from the Internet and tries to determine if it should be allowed on the corporate LAN.

In addition to protecting your sensitive data from outside hackers, most firewall products also include an optional VPN module. The VPN module uses encryption to encode your data before it sends it across the unsecured Internet. But this method has some drawbacks. As a rule, firewalls are fairly expensive and require a lot of knowledge and time to set up. Also, the implementations of encryption standards vary, and interoperability between equipment from different vendors isn't assured. This means that you're well advised to use the same firewall software at all of your locations in order to communicate. In some cases, you'll need proprietary client software in every calling computer to use the firewall's VPN services.

Encrypting data is the most popular and oldest way to send information across the Internet, but it does require special proprietary software. A new way to send sensitive data across the Internet is called *tunneling*. Tunneling allows you to send other protocols, namely IPX, across the IP-only Internet.

SEE ALSO

➤ *There is a description of the structure of the Internet in the section "The New Internet," on page 310.*

➤ *For a more complete description of a firewall, see "Heavy Security," on page 324.*

Point to Point Tunneling Protocol

The first popular tunneling standard was the *Point to Point Tunneling Protocol* (PPTP), developed jointly by U.S. Robotics and Microsoft Corp. The major attraction to PPTP is that it comes free with Windows NT. PPTP allows you to tunnel or encapsulate IPX and NetBEUI packets in a standard TCP/IP dial-up connection or a dedicated Internet connection.

PPTP uses the security policy you have already set up on the network. You don't have to create new security policies or use special encryption software to send data across the Internet. For example, all the user names and passwords you create on your

Windows NT server will work with remote users across the Internet.

A significant feature of PPTP is its ability to connect to your servers using any standard network protocol. The biggest security risk for any network connected to the Internet is installing the TCP/IP protocol on all network servers. Because the Internet uses TCP/IP as its transport, any PC on your network with TCP/IP installed is vulnerable to outside hackers. That's why my favorite Internet security method is not to install the TCP/IP protocol on any server or client PC that has sensitive data. PPTP allows you to connect to a remote server without using TCP/IP on the host PC. For example, you use TCP/IP to connect to the PPTP server on the remote network. The PPTP server strips off the TCP/IP information and uses IPX or NetBEUI to send your requests to the target server. The information is then encapsulated back into a TCP/IP packet and sent back to you across the Internet.

Layer 2 Forwarding

Although PPTP was one of the first tunneling protocol standards, it is not the only one. A new tunneling protocol standard called *Layer 2 Forwarding* (L2F) was developed by Cisco Systems. Like PPTP, L2F encapsulates other protocols inside a TCP/IP packet for transportation across the Internet or any other connection type. The two standards are similar, but they have some differences. L2F does all the tunneling procedures in the router hardware. This means that you must have a router that works with L2F. PPTP, on the other hand, uses special software on the client and server sides to send tunneling information through any TCP/IP router.

In addition to requiring an L2F-compliant router, the Cisco standard runs at a lower level and doesn't require TCP/IP routing to function. L2F also provides additional security for the user names and passwords found in PPTP. As these things happen, the PPTP and L2F standards have been hammered together by a committee of the Internet Engineering Task Force. The result is a new open standard called Layer 2 Tunneling

The value of tunneling?

There is no doubt that tunneling through the Internet can save you money. But at what cost? Internet connections are notoriously unreliable. If you're trying to download your email before getting on an airplane, you want to get on and get off with a fast and reliable link. Forget tunneling. But if you want a connection across country to exchange messages between email servers that have the persistence to retry failed transfers, tunneling across the Internet can work. Be smart about how you use it.

Protocol (L2TP) that combines both vendor standards into a single product. Most remote access and router vendors work with both PPTP and L2F and should also work with the new L2TP.

In a perfect world, you would combine encryption with tunneling to design your VPN. The members of the IETF are aware of this need and have created an open encryption standard called IPsec or IP Security.

Remote Reset

Any remote access device can reach a point at which it becomes stuck and doesn't respond to commands. Big remote access servers are sophisticated systems with multiple CPUs and both hardware- and software-management features. They reset problem devices. But your remote access server might be smaller stuff. If you are using a single port server or several PCs running remote access software, things can get hung up. Nothing can freeze a computer like communications problems. When these devices hang, they need a reboot at the level of the "big red switch" that controls the power to the PC.

Similarly, many people don't want their remote access servers to run all the time; they only want the access server up when they want to call in. The folks from Server Technology Corporation have a telephone-activated power control unit called Remote Power On/Off that solves these problems. If you don't want to leave your remote access server on all the time, this affordable product turns it on when the phone rings and turns it off after the call. But if you do leave your access server on all the time, Remote Power On/Off will drop the AC power after a call, wait a few seconds, and then apply power again, which eliminates frustrating problems with "hung" remotely controlled PCs.

Remote Power On/Off detects an incoming call, provides power to devices plugged into its special wall socket adapter, monitors the status of the telephone line, and drops the power at some specified period of time after the telephone connection is broken. Providing you can disable your PC's memory check in

ROM BIOS to shorten the boot time, this arrangement will work fine for infrequently called systems.

In many offices, the problem is different. Organizations want to keep PCs acting as access servers running, but applications sometimes freeze. A frozen PC can put an organization's remote access capability out of service until someone physically resets the system, which can be a problem at night and on weekends. The Remote Power On/Off product's reboot feature ensures that the access server will come back up with a fresh reboot after every call. You lose only a few seconds of time between calls, and you completely avoid the problem of frozen remote access servers.

Growing and Evolving

While remote access will continue to grow in popularity, it will certainly evolve in form and function. In many areas, Internet service providers will be able to use low-cost urban data networks to provide remote access service from a central site more economically than you can do it yourself. Simultaneously, the presence of the Remote Access Service (RAS) in Microsoft's Windows makes remote access relatively simple to install, even in small networks.

Network Management and Control

The phrase "mission-critical applications"—always spoken in gravely serious tones—is an overused part of marketing pitches for network products. It seems every company aiming to price its products at the high end of the scale touts their reliability and dependability for "mission-critical applications." Yet the amount of overuse this phrase receives actually signals an important fact: Organizations depend upon their networks for productivity, and some companies start to lose money the second a network malfunctions.

Not only do networks represent an investment in wiring, computers, and software totaling thousands of dollars per node, the network is often the production equipment of the business. The local area network system of a modern organization rates as much management attention as the milling and welding machines in an automobile-manufacturing plant or the sales counters of a department store.

Long- and short-term management tasks also include controlling the *total cost of ownership* (TCO) of the network and computing environment. The network is a tool used to develop a competitive business advantage and a tool to improve productivity, but the tool can't overwhelm the value of the work. Control of TCO has become a hot topic for many managers, but it has also become a false front for marketing an old idea in new clothing, the so-called *thin clients*. Thin clients are desktop terminals, typically for Java applications. A different turn on the same idea, called *managed clients*, make a lot more sense.

We'll get to the fact and fancy of TCO later in the chapter, but first let's look at more traditional network management.

Traditional Network Management

Good networks operate invisibly. The servers respond to requests from the client computers quickly and without any special actions on the part of the people using the network's resources. Because designers make these systems transparent, problems of wiring, configuration, design, and deterioration often don't appear or aren't reported until they result in catastrophic failures. The four words "Your network is down!" are

---

That old thin client idea

I wrote a major review of diskless workstations in the December 1989 issue of *PC Magazine*. The idea fell flat then, even though a competitive PC carried a $5,000 price tag and consumers would have welcomed any cost reduction. The concept is back a decade later. This time it will succeed, but not as a replacement for desktop PCs. The best uses of thin clients include portable operation, using the Windows CE operating system, in specialized vertical applications, and as replacements for traditional data entry terminals.

guaranteed to flash-freeze the blood of any network administrator. My goal is to help you avoid unpleasant surprises from your network.

In the management portion of this chapter, I describe the techniques and tools of network management and control. I'll deal with five somewhat overlapping levels of network management systems:

- Management utilities
- Network-wide reporting and control
- Wiring-hub reporting and control
- Protocol analysis and traffic counting
- Statistical analysis

The field of network management systems is confusing primarily because two major categories and several subcategories of products carry the "network management" title. The first category consists of suites of utilities aimed at easing the network manager's burden. These suites, marketed by several companies including Intel, Novell, and Microsoft, typically include network virus protection, backup, server activity monitoring, software inventory control, and software distribution. The suite might also include features such as modem remote control, hardware inventory, and added security control.

These suites of utilities are valuable, but they are only one side of the management story. The other side is network-wide reporting and control. This particularly includes receiving reports and data from routers, Frame Relay networks, and other network backbone devices. IBM's SystemView leads the world in management options and functions. Such management offerings as Bay Networks' Optivity, Cabletron's Spectrum Enterprise, Hewlett-Packard's OpenView, and 3-Com's Transcend are also very complete. Figure 16.1 shows a screen from Transcend Central, 3-Com's centralized network management system.

Frye Computer Systems' Frye Utilities and Novell's ManageWise are very complete hardware-independent software suites. Products from other software companies, including Intel's LANDesk Manager, Microsoft Systems Management Server, and

Symantec's Norton Administrator for Networks, focus on cost of ownership-related functions such as software distribution, inventory, and metering.

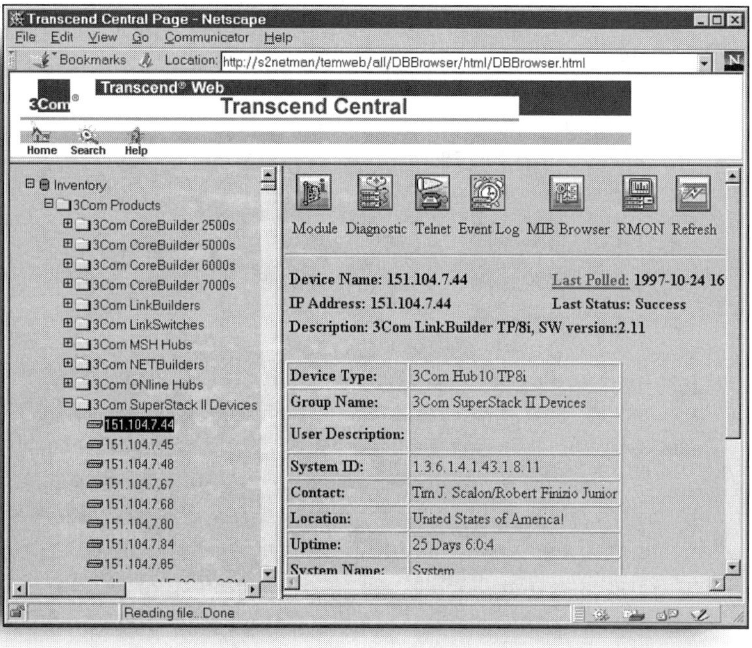

FIGURE 16.1

3-Com's Transcend Central is designed to manage an enterprise network full of routers and other devices. From this front-view screen, you can drill down to see reports from individual devices.

The newest evolution in all network management products is the browser front-end. Whether it's an enterprise network or a single router, you can read its reports and reset critical aspects of its operation through your browser. Converting text-based reports and graphical images into HTML isn't too difficult. The HTML format enables developers to take advantage of the wide availability of browsers on every type of computer to get out from under the burden of developing client software. So, in the case of almost every type of product mentioned in this chapter, if it doesn't work with a browser yet, it will soon.

The browser interface also breaks down the line between products. As an end-user, you don't care much whether the screen you see comes from an SNMP suite or a unique program running in the ROM of a LAN adapter. The commonality of the browser makes it easier to integrate software suites with the hardware-focused configuration and reporting programs that come with a lot of network equipment.

In this chapter we'll work from the top down, first examining the large-scale network reporting and control systems and then visiting some of the utility suites. Finally, we'll tackle TCO on the desktop.

Enterprise Management

Modern enterprise LAN management systems do a lot more than activate your beeper when a server goes down. They offer accounting functions—such as software distribution, license metering, and hardware inventory—that are critical to low overhead and high productivity. Security functions, such as password tracking and virus detection, become even more important when you connect to the Internet. Capacity-planning, trouble-ticketing, and event-logging features all help to justify budgets.

Network control and reporting activities take place at many levels throughout the network, providing readings on pulse points around the network in order to draw a picture of its total health. The largest networks have a hierarchy of devices and programs at several levels reporting status and problems upstream to a central data-gathering and reporting system. But you don't have to put this hierarchy in place all at once. Some products, such as wiring-hub traffic reporting and control systems, generate excellent reports on their own without needing to exchange information with other devices.

The lowest level of network reporting devices consists of hardware boxes with internal microprocessors and programs in ROM that report on the quantity and quality of data passing a particular point in the network. These internal reporting devices include LAN wiring hubs, bridges, routers, remote access servers, print servers, multiplexers, microwave radios, and telephone modems. Their internal processors and programs gather statistical information and send status reports to some intermediate level of management software that may be running on a PC practically anywhere in the network. Figure 16.2 shows a screen that contains an image that shows exactly what is happening on an Ethernet hub as it happens. These programs might provide all the analysis a particular network manager needs, or they might send specified items of information on to higher-level management programs for consolidation.

Management defines products

It's hard to make a product such as a LAN adapter unique while keeping the price down and conforming to standards. So companies such as Hewlett-Packard, Intel, and 3-Com are using management services to differentiate LAN adapters.

FIGURE 16.2

This screen image shows a complete representation of a 3-Com hub. The lights blink and the plugs in the sockets represent the actual connections you would see if you walked to the hub. Other views provide statistics and certain control actions.

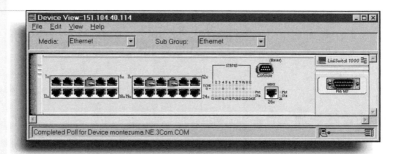

The LAN operating systems in print and file servers can also send special alert messages and periodic status messages on to higher-level management programs running on computers elsewhere in the network. At the highest level of network management activity, application programs complain to management programs about files they can't find or access. The reports from all these levels of hardware and software must be in some common format so that one top-level system can compile them and present them to people who use or respond to them.

Such companies as AT&T, Computer Associates, Digital, Hewlett-Packard, and IBM (under the Tivoli corporate name) market competing grand architectures for network management and control. There was an attempt to standardize network management protocols and procedures within the International Standards Organization. But, as usual, the procedures of the Internet seem to be winning out. An Internet standard management system called SNMP has spread to local area networks and the ubiquitous browser is now a primary way of viewing the health of your network.

SEE ALSO

➤ SNMP is a part of the TCP/IP protocol family described in Chapter 12, starting on page 311.

Alarms and Acronyms

The whole network management and control industry has two factors in common: reliance on the principle of alarms and the use of a bewildering blizzard of acronyms. The concept of alarms is easy to understand; the acronyms take a lot longer to master.

Big systems do applications

Computer Associates calls itself "the second biggest software company in the world." The company has made its mark with management software that monitors the functions of very complex commercial line-of-business applications. Management takes place at all levels from the copper wire to the application program.

Using performance alarms means that you instruct the software to call for your attention only when something abnormal occurs. Typically, you can easily adjust the limits of abnormality. Abnormal events might be defined in terms of more than 30 consecutive Ethernet packet collisions, an unusually small or large number of packets sent within a period of time, or practically any other parameter you want to know about, from the temperature inside an equipment cabinet to the AC line voltage. The network management and control software packages offer responses to alarm situations that range from silently logging the event to calling the number of a pager and displaying special codes that describe the problem on the pager's screen.

Major Management Functions

Formal network management models define fault management, configuration management, performance management, security management, and accounting management as the primary management functions.

- *Fault management* includes detecting problems and taking steps to isolate them, provides messages describing active connections and equipment; it is closely tied to fault management because changing configurations is the primary technique used to isolate network faults.

- *Performance management* includes counting things such as packets, disk access requests, and access to specific programs.

- *Security management* includes alerting managers to unauthorized access attempts at the cable, network, file-server, and resource levels.

- *Accounting management* involves billing people for what they use.

The control and reporting system used online today in many major networks is the Simple Network Management Protocol (SNMP). SNMP was developed and is used by the same federal government and university community that gave us TCP/IP and its suite of protocols. Dr. Jeffrey Case at the University of Tennessee is a leader in the development and use of SNMP.

SNMP works well in the large DoD and commercial networks that use TCP/IP, and there are ways to use SNMP management on even the smallest PC-based LANs. Hewlett-Packard's OpenView SNMP management program for Windows is relabeled and marketed by many companies. Cabletron has an SNMP system called Spectrum that uses artificial-intelligence modules to apply complex rules and react to the reports of network events it receives. Bay Network's Optivity was the original and is still one of the best graphical network management systems. Figure 16.3 shows an Optivity management screen with statistical reporting.

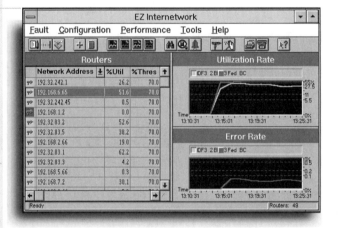

FIGURE 16.3

In this Optivity screen, a specific router is selected on the left while the statistics for that router appear on the right. Statistical reports such as these make it easier to optimize the network architecture and to budget ahead for new equipment and connections.

Segment with the RMON MIB

In previous chapters, I've stressed the need to segment networks to improve performance and reliability. But how do you tell what's going on in the distant segments? The answer is to either buy equipment such as wiring hubs equipped with the RMON MIB or to use a hardware device called a *probe* on the various segments. A probe contains a small processor with software for the RMON MIB. Its sole function is to report on what's happening on network segments.

The devices in an SNMP-managed network consist of agents and management stations. *Agents* are devices that report to the management stations. The major requirement for an agent is that it gather statistical information and store it in a *management information base* or MIB. There are standardized formats for various types of MIBs, and some companies put even more information into what they term MIB extensions. One of the most common MIBs is the Remote Monitoring or RMON MIB. This MIB is used in many devices that can check different LAN segments. Figure 16.4 shows a screen display from an RMON MIB.

Agents can be wiring hubs, routers, file servers, and any other type of network node. It isn't unusual for an agent such as a wiring hub or router to have a separate special-purpose processor for gathering and holding statistical information.

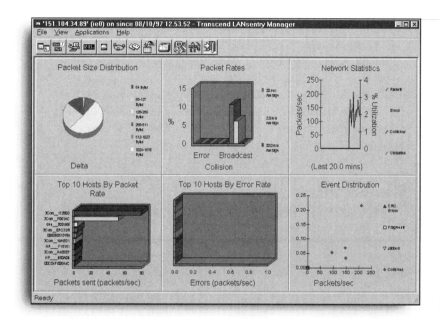

FIGURE 16.4

The report from an RMON MIB contains a wide variety of statistics on the volume and quantity of data monitored by the MIB. This MIB can be found in a variety of network devices including boxes known as *probes* that have no function other than reporting.

SEE ALSO

➤ *You can get an overview of the necessary hardware of networking in the section "Networking's Necessary Hardware," on page 44.*

The *management station* (there can be any number of these on the network) polls each agent and initiates a transmission of the MIB's contents to the management station. Management stations typically run Windows because of its graphical interface, or some version of UNIX because UNIX is commonly associated with the UDP and IP network protocols used to communicate between the agents and management stations. Sun workstations running UNIX are often used as SNMP management stations.

SNMP's drawbacks center around the tendency of some companies to create nonstandard configurations, often called *extensions* to the standard. You can accommodate the extensions by buying additional SNMP monitoring software from the company. If you stick with a single brand name family of equipment, this isn't a big problem, but most networks are a heterogeneous blend of brands, so matching all the extensions can be a hassle.

If you want SNMP in networks that don't use IP as their native transport layer protocol, such as those that use NetWare, you must introduce IP into the network, but in only a limited role.

You assign IP addresses to all monitored devices and to the PCs that will interrogate the MIBs in those devices. SNMP uses processing power and memory economically, is here today, and works well enough to meet the needs of even the largest network systems. If your network has more than a dozen active nodes or if its operation is critical to your business, you should consider installing wiring hubs and other devices with SNMP management.

IBM's NetView

IBM unveiled its network management products in early 1986; it calls its overall system NetView. Although it started out as a proprietary management system centered on IBM's Systems Network Architecture (SNA), NetView is now one of the most eclectic network management systems. NetView management stations can accept data from a variety of platforms ranging from PCs to mainframes and create a wide range of management reports. On the downside, the number of NetView products is bewildering and some of the acronyms and product names (is AIX NetView/6000 catchy enough?) are daunting. Despite its attempt to be all things to all people, NetView is clearly aimed at installations with IBM mainframe connections.

Down to the Desktop

The DMI gets rolling

Despite tremendous pressure from Intel, it took years to get the DMI accepted. Some PC vendors still don't understand it. If you're buying a lot of corporate PCs, I strongly recommend that you buy systems that conform with the DMI 2.0 specification. Your budget will be glad you did.

NetView and SNMP are the grand strategies for management, but other organizations have smaller-scale plans. The Desktop Management Task Force (DMTF), an organization of more than 300 vendors, has defined a Desktop Management Interface (DMI) for network management systems. The DMI provides a sublayer of management integration below the grand strategies. The goal of the DMI is to define how an agent interacts with devices, components, and programs inside a PC to gather and report very detailed information. Companies that support DMI, such as Intel, use NetBIOS, IP, or IPX to bring this information to a central management station.

The Internet Engineering Task Force also recognized the need for simplified management at the desktop level and has developed an SNMP Host Resources MIB. This MIB defines a common set of objects such as drives, adapters, and applications that a PC can manage.

Although it would make sense to integrate the DMI with the Host Resources MIB, progress in this area has been slow. Early DMI programs, such as Intel's LANDesk Gateway/SNMP, have consolidated DMI data and made it available to SNMP management consoles. Other vendors have followed the same path.

ManageWise, LANDesk, and SMS

Novell's ManageWise, Intel's LANDesk, and Microsoft's Systems Management Server (SMS) are three competing network management software systems. They have some overlapping features, but each has a separate focus. If you have a network with both NetWare and NT servers—a very common condition—you will find uses for both ManageWise and SMS. If you have SMS, you probably won't have LANDesk.

Generally, ManageWise is used as a diagnostics tool. Its NetWare Loadable Modules run on servers and report back to an application called the ManageWise Console. SMS works with several different operating systems, although some of its features work only with the various flavors of Windows.

Intel's LANDesk Server Manager Pro (LDSM) is a package that combines specialized hardware and software in one system. It tackles the operation and performance of servers and other control functions. The LDSM hardware enables users to establish in-band (network-based) or out-of-band (modem-based) connections to the server, even when the server is down. The package includes integration with SNMP, dial-up remote control for NT Servers, and the Intelligent Power Module. This module automatically recycles a server's power source. The software includes an impressive variety of programmable alerts, giving administrators options such as pop-up dialog boxes and automatic email.

The hardware and software inventory capabilities of SMS can save you money by keeping track of expensive assets. The system builds a master database of computer hardware and software details. You can use this data to perform a number of administrative tasks, such as determining how many computers you have in your organization or how many copies of a software application are installed, or identifying which computers have the hardware required for a software upgrade.

Maintaining software is a major overhead cost. The cost of having someone walk around to every PC in order to install new drivers or software patches is a heavy burden. With the software distribution capabilities of SMS, you can install, upgrade and configure each computer from a single, central location. You can schedule and distribute individual software files or complete software applications to specific computers, at specified times. SMS even enables you to initiate automated, unattended distribution of software to selected computers. This can be done off-hours, when the majority of users have gone home.

Later in this chapter, we'll also discuss the capability of SMS, and other management products, to limit the actions a user can take on a desktop PC. These limits are another way to keep down management overhead of networked computers.

Down-to-Earth Management

Because few people need the kind of network management system NASA might use to control deep space probes, I'll narrow the focus of this chapter just a bit. Network operating systems such as NetWare and Windows NT include network management utilities, but these utilities don't tell you much, if anything, about the activities of remote printers, communications gateways, mail servers, database servers, routers, and other devices on the LAN. If you want a full picture of the network's activity and health, you have to start at the lowest common denominator: the physical layer of network cabling.

Reporting and Control from the Wiring Hub

As I pointed out in my discussions of 10BASET and Token-Ring wiring topologies, a central wiring hub is a strong pulse point in the network. Because all the traffic goes through the hub—even traffic that bypasses the file server and moves directly between client stations and print or communications servers—a microprocessor in the hub can monitor and report on all network activity. The same processor can also give the network administrator certain levels of control over network connections.

SEE ALSO
➤ *To read more about 10BASET and Token-Ring topologies, turn to pages 140 and 149 respectively.*

Wiring-hub control and management provide a great deal of information. These packages are uniquely independent of the LAN operating system software, and fit into most of the grand management-architecture schemes, or soon will.

These products don't decode the traffic passing through the hubs. More complex devices called protocol analyzers, described later in this chapter, handle the complex decoding chore. Protocol analyzers that capture and decode packets provide some of the same information available through wiring-hub reporting and control systems, but you have to work a lot harder to get the information by those means, and you don't get the "big picture" that wiring-hub systems provide.

The reporting and control systems that operate at the network cable level don't decode packets, so they present no risk to the security of data or passwords. Protocol analyzers have a role in organizations where people develop sophisticated software and network hardware, but reporting and control systems have a role in almost every network. People who use protocol analyzers in place of network reporting and control systems are using a tele-scope to view a football game from the sidelines. They can read the quarterback's lips, but they miss a lot of the action.

It is difficult to break out the added incremental cost for the net-work reporting and control capabilities in wiring-hub systems. Wiring hubs include major elements of the network manage-ment features. Although the initial cost for software and hard-ware is usually several thousand dollars, that single outlay is amortized over all the nodes you have now and all that you add in the future. Because larger networks usually benefit most from reporting and control, their per-node cost is typically very low.

By themselves, these products provide all the network reporting and control capabilities many organizations will ever need, but if you expect your network to grow with multiple servers, gate-ways, bridges, and wide-area connections, you may soon find yourself thinking about adding more layers of reporting.

Looking for SNMP compatibility in all your network components is a smart idea, but installing reporting and control now at
the lowest hardware layer is the smartest move of all.

Adapters at Work

The key element in all protocol-analysis and traffic-counting
tools is the network adapter card that links the computer into
the network. The chip sets on such adapters alert the software to
each passing packet, translate data formats, and move received
data to RAM so the software can work on it. The chip sets also
contain cable-testing functions.

The National Semiconductor chip set on a typical Ethernet
adapter card can report 17 different errors pertaining to transmission control, reception, and packet format. Some of the most
common errors include *runt packets*, which don't contain enough
bits, and *dribble packets*, which contain enough bits but don't end
on an even byte.

When a transmitting Ethernet adapter detects a collision with
another station's packet, it transmits a jam signal of 4 to 6 bytes
of arbitrary data to ensure that all stations detect the collision.
Any receiving adapter reports the jam signal as a collision to any
monitoring software. The LAN traffic counters accept these
reports from Ethernet adapters, or similar types of reports from
ARCnet or Token-Ring adapters, and convert them into useful
charts, graphs, and reports.

Both wiring-hub traffic-management systems and traffic counters operating over LAN adapters provide a practical and broad
view of the network. They measure the force and volume of the
river of data coursing through your network. Figure 16.5 shows
statistics such as packet fragments, jabbering adapters, and other
problems on the wire. But sometimes you need to sample the
quality of the water to get a more detailed picture of what it carries. In networks, you sample the data stream with products
called *protocol analyzers*.

A free net tool

Fluke Corporation has a free tool for
examining the networking activity
inside your PC. Go to
www.fluke.com/nettools
and download the PC Inspector.
This program reports the IP address,
IP mask, domain name, mapped
drives, transport protocol configuration, and client software configuration inside a PC. It also reports and
records all the basic information
about the hardware and software
configuration in the PC. The program includes a nice help database
with detailed troubleshooting information for IP and LAN problems.

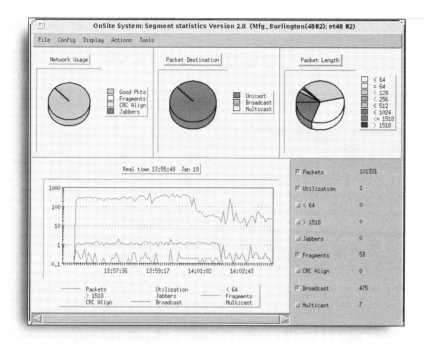

FIGURE 16.5

This screen from the Bay Networks Optivity program shows traffic on the network and breaks it down according to packet fragments, packets from jabbering adapters, packet size, and other categories.

Protocol Analyzers

"I'm not sure what it does, but I knew when I saw it that I just had to have one." That feeling, expressed by a fledgling network manager at a Manhattan bank, represents the feelings of many buyers of LAN diagnostic equipment. For some people, protocol analyzers are powerful tools, but for others they are merely talismans or amulets that confer status and just might ward off network miseries.

Integrated protocol analyzer systems, such as Network General's Sniffer, carry price tags of $10,000 and beyond. But the integrated systems have strong competition from alternative products that are more economical and just as useful for typical network managers. Triticom's LANdecoder family of products consists of reasonably-priced protocol analysis software packages that can run on any PC. However, the products don't work with every brand and type of LAN adapter. The software provides many of the same features as hardware-based analyzers and can

Why protocol analyzers?

I'm convinced that more protocol analyzers are sold as toys than are used as tools. I believe that program developers and a few network troubleshooters need protocol analyzers, but most folks who buy them really don't know what they're seeing. Fortunately, most buyers don't listen to me and buy them anyway. The software products such as Triticom's LANdecoder offer a good value.

run on an inexpensive 486-based notebook. Between the specialized integrated systems and the software products you can find the correct combination of price and capability for your installation. Let's start with a few simple definitions and explanations. What is a protocol, and why does it need analysis anyway?

Protocol = Agreement

A *protocol*, as you may remember, is nothing more than a formal agreement about how computers should format and acknowledge information during a communications session. When products from different companies follow the same protocol, they have the capability to communicate —theoretically, at least.

SEE ALSO

➤ *We discuss transport layer protocols like SPX and TCP on page 173.*

➤ *The IP network layer protocol is described in the section "The Heaven and Hell of IP" on page 317.*

In operation, communications software wraps a data message inside leading and trailing data fields whose format is determined by the protocols that software follows. These data fields form an envelope for the message while it transits the communications link. The sending and receiving systems must use the same protocols so that they know how to read an envelope's address, route it, deliver it, and even get a receipt, regardless of what it contains. If communications over the link break down, reading the leading and trailing fields, and even opening the envelope and decoding the data in the message it frames, might give you clues to the problem.

A *protocol analyzer* is the tool you use to read a protocol-configured packet. Different protocol analyzers exist for all types of communications circuits, including X.25, ISDN, and several specific types of local area network cabling, signaling, and protocol architectures. You can set up analyzers for ATM, Ethernet, and Token-Ring networks. These products typically look like laptop PCs because, in fact, they are simply software running on a laptop. They have screens with flashing displays, and software that can produce graphs and printed reports.

Network protocol analyzers capture data packets flying across a network and use special software to decode them. All LAN protocol analyzers enable you to filter and sort incoming and captured data for easier processing, and the units provide an English-language identification of the protocols in use and an evaluation of any damage to or irregularities in the captured data.

You can use the protocol analyzer to display packets selectively in real-time or to capture activity on the network for later study. You might set filter criteria so the analyzer displays only incoming packets going to or from certain stations, formatted according to specific protocols, or containing certain errors. Setting several filters simultaneously reduces the need for storage capacity in the analyzer. Alternatively, you can enable the analyzer to capture all the data it can hold—thousands of Ethernet packets—and then use the same filters to perform a careful analysis of the captured data. Some analyzer software contains an editor so you can delete unimportant data, enter comments, print reports, and even create files in common database formats. The ease of setting filters and reviewing data is an important criterion for protocol analyzers.

Although their protocol-analysis capabilities are powerful, the function for which most people use these devices is much less sophisticated. The screen display you usually see is a graph of current network activity. My experience is that people giving VIP tours of an organization love to bring visitors past the "network control center" so they can see the marching bar graphs showing network, and presumably corporate, activity. These screens usually include other information as well, such as the number of bytes or bits per second moving across the network, the percentage of maximum network capacity, the number of bad packets, and some measurement of the peak load experienced since the monitor was activated.

Most analyzers can also use a technique called *time domain reflectometry*, or TDR, to test cables for improperly terminated connections. This technique involves sending a signal out on the cable and then watching for and interpreting its echo. The systems can locate the position of open and shorted cable conditions with varying degrees of accuracy. Real TDRs are typically precision devices, often equipped with oscilloscope screens for exact measurement.

Protocol analyzers can generate network traffic too. Some systems, such as Network General's Sniffer, contain a traffic generator that loads the network with a stream of good packets. This activity is useful for checking certain behaviors of adapters and routers, but not for much else.

An important troubleshooting capability, contained in Novell's LANalyzer, enables you to rebroadcast a captured data stream onto the network. Imagine, for example, a network troubleshooter capturing an exchange between a client workstation and a server that contains errant responses from the server. Figure 16.6 shows a LANalyzer screen. The troubleshooter can enter the captured data file, edit out the bad responses, and send the same requests to the server over and over again while trying to isolate the problem. All of this can take place without interrupting activity at the client station. This capability has obvious security implications, which I'll address a little later, but it is certainly a useful troubleshooting tool.

LAN protocol analyzers aren't unique to any particular type of network operating system. You have to pick a product that works with the network adapters and cables in your system. Also, you should choose one that has decoders available for the protocols used by your networking software. For example, if you have a NetWare server, make sure the package has IPX/SPX decoding.

Security

Because they are passive monitoring devices, analyzers don't log onto a server and aren't subject to server-software security. The capability to copy and decode packets as they cross the network means that anyone with a protocol analyzer can easily find and decode packets carrying passwords used as people sign onto servers; in fact, the protocol analyzer can capture any data sent across the network. NetWare and Windows NT encrypt passwords for transmission, but no operating system encrypts data files during transmission; this is typically the job of add-on encryption hardware or special-purpose software. When you give someone a protocol analyzer, that person gains a wide-open tap on the network.

A protocol analyzer can do one thing for you that no other product can: It can decode the contents of captured packets or tokens and display an English-language interpretation, in addition to the hexadecimal code.

Buy What You Need

The first consideration in purchasing these management products is value. Not only should you get what you pay for, you should use what you pay for, too. LAN protocol analyzers are impressive tools—if you need one, there is no substitute—but if you don't need all their power, wiring-hub reporting and control programs or LAN traffic counters can give you an excellent view into your network's operation for a lot less money.

Gathering Statistics at the Server

Mountains of statistics are nothing without interpretation and insight, but with those skills managers can use statistics to move mountains. Networks are dynamic operational systems. You can define their operation in terms of certain measurable parameters. Managers can use those measurements to plan for growth, determine a baseline for comparison, detect problems in early stages, and justify budgets.

A host of modern programs now provides statistical data in both raw and quantified form to LAN administrators. Careful analysis of the data helps administrators create a productive and efficient LAN environment. The products available range from those that check the LAN for circumstances exceeding certain limits to those that soak up every detail of operation they can wring from servers and network adapter cards.

The products producing statistical reports are typically software, although a few have specific hardware components. For the most part, these are third-party, add-on software packages for your LAN that complement any statistical-reporting and management-control capabilities your network operating system already has. Figure 16.6 shows some of the server graphical reports delivered by the Saber Server Manager.

FIGURE 16.6

Saber Server Manager provides a variety of graphs giving a statistical depiction of critical functions within a server.

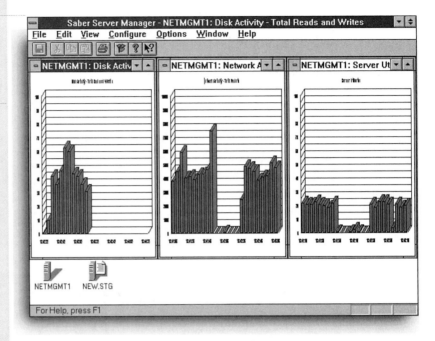

The factors these programs attempt to measure include

- The amount of disk storage space used by particular applications, persons, or cost centers
- The amount of activity in specific programs or files
- The connection time of specific people or client PCs
- The number of print jobs (expressed in several ways)
- Server workloads over a period of time
- Any of a few dozen other parameters

The statistical data you collect with such reporting programs constitutes a day-to-day assessment of your operation that serves as a baseline to assist in LAN troubleshooting and as a platform for planning growth. These programs enable you to compile and format your LAN information so you can see statistics before and after a problem or change. Such information is valuable for finding problems and for projecting requirements and budgets. In addition, programs that create data files in comma-delimited ASCII formats lend themselves to financial-analysis tasks.

Suites of network management programs are made up of many functional utilities that interact, more or less, and work together to present a comprehensive picture of a network's health. The elements of network management software suites range in power from simple programs that monitor the CPU cycles on your network file server to software and hardware inventory programs that can report the interrupt numbers of every adapter in every client PC on your system. Integration within a suite of products can mean a common database of information, a common interface or management program, or even a single console program that ties the reports from isolated programs together.

The network management landscape includes upwards of 15 to 20 islands of utilities (some would argue more). But five basic areas make up the main mass of LAN management: inventory management (including software metering), traffic monitoring, client PC monitoring, server monitoring, and application software distribution. Figure 16.7 shows a screen from a hardware inventory program.

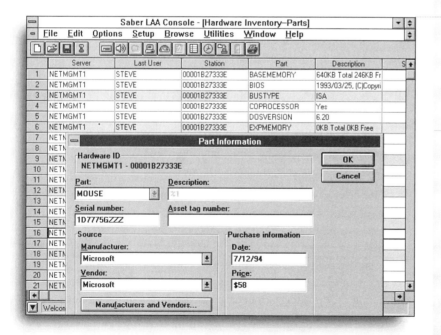

FIGURE 16.7

The Saber suite of management software can provide detailed hardware inventory reports. This screen shows a mouse as part of a hardware inventory.

Like network applications, network utilities are designed to lighten the network administrator's load and to increase productivity by pinpointing problems on your network. Network utilities increase your network awareness. They can help you draw a map of your network, spot needed changes, and diagnose problems so you can eliminate trouble before it starts. Before I get into a description of a few specific management suites, examine the function of the most common suite component: metering software.

LAN Metering Software

LAN metering programs are a subset of general inventory programs, but the topic is worth addressing separately because it is the only area of networking that can keep you out of jail or help you to avoid legal fees and fines! Metering tools give you important information on how the network and network applications are used. If people abuse software licenses, you and your organization can face prosecution. Metering programs have the unique capability to regulate the number of simultaneous users for each application on your network and to establish better security on your LAN at the same time.

Marketing a networked application is a challenging task for many companies. The technology of file sharing isn't a problem anymore; any graduate of a one-semester programming course knows how to write applications that can have simultaneous multiple accesses to the same data file. But LAN piracy is a real threat to the survival of many software companies.

There are two forms of piracy: blatant and subtle. Blatant piracy takes place when someone copies a program from the LAN file server onto a floppy disk and walks out the door with it. LANs are often the scene of subtler piracy, however. When a network administrator buys one single-user copy of a spreadsheet program and lets 12 people access it simultaneously, the company selling that product has been pirated out of a lot of money!

Some software companies try to ignore networks and offer no site-licensing agreements. If you want to use their packages legally at multiple PCs, you need to own multiple copies of each program. Particularly in the case of several federal-government computer contracts, this has resulted in organizations with closets full of shrink-wrapped packages—one for each potential user—while one copy of the program is shared on the network.

Today, most vendors of applications that can work on networks have site-licensing agreements available. Because no one has a perfect solution, the most common licensing agreement is on a "per server" basis. Only the most inexperienced or corrupt administrator would violate this type of license.

Per-server site licenses are expensive for small LANs. Many administrators find that buying a supply of single-copy versions of each program is still the best alternative. But smart network managers also know that it isn't usually economical to have a separate copy of an application program for each person on the network. Seldom does everyone need to use any one application at the same time. Smart network planners and administrators attempt to buy only enough copies or authorized uses of an application to meet the peak demand—but demands have a way of changing.

Some products only audit and report on use; they don't lock people out. The reports show when the demand exceeds the legal supply, so you can take action to correct the situation before it becomes a serious problem. With software metering tools, you can track the number of copies of an application in use and determine the number of copies you should buy for effective LAN management. You can also improve the overall network security and compile statistical data with these products.

Metering products vary in price from $100 to $800 and up, depending on the applications and nodes on your network. You can choose among simple packages that report LAN usage, menuing programs that control applications from behind customized screens, and auditing packages that create extensive reports on every type of network activity.

LAN administrators have a moral and legal responsibility to audit or meter the use of all licensed applications. Software companies lose money when people violate their software licenses by giving more than the allowed number of users access to the program.

Software companies have taken legal action against large corporate LAN pirates, although most cases are settled out of court. The vendors often learn about licensing violations from disgruntled employees looking for some way to strike at a former employer. Large organizations and independent auditing firms usually have software licensing on their internal audit checklists. If the application being audited is misused, there may be fines and discredit for the accused company. But with the audit and control measures established through metering software, license-abuse problems should never arise.

Because metering programs give you a full picture of who uses what resource when, they provide great support for budget requests and operations reports. You can wow the bean-counters by producing professional-looking reports from most of these programs. Add a few month-to-month statistics, put them on an overhead chart, and you may never again have to worry about your budget requests being rejected!

Keep a Low TCO

In 1997, the subject of total cost of ownership was the subject of a lot of hype and speculation. On the one hand, there is evidence that people spend a lot of time tweaking and experimenting with their computers. In many cases, these experiments backfire and IS managers have to spend time restoring configuration files and making things right again.

I don't believe!

I believe in managed PCs if they make life easier for end users and network managers. But I don't believe the "cost savings" promised by various studies. Use managed PC and thin client technologies wisely, but don't expect them to generate big savings that you can take to the bank.

If you believe certain studies, networked PCs can cost nearly ten thousand dollars a year to own. One study by market research firm Gartner Group indicated it would cost 39% less to own and maintain what is called a thin client, such as an Oracle NC, than a Windows 95 PC. The same study estimates it would cost 31% less to use a network server-based solution such as the remote Windows clients sold by Citrix Systems.

For many people, these figures don't stand the test of reason. They seem to attribute costs to the computer that others might consider necessary and a part of doing business. After all, if you somehow stop people from experimenting with the setup of their

PCs, do they suddenly focus only on work and become significantly more productive? Or, do they simply find some other distraction?

TCO Desktop Policy

On the bottom line, the most effective things you can do to control the cost of networked computers are to reduce the amount of walking around by IS professionals and reduce the amount of experimentation by users.

You reduce the walking around by introducing central management of hardware and software. The management suites described earlier in this chapter can perform this kind of management.

Microsoft studied the actions of end-users and came up with the following list of things people do to their systems. These five deadly sins reduce individual productivity and typically require the actions of a professional to correct. Microsoft's SMS and the latest versions of Windows contain software modules aimed at creating a *Zero Administration Workstation (ZAW)*.

- Unintentionally deleting necessary system files from a hard disk
- Modifying the control panel or registry incorrectly
- Introducing incompatibilities or viruses by installing new software
- Experimenting with system settings such as colors, backgrounds, and desktop arrangement
- Installing and using unapproved, job-unrelated software such as games

A technique called *policy management* controls the allowed activities of end users. Basically, it prevents users from committing the sins listed above. This software should eliminate much of the disruption of emergency calls to the IS staff and enhance user productivity. Policy management is a part of TCO-control initiatives from Hewlett-Packard, Intel, Microsoft, Novell, and other companies.

Desktop computer management and network management are key issues as managers feel pressed to investigate and perhaps even to control the total cost of ownership (TCO) of networked PCs. In the last years of the 90's, vendors have rolled out alternative desktop systems designed to reduce the cost of software, maintenance, and maybe acquisition. Sun Microsystems, Oracle and others are promoting the concept of cheaper thin clients that would require less maintenance than a PC. PC vendors are incorporating manageability features into their products.

The market has become a blaze of claims and counter claims as vendors try to gain leverage for their products. There are several alternatives, so let's list them with their pros and cons:

- **Plain old PCs**. Call them "unmanaged" PCs in this context. These familiar machines are open to users' experimentation, require periodic attention from professionals, and sometimes demand customized hardware and software combinations.

- **Managed PCs**. Reducing TCO means reducing walking around, so PCs should be open to management from a central location. The Desktop Management Interface (DMI) specification developed by the Desktop Management Task Force (DMTF) provides a way to remotely inventory system components and system settings. Other management software suites can do similar things, but not from the motherboard BIOS levels.

- **NetPCs**. The NetPC is the first of the so-called *thin clients*. These end-user terminals have few, if any, expansion slots and typically no floppy drives or CD-ROM drives. They do have a local hard disk. All management and configuration of NetPCs is done centrally at the server and users are completely locked out of their systems. If NetPCs are going to be a success, they will ride on Microsoft's Zero Administration for Windows (ZAW) initiative. The server-side technology is a part of Windows NT 5.0 and the client-side software is part of a package called the Zero Administration Kit (ZAK).

- **Windows Terminals**. A WinTerm consists of a display, keyboard, a relatively low-power processor with limited

The thin bottom line

The bottom line is, you're going to use the type of terminals that work best for your applications. If your users need to do the typical jobs of email and word processing, then managed PCs are a good idea. But, specific line-of-business applications might be written for network computers or Windows terminals and work best with these devices. Let the dog wag the tail. Let the application determine the hardware, not the other way around.

memory, parallel and serial ports, and a network connection. Like the remote control devices described in Chapter 15, a WinTerm runs its applications on a central server and only keystrokes and screen images pass over the communications channel. Windows terminals are being marketed primarily as replacements for dumb terminals. You can use Windows terminals to run Windows applications if you connect your machines to a Windows NT server running Citrix Systems' WinFrame.

■ **Network Computer or NC**. The most radical departure from the PC world is the *network computer*, the PR love child of Oracle Corp. and Sun Microsystems. IBM has latched onto the NC as a replacement for standard data entry terminals. The NC is a very thin client with no local storage. Its basic design calls for an 8MB ROM card, a SmartCard slot, infrared and network interfaces, a parallel port, and a pair of PS/2-compatible I/O ports for connecting a mouse and keyboard. In concept, the NC is designed to be both a super browser and a device to run programs written in the Java programming environment. For the most part, NCs are to be used as specialized user terminals for line-of-business applications.

SEE ALSO

➤ *We discuss terminal types in the section "Mainframe and Minicomputer Systems" on page 330.*

■ **Web Terminal**. The web terminal includes a wide range of products such as browser-empowered telephones and subcompact computers running the Windows CE operating system. These devices access web pages customized for small screen and even monochrome screen displays. These devices do the most to improve computing value and productivity by providing more information access in a portable package.

Although those are the definitions of specific types of functional devices, the manufacturers always look for ways to differentiate and add value to their products. These definitions will change as vendors put Java, browser, and policy management capabilities in all hardware.

CHAPTER 16

Network Management Brings Results

Apart from a few dancing histograms and moving bar charts, LAN administrative software may look like pretty dull stuff. It can bury you under mountains of statistics and create deskwork when you might crave technical challenges. Yet these programs can not only save your job by spotting problems, abuses, and trends; they can also enhance your work by supporting your requests for money and people to help operate your LAN.

Network Productivity Tools

It's clear that my favorite phrase is "networks are for sharing," but what you share across the network is changing. Obviously networks are designed to enable you to share devices such as an expensive large format printer or to trade word processing documents with a co-worker, but modern network applications can do a lot more to increase your productivity and flexibility.

A concept called *messaging* is at the core of modern network applications. Messaging systems use a transportation program, often called an *engine* or *service*, running on one or more messaging servers somewhere in the network. The messaging server transports blocks of data between applications running on client PCs. The most common network application to use messaging is electronic mail. Microsoft Mail is based on this model, and uses a service called the Messaging API or MAPI. Lotus has joined with IBM and other vendors to develop Vendor Independent Messaging or VIM.

MAPI won

For all practical purposes, Microsoft drove the challengers from the field (again). Despite its powerful parents, you don't hear much about VIM anymore.

Applications such as network scheduling, electronic forms distribution and tracking, and project tracking interact with the messaging engine. The messages they exchange typically aren't meant for direct human consumption, so messaging is not the same thing as email. However, one of the things messaging helps to implement is email. The capability of applications to pass information about network users, rights, fonts, paths, and other details is increasingly vital to their usefulness. That's the job of messaging. The following sections describe some of the functional applications that messaging makes possible.

The Scheduling Dilemma

In many organizations, scheduling three or more busy people for a meeting, along with arranging for such facilities as a conference room and an overhead projector, can be a frustrating and time-consuming task, requiring any number of phone calls. If one person or facility is not available when the other people or facilities are, a series of negotiations begins. Mathematicians refer to this method of simultaneously handling several unknown factors as "progressive approximation," but whoever has to make all the contacts and coordinate the compromises calls it frustration.

LAN scheduling products simplify this task and often eliminate the frustration. If everyone in the organization uses the scheduling software, one person can access the public calendars of other people and the sign-up sheets for resources. It doesn't take long to determine when everyone involved is free to attend a meeting, and the process does not involve any invasion of privacy. The person planning the meeting doesn't see every detail on a personal calendar—just enough to find the free time.

Personal calendars are at the heart of the group scheduling process. The best scheduling software is useless if people don't cooperate by keeping their personal calendars current. One problem common to all these packages is that they don't provide an easy way to schedule individual resources. Because a group of resources—such as three conference rooms or three slide projectors—usually has only one manager, it's foolish to make that person repeatedly check into a separate personal calendar module to confirm the scheduled use of each room or device. The person scheduling the meeting and the person managing the resources should not have to treat each identical projector, VCR, viewing screen, or meeting room as a separate entity.

Electronic Mail Programs for Productivity

On a practical level, the biggest benefits we get from using electronic mail are that it nearly eliminates telephone tag and that it enables a widespread staff to ignore time zones and office hours. These capabilities do a great deal to improve individual and group productivity and to reduce frustration. The more people in an organization use email—with its capability to store information and deliver it when the recipient is ready to take it—the less they are controlled by the demands of that real-time communications device, the telephone.

Electronic mail systems break the tyranny time holds over communications. For most of recorded history you couldn't engage in real-time communications farther than you could project your voice. The time required to communicate severely limited the quantity and quality of communications. The introduction of electronic devices, particularly the telephone, eliminated the time needed to move a message across distances; but telephone communications brought with them the new requirement of synchronicity—the need to beat the game of telephone tag. For most of this century, if no one answered the phone when it rang, the potentially fast-moving message wasn't delivered.

We work around the problem of synchronicity by using answering machines and facsimile machines. Additionally, many organizations have found relief from telephone tag and discovered a whole new way of communicating through electronic mail. Electronic mail moves messages across long distances quickly, stores messages, and forwards them to you where and when you're ready to receive them.

Intranets break 80/20

Actually, the 80/20 rule is dead. Email in general encourages "skip channel" communications. It goes right along with today's generally flatter organizational hierarchies. Corporate intranets fuzz up the lines between external and internal correspondence. When you share an email system with a parts supplier or an outside accountant, are those people in or out of your system? Email and document transfer are very necessary lubricants for today's "just in time" manufacturing, training, and delivery systems.

The 80/20 rule of office correspondence says that 80% of the words you write are for internal consumption and 20% go outside your organization. Email makes it much easier to create and distribute the internal 80%, and it can invisibly handle distribution to the critically important external 20%, too.

The Basics of Email and Beyond

The basic functions of electronic mail include creating, reading, forwarding, replying to, and issuing receipts for messages. All email packages must do these jobs. Of course, email programs vary significantly in the utilities, menus, and other amenities they provide for creating and receiving messages.

Some of the most useful features in an email system include the following:

- A "message waiting" notification module
- A pop-up window for reading messages
- The option of importing text files into messages
- The option of attaching binary files to outgoing messages
- The option of using standard word processing programs to prepare mail
- Return receipts for messages
- Folders for special subjects

- Encryption during transmission
- Encryption of stored messages
- A central message store
- Rules-based messaging
- Workflow monitoring

The *message store* is a set of files or a database that holds both private user mailboxes and public data, such as calendars and public folders containing discussions, documents, and other shared information. In practice, a server could have physically separate stores for different functions—one for private mailboxes and another for shared information, for example. But to the user, these separate stores usually appear as an integrated store.

Rules-based messaging is a little complicated to set up, but it can save you a lot of time. The best example of rules-based messaging is what I call the "vacation message." For example, imagine you are going on vacation and don't plan to bring your laptop to check your email while you're gone. Think of all the potentially angry clients and the amount of junk mail you'll have to sort through on your return. Fortunately, you can use rules-based messaging to save the day. Sometimes the rules are set in the server of an advanced email system. On the other hand, intelligent email client software like Eudora Pro responds to incoming Internet mail according to specific rules.

Most good email programs have utilities, such as the ones found in Exchange and GroupWise, that automatically send a "vacation" reply to everyone who sends you email while you are away. It even forwards your messages to a designated coworker. You can also use rules-based messaging to perform other neat tricks, such as forwarding all email with the words "help" or "support" displayed in the subject or message body to your technical support department.

One of my favorite utilities in most groupware applications is the *group* or *threaded discussion* application. Unlike standard email, where you are simply sending personal messages to a select set of users, group discussions enable everyone to participate in a discussion and see the responses and messages from their colleagues

Watch those rules

The two best uses of rules are to forward specific email messages to a coworker while you're out of the office and to block delivery of email messages from specific addresses—specifically unwanted advertisements. However, you can go crazy with rules. Many people argue about the value of "I'm on vacation" messages, particularly if the messages don't tell you how to get action while the individual is on vacation!

Online PR

One day in 1997, the stock market fell 554 points. Merrill Lynch Vice Chairman John Steffens jumped into an Internet online question and answer discussion and tossed a little water to feverish investors. The discussion was later posted for reading and the company got a lot of mileage from it. Company-wide or worldwide interactive access is a great PR tool for senior managers, politicians, and leaders. Leverage your technology!

in a threaded format. Group discussions are useful for real-time collaborations; for example, you can have your sales staff vote on a proposal for a new advertising plan. You can also attach binary files to discussion threads and set up a moderator to determine who can post replies and to limit the content of the posts.

Not many groupware applications include a workflow utility in their packages. A *workflow utility* recognizes and manages specific types of document packages. For example, you could create a workflow utility to manage an application for a building permit. Ideally, a would-be builder could initiate the building application through a county web site on the Internet. The web page would become a document that flows, under control of the groupware application, from person to person for action. A workflow utility is a great tool if you want to cut down on the amount of paper in your office and make sure every job gets done.

Another nice feature found in programs, including GroupWise, is the *document management* utility. This feature enables you to post a document to a public folder and enable other users to check it out, make changes, check it back in, or simply make a personal copy. You can also keep track of everyone who has read the document and the changes that were made based on user and date. Document management is a powerful utility for most lawyers' offices and other businesses that have to manage documents.

Groupware solutions are designed to save you time and money, but they also require user participation in order to work effectively. Many people are using the Internet or intranets to perform most of their groupware tasks, but LAN-based solutions still offer more features, are easier to use, and offer Internet/intranet add-ons to protect their place in the market.

Gateways to fax systems work well for sending fax messages from an email system. The major drawback of email/fax systems is the same one that plagues standalone PC/fax systems: an inadequate capability to receive incoming mail. There is no standard way to address a fax message to a particular recipient; someone must use special software to view each incoming fax and route it to the correct person. What's more, incoming fax messages are saved as graphics images, which require a laser printer with a lot of memory to reproduce on paper.

SEE ALSO

➤ *For more on faxing, see page 349.*

Groupware applications have reached the level of real "bet the business" environments. Let's examine three established network applications: Lotus Notes, WordPerfect GroupWise (formerly known as Symmetry and, before that, WordPerfect Office), and Microsoft Exchange.

Lotus Notes and Domino

Lotus released Notes as a network application in 1989, and it has since become a standard of comparison for other workgroup products. Notes is a client/server application that enables users to share information securely over a LAN, telephone line, or wide area network connection. Lotus offers a Notes front end for most popular graphical operating systems, including Windows, OS/2, Macintosh, and UNIX.

The evolution of Notes came in the form of a family of products called Domino. Domino includes a database engine and many services. The Domino translation engine translates Notes documents into HTML so that users can get at messages and services through a browser without the special client software. In addition to translating files, Domino can also provide HTML and graphics files from its file system. Overall, Domino is an email, scheduling, database, and web server system. This brief description barely scratches the surface of what Domino can be, but it is a complex system requiring a great deal of local management, configuring, and some customized programming.

Replication, meaning "copying", is a busy word in the Notes and Domino architecture. Figure 17.1 shows the replication settings for a Notes client. Notes servers continually replicate databases among themselves and among users. Users can set rules describing what portions of a database they want to replicate locally. A Notes database is an object storage facility that users can use to access, track, and organize information on the network. Users connected to the same network, whether they are local network clients or mobile users who only occasionally connect to the network via a modem and a phone line, can replicate from the Notes database structure.

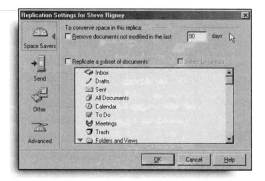

The word *database*, although technically correct, doesn't convey the actual uses of the Notes/Domino structure. The databases concerned go far beyond the typical concept of files and records to include sophisticated tools for making useful forms, adding information, and arranging information. As the screen in Figure 17.2 shows, the database approach means that you don't have to select specific functions such as scheduling, discussion, or email. Those differences between functions still exist, but they are less visible to users under Notes than under GroupWise or any Exchange client. News update services, online discussion groups with threading, lists of sales leads, and electronic mail are all services commonly based on Notes databases.

Users of Lotus Notes can send any document to any Notes database, and all email is stored in a Notes database. In addition to text, you can use Notes email to send hypertext documents, OLE embedded documents, and various forms and applications. This flexibility means people can create messages that include graphics and enhanced text to add spark to their information. Because Lotus complies with the Vendor Independent Messaging (VIM) standard, other email systems on the network can easily exchange messages with Notes.

Novell's GroupWise

Novell's GroupWise combines email, personal and group scheduling, workflow routing, and rules-based message management,

into a single application. The screen in Figure 17.3 shows the
GroupWise inbox and the activity options. Like Lotus, Novell
provides client software for Windows, Macintosh, and UNIX-
based computers. Like Exchange, GroupWise is primarily an
email server that provides some groupware applications for
group scheduling, basic workflow, and keeping track of tasks.
Although the capability to use a browser to connect to your
GroupWise server is a nice feature, you can't perform all the
same tasks through the browser that you can from Novell's proprietary Windows-based client.

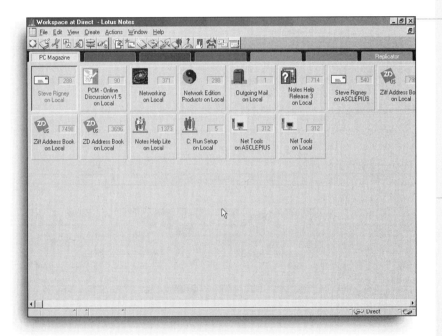

FIGURE 17.2

This Notes user screen provides access to locally replicated databases of email,
discussion groups, address
books, and to similar databases housed on a server. Users
would typically elect to keep a
database full of graphical
images on the server, but
locally replicate a database of
email messages.

GroupWise is tightly integrated with Novell Directory Services
(NDS). NDS is much more powerful than NT's original domain
structure and you can easily keep track of all of your email
addressees across a WAN. You can use a single management
console to define all aspects of GroupWise from post office
name to user access rights.

GroupWise enables you to send email to local and remote users
across heterogeneous mail systems using the Simple MAPI protocol. You can send and receive network fax messages using the

email front end. Under Windows, you can also create electronic messages and link them to certain applications so that an icon in the message can automatically launch a Windows application. This is a lot easier than attaching a binary file and hoping the recipient will figure out the file format and have the correct application to run it. Figure 17.4 shows Microsoft's Outlook, the most popular Exchange client software, and the functional selections.

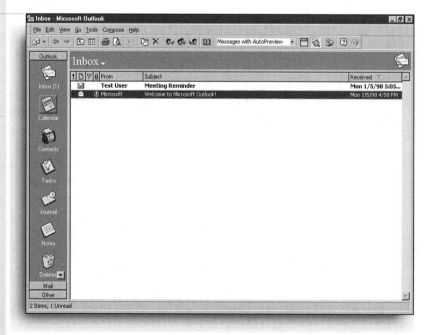

Both Notes and GroupWise are designed to keep track of and access data no matter where it is stored on the network; however, Notes offers stronger database features for storing different file formats and information. With its replicating database structure, Notes delivers up-to-date information to every client, anywhere on the network.

Like Exchange, GroupWise comes with all the major post office protocols including POP3, SMTP, IMAP, and LDAP. The product also provides gateways you can use to connect your GroupWise server to other messaging systems, such as cc:Mail, MSMail, and Lotus Notes.

SEE ALSO

➤ *POP3 and the other mail protocols are part of the TCP/IP suite of protocols described on page 312.*

Microsoft Exchange

It didn't take long for Microsoft to jump on the network application bandwagon. Microsoft Exchange combines messaging and information-sharing into a single product that ties directly to your operating system. Within Exchange, public folders enable people to create discussion groups and shared pools of information. The features of Exchange include an unlimited message store size, support for the IMAP and LDAP protocols, enhanced security, and fast online data backup.

Exchange handles scheduling well, but you need Microsoft's Outlook software on the client PCs to use it. Outlook provides a personal calendar that you can use to create meetings and invite other attendees. The scheduler can automatically determine whether a person is free for a planned meeting by consulting his or her personal calendar.

You can perform all the messaging and groupware tasks using Microsoft Outlook as well as your favorite web browser. Microsoft has produced "mail-enabled" applications, so you can send a message or attachment without switching to another email application. Unlike GroupWise and Notes, Exchange is strongly tied to the Windows operating system and applications, especially to those developed by Microsoft. Figure 17.5 illustrates how Exchange gathers information about the intended use of the system in order to configure the environment.

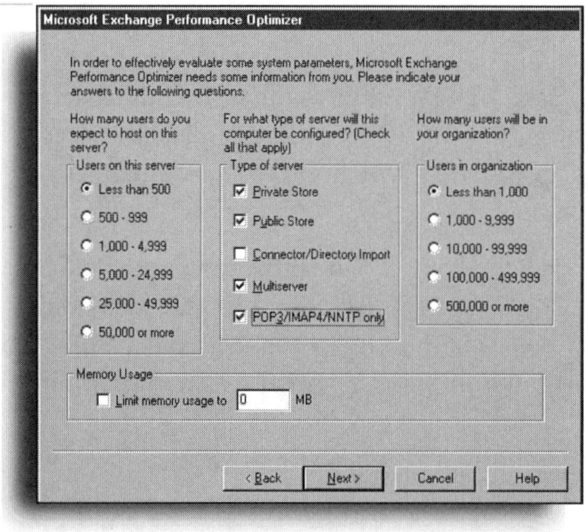

FIGURE 17.5

The Exchange program uses information you provide to initially set up the networking environment with sufficient storage, data buffers, and other capabilities. As your needs grow, the system adjusts.

Microsoft = environment

Although Exchange is merely competitive with Notes and GroupWise in terms of features, the combination of services within Windows is hard to beat as an application development environment. The messaging services, communications services, database services, and other integrated features of Windows make it a great place to build a line of business applications.

Exchange comes with a copy of Microsoft Outlook 97 that is its client of choice for sending and receiving email. However, you can also use your existing Internet email client, such as Eudora, to connect to an Exchange mailbox. You can also use any web browser to read your email messages. Like Lotus Notes, Exchange keeps a copy of your messages on both your client PC and the server.

The Internet Influence

The electronic messaging industry has split into two factions: those advocating solutions based entirely on Internet standards and those promoting proprietary designs with new open interfaces. Internet zealots want to use web servers as replacements for the traditional file server, with browsers as the interface to virtually every application. Proprietary vendors such as Lotus and Microsoft have in turn promised to make their messaging servers integrate with clients that use Internet protocols, but they insist that such clients cannot provide the same level of service as proprietary clients. Generally, proprietary clients can take greater advantage of server-based rules and sophisticated replication models.

Internet standards include Post Office Protocol (POP), Internet Message Access Protocol (IMAP) and Multipurpose Internet

Mail Extension (MIME). IMAP is replacing POP; much IMAP software is distributed as freeware and supported via email and Usenet. Sun and DEC are the leading Internet-focused messaging vendors.

The Post Office Protocol is the oldest and most widely used email standard in the Internet family. Internet service providers typically offer customers POP3 (the third major standards revision) Internet mail service. You can get POP3 client software for practically every combination of hardware and software. The most popular for PCs and Macintosh systems is Qualcomm's Eudora.

POP servers operate in an economical store-and-forward fashion. The servers exchange mail across the Internet and hold incoming mail for their clients. The client software initiates a connection to the server and logs in. After authentication, the POP server transfers everything in its queue that is addressed to the client, and then most POP servers clear the queue. The interchange is quick and efficient but not flexible or repeatable. If you lose the hard disk on your client computer, you've lost your email. Or if you want to see previously received mail from a second computer, you can't. Some vendors have workarounds that can tell the server not to delete messages, but nothing they offer approaches the replication capabilities of Notes or Exchange.

The Internet Message Access Protocol (IMAP) is replacing POP. IMAP4, an emerging standard, continues the evolution of a client/server messaging system using remote procedure calls. An IMAP server does a lot more for the client than a POP server does. IMAP client programs can give the user choices about what categories of messages to draw from the server, where to store messages, and what the server should do with specific categories of read messages.

The Multipurpose Internet Mail Extensions (MIME) give Internet email users the capability to attach files to messages. The most sophisticated MIME extensions help the client PC select the correct application to view or execute the file. In conjunction with IMAP, MIME provides a way to create rich and useful messages. MIME is a feature of new IMAP clients.

The Internet dilutes proprietary products

You'll find that the once-proprietary products such as Notes, Exchange, and GroupWise now have POP, IMAP, and NNTP capabilities. You might be able to do a little more with the proprietary clients, but the Internet protocols are useful.

Similarly, the Network News Transfer Protocol (NNTP) is part of many browsers. NNTP sets up the structure for the threaded discussions carried on in Internet newsgroups. MIME does not work with NNTP, however.

The Internet standards enable interoperability, product interchangeability, and vendor independence. On the other hand, most pure Internet mail products can't match the features of the proprietary products.

The Internet standards are pretty basic stuff. They include no standards for extended groupware functions such as calendaring and replication. The Internet standard mail products are starting the race several laps behind and will have to jump a few fences to catch up. Mail products are highly visible and have to provide a lot of functionality. Users want messaging products that use standards-based, general-purpose directories rather than have to create their own directories. Strong authentication, digital signatures, and message encryption will quickly become baseline requirements in terms of security. Enterprise customers are also asking for integrated scheduling and calendaring, discussions based on public folders, and better management capabilities. Likewise, directory services must be more robust than the simple address books that once typified messaging systems.

Where stores of email messages were once shared files, the servers must now use single-instance storage. In other words, the email system should maintain only a single copy of a message intended for many recipients. Many message stores now provide transaction capabilities that enable managers to restore a messaging system to its pre-crash state in cases of disaster recovery. This is all challenging technology.

Vendors such as Lotus, Microsoft, and Novell have feature-rich products based on closed protocols. But to enable these features, vendors have employed closed protocols. Choosing feature-rich, but proprietary, products involves sacrificing degrees of interoperability, product interchangeability, and vendor independence.

To remain competitive, Lotus, Microsoft, and Novell are adding Internet standards support to their products, creating multiprotocol servers that support both existing proprietary protocols and

Internet standards. Such standards support gives customers choices when it comes to the protocols and products they use. But customers must understand the long-term implications of such decisions.

Lotus, Microsoft, and Novell have software modules conforming to standards such as IMAP4. But those same vendors point to the extended features Notes, Exchange, and GroupWise provide as the primary reasons customers should buy and use those products. It's also safe to assume that Lotus, Microsoft, and Novell will continue to extend their solutions, adding proprietary features in an effort to remain competitive. In other words, just because a vendor conforms to IMAP4, you shouldn't assume that you won't end up locked into a vendor-specific solution. If a feature such as integrated calendaring or replication is important to you, then it may well be worth investing in vendor-specific technology to solve a pressing business problem.

Your decision on whether to invest in a back-end email infrastructure based on Internet technologies, or to trust the more proprietary products, depends upon how much you have invested or plan to invest in the overhead of the Internet, and on the services you must have. On the Internet side, do you intend to give everyone access to a primary and a backup DNS server? Is your IP addressing scheme up to date? Do you use the Dynamic Host Configuration Protocol (DHCP) to manage IP addresses? Are you comfortable with UNIX? Even if the answer to each of these questions is "no" for now, will the pressure of a corporate intranet push you in these directions in the near future? If so, then you are a candidate for mail systems based on Internet technology.

Glossary

access method A protocol that determines which device in a local area network has access to the transmission media at any instant. CSMA/CD is an example of an access method. IBM uses the same term for specific kinds of communications software that include protocols for exchanging data, constructing files, and other functions.

access protocol The traffic rules that LAN workstations abide by to avoid data collisions when sending signals over shared network media; also referred to as the *media-access control (MAC) protocol.* Common examples are carrier sense multiple access (CSMA) and token passing.

ACK A positive acknowledgment control character. This character is exchanged between system components when data has been received without error. The control character is also used as an affirmative response for setting up a communications exchange. ACK is also used as the name of a message containing an acknowledgment.

acoustic coupler The portion of a modem that physically holds a telephone handset in two rubber cups. The cups house a small microphone and speaker that "talk" and "listen" to the telephone handset.

ADCCP (Advanced Data Communications Control Procedures) A bit-oriented ANSI-standard communications protocol. It is a link-layer protocol.

A/D converter A device that converts analog signals to digital.

address A unique memory location. Network interface cards and CPUs often use shared addresses in RAM to move data from each card to the PC's processor. The term can also refer to the unique identifier for a particular node in a network.

Address Resolution Protocol (ARP) A protocol within the Transmission Control Protocol/Internet Protocol (TCP/IP) suite that "maps" IP addresses to Ethernet addresses. TCP/IP requires ARP for use with Ethernet.

Advanced Communications Function (ACF) An IBM program package to allow sharing computer resources through communications links. It supports SNA.

Advanced Communications Service A large data communications network developed by AT&T.

AFP (AppleTalk File Protocol) Apple's network protocol, used to provide access between file servers and clients in an AppleShare network. AFP is also used by Novell's products for the Macintosh.

alphanumeric Characters made up of letters and numbers; usually contrasted with graphics characters made up of dots in terminal emulation.

analog Commonly refers to transmission methods developed to transmit voice signals. These methods were designed only for the bandwidth of the human voice (up to about 3 kHz); this limits their capability to pass high-speed digital signals.

ANSI (American National Standards Institute) An organization that develops and publishes standards for codes, alphabets, and signaling schemes.

API (application program interface) A set of standard software interrupts, calls, and data formats that application programs use to initiate contact with network services, mainframe communications programs, or other program-to-program communications. For example, applications use APIs to call services that transport data across a network.

APPC (Advanced Program-to-Program Communications) An IBM protocol analogous to the OSI model's session layer; it sets up the necessary conditions that enable application programs to send data to each other through the network.

APPC/PC An IBM product that implements APPC on a PC.

APPN (Advanced Peer-to-Peer Networking) An addition to IBM's SNA communication, APPN provides the most efficient route for establishing direct communication between users anywhere on the network.

AppleTalk An Apple networking system that can transfer data at a rate of 230 kilobytes per second over shielded twisted-pair wire. Superseded by the term *LocalTalk*.

application layer The highest (seventh) level of the OSI model. It describes the way that application programs interact with the network operating system.

applications processor A special-purpose computer that enables a telephone system to furnish special services such as voice mail, messaging services, and electronic mail.

ARCnet (Attached Resources Computing) A networking architecture (marketed by Datapoint Corp. and other vendors) using a token-passing bus architecture, usually on coaxial cable.

ARP (Address Resolution Protocol) A TCP/IP protocol used to obtain a node's physical address when only its logical IP address is known. An ARP request with the IP address is broadcast onto the network, and the node with that address responds by sending back its hardware address so that packets can be transmitted. Reverse ARP, or RARP, is used by a diskless workstation to obtain its logical IP address.

ARPANET (Advanced Research Projects Agency Network) A network originally sponsored by the Defense Advanced Research Projects Agency (DARPA) to link universities and government research centers. The TCP/IP protocols were pioneered on ARPANET.

ARQ A control code that calls for the retransmission of a block of data.

ASCII (American Standard Code for Information Interchange) The data alphabet used in the IBM PC to determine the composition of the 7-bit string of 0s and 1s that represents each character (alphabetic, numeric, or special).

ASR (automatic send/receive) A term left over from teleprinters that punched messages on paper tape. Now, it is sometimes used to indicate any terminal that has storage capability.

asynchronous A method of transmission in which the time intervals between characters do not have to be equal. Start and stop bits are added to coordinate the transfer of characters.

attenuation The decrease in power of a signal transmitted over a wire, measured in decibels. As attenuation increases, the signal decreases.

automatic number identification (ANI) A feature that passes a caller's ten-digit telephone number over the network to the customer's premises so that the caller can be identified.

background program (background mode) A program that performs its functions while the user is working with a different program. Communications programs often operate in background mode. They can receive messages while the user works with other programs. The messages are stored for later display.

balun (BALanced UNbalanced) An impedance-matching device that connects a balanced line (such as a twisted-pair line) and an unbalanced line (such as a coaxial cable).

bandwidth The range of frequencies a circuit will pass. Analog circuits typically have a bandwidth limited to that of the human voice (about 300 Hz to 3 kHz). The square waves of a digital signal require a higher bandwidth. The higher the transmission rate, the greater the bandwidth requirement. Fiber-optic and coaxial cables have excellent bandwidths. Also, in common usage, *bandwidth* refers to the upper limit of the rate that information can be transferred over a network.

base address The first address in a series of addresses in memory, often used to describe the beginning of a network interface card's I/O space.

baseband A network that transmits signals as a direct-current pulse rather than as variations in a radio-frequency signal.

basic-rate interface (BRI) The ISDN standard governing how a customer's desktop terminals and telephones can connect to the ISDN switch. It specifies two B-channels that allow 64-kilobit-per-second simultaneous voice and data service, and one D-channel that carries call information and customer data at 16 kbps.

baud A measure of transmission speed; the reciprocal of the time duration of the shortest signal element in a transmission. In RS-232C ASCII, the signaling element is 1 bit.

BBS (bulletin board system) An electronic message system.

BCD (binary-coded decimal) A coding scheme using a 6-bit (six-level) code.

B-channel A "bearer" channel that carries voice or data at 64 kilobits per second in either direction and is circuit-switched.

benchmark test A program used to measure system speed or throughput.

BIND The Berkley Internet Name Domain is the most popular implementation of the Domain Name Service (DNS). This implementation follows the …username@domain style of addressing. The DNS/BIND process links the human-readable name to an IP address. Bind is also a term frequently used in WINDOWS or other operating systems to describe a condition when a protocol is "bound" to a card or to an upper layer as part of a complete stack.

Bindery A database maintained by Novell's NetWare operating system that holds information on users, servers, and other elements of the network.

Bisynchronous Communications Also abbreviated as BSC, this protocol is one of the two commonly used methods of encoding data for transmission between devices in IBM mainframe computer systems. Data characters are gathered in a package called a *frame*, which is marked by 2 synchronization bits (bisync). The more modern protocol is SDLC.

bit The smallest unit of information. In digital signaling, this commonly refers to a 0 or a 1.

block A number of characters transmitted as a group.

BNC connector A small coaxial connector with a half-twist locking shell.

boot ROM A read-only memory chip allowing a workstation to communicate with the file server and to read a DOS boot program from the server. Stations can thus operate on the network without having a disk drive.

bps Bits per second.

bridge An interconnection device, sometimes working within a PC and sometimes within a special-purpose hardware device, that can connect LANs using similar or dissimilar data links such as

Ethernet, Token-Ring, and X.25. Bridges link LANs at the data-link layer of the OSI model. Modern bridges read and filter data packets and frames, and they pass traffic only if the address is on the same segment of the network cable as the originating station.

broadband Refers to a network that carries information riding on carrier waves rather than directly as pulses, providing greater capacity at the cost of higher complexity.

broadcast To send a message to all stations or an entire class of stations connected to the network.

brouter A device that combines the functions of a bridge and a router. Brouters can route one or more protocols, such as TCP/IP and XNS, and bridge all other traffic. Contrast with *bridge*, *router*, and *gateway*.

buffer A temporary storage space. Data may be stored in a buffer as it is received, before or after transmission. A buffer may be used to compensate for the differences between the speed of transmission and the speed of processing.

buffered repeater A device that amplifies and regenerates signals so they can travel farther along a cable. This type of repeater also controls the flow of messages to prevent collisions.

bus topology A "broadcast" arrangement in which all network stations receive the same message through the cable at the same time.

byte A group of 8 bits.

C A programming language used predominantly by professional programmers to write applications software.

cache An amount of RAM set aside to hold data that is expected to be accessed again. The second access, which finds the data in RAM, is very fast.

call packet A block of data carrying addressing and other information that is needed to establish an X.25 switched virtual circuit (SVC).

carrier signal A tone or radio signal modulated by data, usually for long-distance transmission.

CCITT X.25 Recommendation An international standard defining packet-switched communication protocols for a public or private network. The recommendation is prepared by the Comite Consultatif International Telegraphique et Telephonique (CCITT). Along with other CCITT recommendations, the X.25 Recommendation defines the physical-, data-link-, and network-layer protocols necessary to interface with X.25 networks. The CCITT X.25 Recommendation is supported by most X.25 equipment vendors, but a new CCITT X.25 Recommendation is published every four years.

CCS 7 A network signaling standard for ISDN that incorporates information from databases in order to offer advanced network services.

central office (CO) The telephone-switching location nearest to the customer's premises. It serves the businesses and residences connected to its loop lines.

channel A path between sender and receiver that carries one stream of information (a two-way path is a *circuit*).

CHAP/PAP (Challenge Handshake and Authentication Protocol/Password Authentication Protocol) Standard authentication protocol for PPP connections.

character One letter, number, or special code.

CICS (Customer Information Control System) This IBM software runs on a mainframe and makes a variety of services available for application programs. It furnishes easy ways for programs to enter mainframe files and find data within them.

CIFS Common Internet File System, a distributed file and printer system used by Microsoft networking and, specifically, by NT/Windows 95 networks over TCP/IP. Unlike NFS (see below) this renamed SMB file system retains the ability to perform the full set of client-server NOS functions over the Internet including print queuing, file locking, and administration

circuit switching A method of communicating in which a dedicated communications path is established between two devices, the bandwidth is guaranteed, and the delay is essentially limited to propagation time. The telephone system uses circuit switching.

clear packet A block of data containing a command that performs the equivalent of hanging up the telephone.

client/server computing A computing system in which processing can be distributed among "clients" on the network that request information and one or more network "servers" that store data, let clients share data and programs, help in printing operations, and so on. The system can accommodate standalone applications (word processing), applications requiring data from the server (spreadsheets), applications that use server capabilities to exchange information among users (electronic mail), and applications providing true client/server teamwork (databases, especially those based on Structured Query Language, or SQL). Before client/server computing, a server would download an entire database to a client machine for processing. SQL database applications divide the work between machines, letting the database stay on the server.

cluster controller A computer that sits between a group of terminals and the mainframe, gathering messages and multiplexing over a single link to the mainframe.

CMIP (Common Management Information Protocol) An OSI-based structure for formatting messages and for transmitting information between data-collection programs and reporting devices. This was developed by the International Standards Organization and designated as ISO 9596.

CMOT (CMIP Over TCP/IP) An Internet standard defining the use of CMIP for managing TCP/IP networks.

coax or coaxial cable A type of network media. Coaxial cable contains a copper inner conductor surrounded by plastic insulation and then a woven copper or foil shield.

codec (coder/decoder) A device that transforms analog voice signals into a digital bit stream (coder) and digital signals into analog voice (decoder) using pulse-code modulation.

collision An attempt by two units to send a message at one time on a single channel. In some networks, the detection of a collision causes all senders to stop transmissions, while in others the collision is noticed when the receiving station fails to acknowledge the data.

common carrier A transmission company (such as a telephone company) that serves the general public.

communications controller A programmable computer dedicated to data communications and serving as the "front end" in the IBM SNA network.

concentrator See *wiring hub*.

contention The condition when two or more stations attempt to use the same channel at the same time.

control character A character used for special signaling; often not printed or displayed, but causing special functions such as the movement of paper in a printer, the blanking of a display screen, or "handshaking" between communicating devices to control the flow of data.

COW interface (character-oriented Windows interface) An SAA-compatible user interface for OS/2 applications.

cps Characters per second.

CPU (central processing unit) The functional "brain" of a computer; the element that does the actual adding and subtracting of 0s and 1s that is essential to computing.

CRC (cyclic redundancy check) A numeric value derived from the bits in a message. The transmitting station uses one of several formulas to produce a number that is attached to the message. The receiving station applies the same formula and should derive the same number. If the numbers are not the same, an error condition is declared.

crosstalk The spillover of a signal from one channel to another. In data communications it is very disruptive. Usually, careful adjustment of the circuits will eliminate crosstalk.

CRT (cathode ray tube) A video screen.

CSMA (carrier sense multiple access) A media-sharing scheme in which stations listen in to what's happening on the network media; if the cable is not in use, a station is permitted to transmit its message. CSMA is often combined with a means of performing collision detection, hence *CSMA/CD*.

current loop An electrical interface that is sensitive to current changes rather than voltage swings; used with older teleprinter equipment.

cursor The symbol indicating the place on the video screen where the next character will appear.

customer premises equipment (CPE) A general term for the telephones, computers, private branch exchanges, and other hardware located on the end user's side of the network boundary, established by the Computer Inquiry II action of the Federal Communications Commission.

D/A converter A device that changes digital pulses into analog signals.

Data Access Protocol A specialized protocol used by Digital Equipment Corp.

datagram A packet of computer-generated information that minimally contains the source and destination addresses of the computers in communication. Protocols, like TCP/IP, often integrate datagrams with higher levels of protocols to assure complete transmission.

data-link control A communications layer in SNA that manages the physical data circuits.

data-link layer The second layer of the OSI model. Protocols functioning in this layer manage the flow of data leaving a network device and work with the receiving station to ensure that the data arrives safely.

data packet In X.25, a block of data that transports full-duplex information via an X.25 switched virtual circuit (SVC) or permanent virtual circuit (PVC). X.25 data packets may contain up to 1,024 bytes of user data, but the most common size is 128 bytes (the X.25 default).

data set 1. A file, a "set" of data. **2.** The name the telephone company often uses for a modem.

DB-25 The designation of a standard plug-and-jack set used in RS-232C wiring: 25-pin connectors, with 13 pins in one row and 12 in the other row.

DCE (data communications equipment) Refers to any X.25 network component that implements the CCITT X.25 standard.

D-channel The "data" channel of an ISDN interface, used to carry control signals and customer call data in a packet-switched mode. In the basic-rate interface (BRI), the D-channel operates at 16 kilobits per second; in the primary-rate interface (PRI), the D-channel is used at 64 kbps.

DDCMP (Digital Data Communications Message Protocol) A byte-oriented, link-layer protocol from Digital Equipment Corp., used to transmit messages over a communications line.

DDD (direct distance dialing) Use of the common long-distance telephone system.

DECnet A communications protocol and line of networking products from Digital Equipment Corp., compatible with Ethernet and a wide range of systems.

delay Commonly, a pause in activity. Delay can also be a kind of distortion on a communications circuit. Specifically, it is the property of an electrical circuit that slows down and distorts high-frequency signals. Devices called *equalizers* slow down the lower frequencies and "equalize" the signal.

demodulation The process of retrieving data from a modulated carrier wave; the reverse of *modulation*.

DHCP (Dynamic Host Configuration Protocol) A protocol for automatic TCP/IP configuration that provides static and dynamic address allocation and management.

dial-up line A communications circuit established by dialing a destination over a commercial telephone system.

digital In common use, on/off signaling; signals consist of 0s and 1s instead of a great multitude of analog-modulated frequencies.

disk duplexing A fault-tolerant technique that writes simultaneously to two hard disks using different controllers.

disk mirroring A fault-tolerant technique that writes data simultaneously to two hard disks using the same controller.

DISOSS (Distributed Office Supported System) An integrated package of electronic-mail and document-preparation programs from IBM, designed for IBM mainframe computer systems.

distortion Any change to the transmitted signal. Distortion can be caused by crosstalk, delay, attenuation, or other factors.

Distributed Systems Architecture (DSA) A Honeywell architecture that conforms to the Open Systems Interconnection model proposed by the ISO. It supports X.25 for packet switching and X.21 for packet-switched and circuit-switched network protocols.

DMI The Desktop Management Interface specification, a development of the Desktop Management Task Force which tracks system components inside PCs for management purposes.

DNS A Domain Name System server relates a human friendly (although with a defined structure) name to an IP address. Throughout the Internet and inside corporate intranets, hierarchies of DNS servers consult internal databases and provide references in reply to queries from client computers.

DQDB (Distributed Queue Dual Bus) A proposed IEEE 802.6 standard for metropolitan-area networks (MANs).

driver A software program that interfaces between portions of the LAN software and the hardware on the network interface card.

DSL A Digital Subscriber Line connection is a digital connection between a customer facility and a telephone company central office. The connection typically offers data rates of several megabits per second in the download direction even though the service is designed to use existing telephone wires.

DTE (data terminal equipment) Refers to any end-user device that can access an X.25 network using the CCITT X.25 standard, LAP/LAB, and X.25 PAP.

duplex 1. In communications circuits, the ability to transmit and receive at the same time; also referred to as *full duplex*. Half-duplex circuits can receive only or transmit only. **2.** In terminals, a choice between displaying locally generated characters and echoed characters.

EBCDIC (Extended Binary Coded Decimal Interchange Code) The data alphabet used in all IBM computers except the PC; it determines the composition of the 8-bit string of 0s and 1s representing each character (alphabetic, numeric, or special).

echoplex A method of transmission in which characters are echoed from the distant end and the echoes are presented on the terminal; this provides a constant check of the communications circuit to the user.

echo suppressor A device used to eliminate the echo effect of long-distance voice transmission circuits. This suppressor must be disabled for full-duplex data transmission; the modem answer tones turn the suppressor off automatically.

ECMA (European Computer Manufacturers' Association) A trade association that provides input to international standards-forming organizations.

EDI (electronic data interchange) The communication of orders, invoices, and similar transactions electronically between organizations.

EIA (Electronic Industries Association) An organization of U.S. manufacturers of electronic parts and equipment. The organization develops industry standards for the interface between data-processing and communications equipment.

EISA (Extended Industry Standard Architecture) A PC bus system that serves as an alternative to IBM's Micro Channel Architecture (MCA). The EISA architecture, backed by an industry consortium headed by Compaq, is compatible with the IBM AT bus; MCA is not.

802.X The Institute of Electrical and Electronics Engineers (IEEE) committee that developed a set of standards describing the cabling, electrical topology, physical topology, and access scheme of network products; in other words, the 802.X standards define the physical and data-link layers of LAN architectures. IEEE 802.3 is the work of an 802 subcommittee that describes the cabling and signaling for a system nearly identical to classic Ethernet. IEEE 802.5 comes from another subcommittee and similarly describes IBM's Token-Ring architecture.

elevator seeking A method of optimizing the movement of the heads on the hard disk in a file server.

EMA (Enterprise Management Architecture) Digital Equipment Corp.'s company-specific architecture, conforming to ISO's CMIP.

emulation Simulation of a system, function, or program.

equalization Balancing of a circuit so that it passes all frequencies with equal efficiency.

Ethernet A network cable and access protocol scheme originally developed by Xerox. Now the dominant LAN topology.

EtherTalk 1. The Apple Ethernet adapter for the Macintosh II computer. **2.** The software driver used by the Macintosh to communicate with Ethernet adapters.

facsimile (fax) The transmission of page images by a system that is concerned with patterns of light and dark rather than with specific characters. Older systems use analog signals; newer devices use digital signals and may interact with computers and other digital devices.

fault A physical or logical break in a communications link.

fault management One of the five basic categories of network management defined by the International Standards Organization (ISO). Fault management is used for the detection, isolation, and correction of faults on the network.

fault tolerance A method of ensuring continued operation through redundancy and diversity.

FCC Federal Communications Commission.

FDDI (Fiber Distributed Data Interface) A specification for fiber-optic networks operating at 100 megabits per second. FDDI uses wiring hubs, and the hubs are prime candidates to serve as network monitoring and control devices.

FEP (front-end processor) A computer that sits between groups of cluster controllers and the mainframe, concentrating signals before they are transmitted to the mainframe.

fiber optics A data-transmission method that uses light pulses sent over glass cables.

field A particular position within a message frame. Positions are labeled as the control field, flag field, and so on. Bits in each message have a meaning for stations on the network.

file lock See *locking*.

file server A type of server that holds files in private and shared directories for LAN users. See *server*.

flow control A convention used to regulate communications between two nodes. Hardware and software techniques are available.

foreign exchange A telephone line that represents a local number in a calling area quite removed from the telephone's actual termination. If your office is in the suburbs but many of your customers are in the city, you might have a foreign-exchange line with a city telephone office.

four-wire circuit A transmission arrangement where two half-duplex circuits (two wires each) are combined to make one full-duplex circuit.

frame A data packet on a Token-Ring network. Also denotes a data packet on other networks such as X.25 or SNA.

frequency-agile modem A modem used on some broadband systems that can shift frequencies to communicate with stations in different dedicated bands.

frequency converter In broadband cable systems, the device that translates between the transmitting and receiving frequencies.

frequency-division multiplexing A technique for combining many signals on one circuit by separating them in frequency.

frequency-shift keying A transmission method using two different frequencies that are shifted to represent the digital 0s and 1s; used in some common modems.

FTAM (File Transfer Access and Management) An OSI protocol that provides access to files stored on dissimilar systems.

FTP (File Transfer Protocol) A protocol that describes how one computer can host other computers to allow transferring files in either direction. Users can see directories of either computer on the host and perform limited file-management functions. Software for the FTP client function is usually a part of TCP/IP packages for the PC; some vendors also provide FTP host software for the PC. See *TFTP*.

full duplex The ability for communications to flow both ways over a communications link at the same time.

functional-management layer A communications layer in SNA that formats presentations.

gateway A device that serves as a shared point of entry from a local area network into a larger information resource such as a large packet-switched information network or a mainframe computer.

GOSIP (Government OSI Profile) The U.S. government's version of the OSI protocols. GOSIP compliance is typically a requirement in government networking purchases.

ground An electrically neutral contact point.

half duplex 1. Alternating transmissions; each station can either transmit or receive, not both simultaneously. **2.** In terminals, describes the condition when a terminal displays its own transmissions instead of a remote-end echo. **3.** The configuration option in some modems allowing local character echo.

handshaking Exchange of control codes or specific characters to control data flow.

HDLC (High-level Data Link Control) A comprehensive standard developed by the International Standards Organization (ISO). It is a bit-oriented link-layer protocol.

high-speed modem A modem operating at speeds from 2,400 to 9,600 bits per second.

HLLAPI (High-Level-Language Application Program Interface) A scripting language (that is, a set of verbs) that allows programmers to build transparent interfaces between 3270 terminals and applications on IBM mainframes.

HotFix A Novell program that dynamically marks defective blocks on the hard disk so they will not be used.

Hz (hertz) Cycles per second.

IAB The Internet Architecture Board guides (as much as possible) the development of the Internet infrastructure. It has two working bodies, the Internet Engineering Task Force (IETF) and Internet Research Task Force (IRTF).

ICMP (Internet Control Message Protocol) The TCP/IP process that provides the set of functions used for network-layer management and control.

IEEE 802 A large family of standards for the physical and electrical connections in local area networks, developed by the IEEE (Institute of Electrical and Electronics Engineers).

IEEE 802.1D An IEEE media-access-control-level standard for interLAN bridges linking IEEE 802.3, 802.4, and 802.5 networks.

IEEE 802.2 An IEEE standard for data-link-layer software and firmware for use with IEEE 802.3, 802.4, and 802.5 networks.

IEEE 802.3 1Base5 An IEEE specification matching the older AT&T StarLAN product. It designates a 1-megabit-per-second signaling rate, a baseband signaling technique, and a maximum cable-segment distance of 500 meters.

IEEE 802.3 10Base2 This IEEE specification matches the thin Ethernet cabling. It designates a 10-megabit-per-second signaling rate, a baseband signaling technique, and a maximum cable-segment distance of 185 (nearly 200) meters.

IEEE 802.3 10BaseT An IEEE standard describing 10-megabit-per-second twisted-pair Ethernet wiring using baseband signaling. This system requires a wiring hub.

IEEE 802.3 10Broad36 This IEEE specification describes a long-distance type of Ethernet cabling with a 10-megabit-per-second signaling rate, a broadband signaling technique, and a maximum cable-segment distance of 3,600 meters.

IEEE 802.4 This IEEE specification describes a LAN using 10-megabit-per-second signaling, token-passing media-access control, and a physical bus topology. It is typically used as part of networks following the Manufacturing Automation Protocol (MAP) developed by General Motors. This is sometimes confused with ARCnet, but it is not the same.

IEEE 802.5 This IEEE specification describes a LAN using 4- or 16-megabit-per-second signaling, token-passing media-access control, and a physical ring topology. It is used by IBM's Token-Ring systems.

IEEE 802.6 This IEEE standard for metropolitan-area networks (MANs) describes what is called a Distributed Queue Dual Bus (DQDB). The DQDB topology includes two parallel runs of cable—typically fiber-optic cable—linking each node (typically a router for a LAN segment) using signaling rates in the range of 100 megabits per second.

IETF The Internet Engineering Task Force is one of two technical working groups of the Internet Activities Board. It focuses on developing and evolving standards for the Internet.

IGRP (Interior Gateway Routing Protocol) A distance-vector routing protocol developed by Cisco Systems for use in large, heterogeneous networks.

IMAP4 (Internet Message Access Protocol, Version 4) An evolving application protocol that allows a client to access and manipulate e-mail messages on a server. More sophisticated than POP3, IMAP4 allows an off-line client to synchronize a mailbox with a server.

impedance An electrical property of a cable, combining capacitance, inductance, and resistance, and measured in ohms.

IND$FILE A mainframe editing utility, commonly used to make PC-to-mainframe file transfers; a logical unit in an SNA network that addresses and interacts with the host.

interface An interconnection point, usually between pieces of equipment.

Internet A collection of networks and gateways including ARPAnet, MILnet, and NSFnet (National Science Foundation net). Internet uses TCP/IP protocols.

interrupt A signal that suspends a program temporarily, transferring control to the operating system when input or output is required. Interrupts may have priority levels, and higher-priority interrupts take precedence in processing.

Intranet An IP-based network serving an organization and it's business partners. It often includes Web servers, mail servers, and other services found on the Internet, but the communications channels have limited access.

I/O Input/output.

I/O bound A condition where the operation of the I/O port is the limiting factor in program execution.

IP (Internet Protocol) A standard describing software that keeps track of the Internet address for different nodes, routes outgoing messages, and recognizes incoming messages.

IPX (Internet Packet Exchange) NetWare's native LAN communications protocol, used to move data between server or workstation programs running on different network nodes. IPX packets are encapsulated and carried by the packets used in Ethernet and the similar frames used in Token-Ring networks.

IRQ (interrupt request) A computer instruction that causes an interruption of a program for an I/O task.

ISDN (Integrated Services Digital Network) As officially defined by the CCITT, "a limited set of standard interfaces to a digital communications network." The result is a network that offers end users voice, data, and certain image services on end-to-end digital circuits.

ISO (International Standards Organization) An international technical standards organization that developed the Open Systems Interconnection (OSI) model.

ISP An Internet Service Provider establishes wide bandwidth connections in to the Internet, subdivides those connections, and sells slower connections to individuals and organizations. An ISP typically also offers services such as Web site hosting.

jam signal A signal generated by a card to ensure that other cards know that a packet collision has taken place.

jumper A plastic-and-metal shorting bar that slides over two or more electrical contacts to set certain conditions for operation.

k Used in this book to represent a kilobyte (1,024 bytes).

Kerberos An authentication system developed at the Massachusetts Institute of Technology that uses symmetric key cryptography to ensure authentication and security. NT 5 uses Kerberos security in place of the NTLM security system of previous versions (but still supports the NTLM system for backwards compatibility).

kernel The heart of an operating system, containing the basic scheduling and interrupt handling, but not the higher-level services, such as the file system.

LAN Manager A now defunct multiuser network operating system codeveloped by Microsoft and 3Com.

LAN Manager/X (LM/X) LAN Manager for the Unix environment.

LAN Server IBM's proprietary OS/2-based network operating system. LAN Server is compatible with LAN Manager, codeveloped by Microsoft and 3Com.

LAP-B Link access procedure (balanced), the most common data-link control protocol used to interface X.25 DTEs with X.25 DCEs. X.25 also specifies a *LAP*, or link access procedure (not balanced). Both LAP and LAP-B are full-duplex, point-to-point bit-synchronous protocols. The unit of data transmission is called a *frame*; frames may contain one or more X.25 packets.

latency If a communications system significantly delays the passage of packets, it is said to have high latency. High latency is particularly bad for transaction processes which "ping pong" back and forth during the course of its operation. The TCP/IP protocol is designed to minimize the effects of latency in the passage of streaming data such as sound and video.

LDAP (Lightweight Directory Access Protocol) An emerging directory service protocol backed by Netscape and other vendors, designed to identify all network resources to clients using a subset of the X.500 directory standard. LDAP is specifically targeted at simple applications like Web browsers and other Internet software.

leased line A communications circuit reserved for the permanent use of a customer; also called *private line*.

light-wave communications Usually, communications using fiber-optic cables and light generated by lasers or light-emitting diodes (LEDs). The phrase can also refer to systems using modulated light beams passing through the air between buildings or other adjacent locations.

link layer The second layer in the OSI architecture. This layer performs the function of taking data from the higher layers, creating packets, and sending them accurately out through the physical layer.

local Refers to programs, files, peripherals, and computational power accessed directly in the user's own machine rather than through the network.

local area network (LAN) A computer communications system limited to no more than a few miles and using high-speed connections (2 to 100 megabits per second).

local area transport (LAT) A DECnet protocol used for terminal-to-host communications.

local loop The connection between a customer's premises and the telephone company's central office.

LocalTalk The 230.4-kilobit-per-second media-access method developed by Apple Computer for use with its Macintosh computer.

locking A method of protecting shared data. When an application program opens a file, *file locking* either prevents simultaneous access by a second program or limits such access to "read only." DOS Versions 3.0 and higher allow an application to lock a range of bytes in a file for various purposes. Since DBMS programs interpret this range of bytes as a record, this is called *record locking.*

low-speed modem A modem operating at speeds up to 600 bits per second.

LU 6.2 (Logical Unit 6.2) In IBM's SNA scheme, a software product that implements the session-layer conversation specified in the Advanced Program-to-Program Communications (APPC) protocol.

MAC (media-access control) See *access protocol.*

mainframe A large centralized computer.

MAN (metropolitan-area network) A public high-speed network (100 megabits per second or more) capable of voice and data transmission over a range of 25 to 50 miles (40 to 80 kilometers).

MAP (Manufacturing Automation Protocol) A token-passing bus LAN originally designed by General Motors and now adopted as a subset of the IEEE 802.3 standards.

mark A signaling condition equal to a binary 1.

MAU See *medium attachment unit* and *Multistation Access Unit.*

MCA (Micro Channel Architecture) The basis for IBM Micro Channel bus, used in high-end models of IBM's PS/2 series of personal computers.

media Plural of *medium*; the cabling or wiring used to carry network signals. Typical examples are coax, fiber-optic, and twisted-pair wire.

media-sharing LAN A network in which all nodes share the cable using a media-access control (MAC) scheme. Contrast with *circuit switching* or *packet switching.*

medium attachment unit (MAU) A transceiver that attaches to the AUI port on an Ethernet adapter and provides electrical and mechanical attachments to fiber-optic, twisted-pair, or other media.

medium-speed modem A modem operating between 600 and 2,400 bits per second.

message switching A routing technique using a message store-and-forward system. No dedicated path is established. Rather, each message contains a destination address and is passed from source to destination through intermediate nodes. At each node, the entire message is received, stored briefly, and then passed on to the next node.

MHS (Message Handling Service) A program developed by Action Technologies and marketed by that firm and Novell to exchange files with other programs and send files out through gateways to other computers and networks. It is used particularly to link dissimilar electronic-mail systems.

MIB (management information base) A directory listing the logical names of all information resources residing in a network and pertinent to the network's management.

midsplit A type of broadband cable system in which the available frequencies are split into two groups, one for transmission and one for reception. This requires a frequency converter.

MIF (management information file) A file used by the Desktop Management Interface for describing components.

MIME (Multipurpose Internet Mail Extensions) A set of extensions to SMTP designed for transmitting non-text e-mail message attachments.

modem (modulator/demodulator) A device that translates between electrical signals and some other means of signaling. Typically a modem translates between direct-current signals from a computer or terminal and analog signals sent over telephone lines. Other modems handle radio frequencies and light waves.

modem eliminator A wiring device designed to replace two modems; it connects equipment over a distance of up to several hundred feet. In asynchronous systems, this is a simple cable.

modulation A process of varying signals to represent intelligent information. The frequency, amplitude, or phase of a signal may be modulated to represent an analog or digital signal.

MP, MPPP, or MLPPP Regardless of how you abbreviate it, the Multilink protocol provides for data compression, error control, and methods for handling multiple transmission protocols. MP supercedes the PPP and older *Serial Line Internet Protocol* (SLIP) protocols.

multiple name spaces The association of several names or other pieces of information with the same file. This allows renaming files and designating them for dissimilar computer systems such as the PC and the Mac.

multipoint line A single communications link for two or more devices shared by one computer and more than one terminal. Use of this line requires a polling mechanism. It is also called a *multidrop line*.

Multistation Access Unit (MAU) IBM's name for a Token-Ring wiring concentrator.

NAK A control code indicating that a character or block of data was not properly received. The name stands for *negative acknowledgement*. See *ACK*.

Namespace A namespace is a collection of unique domain names. The Internet ".com" domain, for example, is a namespace that represents all commercial enterprises.

NAT (Network Address Translation) The NAT function can map internal IP addresses (illegal or non-routable/private) to legitimate Internet addresses either many-to-one or one-to-one.

Some firewalls and routers offer a type of NAT, often many-to-one, to provide a powerful, secure proxy interface to the Internet.

Named Pipes A technique used for communications between applications operating on the same computer or across the network. It includes a relatively easy-to-use API, providing application programmers with a simple way to create interprogram communications using routines similar to disk-file opening, reading, and writing.

N connector The large-diameter connector used with thick Ethernet cable.

NCP 1. (NetWare Core Protocol) The data format of the requests NetWare uses to access files. **2.** (Network Control Program) Special IBM software that runs in a front-end processor and works with VTAM on the host computer to link the application programs and terminal controllers.

NDIS (Network Driver Interface Specification) A device driver specification codeveloped by Microsoft and 3Com. Besides providing hardware and protocol independence for network drivers, NDIS supports both DOS and OS/2, and it offers protocol multiplexing so that multiple protocol stacks can coexist in the same host.

NetBEUI (NetBIOS Extended User Interface) An enhanced version of the NetBIOS protocol used by network operating systems such as LAN Manager, LAN Server, Windows for Workgroups and Windows NT. It formalizes the interface for programmers and adds more functions.

NetBIOS (Network Basic Input/Output System) A layer of software originally developed by IBM and Sytek to link a network operating system with specific hardware. It can also open communications between workstations on a network at the transport layer. Today, many vendors either provide a version of NetBIOS to interface with their hardware or emulate its transport-layer communications services in their network products.

NetVIEW IBM's company-specific network-management and control architecture. This architecture relies heavily on mainframe data-collection programs and also incorporates PC-level products running under OS/2.

NetWare A popular series of network operating systems and related products made by Novell.

network A continuing connection between two or more computers that facilitates sharing files and resources.

network-addressable unit (NAU) In SNA, a device that can be the source and destination of messages.

network layer The third level of the OSI model, containing the logic and rules that determine the path to be taken by data flowing through a network; not important in small LANs.

NFS (Network File System) One of many distributed-file-system protocols that allow a computer on a network to use the files and peripherals of another networked computer as if they were local. This protocol was developed by Sun Microsystems and adopted by other vendors.

NLMs (NetWare Loadable Modules) Applications and drivers that run in a server under Novell's NetWare 386 and can be loaded or unloaded on the fly. In other networks, such applications could require dedicated PCs.

NMP (Network Management Protocol) An AT&T-developed set of protocols designed to exchange information with and control the devices that govern various components of a network, including modems and T1 multiplexers.

NNTP (Network News Transport Protocol) An extension of the TCP/IP protocol that provides a network news transport service.

node A connection or switching point on the network.

ODI (Open Data-link Interface) A standard interface for transport protocols, allowing them to share a single network card without any conflicts.

OfficeVision IBM's set of applications designed to bring a uniform user interface to the company's various lines of computing products. OfficeVision works in conjunction with IBM's Systems Application Architecture.

online Connected to a network or a host computer system.

ONMS (Open Network Management System) Digital Communications Associates' architecture for products conforming to ISO's CMIP.

Open Systems Interconnection (OSI) reference model A model for networks developed by the International Standards Organization, dividing the network functions into seven connected layers. Each layer builds on the services provided by those under it.

OpenView Hewlett-Packard's suite of a network-management application, a server platform, and support services. OpenView is based on HP-UX, which complies with AT&T's Unix system.

OPT (Open Protocol Technology) Novell's strategy for complete protocol independence. NetWare supports multivendor hardware with this approach.

OSF (Open Software Foundation) A consortium of industry leaders working to standardize the Unix operating system.

OSI See *Open Systems Interconnection*.

OSPF (Open Shortest Path First) A link-state routing protocol used to determine the least expensive path for routing a message by examining the number of routers, transmission speed, delays and route cost.

OS/2 (Operating System/2) An operating system developed by IBM and Microsoft for use with Intel's microprocessors.

Unlike its predecessor, DOS, OS/2 is a multitasking operating system.

OS/2 Extended Edition IBM's proprietary version of OS/2; it includes built-in communications and database-management facilities.

OverVIEW Proteon's architecture for products conforming to SNMP.

packet A block of data sent over the network transmitting the identities of the sending and receiving stations, error-control information, and a message.

packet filter A feature of a bridge that compares each packet received with specifications set by the network administrator. If the packet matches the specifications, the bridge can either forward or reject it. Packet filters let the administrator limit protocol-specific traffic to one network segment, isolate electronic-mail domains, and perform many other traffic-control functions.

packet switching A transmission technique that maximizes the use of digital transmission facilities by transmitting packets of digital data from many customers simultaneously on a single communications channel.

PAD (packet assembler/disassembler) An X.25 PAD. A hardware-and-software device, sometimes inside a PC, that provides users access to an X.25 network. CCITT Recommendations X.3, X.28, and X.29 define the PAD parameters, terminal-to-PAD interface, and PAD-to-X.25 host interface.

PAP (packet-level procedure) A protocol for the transfer of packets between an X.25 DTE and an X.25 DCE. X.25 PAP is a full-duplex protocol that supports data sequencing, flow control, accountability, and error detection and recovery.

parallel transmission Simultaneous transmission of bits down parallel wires; for example, *byte parallel transmission* requires eight wires. See *serial port*.

parity In ASCII, a check of the total number of 1 bits (as opposed to 0's) in a character's binary representation. A final eighth bit is set so that the count, when transmitted, is always even or always odd. This even or odd state can easily be checked at the receiving end; an incorrect parity bit can help reveal errors in the transmission.

passive head end A device that connects the two broadband cables of a dual-cable system. It does not provide frequency translation.

PBX (private branch exchange) A telephone system serving a specific location. Many PBX systems can carry computer data without the use of modems.

PDS (Premise Distribution System) AT&T's proprietary buildingwide telecommunications cabling system.

peer-to-peer resource sharing An architecture that lets any station contribute resources to the network while still running local application programs.

physical layer The lowest layer of the OSI model. It consists of network wiring and cable and the interface hardware that sends and receives signals over the network.

PING (Packet Internet Groper) An exercise and diagnostic program associated with TCP/IP and used to test the Internet communications channel between stations.

pipe A communications process within the operating system that acts as an interface between a computer's devices (keyboard, disk drives, memory, and so on) and an applications program. A pipe simplifies the development of application programs by "buffering" a program from the intricacies of the hardware or the software that controls the hardware; the application developer writes code to a single pipe, not to several individual devices. A pipe is also used for program-to-program communications.

polling A method of controlling the transmission sequence of communicating devices on a shared circuit by sending an inquiry to each device asking whether it wishes to transmit.

POP3 (Post Office Protocol, Version 3) A simple application protocol used to retrieve email from mail servers.

PPP (Point-to-Point Protocol) A protocol that allows the user to connect directly onto the Internet using a standard telephone line and high-speed modem. Features error detection and data protection, unlike older internetworking systems such as SLIP. See also *MP*.

presentation layer The sixth layer of the OSI model, which formats data for screen presentation and translates incompatible file formats.

Presentation Manager The portion of the operating system OS/2 providing users with a graphical-based rather than character-based interface. The screens are similar to those of Microsoft Windows.

primary-rate interface (PRI) In ISDN, the specification for the interface at each end of the high-volume trunks linking PBX and central-office facilities or connecting network switches to each other. The primary rate consists of 23 B or "bearer" channels (operating at 64 kilobits per second) and a D or "data" channel (also functioning at 64 kbps). The combined signal-carrying capacity is 1.544 megabits per second—equivalent to that of a type T1 channel.

print server A computer on the network that makes one or more attached printers available to other users. The server usually requires a hard disk to spool the print jobs while they wait in a queue for the printer.

print spooler The software that holds print jobs sent to a shared printer over a network when the printer is busy. Each file is saved in temporary storage and then printed when the shared printer is available.

PROFS (Professional Office System) Interactive productivity software developed by IBM that runs under the VM/CMS mainframe system. PROFS is frequently used for electronic mail.

propagation delay The delay between the time a signal enters a channel and the time it is received. This is normally insignificant in local area networks, but it becomes a major factor in satellite communications.

protocol A specification that describes the rules and procedures that products should follow to perform activities on a network, such as transmitting data. If they use the same protocols, products from different vendors can communicate on the same network.

proxy server A proxy server is a style of security firewall which interfaces the Internet with a single address on behalf of an entire intranet of workstations, hence the name "proxy." The popular HTML-layer proxy deals with files and most HTML proxy firewalls provide the added benefit of a speedy local cache of previously loaded WEB pages. Other proxy firewalls operate at layer 5 (the SOCKS proxy) and layer 3 (the NAT proxy).

PSDN Packet-switched data network.

PU (physical unit) In an SNA network, usually a terminal or printer connected to the controller.

public data network A commercially owned or national-monopoly packet-switched network, publicly available as a service to data-processing users.

pulse-code modulation (PCM) A common method for digitizing voice signals. The bandwidth required for a single digitized voice channel is 64 kilobits per second.

PVC See *VC (virtual circuit)*.

query language A programming language designed to make it easier to specify what information a user wants to retrieve from a database.

queue A list formed by items in a system waiting for service. An example is a *print queue* of documents to be printed in a network print server.

RAM (random access memory) Also known as *read-write memory*; the memory used to execute application programs.

record locking A feature that excludes other users from accessing (or sometimes just writing to) a record in a file while the first user is accessing that record.

redirector A software module loaded into every network workstation; it captures application programs' requests for file- and equipment-sharing services and routes them through the network for action.

repeater A device that amplifies and regenerates signals so they can travel on additional cable segments.

restart packet A block of data that notifies X.25 DTEs that an irrecoverable error exists within the X.25 network. Restart packets clear all existing SVCs and resynchronize all existing PVCs between an X.25 DTE and X.25 DCE.

reverse channel An answer-back channel provided during half-duplex operation. It allows the receiving modem to send low-speed acknowledgments to the transmitting modem without breaking the half-duplex mode. This is also used to arrange the turnaround between modems so that one ceases transmitting and the other can begin.

RF (radio frequency) A generic term referring to the technology used in cable television and broadband networks. It uses electromagnetic waveforms, usually in the megahertz (MHz) range, for transmission.

RFC This term means "Request for Comments," but it has grown into a complete process of developing standards for protocols. Today, the RFC process has resulted in the establishment of more than 50 IETF Standards or STDs. Use any Internet search engine to find STD0001 for a complete and current list of STDs.

RFS (Remote File Service) One of the many distributed-file-system network protocols that allow one computer to use the files and peripherals of another as if they were local. Developed by AT&T and adopted by other vendors as a part of Unix V.

ring A network connection method that routes messages through each station on the network in turn. Most ring networks use a token-passing protocol, which allows any station to put a message on the network when it receives a special bit pattern.

RIP (Routing Information Protocol) The simplest routing protocol, RIP finds the shortest path between two points on a network in terms of "hops." OSPF AND IGRP are more advanced routing protocols.

RJE (Remote Job Entry) A method of submitting work to an IBM mainframe in a batch format. Though superseded by the 3270 system, it is still widely used in some installations.

RJ-11/RJ-45 Designations for commonly used modular telephone connectors. RJ-11 is the 8-pin connector used in most voice connections. RJ-45 is the 8-pin connector used for data transmission over twisted-pair telephone wire.

RO (receive-only) Refers to a one-way device such as a printer, plotter, or graphics display.

ROM (read-only memory) Memory containing preloaded programs that cannot be rewritten or changed by the CPU.

router An interconnection device that is similar to a bridge but serves packets or frames containing certain protocols. Routers link LANs at the network layer of the OSI model. Modern routers handle multiple protocol stacks simultaneously and move packets or frames onto the right links for their destinations. For example, an X.25 router will wrap an Ethernet packet back into an Ethernet system.

RPC (Remote Procedure Call) A set of software tools developed by a consortium of manufacturers and designed to assist developers in creating distributed applications. These tools automatically generate the code for both sides of the program (client and server) and let the programmer concentrate on other portions of the application.

RS-232C An electrical standard for the interconnection of equipment established by the Electrical Industries Association; the same as the CCITT code V.24. RS-232C is used for serial ports.

RS-449 An EIA standard that applies to binary, serial synchronous, or asynchronous communications systems.

RU (request unit or response unit) A message that makes a request or responds to one during a session.

SAA (Systems Application Architecture) A set of specifications written by IBM describing how users, application programs, and communications programs interface. SAA represents an attempt to standardize the look and feel of applications and the methods they use to communicate.

SDLC (synchronous data link control) The data-link layer of SNA, SDLC is a more efficient method than the older bisync protocol when it comes to packaging data for transmission between computers. Packets of data are sent over the line without the overhead created by synchronization and other padding bits.

serial port An I/O port that transmits data 1 bit at a time; contrasted with a *parallel transmission*, which transmits multiple

bits (usually 8) simultaneously. RS-232C is a common serial signaling protocol.

server 1. A computer with a large power supply and cabinet capacity. **2.** Any computer on a network that makes file, print, or communications services available to other network stations.

session The name for the connection between a mainframe terminal (or a PC emulating a mainframe terminal) and the mainframe itself when they are communicating. The number of sessions that can be run simultaneously through a LAN gateway is limited by the gateway software and the hardware configuration.

session layer The fifth layer of the OSI model, which sets up the conditions whereby individual nodes on the network can communicate or send data to each other. The functions of this layer are used for many purposes, including determining which side may transmit during half-duplex communications.

SFT (system fault tolerance) The capability to recover from or avoid a system crash. Novell uses a Transaction Tracking System (TTS), disk mirroring, and disk duplexing as its system recovery methods.

SLIP (Serial Line Internet Protocol) A communications protocol designed to run IP over serial lines.

SMB (Server Message Block) A distributed-file-system network protocol that allows one computer to use the files and peripherals of another as if they were local. Developed by Microsoft and adopted by IBM and many other vendors.

SMTP (Simple Mail Transfer Protocol) A protocol that describes an electronic mail system with both host and user sections. Many companies sell host software (usually for Unix) that will exchange SMTP mail with proprietary mail systems, such as IBM's PROFS. The user software is often included as a utility in TCP/IP packages for the PC.

SNA (Systems Network Architecture) IBM's scheme for connecting its computerized products so that they can communicate and share data.

SNADS (SNA Distribution Services) An IBM protocol that allows the distribution of electronic mail and attached documents through an SNA network.

SNMP (Simple Network Management Protocol) A structure for formatting messages and for transmitting information between reporting devices and data-collection programs; developed jointly by the Department of Defense, industry, and the academic community as part of the TCP/IP protocol suite.

space The signal condition that equals a binary 0.

SPX (Sequenced Packet Exchange) An enhanced set of commands implemented on top of IPX to create a true transport-layer interface. SPX provides more functions than IPX, including guaranteed packet delivery.

SQL (Structured Query Language) A formal data sublanguage for specifying common database operations such as retrieving, adding, changing, or deleting records. SQL is pronounced "sequel."

STA (Spanning Tree Algorithm) A technique based on an IEEE 802.1 standard that detects and eliminates logical loops in a bridged network. When multiple paths exist, STA lets a bridge use only the most efficient one. If that path fails, STA automatically reconfigures the network so that another path becomes active, sustaining network operations.

StarLAN A networking system developed by AT&T that uses CSMA protocols on twisted-pair telephone wire; a subset of 802.3. Now obsolete.

start bit A data bit used in asynchronous transmission to signal the beginning of a character and indicate that the channel is in use. It is a space signal lasting only for the duration of 1 bit.

star topology A network connection method that hooks up all links to a central node.

STDs IETF standards describe over 50 protocols and procedures. Use any Internet search engine to find STD0001, the complete and current list of STDs.

stop bit A data bit used in asynchronous transmission to signal the end of a character and indicate that the channel is idle. It is a mark signal lasting at least for the duration of 1 bit.

store and forward See *message switching*.

Streams An architecture introduced with Unix System V, Release 3.2, that provides for flexible and layered communication paths between processes (programs) and device drivers. Many companies market applications and devices that can integrate through Streams protocols.

strobe An electrical pulse used to call for the transfer of information.

SVC See *VC (virtual circuit)*.

sync character A character (two or more in bisync) sent from a transmitting station for synchronizing the clocks in transmitting and receiving stations.

synchronous Refers to a transmission system in which characters are synchronized by the transmission of initial sync characters and a common clock signal. No stop or start bits are used.

T1 A 1.544-megabit-per-second communications circuit provided by long-distance communications carriers for voice or data transmission. T1 lines are typically divided into 24 64-kilobit channels.

tap A connector that couples to a cable without blocking the passage of signals down the cable.

TCAM (Telecommunications Access Method) An IBM system for controlling communications.

T-connector A coaxial connector, shaped like a T, that connects two thin Ethernet cables while supplying an additional connector for a network interface card.

TCP (Transmission Control Protocol) A specification for software that bundles and unbundles sent and received data into packets, manages the transmission of packets on a network, and checks for errors.

TCP/IP (Transmission Control Protocol/Internet Protocol) A set of communications protocols that has evolved since the late 1970s, when it was first developed by the Department of Defense (DOD). Because programs supporting these protocols are available on so many different computer systems, they have become an excellent way to connect different types of computers over networks.

Telex An international messaging service, marketed in the United States by Western Union.

TELNET A terminal-emulation protocol. Software supporting TELNET usually comes as a utility in a TCP/IP package, and all TELNET programs provide DEC VT-100 terminal emulation. Many companies either provide or allow other add-in emulators.

10Base2 IEEE's specifications for running Ethernet over thin coaxial cable.

10Base5 IEEE's specifications for running Ethernet over thick coaxial cable.

10BaseT IEEE's specifications for running Ethernet over unshielded twisted-pair wiring.

terminal adapter (TA) An ISDN phone or a PC card that emulates one. Devices on the end of a basic-rate interface line are known as *terminals*.

terminator A resistor used at each end of an Ethernet cable to ensure that signals do not reflect back and cause errors. It is usually attached to an electrical ground at one end.

TFTP (Trivial File Transfer Protocol) A simplified version of FTP that transfers files but does not provide password protection or user-directory capability. It is associated with the TCP/IP family of protocols.

thick Ethernet A cabling system using relatively stiff, large-diameter cable to connect transceivers. The transceivers connect to the nodes through flexible multiwire cable.

thin Ethernet A cabling system using a thin and flexible coaxial cable to connect each node to the next node in line.

3174, 3270, and so on Appear at the end of the alphabet in this glossary.

3+Open A family of 3Com networking products built around the LAN Manager file/print server. 3+Open includes connectivity, messaging, and network management services.

TIC (Token-Ring Interface Coupler) An IBM device that allows a controller or processor to attach directly to a Token-Ring network. This is an optional part of several IBM terminal cluster controllers and front-end processors.

time-division multiplexing (TDM) A method of placing a number of signals on one communications circuit by allocating the available time among competing stations. Allocations may be on a microsecond basis.

time domain reflectometry (TDR) A method of sending a radio pulse down a wire or cable to detect a shorted or open condition. High-priced devices can pinpoint a fault within inches; lower-priced devices often provide widely varying results when they try to pinpoint the distance to a fault.

T interface A standard basic-rate interface using four copper wires.

token passing An access protocol in which a special message (token) circulates among the network nodes, giving them permission to transmit.

Token-Ring The wire and the access protocol scheme whereby stations relay packets in a logical ring configuration. This architecture, pioneered by IBM, is described in the IEEE 802.5 standards.

TOP (Technical and Office Protocol) An implementation of OSI standards in office and engineering environments. TOP, developed by Boeing and other firms, employs Ethernet specifications.

topology The map or plan of the network. The physical topology describes how the wires or cables are laid out, and the logical or electrical topology describes how the messages flow.

TP-4 (Transport Protocol 4) An OSI layer-4 protocol developed by the National Bureau of Standards.

Traceroute An excercise/diagnostic program which extends PING to include the roundtrip times not only to the destination host but to all intermediate routers, as well. Traceroute is a very revealing facility to analyze Internet service problems.

transceiver A communicating device capable of transmitting and receiving.

transmission control The layer in SNA that controls sessions and manages communications.

transport layer The fourth layer of the OSI model. Software in this layer checks the integrity of and formats the data carried by the physical layer (1), managed by the data layer (2), and perhaps routed by the network layer (3).

tree Refers to a network arrangement in which the stations are attached to a common branch or data bus.

TTS (Transaction Tracking System) A log of all file activity in NetWare.

twisted-pair Ethernet See *IEEE 802.3 10BaseT.*

twisted-pair wiring Cable comprised of two wires twisted together at six turns per inch to provide electrical self-shielding. Some telephone wire—but by no means all—is twisted-pair.

Type 3 cable An unshielded twisted-pair wire that meets IBM specifications for use in 4-megabit-per-second Token-Ring networks.

UDP (User Datagram Protocol) A TCP/IP protocol describing how messages reach application programs within a destination computer. This protocol is normally bundled with IP-layer software.

U interface A standard basic-rate interface using two copper wires.

Unix A multitasking, multiuser operating system for minicomputers that was developed by AT&T and has enjoyed popularity among engineering and technical professionals. Unix is finding new uses as the basis of file-server operating systems for networks of PCs.

UNMA (Unified Network Management Architecture) AT&T's company-specific architecture conforming to the ISO's CMIP.

UUCP (Unix-to-Unix Copy Program) A standard Unix utility used for information exchange between two Unix nodes.

VAN (value-added network) A privately owned packet-switched network whose services are sold to the public. See *PSDN.*

VC (virtual circuit) An X.25 VC is a PAP logical connection between an X.25 DTE and an X.25 DCE. X.25 supports both *switched VCs* (SVCs) and *permanent VCs* (PVCs). SVCs are analogous to dial-up lines; that is, they allow a particular X.25 DTE to establish a connection with different X.25 DTEs on a per-call basis. By contrast, PVCs are analogous to leased lines because they always connect two X.25 DTEs.

VINES (Virtual Networking Software) A Unix-based network operating system from Banyan Systems.

virtual circuit A temporary connection path, set up between two points by software and packet switching, that appears to the user to be available as a dedicated circuit. This "phantom" circuit can be maintained indefinitely or can be ended at will.

voice channel A transmission path usually limited to passing the bandwidth of the human voice.

VTAM (Virtual Telecommunications Access Method) An IBM standard for software that runs on the host mainframe computer and works with the Network Control Program to establish communications between the host and the cluster controllers. Among other things, VTAM sets the pacing and LU characteristics.

WAN (wide-area network) A type of network that connects computers over areas potentially as wide as the entire world.

wideband Refers to a channel or transmission medium capable of passing more frequencies than a standard 3-kHz voice channel.

WINS The Windows Internet Naming Service protocol, developed by Microsoft, uses a database of client names and associates those names with IP addresses. WINS supports the use of CIFS (SMB) and NetBIOS over TCP/IP (RFC1001-1002), Microsoft's NT network operating system, by managing connections through NetBIOS names over a TCP/IP network.

wiring hub A cabinet, usually mounted in a wiring closet, that holds connection modules for various kinds of cabling. The hub contains electronic circuits that re-time and repeat the signals on the cable. The hub may also contain a microprocessor board that monitors and reports on network activity.

X.25 A standard describing how data is on packet-switched networks. X.25 provides high reliability. Frame relay is replacing X.25. The protocol of Frame Relay transfers the error control from each node to the endpoints which significantly improves the throughput by eliminating the full packet assembly/error-checking/disassembly at each intervening node.

X.400 The CCITT designation for an international electronic-mail distribution system.

X.500 The CCITT designation for a directory standard to coordinate the dispersed file directories of different systems.

XNS (Xerox Network Services) A multi-layer protocol system developed by Xerox and adopted, at least in part, by Novell and other vendors. XNS is one of the many distributed-file-system protocols that allow network stations to use other computers' files and peripherals as if they were local.

X/Open A consortium of computer-industry vendors, chartered to specify an open system platform based on the Unix operating system.

X Window A network-based windowing system that provides a programmatic interface for graphic window displays. X Window permits graphics produced on one networked workstation to be displayed on another.

3174 A new version of the 3274 terminal cluster controller.

3270 The generic name for the family of interoperable IBM system components —terminals, printers, and terminal cluster controllers—that can be used to communicate with a mainframe by means of the SNA or bisync protocols. All of these components have four-digit names, some of which begin with the digits 327.

3274/3276 The most commonly used cluster controller. This device links as many as 32 3270-type terminals and printers to a mainframe front-end processor.

3278 The most commonly used terminal in the 3270 family. It features a monochrome display and offers a limited graphics set.

3279 A color terminal that is part of the 3270 family.

3287 The current series of printers in the 3270 equipment family.

3705 A common front-end processor, typically used to link several 3274s to a mainframe.

3725 A common front-end processor, intended for linking groups of cluster controllers to a mainframe.

3745 A new communications controller that combines the functions of a cluster controller and a front-end processor. The 3745 can interface simultaneously with as many as 8 Token-Ring networks, 512 terminals or printers, and 16 1.544-megabit-per-second communications lines.

What's on the Web Page?

The *Using Networks* web pages contain tips, stories, diagrams, and lots of World Wide Web links to networking vendors, networking and communications special interest groups, and other sources of information on networking products and technologies.

The series of pages can be accessed by going to www.mcp.com, clicking Downloads, and entering the ISBN number of this book (0-7897-1596-1).

The pages are designed specifically for readers of this book and contain updates and information related to the book and its organization.

Index

Symbols